THE

INTERVIEWS

THE

INTERVIEWS

EDITED BY

JANN S. WENNER AND JOE LEVY

Introduction by Jann S. Wenner

BACK BAY BOOKS

Little, Brown and Company

NEW YORK · BOSTON · LONDON

Back Bay Books / Little, Brown and Company
Hachette Book Group USA
237 Park Avenue, New York, NY 10017
Visit our Web site at www.HachetteBookGroupUSA.com

First Edition: November 2007

ISBN 978-0-316-00526-5
LCCN 2007931330

10 9 8 7 6 5 4 3 2 1

Q-MART

Printed in the United States of America

CONTENTS

Contents

Contents

INTRODUCTION

On August 14, 1968, the Who finished a show at the Fillmore West with "My Generation." Pete Townshend did not smash his guitar—not that night—and I wanted to know why. So I made my way backstage to ask him if he'd sit for an interview with *Rolling Stone*.

I wanted to know much more, in fact: where Pete grew up, what shaped his music, what his relationship with Roger Daltrey was like, what he thought rock & roll could accomplish, what his plans for the band were. We went back to my house, started talking at two A.M. and finished sometime after dawn. Pete was articulate, passionate, and lost in his own thoughts (at one point, he asked if I'd dosed his orange juice with LSD; I hadn't). He talked about the Who's next album, a project he was then calling "Deaf, Dumb, and Blind Boy." A year or so later, he told me it was the first time he'd ever sketched out the whole plan for *Tommy,* even for himself.

That was the first fully realized *Rolling Stone* Interview. We'd included Q&A's starting with the first issue of the magazine—one of our goals had always been delivering the voices of the artists behind the music—but this went deeper. It accomplished everything I loved about the in-depth interviews with writers in *The Paris Review*—it brought you into the working process of the artist—and it also opened up the private life and aspirations of a defining force in popular culture, the way the *Playboy* Interview did. In those days, *The Paris Review* and *Playboy* were the only places you could read a thoughtful, in-depth magazine interview, and no one was bringing the same rigor and seriousness of purpose to rock & roll.

Rolling Stone was different. From the start, we were devoted not only to rock & roll but to the culture and politics that surrounded the music, that shaped it and were shaped by it. And though we knew how to have fun (we did, after all, offer a roach clip as a subscription premium with our February 24, 1968, issue [RS 6]), we were all about seriousness of purpose. These were not casual interviews. Our reporters researched their subjects deeply, and the musicians we spoke with responded. They were bored by the short-form interviews they did with fan magazines and radio stations. We presented them with a new opportunity to articulate what they were thinking and doing, to communicate with their audience in a direct and unfiltered way.

The *Rolling Stone* Interview gained prestige quickly. Prestige and size—nowhere else could you read ten or fifteen pages of Jerry Garcia talking about his childhood, the first music he loved, his experiences in the army, and the days of the Acid Tests. And we spoke not just with musicians but with writers, directors, philosophers, presidents and religious leaders as well.

Sometimes these interviews lasted for hours; sometimes they stretched over days or even months. Over a period of weeks in 1969, Jerry Hopkins spoke with Jim Morrison at the Doors' management office in Los Angeles, a nearby bar, and a strip club where Morrison was a regular. In 1973, Johnny Cash was so pleased that the magazine wanted to speak with him at the ripe old age of forty ("I've often read those interviews and wondered if they'd be interested in someone like me," he said) that he sat with Robert Hilburn in his Las Vegas hotel suite after finishing a midnight show, then invited Hilburn back for more the following morning over breakfast. Neil Young broke a years-long silence in 1975 to talk with Cameron Crowe (the coup landed Cameron a staff job); they talked for so long Cameron ran out of tapes and Neil had to give him some cassettes that had alternate takes of his songs on them. (Yes, he recorded over them, but later he did also capture a long band rehearsal of then-unreleased "Cortez the Killer.") I remember the interview that Charles Reich—the author of *The Greening of America* and a Yale law professor—and I conducted with Jerry Garcia in 1971. We spent hours in the July heat on the front lawn of Jerry's house near Mount Tamalpais in northern California, overlooking the Pacific Ocean. A few days later, Reich attended a Grateful Dead recording session to get more, and then he went back a few weeks after that to talk with Jerry for another two hours. In the fall, I spent four more hours giving the whole thing a more journalistic perspective. The result—both far ranging and incredibly specific—ran in two issues of the magazine and eventually was published in book form.

From the start, our subjects were explorers, discussing things for the first time. And we were exploring right along with them, finding new journalistic territory as we went. We were hungry for insights, for the stories of how the music and culture we loved came to be, and who the people who made it were. We wanted revelations, and we got them. In December of 1970, I interviewed John Lennon in New York at the time of the release of his first solo album, *Plastic Ono Band* (still one of the most painfully honest and greatest rock records ever made). *Rolling Stone* already had a long history with John and Yoko (when the cover of their *Two Virgins* album was banned, *Rolling Stone* cofounder Ralph J. Gleason had the idea of putting it on the cover of our first anniversary issue [RS 22]). Lennon chose the magazine to discuss the devastating pain behind the dissolution of the Beatles.

Remember that the Beatles had been hermetically protected for years, and however much their image had changed, much of the world clung to the fantasy that they were the same clean-cut boys who'd worn matching suits on *The Ed Sullivan Show*. Lennon's *Rolling Stone* Interview ended all that. He lifted the curtain on the "orgies" that accompanied life on the road ("The Beatles tours were like the Fellini film *Satyricon*"), spoke frankly about the band's drug use ("*Help* was where we turned onto pot and we dropped drink, simple as that") and went through the Beatles catalog song by song, the first time he'd ever discussed the band's music in this kind of detail ("'Yesterday' I had nothing to do with.... 'Eleanor Rigby' I wrote a good half of the lyrics or more"). For weeks afterward it was everywhere, because none of the other Beatles had yet publicly explained the breakup of the band. The effect was shocking. "One has to completely humiliate oneself to be what the Beatles were," Lennon said. "And that's what I'm saying with this album—I *remember* what it's all about now, you *fuckers, fuck you all!* That's what I'm saying: 'You don't get me twice.'"

That strong, unfiltered voice was everything I wanted the *Rolling Stone* Interview to be. The best interviews of the past forty years—excerpts of which are collected in this volume—are documents of the individuals and of the times. They are visits as well as interviews, and they bring you face-to-face with the person talking. While we clean up the syntax to make it more readable—remove the *ums, ahs* and repetitions—we also preserve the speech and idiosyncrasies of the subject. Over the years, I stressed to editors and writers that the interviewer has to establish himself as a stand-in for the reader—show a little bit but not too much of his own personality, and know when not to get in his subject's, or the reader's, way. An interviewer gets to go somewhere every reader would love to, whether it's the dressing room after a show or a private home, and he has to deliver that experience to the reader. Sometimes that means bonding with the subject; sometimes it means challenging the subject. The *Rolling Stone* Interview thrives on both drama and informality. And above all intimacy.

Reading over this collection, I'm struck by how many intimate moments our subjects chose to share with us, and with our readers: Jack Nicholson recalling the moment he learned the woman he thought was his sister was in fact his mother; Axl Rose sharing his recovered memories of child abuse; Robin Williams sitting for an interview just months after the death of his father and discussing the end of his first marriage; Courtney Love talking with David Fricke less than six months after the suicide of her husband, Kurt Cobain. ("If I start to cry," she told Fricke, "I will probably get up and leave the room. Don't be offended." Except that when she did start to cry, she just kept talking.)

Though he has a reputation as reticent, Bob Dylan has proved one of our most rewarding interview subjects. I remember how hard I worked to land a Dylan interview when the magazine started. He had little interest in talking with the press, and I wrote to him for nearly two years asking for a meeting. On a trip to New York in 1969, I returned to my hotel and found a phone message that a "Mr. Dillon" had called. I thought I'd missed my chance, but a few months later, I was back in New York and there was a knock at the door. I opened it to find Dylan in the hallway. He'd come to check me out, and when he was comfortable enough, we began Dylan's first *Rolling Stone* Interview. Over the years, as Dylan changed masks and passions again and again, we've sent numerous writers to talk with him, always striving to find the right match for what was going on in his life and career. Among the best were a pair of 1978 interviews with Jonathan Cott, full of mysticism, and a frank sit-down with Kurt Loder in 1984 at the time of *Infidels*. (You can find them in a collection we put together in 2006, *Bob Dylan: The Essential Interviews*, from Wenner Books.) The interview we've chosen here was conducted in 2001 by Mikal Gilmore after the release of *"Love & Theft,"* an album that stood with Dylan's best work of the sixties. The interview is filled with the remarkable perspective (to say nothing of the clear, ringing language) that Dylan would bring to his autobiography, *Chronicles,* three years later: "Every one of the records I've made has emanated from the entire panorama of what America is to me. America, to me, is a rising tide that lifts all ships, and I've never really sought inspiration from other types of music."

A similar perspective graces the interviews with Mick Jagger and Keith Richards. Keith has long been a favorite assignment for *Rolling Stone* writers because he's one of rock's great raconteurs. In 2002, as the Stones celebrated their fortieth year, he talked with David Fricke about longevity and mortality: "We're fighting people's misconceptions about what rock & roll is supposed to be. You're supposed to do it when you're twenty, twenty-five—as if you're a tennis player and you have three hip surgeries and you're done. We play rock & roll because it's what turned us on. Muddy Waters and Howlin' Wolf—the idea of retiring was ludicrous to them. You keep going—and why not?"

Mick, on the other hand, does not relish interviews. He's reluctant to look back, to be introspective or too self-involved. In 1994, though, he agreed to sit for a long interview, which we both saw as an opportunity to set it all down as a matter of history. It took over a year to put together. I joined him at tour stops in Palm Beach, Montreal, and Cologne, trailing him to better understand his routine—his vocal exercises, his preshow preparations—and I also talked to Keith, Charlie Watts and Ron Wood to find out what they would ask him. In our interviews, he went through the classic Stones albums track by track for the first time, he talked about his childhood, and he discussed the rewards and difficulties of his longtime partnership with Keith, whom he's known since childhood. "When Keith was taking heroin, it was very difficult to work. He still was creative, but it took a long time. And everyone else was taking drugs and drinking a tremendous amount, too. And it affected everyone in certain ways. But I've never really talked to Keith about this stuff. So I have no idea what he feels.... I'm always second-guessing. I tell you something, I probably read it in *Rolling Stone.*"

In October of 2005, I went to Cancún, Mexico, to conduct the *Rolling Stone* Interview with Bono. I'd spent weeks preparing, speaking with the Edge and U2's manager, Paul McGuinness, to get their insights into Bono's character, meeting with the editors here to hone my list of questions, going back through past interviews. In Cancún, in the bedroom of a house Bono and his wife, Ali, had rented with their family for a weeklong break from touring, we talked for ten hours. We talked about his faith and religious practice. We talked about how he'd developed as a performer. We went back and forth over his progress in debt relief for the third world and his campaign against AIDS in Africa, which had aligned him with the Bush administration. And I pushed him hard on his relationship with his father, a strong man with whom he'd clashed during his childhood. "Do you ever feel guilty about how you treated him?" I asked him. "No," he said. "Not until I fucking met you!" Later, he would remember it as a moment of personal revelation. Bono is, without doubt, one of the most articulate and passionate figures in rock & roll. Still, he wasn't content with his answers on some matters, so he came by the office two weeks later when U2 was in New York to play Madison Square Garden, and we spent two more hours going over details. The result was one of the finest interviews we've ever printed.

The *Rolling Stone* Interview does not confine itself to music. Over the years, *Rolling Stone* has earned a reputation for its innovative and in-depth coverage of politics, which I'm proud to say is both deeply informed and fervently committed. We've opposed America's misguided wars, from Vietnam to Iraq, and long stood for gun control, protecting the environment, a sane and responsible drug policy and economic justice. When we interview politicians, we avoid the news cycle and gotcha questions. We deliver what the political press never has time for: an attempt to discover who these people are, what they're like, and what were the experiences and beliefs that shaped their thinking. There have been three *Rolling Stone* Interviews with Bill Clinton, the first in 1992 during his first presidential campaign. It was informal—the candidate wore khakis and met Hunter S. Thompson, P. J. O'Rourke, William Greider and me at one of his favorite Little Rock spots, Doe's Eat Place. The second took place in the White House dining room, and Clinton lost his temper, exploding over what he characterized as the "knee-jerk liberal press" continually questioning his commitment to his own ideals. "I am sick and tired of it, and you can put that in the damn article," he shouted. We did, and many others picked up the thundering rebuke in articles of their own. I asked Clinton about his temper in 2000, when I conducted the third interview (which you'll find here) in the private residence at the White House and on *Air Force One* as the president was on his way to a campaign stop on behalf of Al Gore. "One of the things I had to learn," Clinton said, "it took me almost my whole first term to learn it—was that, at some point, presidents are not permitted to have personal feelings. When you manifest your anger in public, it should be on behalf of the American people and the values that they believe in."

Taken together, the forty interviews in this collection form a cultural history of our times, as narrated by the most important people of our times. You'll find here rock & roll pioneers like Tina Turner, Ray Charles and Johnny Cash. You'll find the crucial voices of the Sixties: Lennon, Jagger, Dylan, Townshend and Jerry Garcia, some caught at the start of their careers and others sharing the perspective of several decades of ups and downs. You'll find the great songwriters of the seventies (Neil Young and Joni Mitchell), the Eighties (Bruce Springsteen and Bono), the Nineties (Kurt Cobain) and today (Eminem). You'll find great directors like Francis Ford Coppola, George Lucas, Clint Eastwood and Spike Lee. You'll find writers who helped shaped generations of readers (and *Rolling Stone* itself), like Hunter S. Thompson and Tom Wolfe. You'll find cultural heroes who rarely granted interviews, like Johnny Carson, and great interviewers who had the tables turned on them, like Oriana Fallaci. And, not content to speak with presidents, we also spoke with God, in the person of the Dalai Lama.

Times have changed. You can no longer stroll up to Pete Townshend after a show and ask if he has time for an interview. But one thing remains the same: The *Rolling Stone* Interview is still the most intimate, penetrating, and perceptive conversation going.

Jann S. Wenner
New York City
September 13, 2007

THE

INTERVIEWS

PETE TOWNSHEND

by Jann S. Wenner

September 28, 1968

The end of your act goes to "My Generation," like you usually do, and that's where you usually smash your guitar. You didn't tonight—why not?

Well, there is a reason, not really anything that's really worth talking about. But I'll explain the pattern of thought which went into it.

I've obviously broken a lot of guitars, and I've brought eight or nine of that particular guitar I was using tonight and I could very easily have broken it and have plenty more for the future. But I just suddenly decided before I went on that if there was anywhere in the world I should be able to walk off the stage without breaking a guitar if I didn't want to, it would be the Fillmore.

I decided in advance that I didn't want to smash the guitar, so I didn't, not because I liked it or because I've decided I'm going to stop doing it or anything. I just kind of decided about the actual situation; it forced me to see if I could have gotten away with it in advance. And I think that's why "My Generation" was such a down number at the end. I didn't really want to play it, you know, at all. I didn't even want people to expect it to happen, because I just wasn't going to do it.

But Keith still dumped over his drum kit like he usually does.

Yeah, but it was an incredible personal thing with me. I've often gone on the stage with a guitar and said, "Tonight I'm not going to smash a guitar and I don't give a shit"—you know what the pressure is on me—whether I feel like doing it musically or whatever, I'm just not going to do it. And I've gone on, and *every* time I've done it. The actual performance has always been bigger than my own patterns of thought.

Tonight, for some reason, I went on and I said, "I'm not going to break it," and I didn't. And I don't know how, I don't really know why I didn't. But I didn't, you know, and it's the first time. I mean, I've said it millions of times before, and nothing has happened.

I imagine it gets to be a drag talking about why you smash your guitar.

No, it doesn't get to be a drag to talk about it. Sometimes it gets a drag to do it. I can explain it, I can justify it and I can enhance it, and I can do a lot of things, dramatize it and literalize it. Basically it's a gesture which happens on the spur of the moment. I think, with guitar smashing, just like performance itself; it's a performance, it's an act, it's an instant and it really is meaningless.

When did you start smashing guitars?

It happened by complete accident the first time. We were just kicking around in a club which we played every Tuesday, and I was playing the guitar and it hit the ceiling. It broke, and it kind of shocked me 'cause I wasn't ready for it to go. I didn't particularly want it to go, but it went.

And I was expecting an incredible thing, it being so precious to me, and I was expecting everybody to go, "Wow, he's broken his guitar, he's broken his guitar," but nobody did anything, which made me kind of angry in a way and determined to get this precious event noticed by the audience. I proceeded to make a big thing of breaking the guitar. I pounded all over the stage with it, and I threw the bits on the stage, and I picked up my spare guitar and carried on as though I really meant to do it.

Were you happy about it?

Deep inside I was very unhappy because the thing had got broken. It got around, and the next week the people came, and they came up to me and they said, "Oh, we heard all about it, man; it's 'bout time someone gave it to a guitar," and all this kind of stuff. It kind of grew from there; we'd go to another town and people would say, "Oh yeah, we heard that you smashed a guitar." It built and built and built and built and built and built until one day, a very important daily newspaper came to see us and said, "Oh, we hear you're the group that smashes their guitars up. Well, we hope you're going to do it tonight because we're from the *Daily Mail*. If you do, you'll probably make the front pages."

This was only going to be like the second guitar I'd ever broken, seriously. I went to my manager, Kit Lambert, and I said, you know, "Can we afford it, can we afford it, it's for publicity." He said, "Yes, we can afford it, if we can get the *Daily Mail*." I did it, and of course the *Daily Mail* didn't buy the photograph and didn't want to know about the story. After that I was into it up to my neck and have been doing it since.

Was it inevitable that you were going to start smashing guitars?

It was due to happen because I was getting to the point where I'd play and I'd play, and I mean, I still can't play how I'd like to play. *Then* it was worse. I couldn't play the guitar; I'd listen to great music, I'd listen to all the people I dug, time and time again. When the Who first started we were playing blues, and I dug the blues and I knew what I was supposed to be playing, but I couldn't play it. I couldn't get it out. I knew what I had to play; it was in my head. I could hear the notes in my head, but I couldn't get them out on the guitar. I knew the music, and I knew the feeling of the thing and the drive and the direction and everything.

It used to frustrate me incredibly. I used to try and make up visually for what I couldn't play as a musician. I used to get into very incredible visual things where in order just to make one chord more lethal, I'd make it a really lethal-looking thing, whereas really, it's just going to be picked normally. I'd hold my arm up in the air and bring it down so it really looked lethal, even if it didn't sound too lethal. Anyway, this got bigger and bigger and bigger and bigger until eventually I was setting myself incredible tasks.

How did this affect your guitar playing?

Instead I said, "All right, you're not capable of doing it musically, you've got to do it visually." I became a huge, visual thing. In fact, I forgot all about the guitar because my visual thing was more my music than the actual guitar. I got to jump about, and the guitar became unimportant. I banged it and I let it feed back and scraped it and rubbed it up against the microphone, did anything; it wasn't part of my act, even. It didn't deserve any credit or any respect. I used to bang it and hit it against walls and throw it on the floor at the end of the act.

And one day it broke. It just wasn't part of my thing, and ever since then I've never really regarded myself as a guitarist. When people come up to me and say like, "Who's your favorite guitarist?" I say, "I know who my favorite guitarist is, but asking me, as a guitarist, forget it because I don't make guitar-type comments. I don't talk guitar talk, I just throw the thing around." Today still, I'm learning. If I play a solo, it's a game to me because I can't play what I want to play. That's the thing: I can't get it out because I don't practice. When I should be practicing, I'm writing songs, and when I'm writing songs, I should be practicing.

You said you spend most of your time writing songs in your basement.

A lot of writing I do on tour. I do a lot on airplanes. At home, I write a lot, obviously. When I write a song, what I usually do is work the lyric out first from some basic idea that I had, and then I get an acoustic guitar and I sit by the tape recorder and I try to bang it out as it comes. Try to let the music come with the lyrics. If I dig it, I want to add things to it, like I'll add bass guitar or drums or another voice. This is really for my own amusement that I do this.

I'm working on the lyrics now for the next album. The album concept in general is complex. I don't know if I can explain it in my condition, at the moment. But it's derived as a result of quite a few things. We've been talking about doing an opera, we've been talking about doing like albums, we've been talking about a whole lot of things and what has basically happened is that we've condensed all of these ideas, all this energy and all these gimmicks, and whatever we've decided on for future albums, into one juicy package. The package I hope is going to be called "Deaf, Dumb and Blind Boy." It's a story about a kid that's born deaf, dumb and blind and what happens to him throughout his life. The deaf, dumb and blind boy is played by the Who, the musical entity. He's represented musically, represented by a theme which we play, which starts off the opera itself, and then there's a song describing the deaf, dumb and blind boy. But what it's really all about is the fact that because the boy is "D, D & B," he's seeing things basically as vibrations which we translate as music. That's really what we want to do: create this feeling that when you listen to the music you can actually become aware of the boy, and aware of what he is all about, because we are creating him as we play.

Yes, it's a pretty far-out thing, actually. But it's very, very endearing to me because the thing is…inside; the boy sees things musically and in dreams, and nothing has got any weight at all. He is touched from the outside, and he feels his mother's touch, he feels his father's touch, but he just interprets them as music. His father

7

gets pretty upset that his kid is deaf, dumb and blind. He wants a kid that will play football and God knows what.

One night he comes in and he's drunk, and he sits over the kid's bed and he looks at him and he starts to talk to him, and the kid just smiles up, and his father is trying to get through to him, telling him about how the other dads have a kid that they can take to football and they can teach them to play football and all this kind of crap, and he starts to say, "Can you hear me?" The kid, of course, can't hear him. He's groovin' in this musical thing, this incredible musical thing; he'll be out of his mind. Then there's his father outside, outside of his body, and this song is going to be written by John. I hope John will write this song about the father who is really uptight now.

The kid won't respond, he just smiles. The father starts to hit him, and at this moment the whole thing becomes incredibly realistic. On one side you have the dreamy music of the boy wasting through his nothing life. And on the other you have the reality of the father outside, uptight, but now you've got blows, you've got communication. The father is hitting the kid; musically then I want the thing to break out, hand it over to Keith — "This is your scene, man, take it from here."

And the kid doesn't catch the violence. He just knows that some sensation is happening. He doesn't feel the pain, he doesn't associate it with anything. He just accepts it.

A similar situation happens later on in the opera, where the father starts to get the mother to take the kid away from home to an uncle. The uncle is a bit of a perv, you know. He plays with the kid's body while the kid is out. And at this particular time the child has heard his own name; his mother called him. And he managed to hear the word: "Tommy." He's really got this big thing about his name, whatever his name is going to be, you know, "Tommy." And he gets really hung up on his own name. He decides that this is the king and this is the goal. Tommy is the thing, man.

He's going through this, and the uncle comes in and starts to go through a scene with the kid's body, you know, and the boy experiences sexual vibrations, you know, sexual experience, and again it's just basic music; it's interpreted as music, and it is nothing more than music. It's got no association with sleaziness or with undercover or with any of the things normally associated with sex. None of the romance, none of the visual stimulus, none of the sound stimulus. Just basic touch. It's *meaningless*. Or not meaningless; you just don't react, you know. Slowly but surely the kid starts to get it together, out of this simplicity, this incredible simplicity in his mind. He starts to realize that he can see, and he can hear, and he can speak; they are there, and they are happening all the time. And that all the time he has been able to hear and see. All the time it's been there in front of him, for him to see.

This is the difficult jump. It's going to be extremely difficult, but we want to try to do it musically. At this point, the theme, which has been the boy, starts to change. You start to realize that he is coming to the point where he is going to get over the top, he's going to get over his hang-ups. You're gonna stop monkeying around with songs about people being tinkered with, and with Father's getting uptight, with Mother's getting precious and things, and you're gonna get down to the fact of what is going to happen to the kid.

The music has got to explain what happens, that the boy elevates and finds something which is incredible. To us, it's nothing to be able to see and hear and speak, but to him, it's absolutely incredible and overwhelming; this is what we want to do musically. Lyrically, it's quite easy to do it; in fact, I've written it out several times. It makes great poetry, but so much depends on the music, so much. I'm hoping that we can do it. The lyrics are going to be okay, but every pitfall of what we're trying to say lies in the music, lies in the way we play the music, the way we interpret, the way things are going during the opera.

The main characters are going to be the boy and his musical things; he's got a mother and father and an uncle. There is a doctor involved who tries to do some psychiatric treatment on the kid which is only partly successful. The first two big events are when he hears his mother calling him and hears the word "Tommy," and he

devotes a whole part of his life to this one word. The second important event is when he sees himself in a mirror, suddenly seeing himself for the first time. He takes an immediate back step, bases his
whole life around his own image. The whole thing then becomes
incredibly introverted. The music and the lyrics become introverted, and he starts to talk about himself, starts to talk about his
beauty. Not knowing, of course, that what he saw was him but still
regarding it as something which belonged to him, and of course it
did all of the time anyway.

*This theme, not so dramatically, seems to be repeated in so many songs that
you've written and the Who have performed—a young cat, our age, becoming an outcast from a very ordinary sort of circumstance. Not a "Desolation
Row" scene, but a very common set of middle-class situations. Why does this
repeat itself?*

I don't know. I never really thought about that.

*There's a boy with pimple problems and a chick with perspiration troubles
and so on.*

Most of those things just come from me. Like this idea I'm talking
about right now, comes from me. These things are my ideas, it's
probably why they all come out the same; they've all got the same
fuckups, I'm sure.

  I can't get my family together, you see. My family were musicians.
They were essentially middle class, they were musicians, and I spent
a lot of time with them when other kids' parents were at work, and
I spent a lot of time *away* from them when other kids had parents,
you know. That was the way it came together. They were always out
for long periods. But they were always home for long periods, too.
They were always very respectable—nobody ever stopped making me play the guitar and nobody ever stopped me smoking pot,
although they advised me against it.

  They didn't stop me from doing anything that I wanted to do. I had my first fuck in the drawing room of my mother's house. The whole incredible thing about my parents is that I just can't place their effect on me, and yet I know that it's there. I can't say how they affected me. When people find out that my parents are musicians, they ask how it affected me. Fucked if I know; musically, I can't place it, and I can't place it in any other way. But I don't even feel myself aware of a class structure, or an age structure, and yet I perpetually write about age structures and class structures. On the surface I feel much more concerned with racial problems and politics. Inside I'm much more into basic stuff.

You must have thought about where it comes from if it's not your parents. Was it the scene around you when you were young?

One of the things which has impressed me most in life was the mod movement in England, which was an incredible youthful thing. It was a movement of young people, much bigger than the hippie thing, the underground and all these things. It was an army, a powerful, aggressive army of teenagers with transport. Man, with these scooters and with their own way of dressing. It was acceptable, this was important; their way of dressing was hip, it was fashionable, it was clean and it was groovy. You could be a bank clerk, man, it was acceptable. You got them on your own ground. They thought, "Well, there's a smart young lad." And also you were hip, you didn't get people uptight. That was the good thing about it. To be a mod, you had to have short hair, money enough to buy a real smart suit, good shoes, good shirts; you had to be able to dance like a madman. You had to be in possession of plenty of pills all the time and always be pilled up. You had to have a scooter covered in lamps. You had to have like an army anorak to wear on the scooter. And that was being a mod, and that was the end of the story.

The groups that you liked when you were a mod were the Who. That's the story of why I dig the mods, man, because we were mods and that's how we happened. That's my generation, that's how the song "My Generation" happened, because of the mods. The mods could appreciate the Beatles' taste. They could appreciate their haircuts, their peculiar kinky things that they had going at the time.

What would happen is that the phenomena of the Who could invoke action. The sheer fact that four mods could actually form themselves into a group which sounded quite good, considering that most mods were lower-class garbagemen, you know, with enough money to buy himself Sunday best, you know, their people. Nowadays, okay, there are quite a few mod groups. But mods aren't the kind of people that could play the guitar, and it was just groovy for them to have a group. Our music at the time was representative of what the mods dug, and it was meaningless rubbish.

We used to play, for example, "Heat Wave," a very long version of "Smokestack Lightning," and that song we sang tonight, "Young Man Blues," fairly inconsequential kind of music which they could identify with and perhaps something where you banged your feet on the third beat or clapped your hands on the fifth beat, something so that you get the thing to go by. I mean, they used to like all kinds of things. They were mods and we're mods and we dig them. We used to make sure that if there was a riot, a mod-rocker riot, we would be playing in the area. That was a place called Brighton.

By the sea?

Yes. That's where they used to assemble. We'd always be playing there. And we got associated with the whole thing, and we got into the spirit of the whole thing. And, of course, rock & roll, the words wouldn't even be mentioned; the fact that music would have any part of the movement was terrible. The music would come from the actual drive of the youth combination itself.

You see, as individuals these people were nothing. They were the lowest, they were England's lowest common denominators. Not only were they young, they were also lower-class young. They had to submit to the middle-class way of dressing and way of speaking and way of acting in order to get the very jobs which kept them alive.

They had to do everything in terms of what existed already around them. That made their way of getting something across that much more latently effective, the fact that they were hip and yet still, as far as Granddad was concerned, exactly the same. It made the whole gesture so much more vital. It was incredible. As a force, they were unbelievable. That was the Bulge, that was England's Bulge; all the war babies, all the old soldiers coming back from war and screwing until they were blue in the face—this was the result. Thousands and thousands of kids, too many kids, not enough teachers, not enough parents, not enough pills to go around. Everybody just grooving on being a mod.

I forget if I read this or whether it is something [producer and engineer] Glyn Johns told me. You and the group came out of this rough, tough area, were very restless and had this thing: You were going to show everybody; you were a kid with a big nose, and you were going to make all these people love it, love your big nose.

That was probably a mixture of what Glyn told you and an article I wrote. In fact, Glyn was exactly the kind of person I wanted to show. Glyn used to be one of the people who, right when I walked in, he'd be on the stage singing. I'd walk in because I dug his group. I'd often go to see him, and he would announce through the microphone, "Look at that bloke in the audience with that huge nose," and of course the whole audience would turn around and look at me, and that would be acknowledgment from Glyn.

When I was in school the geezers that were snappy dressers and got chicks like years before I ever even thought they existed would always like to talk about my nose. This seemed to be the biggest thing in my life: my fucking nose, man. Whenever my dad got drunk, he'd come up to me and say, "Look, son, you know, looks aren't everything," and shit like this. He's getting drunk, and he's ashamed of me because I've got a huge nose, and he's trying to make me feel good. I know it's huge, and of course it became incredible, and I became an enemy of society. I had to get over this thing. I've done it, and I never believe it to this day, but I do not think about my nose anymore. And if I had said this when I was a kid, if I ever said to myself, "One of these days you'll go through a whole day without once thinking that your nose is the biggest in the world, man"—you know, I'd have laughed.

It was huge. At that time, it was the reason I did everything. It's the reason I played the guitar—because of my nose. The reason I wrote songs was because of my nose, everything, so much. I eventually admitted something in an article where I summed it up far more logically in terms of what I do today. I said that what I wanted to do was distract attention from my nose to my body and make people look at my body, instead of at my face—turn my body into a machine. But by the time I was into visual things like that, anyway, I'd forgotten all about my nose and a big ego trip, and I thought, well, if I've got a big nose, it's a groove and it's the greatest thing that can happen because, I don't know, it's like a lighthouse or something. The whole trip had changed by then, anyway.

JIM MORRISON
by Jerry Hopkins

July 26, 1969

How did you start this... decide you were going to be a performer?

I think I had a suppressed desire to do something like this ever since I heard...y'see, the birth of rock & roll coincided with my adolescence, my coming into awareness. It was a real turn-on, although at the time I could never allow myself to rationally fantasize about ever doing it myself. I guess all that time I was unconsciously accumulating inclination and listening. So when it finally happened, my subconscious had prepared the whole thing.

I didn't think about it. It was just there. I never did any singing. I never even conceived it. I thought I was going to be a writer or a sociologist, maybe write plays. I never went to concerts—one or two at most. I saw a few things on TV, but I'd never been a part of it all. But I heard in my head a whole concert situation, with a band and singing and an audience—a large audience. Those first five or six songs I wrote, I was just taking notes at a fantastic rock concert that was going on inside my head. And once I had written the songs, I had to sing them.

When was this?

About three years ago. I wasn't in a group or anything. I just got out of college and I went down to the beach. I wasn't doing much of anything. I was free for the first time. I had been going to school, constantly, for fifteen years. It was a beautiful hot summer and I just started hearing songs. I think I still have the notebook with those songs written in it. This kind of mythic concert that I heard...I'd like to try and reproduce it sometime, either in actuality or on record. I'd like to reproduce what I heard on the beach that day.

Had you ever played any musical instrument?

When I was a kid I tried piano for a while, but I didn't have the discipline to keep up with it.

How long did you take piano?

Only a few months. I think I got to about the third-grade book.

Any desire now to play an instrument?

Not really. I play maracas. I can play a few songs on the piano. Just my own inventions, so it's not really music; it's noise. I can play one song. But it's got only two changes in it. Two chords, so it's pretty basic stuff. I would like to be able to play guitar, but I don't have any feeling for it.

When did you start writing poetry?

Oh, I think around the fifth or sixth grade I wrote a poem called "The Pony Express." That was the first I can remember. It was one of those ballad-type poems. I never could get it together, though. I always wanted to write, but I always figured it'd be no good unless somehow the hand just took the pen and started moving without me really having anything to do with it. Like, automatic writing. But it just never happened. I wrote a few poems, of course.

Like, "Horse Latitudes," I wrote when I was in high school. I kept a lot of notebooks through high school and college and then when

I left school for some dumb reason—maybe it was wise—I threw them all away. There's nothing I can think of I'd rather have in my possession right now than those two or three lost notebooks. I was thinking of being hypnotized or taking sodium Pentothal to try to remember, because I wrote in those books night after night. But maybe if I'd never thrown them away, I'd never have written anything original—because they were mainly accumulations of things that I'd read or heard, like quotes from books. I think if I'd never gotten rid of them I'd never been free.

A question you've been asked before countless times: do you see yourself in a political role? I'm throwing a quote of yours back at you, in which you described the Doors as "erotic politicians."

It was just that I've been aware of the national media while growing up. They were always around the house and so I started reading them. And so I became aware gradually, just by osmosis, of their style, their approach to reality. When I got into the music field, I was interested in securing kind of a place in that world, and so I was turning keys and I just knew instinctively how to do it. They look for catchy phrases and quotes they can use for captions, something to base an article on to give it an immediate response. It's the kind of term that does mean something, but it's impossible to explain. If I tried to explain what it means to me, it would lose all its force as a catchword.

Deliberate media manipulation, right? Two questions come to me. Why did you pick that phrase over others? And do you think it's pretty easy to manipulate the media?

I don't know if it's easy, because it can turn on you. But, well, that was just one reporter, y'see. I was just answering his question. Since then a lot of people have picked up on it—that phrase—and have made it pretty heavy, but actually I was just...I knew the guy would use it and I knew what the picture painted would be. I knew that a few key phrases is all anyone ever retains from an article. So I wanted a phrase that would stick in the mind.

I do think it's more difficult to manipulate TV and film than it is the press. The press has been easy for me in a way, because I am biased toward writing and I understand writing and the mind of writers; we are dealing with the same medium, the printed word. So that's been fairly easy. But television and films are much more difficult and I'm still learning. Each time I go on TV I get a little more relaxed and a little more able to communicate openly, and control it. It's an interesting process.

Does this explain your fascination with film?

I'm interested in film because to me it's the closest approximation in art that we have to the actual flow of consciousness, in both dream life and in the everyday perception of the world.

You're getting more involved in film all the time . . .

Yeah, but there's only one we've completed — *Feast of Friends,* which was made at the end of a spiritual, cultural renaissance that's just about over now.

How much in 'Feast of Friends' is you? Aside from what we see. The technical aspects . . . putting the film together . . . how much of that did you do?

In conception, it was a very small crew following us around for three or four months in a lot of concerts, culminating in the Hollywood Bowl [summer 1968]. Then the group went to Europe on a short tour and while we were there, Frank Lisciandro and Paul Ferrara, the editor and photographer, started hacking it together. We returned, we looked at the rough cut and showed it to people. No one liked it very much and a lot of people were ready to abandon the project. I was almost of that opinion, too. But Frank and Paul wanted a chance so we let them. I worked with them in the refining of the editing and

I made some good suggestions on the form it should take and after a few more...after paring down the material, I think we got an interesting film out of it.

I think it's a timeless film. I'm glad it exists. I want to look at it through the years from time to time and look back on what we were doing. Y'know, it's interesting...the first time I saw the film I was rather taken aback, because being onstage and one of the central figures in the film, I only saw it from my point of view. Then, to see a series of events that I thought I had some control over...to see it as it actually was...I suddenly realized in a way I was just a puppet of a lot of forces I only vaguely understood. It was kind of shocking.

I think of one part of the film, a performance sequence, in which you're flat on your back, still singing...which represents how theatrical you've gotten in your performance. How did that theatricality develop? Was it a conscious thing?

I think in a club, histrionics would be a little out of place, because the room is too small and it would be a little grotesque. In a large concert situation, I think it's just...necessary, because it gets to be more than just a musical event. It turns into a little bit of a spectacle. And it's different every time. I don't think any one performance is like any other. I can't answer that very well. I'm not too conscious of what's happening. I don't like to be too objective about it. I like to let each thing happen—direct it a little consciously, maybe, but just kind of follow the vibrations I get in each particular circumstance. We don't plan theatrics. We hardly ever know which set we'll play.

I'm hesitant to bring it up, because so bloody much has been made of it, and I guess I want your reaction to that as well as the truth of the matter...the Oedipus section of "The End." Just what does this song mean to you?

Let's see...Oedipus is a Greek myth. Sophocles wrote about it. I don't know who before that. It's about a man who inadvertently killed his father and married his mother. Yeah, I'd say there was a similarity, definitely. But to tell you the truth, every time I hear that song, it means something else to me. I really don't know what I was trying to say. It just started out as a simple goodbye song.

Goodbye to whom, or to what?

Probably just to a girl, but I could see how it could be goodbye to a kind of childhood. I really don't know. I think it's sufficiently complex and universal in its imagery that it could be almost anything you want it to be.

I don't care what critics write about it, or anything like that, but one thing that disturbed me...I went to a movie one night in Westwood and I was in a bookstore or some shop where they sell pottery and calendars and gadgets, y'know...and a very attractive, intelligent—intelligent in the sense of aware and open—girl thought she recognized me and she came to say hello. And she was asking about that particular song. She was just out for a little stroll with a nurse. She was on leave just, just for an hour or so, from the UCLA Neuropsychiatric Institute. She lived there and was just out for a walk. Apparently she had been a student at UCLA and freaked on heavy drugs or something and either committed herself or someone picked up on her and put her there. Anyway, she said that song was really a favorite of a lot of kids in her ward. At first I thought: Oh, man...and this was after I talked with her for a while, saying it could mean a lot of things, kind of a maze or a puzzle to think about, everybody should relate it to their own situation. I didn't realize people took songs so seriously and it made me wonder whether I ought to consider the consequences. That's kind of ridiculous, because I do it myself; you don't think of the consequences and you can't.

Getting back to your film, then, there's some of the most incredible footage I've ever seen of an audience rushing a performer. What do you think in a situation like that?

It's just a lot of fun [*laughs*]. It actually looks a lot more exciting than it really is. Film compresses everything. It packs a lot of energy into a small...anytime you put a form on reality, it's going to look more intense. Truthfully, a lot of times it was very exciting, a lot of fun. I enjoy it or I wouldn't do it.

You said the other day that you like to get people up out of their seats, but not intentionally create a chaos situation...

It's never gotten out of control, actually. It's pretty playful, really. We have fun, the kids have fun, the cops have fun. It's kind of a weird triangle. We just think about going out to play good music. Sometimes I'll extend myself and work people up a little bit, but usually we're out there trying to make good music and that's it. Each time it's different. There are varying degrees of fever in an auditorium waiting for you. So you go out onstage and you're met with this rush of energy potential. You never know what it's going to be.

What do you mean you'll sometimes extend yourself...work the people up a bit?

Let's just say I was testing the bounds of reality. I was curious to see what would happen. That's all it was: just curiosity.

There is a quote attributed to you. It appears in print a lot. It goes: "I'm interested in anything about revolt, disorder, chaos..."

"...especially activity that appears to have no meaning."

Right. That one. Is this another example of media manipulation? Did you make that one up for a newspaper guy?

Yes, definitely. But it's true, too. Who isn't fascinated with chaos? More than that, though, I am interested in activity that has no meaning, and all I mean by that is free activity. Play. Activity that has nothing in it except just what it is. No repercussions. No motivation.

Free...activity. I think there should be a national carnival much the same as Mardi Gras in Rio. There should be a week of national hilarity...a cessation of all work, all business, all discrimination, all authority. A week of total freedom. That'd be a start. Of course, the power structure wouldn't really alter. But someone off the streets—I don't know how they'd pick him, at random perhaps—would become president. Someone else would become vice president. Others would become senators, congressmen, on the Supreme Court, policemen. It would just last for a week and then go back to the way it was. I think we need it. Yeah. Something like that.

This may be insulting, but I have a feeling I'm being put on...

A little bit. But I don't know. People would have to be real for a week. And it might help the rest of the year. There would have to be some form of ritual to it. I think something like that is really needed.

You've twice said that you think you successfully manipulated the press. How much of this interview was manipulated?

You can't ever get around the fact that what you say could possibly turn up in print sometime, so you have that in the back of your mind. I've tried to forget it.

Is there some other area you'd like to get into?

How about...feel like discussing alcohol? Just a short dialogue. No long rap. Alcohol as opposed to drugs?

Okay. Part of the mythology has you playing the role of a heavy juicer.

On a very basic level, I love drinking. But I can't see drinking just milk or water or Coca-Cola. It just ruins it for me. You have to have wine or beer to complete a meal. [*Long pause*]

That's all you want to say? [Laughter]

Getting drunk…you're in complete control up to a point. It's your choice, every time you take a sip. You have a lot of small choices. It's like…I guess it's the difference between suicide and slow capitulation.

What's that mean?

I don't know, man. Let's go next door and get a drink.

PHIL SPECTOR

by Jann S. Wenner

November 1, 1969

You worked at Atlantic, a white-owned company, dealing primarily with black music. Was there any resentment from the artists?

Oh yeah, man, "We bought your home, goddamn, and don't you forget it, boy. You livin' in the house we paid for, you drivin' a Cadillac we got, man. It's ours. You stole it from us."

You heard that from the beginning of time. All the Drifters were gettin' was $150 a week and they never got any royalties. It wasn't that Atlantic didn't pay them; it was that everybody screwed everybody in those days. I mean I was in the Teddy Bears and what did we get—one penny a record royalties!

What has disappeared completely is the black groups, other than what you have comin' out of Motown and your other few—and I don't mean Stax-Volt because I don't consider that what I'm talking about. The group on the corner has disappeared. It's turned into a white psychedelic or a guitar group, there are thousands of them. There used to be hundreds and hundreds of black groups singin' harmony with a great lead singer and you'd go in and record them.

You used to go down to Jefferson High or 49th and Broadway and could get sixteen groups. Today you can't find them; they're either involved in the militant thing or they just passed, like it's not their bag anymore, or like it's just disappeared. It's not the big thing to get together after school and harmonize. And it used to be a real big thing. It was very important. I guess they just got tired of knocking on record doors, and they saw that a whole new regime had taken over.

This is why you have the music business dominated in the black area by just two companies. Because there is just really no place for them to go. They've just sort of disbanded. Other than Motown you don't see any groups, colored groups. The Dells happened for a while on that Cadet label from Chicago or whatever. That's where black *something* has affected it. I don't know if it's black militancy or whatever, but something has definitely effected the complete destruction of the black groups that used to be dominating the record industry.

How has that changed the music?

It's changed the music drastically. It's given birth to English groups to come along and do it like Eric Burdon. It's also given birth for the Stones and the Beatles to come along and do it—not that they wouldn't have done it otherwise—but the first place the Beatles wanted to see when they came to America, 'cause I came over on the plane with them, was the Apollo Theater.

As bad as a record as "Book of Love" by the Monotones is, you can hear a lot of "Book of Love" in the Beatles' "Why Don't We Do It in the Road?" I think you hear a lot of that dumb, great-yet-nonsensical stuff that makes it—even though it's silly. It's got the same nonsense.

I believe that the English kids have soul. Really soul. When I watch Walter Cronkite or *Victory at Sea,* or *You Are There*—any of those programs, I see bombs flying all over England and little kids running. Now that's probably Paul McCartney running. You know, 'cause that's where the bombs fell. They say soul comes through suffering. Slavery for the blacks. And gettin' your ass bombed off is another way of gettin' some soul, so I would say that these English cats have a lot of soul legitimately. You're gonna have Dave Clark in there who don't know too much about it, and just like you're gonna have a Rosy and the Originals in America who don't know too much about it.

What artist do you really feel has not been recorded right that you'd like to record?

Bob Dylan.

How would you record him?

I'd do a Dylan opera with him. I'd produce him. You see, he's never been produced. He's always gone into the studio on the strength of his lyrics, and they have sold enough records to cover up every-thing—all the honesty of his records. But he's never really made a production. He doesn't really have to.

His favorite song is "Like a Rolling Stone," and it stands to reason because that's his grooviest song, as far as songs go. It may not be his grooviest message. It may not be the greatest thing he ever wrote, but I can see why he gets the most satisfaction out of it, because rewriting "La Bamba" chord changes is always a lot of fun and any time you can make a Number One record and rewrite those kind of changes, it is very satisfying.

I would like him to just say something that could live recording-wise forever. I would have enjoyed recording *John Wesley Harding* in its own way. He doesn't really have the time nor do any of his producers necessarily have the ambition or talent to really overrule him and debate with him. I would imagine with Albert Grossman there is a situation of business control just like it would be with Elvis Presley and Colonel Parker. Assume that there is no control, then somebody should be much more forceful. Maybe nobody has the guts, balls or the ambition to get in there, but there is no reason unless Dylan didn't want it. But there is a way he could have been made to want it.

There is no reason why Dylan can't be recorded in a very certain way and a very beautiful way where you can just sit back and say "wow" about everything—not just him and the song—just every-thing.

How would you have done 'John Wesley Harding'?

There is a way to do it. He's so great on it and he is so honest that it's just like going into the studio with twelve of Stephen Foster's songs. There's so much you can do. There is so much you can do with Dylan; he gives you so much to work with. That's probably why he sells so many records without trying so very hard in the studio.

It's also probably why the Beatles...well it's obvious that Paul McCartney and John Lennon may be the greatest rock & roll sing-ers that we've ever had. They may be the greatest singers of the last ten years—they really may be! I mean there is a reason for the Beatles other than the fact that they're like Rogers and Hart and Hammerstein, Gershwin and all of 'em. They are *great, great* sing-ers. They can do anything with their voices.

Many of the artists today just sing, they don't really interpret any-thing. I mean the Doors don't interpret. They're not interpreters of music. They always sing ideas. The Beach Boys have always sung ideas—they've never been interpreters. The Beatles interpret; "Yes-terday" meant something. Whereas "Good Vibrations" was a nice idea on which everybody sort of grooved.

What did you think of 'Beggar's Banquet'?

Well, they're just makin' hit records now. There was a time when the Stones were really writing *contributions*. See that's a big word to me—"contributions."

What were the songs at the time?

"Satisfaction" was a contribution. They've had a few contributions. See, there's a difference: other than one or two numbers, Johnny Rivers is *not* a contribution to music, he never will be, he never can be. I don't care if all the Johnny Rivers fans say "boo." Just like Murray Roman will never be a comedian. There's just certain people that just don't have it. Moby Grape will never be a contribution. There are a lot of groups that will never be a contribution. 'Cause if you listen to just one Muddy Waters record you've heard everything Moby Grape's ever gonna do. Or if you listen to one Jimmy Reed record you've heard everything they may want to do.

The big word is "contribution," and the Stones lately have not been—although they have been writing groovy hit things—contributing anymore. You have a time when they were contributing *all* of it. Everything was contribution. They'll go down as a contribution. They'll be listed as a contributing force in music. An important influence. It's not a put-down on them, because *nobody* can keep up that pace.

What about John Lennon?

I haven't spoken to Lennon in some time so I don't know where he's at now. But I have a feeling that Yoko may not be the greatest influence on him. I mean, I don't know, but I have a feeling that he's a far greater talent than she is.

You know, a multimillionaire in his position just doesn't get caught in an English apartment house by the cops on a dope charge unless you're just blowing your mind or somebody is just really giving you a fucking. I mean you have dogs, you have bodyguards, you got *something* to protect you. Everybody knows the Beatles were immune. Everybody knows that George Harrison was at the Stones' party the night they got busted, and they let Harrison leave and then they went in and made the bust. I mean it was like the Queen said, "Leave them alone."

So Lennon must really have been causing a disturbance or somebody must have been setting him up to get busted, 'cause it ain't no medal of honor. Like it's no medal of honor to get the clap. Being busted for marijuana don't mean nothin'—it's just a waste of time, if anything. It wasted his time. It may have even caused…miscarriages.

It's almost like a weird thing to see just how bizarre he can get before he really blows it or he just teaches everybody something.

You came over with the Beatles when they first came over to the States. What was that like?

It was a lot of fun. It was probably the only time I flew that I wasn't afraid, because I knew they weren't goin' to get killed in a plane. That plane was really an awful trip. I mean there were twenty-eight or thirty minutes where that plane dropped thousands of feet over the ocean. It scared the shit out of me, but there were 149 people on board who were all press and Beatles' right-hand men, and left-hand men, and we just sat up there and talked about the Apollo and all that jive. Lennon was with his first wife, and he was very quiet. Paul asked a lot of questions, George was wonderful. It was a nice trip.

I'd just been in England for a couple of weeks and I went by their apartment, and they were leaving and said why don't you come back with us. It's really funny, but they were terribly frightened to get off the plane.

They were terribly frightened of America. They even said, "You go first." 'Cause the whole thing about Kennedy scared them very, very much. They really thought it would be possible for somebody to be there and want to kill them, because they were just very shocked. The assassination really dented them tremendously—their image of America. Just like it dented everybody's image of the Secret Service.

What are you gonna do with the stuff you're workin' on now? How does that differ from the last work you did with Ike and Tina Turner?

Don't know. I will go in many directions—some experimental—some not. Today "River Deep—Mountain High" could be a Number One record. I think when it came out, it was just like my farewell. I was just sayin' goodbye, and I just wanted to go crazy, you know, for a few minutes—four minutes on wax, that's all it was. I loved it, and I enjoyed making it, but I didn't really think there was anything for the public…nobody had really gotten into it enough yet; it really hadn't exploded the way it's exploding today with all the sounds and they're really freaking out with the electronical stuff. Today "River Deep—Mountain High" would probably be a very important sales record. When I made it, it couldn't be—so, I don't know. I got what I wanted out of it.

You see, I don't have a sound, a Phil Spector sound—I have a style, and my style is just a particular way of making records—as opposed to Lou Adler or any of the other record producers who follow the artist's style. I create a style and call it a sound or a style; I call it a *style* because it's a way of doing it.

My style is that I know things about recording that other people just don't know. It's simple and clear, and it's easy for me to make hits. I think the *River Deep* LP would be a nice way to start off because it's a record that Tina deserves to be heard on—she was sensational on that record. A record that was Number One in England deserves to be Number One in America. If so many people are doing the song today, it means it's ready.

How did your association with Ike and Tina first come about?

They were introduced to me. Somebody told me to see them, and their in-person act just killed me. I mean, they were just sensational.

Have you seen it lately?

Yeah, I saw them at the Factory, of all places. They were…well, I always loved Tina. I never knew how great she was. She *real*-ly is as great as Aretha is. I mean, in her own bag she is sensational, and Joplin and all that, but I couldn't figure out how to get her on record.

What do you think the difference is going to be between the audience today and the audience's reaction to music today, as compared to five years ago?

I don't know. Everybody's a helluva lot hipper today. I'll tell you that. There's thirteen-year-old whores walkin' the streets now. It wouldn't have happened as much five years ago. Not thirteen-year-old drug addicts. It's a lot different today. I tell you, the whole world is a dropout. I mean, everybody's a fuck-off. Everybody's mini-skirted, everybody's hip, everybody reads *all* the books. How in the hell you gonna overcome all that? Sophistication, hipness, everything. They're really *very* hip today.

The music business is so different than any other business. You know, Frank Sinatra has a hit. Sister Dominique or whatever her name is, has a hit. I can show you six groups out there today who are opposite. I mean the Archies have a hit at the same time the Beatles do, hit really doesn't mean anything.

Now who's buyin' the Archies' records? That's what I can't understand, and who bought all the Monkees' records—same cats who bought all the Stones records? If they're not, then that makes the buyin' public so big... 'Cause the four million that bought the Monkees and the six million that bought the Beatles are different, then there's 10 million kids buying records. That's a helluva lot of a better throw at the dice. I'd rather have a chance out of 10 million times instead of 6 million times, so it probably will be easier.

How are you cutting with the Check Mates?

I don't know yet. All different ways. Very commercial records. Good records. Easy records. Soulful records. Some have depth, some don't have...

Does it worry you at all, that there's been a change?

Well, anything that deteriorates music bothers me a little bit. I mean, if when Beethoven lost his hearing, if I was alive, it would have bothered me. I have to be affected by it. It bothers me that some music is very boring. I hear a lot of disc jockeys saying, "Let's throw this shit out." I hear them saying there are so many fucking groups—so boring. I hear this so much, that I believe it. If it's true then yeah, it bothers me. It bothers me enough to get back in.

JOHN LENNON

by Jann S. Wenner

January 21, 1971

What do you think of your album 'Plastic Ono Band'?

I think it's the best thing I've ever done. I think it's realistic, and it's true to the me that has been developing over the years from my life. "I'm a Loser," "Help," "Strawberry Fields," they are all personal records. I always wrote about me when I could. I didn't really enjoy writing third-person songs about people who lived in concrete flats and things like that. I like first-person music. But because of my hang-ups and many other things, I would only now and then specifically write about me. Now I wrote all about me, and that's why I like it. It's me! And nobody else. That's why I like it. It's real, that's all.

I don't know about anything else, really, and the few true songs I ever wrote were like "Help" and "Strawberry Fields." I can't think of them all offhand. They were the ones I always considered my best songs. They were the ones I really wrote from experience and not projecting myself into a situation and writing a nice story about it. I always found that phony, but I'd find occasion to do it because I'd have to produce so much work, or because I'd be so hung up, I couldn't even think about myself.

On this album, there is practically no imagery at all.

Because there was none in my head. There were no hallucinations in my head.

There are no "newspaper taxis."

Actually, that's Paul's line. I was consciously writing poetry, and that's self-conscious poetry. But the poetry on this album is superior to anything I've done because it's not self-conscious, in that way. I had least trouble writing the songs of all time.

YOKO: There's no bullshit.

JOHN: There's no bullshit.

The arrangements are also simple and very sparse.

I always liked simple rock and nothing else. I was influenced by acid and got psychedelic, like the whole generation, but really, I like rock & roll, and I express myself best in rock.

How did you put together that litany in "God"?

What's "litany"?

"I don't believe in magic," that series of statements.

Well, like a lot of the words; it just came out of me mouth. "God" was put together from three songs, almost. I had the idea that "God is the concept by which we measure pain," so that when you have a word like that, you just sit down and sing the first tune that comes into your head, and the tune is simple because I like that kind of music, and then I just rolled into it. It was just going on in my head and I got by the first three or four, the rest just came out. Whatever came out.

When did you know that you were going to be working towards "I don't believe in Beatles"?

I don't know when I realized that I was putting down all these things I didn't believe in. So I could have gone on, it was like a Christmas card list: Where do I end? Churchill? Hoover? I thought I had to stop.

YOKO: He was going to have a do-it-yourself type of thing.

JOHN: Yes, I was going to leave a gap and just fill in your own words: whoever you don't believe in. It had just got out of hand, and Beatles was the final thing because I no longer believe in myth, and Beatles is another myth.

I don't believe in it. The dream is over. I'm not just talking about the Beatles, I'm talking about the generation thing. It's over, and we gotta—I have to personally—get down to so-called reality.

When did you become aware that the song would be the one that is played the most?

I didn't know that. I don't know. I'll be able to tell in a week or so what's going on, because they [the radio] started off playing "Look at Me" because it was easy, and they probably thought it was the Beatles or something. So I don't know if that is the one. Well, that's the one; "God" and "Working Class Hero" probably are the best whatevers—sort of ideas or feelings—on the record.

Why did you choose or refer to Zimmerman, not Dylan.

Because Dylan is bullshit. Zimmerman is his name. You see, I don't believe in Dylan, and I don't believe in Tom Jones, either, in that way. Zimmerman is his name. My name isn't John Beatle. It's John Lennon. Just like that.

Always the Beatles were talked about — and the Beatles talked about themselves — as being four parts of the same person. What's happened to those four parts?

They remembered that they were four individuals. You see, we believed the Beatles myth, too. I don't know whether the others still believe it. We were four guys...I met Paul, and said, "You want to join me band?" Then George joined and then Ringo joined. We were just a band that made it very, very big, that's all. Our best work was never recorded.

Why?

Because we were performers — in spite of what Mick says about us — in Liverpool, Hamburg and other dance halls. What we generated was fantastic, when we played straight rock, and there was nobody to touch us in Britain. As soon as we made it, we made it, but the edges were knocked off.

You know, Brian [Epstein, the Beatles' manager] put us in suits and all that, and we made it very, very big. But we sold out, you know. The music was dead before we even went on the theater tour of Britain. We were feeling shit already, because we had to reduce an hour or two hours' playing, which we were glad about in one way, to twenty minutes, and we would go on and repeat the same twenty minutes every night.

The Beatles' music died then, as musicians. That's why we never improved as musicians; we killed ourselves then to make it. And that was the end of it. George and I are more inclined to say that; we always missed the club dates because that's when we were playing music, and then later on we became technically efficient recording artists — which was another thing — because we were competent people, and whatever media you put us in we can produce something worthwhile.

How did you choose the musicians you use on this record?

I'm a very nervous person, really, I'm not as bigheaded as this tape sounds; this is me projecting through the fear, so I choose people that I know, rather than strangers.

Why do you get along with Ringo?

Because in spite of all the things, the Beatles could really play music together when they weren't uptight, and if I get a thing going, Ringo knows where to go, just like that, and he does well. We've played together so long that it fits. That's the only thing I some-times miss—just being able to sort of blink or make a certain noise and I know they'll all know where we are going on an ad lib thing. But I don't miss it that much.

How do you rate yourself as a guitarist?

Well, it depends on what kind of guitarist. I'm okay, I'm not techni-cally good, but I can make it fucking howl and move. I was rhythm guitarist. It's an important job. I can make a band drive.

How do you rate George?

He's pretty good. [*Laughs*] I prefer myself. I have to be honest, you know. I'm really very embarrassed about my guitar playing, in one way, because it's very poor. I can never move, but I can make a gui-tar speak.

You say you can make the guitar speak; what songs have you done that on?

Listen to "Why" on Yoko's album [or] "I Found Out." I think it's nice. It drives along. Ask Eric Clapton, he thinks I can play, ask him. You see, a lot of you people want technical things; it's like wanting tech-nical films. Most critics of rock & roll, and guitarists, are in the stage of the Fifties when they wanted a technically perfect film finished for them, and then they would feel happy.

I'm a cinema verité guitarist; I'm a musician, and you have to break down your barriers to hear what I'm playing. There's a nice little bit I played, they had it on the back of *Abbey Road*. Paul gave us each a piece; there is a little break where Paul plays, George plays and I played. And there is one bit, one of those where it stops, one of those "carry that weights" where it suddenly goes boom, boom on the drums, and then we all take it in turns to play. I'm the third one on it.

I have a definite style of playing. I've always had. But I was overshadowed. They call George the invisible singer. I'm the invisible guitarist.

You said you played slide guitar on "Get Back."

Yes, I played the solo on that. When Paul was feeling kindly, he would give me a solo! Maybe if he was feeling guilty that he had most of the A side or something, he would give me a solo. And I played the solo on that. I think George produced some beautiful guitar playing. But I think he's too hung up to really let go, but so is Eric, really. Maybe he's changed. They're all so hung up. We all are, that's the problem. I really like B.B. King.

I would like to ask a question about Paul and go through that. When we went and saw 'Let It Be' in San Francisco, what was your feeling?

I felt sad, you know. Also I felt...that film was set up by Paul for Paul. That is one of the main reasons the Beatles ended. I can't speak for George, but I pretty damn well know we got fed up of being sidemen for Paul.

After Brian died, that's what happened, that's what began to happen to us. The camera work was set up to show Paul and not anybody else. And that's how I felt about it. On top of that, the people that cut it did it as if Paul is God and we are just lyin' around there. And that's what I felt. And I knew there were some shots of Yoko and me that had been just chopped out of the film for no other reason than the people were oriented for Englebert Humperdinck. I felt sick.

How would you trace the breakup of the Beatles?

After Brian died, we collapsed. Paul took over and supposedly led us. But what is leading us when we went round in circles? We broke up then. That was the disintegration.

When did you first feel that the Beatles had broken up? When did that idea first hit you?

I don't remember, you know. I was in my own pain. I wasn't noticing, really. I just did it like a job. The Beatles broke up after Brian died; we made the double album, the set. It's like if you took each track off it and made it all mine and all George's. It's like I told you many times, it was just me and a backing group, Paul and a backing group, and I enjoyed it. We broke up then.

What was your feeling when Brian died?

The feeling that anybody has when somebody close to them dies. There is a sort of little hysterical sort of hee, hee, I'm glad it's not me or something in it, the funny feeling when somebody close to you dies. I don't know whether you've had it, but I've had a lot of people die around me, and the other feeling is, "What the fuck? What can I do?"

I knew that we were in trouble then. I didn't really have any misconceptions about our ability to do anything other than play music, and I was scared. I thought, "We've fuckin' had it."

What were the events that sort of immediately happened after Brian died?

Well, we went with Maharishi. . . . I remember being in Wales, and then, I can't remember, though. I will probably have to have a bloody primal to remember this. I don't remember. It just all happened.

How did Paul react?

I don't know how the others took it, it's no good asking me...it's like asking me how *you* took it. I don't know. I'm in me own head, I can't be in anybody else's. I don't know really what George, Paul or Ringo think anymore. I know them pretty well, but I don't know anybody that well. Yoko, I know about the best. I don't know how they felt. It was my own thing. We were all just dazed.

So Brian died, and then you said what happened was that Paul started to take over.

That's right. I don't know how much of this I want to put out. Paul had an impression, he has it now like a parent, that we should be thankful for what he did for keeping the Beatles going. But when you look back upon it objectively, he kept it going for his own sake. Was it for my sake Paul struggled?

Paul made an attempt to carry on as if Brian hadn't died by saying, "Now, now, boys, we're going to make a record." Being the kind of person I am, I thought, well, we're going to make a record all right, so I'll go along, so we went and made a record. And that's when we made *Magical Mystery Tour*. That was the real...

Paul had a tendency to come along and say, well, he's written these ten songs, let's record now. And I said, "Well, give us a few days, and I'll knock a few off," or something like that. *Magical Mystery Tour* was something he had worked out with Mal [Evans, the Beatles' personal assistant], and he showed me what his idea was and this is how it went, it went around like this, the story and how he had it all...the production and everything.

Paul said, "Well, here's the segment, you write a little piece for that," and I thought, bloody hell, so I ran off and I wrote the dream sequence for the fat woman and all the thing with the spaghetti. Then George and I were sort of grumbling about the fuckin' movie, and we thought we better do it, and we had the feeling that we owed it to the public to do these things.

When did your songwriting partnership with Paul end?

That ended...I don't know, around 1962, or something, I don't know. If you give me the albums I can tell you exactly who wrote what, and which line. We sometimes wrote together. All our best work—apart from the early days, like "I Want to Hold Your Hand," we wrote together and things like that—we wrote apart always. The "One after 909," on the *Let It Be* LP, I wrote when I was seventeen or eighteen. We always wrote separately, but we wrote together because we enjoyed it a lot sometimes, and also because they would say, well, you're going to make an album, get together and knock off a few songs, just like a job.

You said you quit the Beatles first.

Yes.

How?

I said to Paul, "I'm leaving."

I knew on the flight over to Toronto or before we went to Toronto: I told Allen [Klein, the Beatles' manager] I was leaving, I told Eric Clapton and Klaus [Voormann] that I was leaving then, but that I would probably like to use them as a group. I hadn't decided how to do it—to have a permanent new group or what—then, later on, I thought, fuck, I'm not going to get stuck with another set of people, whoever they are.

I announced it to myself and the people around me on the way to Toronto a few days before. And on the plane—Klein came with me—I told Allen, "It's over." When I got back, there were a few meetings, and Allen said, well, cool it, cool it, there was a lot to do, businesswise, you know, and it would not have been suitable at the time.

Then we were discussing something in the office with Paul, and Paul said something or other about the Beatles doing something, and I kept saying, "No, no, no," to everything he said. So it came to a point where I had to say something, of course, and Paul said, "What do you mean?"

I said, "I mean the group is over, I'm leaving."

Allen was there, and he will remember exactly and Yoko will, but this is exactly how I see it. Allen was saying, don't tell. He didn't want me to tell Paul even. So I said, "It's out," I couldn't stop it, it came out. Paul and Allen both said that they were glad that I wasn't going to announce it, that I wasn't going to make an event out of it. I don't know whether Paul said, "Don't tell anybody," but he was darned pleased that I wasn't going to. He said, "Oh, that means nothing really happened if you're not going to say anything."

So that's what happened. So, like anybody when you say divorce, their face goes all sorts of colors. It's like he knew really that this was the final thing; and six months later he comes out with whatever. I was a fool not to do it, not to do what Paul did, which was use it to sell a record.

You were really angry with Paul?

No, I wasn't angry.

Well, when he came out with this "I'm *leaving."*

No, I wasn't angry—shit, he's a good PR man, that's all. He's about the best in the world, probably. He really does a job. I wasn't angry. We were all hurt that he didn't tell us that was what he was going to do.

I think he claims that he didn't mean that to happen, but that's bullshit. He called me in the afternoon of that day and said, "I'm doing what you and Yoko were doing last year." I said, good, you know, because that time last year they were all looking at Yoko and me as if we were strange, trying to make our life together instead of being fab, fat myths. So he rang me up that day and said, I'm doing what you and Yoko are doing, I'm putting out an album, and I'm leaving the group, *too,* he said. I said, good. I was feeling a little strange because *he* was saying it this time, although it was a year later, and I said, "Good," because he was the one that wanted the Beatles most, and then the midnight papers came out.

How did you feel then?

I was cursing because I hadn't done it. I wanted to do it, I should have done it. Ah, damn, shit, what a fool I was. But there were many pressures at that time with the Northern Songs fight going on; it would have upset the whole thing if I would have said that.

How did you feel when you found out that Dick James [the Beatles' music publisher] had sold his shares in your own company, Northern Songs? Did you feel betrayed?

Sure I did. He's another one of those people who think they made us. They didn't. I'd like to hear Dick James' music and I'd like to hear George Martin's music, please, just play me some. Dick James actually has said that.

What?

That he *made* us. People are under a delusion that *they* made *us,* when in fact *we* made *them.*

How did you get Allen Klein into Apple?

The same as I get anything I want. The same as you get what you want. I'm not telling you; just work at it, get on the phone, a little word here and a little word there, and do it.

What was Paul's reaction?

You see, a lot of people, like the Dick Jameses, Derek Taylors and Peter Browns, all of them, they think they're the Beatles, and Neil

[Aspinal] and all of them. Well, I say, fuck 'em, you know, and after working with genius for ten, fifteen years they begin to think they're it. They're not.

Do you think you're a genius?

Yes, if there is such a thing as one, I am one.

When did you first realize that?

When I was about twelve. I used to think I must be a genius, but nobody's noticed. I used to wonder whether I'm a genius or I'm not, which is it? I used to think, well, I can't be mad because nobody's put me away; therefore, I'm a genius. A genius is a form of madness, and we're all that way, you know, and I used to be a bit coy about it, like my guitar playing.

If there is such a thing as genius—which is what...what the fuck is it?—I am one, and if there isn't, I don't care. I used to think it when I was a kid, writing me poetry and doing me paintings. I didn't become something when the Beatles made it, or when you heard about me, I've been like this all me life. Genius is pain, too.

You say that the dream is over. Part of the dream was that the Beatles were God or that the Beatles were the messengers of God, and, of course, yourself as God...

Yeah. Well, if there is a God, we're all it.

When did you first start getting the reactions from people who listened to the records, sort of the spiritual reaction?

There is a guy in England, William Mann, who was the first intellectual who reviewed the Beatles in the *Times* and got people talking about us in that intellectual way. He wrote about aeolian cadences and all sorts of musical terms, and he is a bullshitter. But he made us credible with intellectuals. He wrote about Paul's last album as if it were written by Beethoven or something. He's still writing the same shit. But it did us a lot of good in that way, because people in all the middle classes and intellectuals were all going, "Oooh."

When did somebody first come up to you about this thing about John Lennon as God?

About what to do and all of that? Like "You tell us, Guru"? Probably after acid. Maybe after *Rubber Soul*. I can't remember it exactly happening. We just took that position. I mean, we started putting out messages. Like "The Word Is Love" and things like that. I write messages, you know. See, when you start putting out messages, people start asking you, "What's the message?"

How did you first get involved in LSD?

A dentist in London laid it on George, me and wives, without telling us, at a dinner party at his house. He was a friend of George's and our dentist at the time, and he just put it in our coffee or something. He didn't know what it was; it's all the same thing with that sort of middle-class London swinger, or whatever. They had all heard about it, and they didn't know it was different from pot or pills, and they gave us it. He said, "I advise you not to leave," and we all thought he was trying to keep us for an orgy in his house, and we didn't want to know, and we went to the Ad Lib and these discotheques, and there were these incredible things going on.

It was insane, going around London. When we went to the club we thought it was on fire, and then we thought it was a premiere and it was just an ordinary light outside. We thought, "Shit, what's going on here?" We were cackling in the streets, and people were shouting, "Let's break a window," you know; it was just insane. We were just out of our heads. When we finally got on the lift [elevator], we all thought there was a fire, but there was just a little red light. We were all screaming like that, and we were all hot and hysterical, and when we all arrived on the floor, because this was a discotheque that was up a building, the lift stopped and the door opened and we were all [*John demonstrates by screaming*] . . .

I had read somebody describing the effects of opium in the old days, and I thought, "Fuck! It's happening," and then we went to the Ad Lib and all of that, and then some singer came up to me and said, "Can I sit next to you?" And I said, "Only if you don't talk," because I just couldn't think.

This seemed to go on all night. I can't remember the details. George somehow or another managed to drive us home in his Mini. We were going about ten miles an hour, but it seemed like a thousand, and Patti was saying, let's jump out and play football. I was getting all these sort of hysterical jokes coming out like speed, because I was always on that, too.

God, it was just terrifying, but it was fantastic. I did some drawings at the time, I've got them somewhere, of four faces saying, "We all agree with you!" I gave them to Ringo, the originals. I did a lot of drawing that night. And then George's house seemed to be just like a big submarine. I was driving it, they all went to bed, I was carrying on in it; it seemed to float above his wall which was eighteen foot, and I was driving it.

When you came down, what did you think?

I was pretty stoned for a month or two. The second time we had it was in L.A. We were on tour in one of those houses, Doris Day's house or wherever it was we used to stay, and the three of us took it, Ringo, George and I. Maybe Neil and a couple of the Byrds—what's his name, the one in the Stills and Nash thing, Crosby and the other guy, who used to do the lead. McGuinn. I think they came, I'm not sure, on a few trips. But there was a reporter, Don Short. We were in the garden; it was only our second one, and we still didn't know anything about doing it in a nice place and cool it. Then they saw the reporter and thought, "How do we act?" We were terrified waiting for him to go, and he wondered why we couldn't come over.

Neil, who never had acid either, had taken it, and he would have to play road manager, and we said go get rid of Don Short, and he didn't know what to do.

Peter Fonda came, and that was another thing. He kept saying [*in a whisper*], "I know what it's like to be dead," and we said, "What?" and he kept saying it. We were saying, "For Christ's sake, shut up, we don't care, we don't want to know," and he kept going on about it. That's how I wrote "She Said, She Said" — "I know what's it's like to be dead." It was a sad song, an acidy song, I suppose. "When I was a little boy"...you see, a lot of early childhood was coming out, anyway.

So LSD started for you in 1964: How long did it go on?

It went on for years, I must have had a thousand trips.

Literally a thousand, *or a couple of hundred?*

A thousand. I used to just eat it all the time. I never took it in the studio. Once I thought I was taking some uppers, and I was not in the state of handling it. I can't remember what album it was, but I took it and I just noticed...I suddenly got so scared on the mike. I thought I felt ill, and I thought I was going to crack. I said, I must get some air. They all took me upstairs on the roof and George Martin was looking at me funny, and then it dawned on me I must have taken acid. I said, "Well, I can't go on, you'll have to do it and I'll just stay and watch." You know, I got very nervous just watching them all. *I was saying, "Is it all right?"* And they were saying, "Yeah." They had all been very kind, and they carried on making the record.

The other Beatles didn't get into LSD as much as you did?

George did. In L.A., the second time we took it, Paul felt very out of it because we are all a bit slightly cruel, sort of, "We're taking it, and *you're* not." But we kept *seeing him,* you know. We couldn't eat our food. I just couldn't manage it, just picking it up with our hands. There were all these people serving us in the house, and we were knocking food on the floor and all of that. It was a long time before Paul took it. Then there was the big announcement.

Right.

So, I think George was pretty heavy on it; we are probably the most cracked. Paul is a bit more stable than George and I.

And straight?

I don't know about straight. Stable. I think LSD profoundly shocked him, and Ringo. I think maybe they *regret* it.

Did you have many bad trips?

I had many. Jesus Christ, I stopped taking it because of that. I just couldn't stand it.

You got too afraid to take it?

It got like that, but then I stopped it for I don't know how long, and then I started taking it again just before I met Yoko. Derek came over and...you see, I got the message that I should destroy my ego, and I did, you know. I was reading that stupid book of Leary's; we were going through a whole game that everybody went through, and I destroyed myself. I was slowly putting myself together round about Maharishi time. Bit by bit over a two-year period, I had destroyed me ego.

I didn't believe I could do anything and let people make me, and let them all just do what they wanted. I just was nothing. I was shit. Then Derek tripped me out at his house after he got back from L.A. He sort of said, "You're all right," and pointed out which songs I had written. "You wrote this," and "You said this," and "You are intelligent, don't be frightened."

The next week I went to Derek's with Yoko and we tripped again, and she filled me completely to realize that I was me and that it's all right. That was it; I started fighting again, being a loudmouth again and saying, "I *can* do this, fuck it, this is what I want, you know. I want it and don't put me down." I did this, so that's where I am now.

At some point, right between 'Help' and 'Hard Day's Night,' you got into drugs and got into doing drug songs?

A Hard Day's Night I was on pills; that's drugs, that's bigger drugs than pot. Started on pills when I was fifteen, no, since I was seventeen, since I became a musician. The only way to survive in Hamburg, to play eight hours a night, was to take pills. The waiters gave you them—the pills and drink. I was a fucking dropped-down drunk in art school. *Help* was where we turned on to pot and we dropped drink, simple as that. I've always needed a drug to survive. The others, too, but I always had more, more pills, more of everything because I'm more crazy, probably.

There's a lot of obvious LSD things you did in the music.

Yes.

How do you think that affected your conception of the music? In general.

It was only another mirror. It wasn't a miracle. It was more of a visual thing and a therapy, looking at yourself a bit. It did all that. You know, I don't quite remember. But it didn't write the music; neither did Janov or Maharishi in the same terms. I write the music in the circumstances in which I'm in, whether it's on acid or in the water.

The Hunter Davies book, the "authorized biography," says...

It was written in [London] *Sunday Times* sort of fab form. And no home truths were written. My auntie knocked out all the truth bits from my childhood, and my mother and I allowed it, which was my cop-out, et cetera. There was nothing about orgies and the shit that happened on tour. I wanted a real book to come out, but we all had wives and didn't want to hurt their feelings. End of that one. Because they still have wives.

The Beatles tours were like the Fellini film *Satyricon*. We had that image. Man, our tours were like something else; if you could get on our tours, you were in. They were *Satyricon*, all right.

Would you go to a town...hotel...

Wherever we went, there was always a whole scene going; we had our four separate bedrooms. We tried to keep them out of our room. Derek's and Neil's rooms were always full of junk and whores and who-the-fuck-knows-what, and policemen with it. *Satyricon*! We had to do something. What do you do when the pill doesn't wear off and it's time to go? I used to be up all night with Derek, whether there was anybody there or not, I could never sleep, such a heavy scene it was. They didn't call them groupies then, they called it something else, and if we couldn't get groupies, we would have whores and everything, whatever was going.

Who would arrange all that stuff?

Derek and Neil, that was their job, and Mal, but I'm not going into all that.

Like businessmen at a convention.

When we hit town, we hit it. There was no pissing about. There's photographs of me crawling about in Amsterdam on my knees coming out of whorehouses and things like that. The police escorted me to the places because they never wanted a big scandal, you see. I don't really want to talk about it because it will hurt Yoko. And it's not fair. Suffice to say that they were *Satyricon* on tour and that's it, because I don't want to hurt their feelings, or the other people's girls either. It's just not fair.

What else was left out of the Hunter Davies book?

That I don't know because I can't remember it. There is a better book on the Beatles by Michael Brown, *Love Me Do.* That was a true book. He wrote how we were, which was bastards. You can't be anything else in such a pressurized situation, and we took it out on people like Neil, Derek and Mal. That's why underneath their facade, they resent us, but they can never show it, and they won't believe it when they read it. They took a lot of shit from us because we were in such a shitty position. It was hard work, and somebody had to take it. Those things are left out by Davies, about what bastards we were. Fuckin' big bastards, that's what the Beatles were. You have to be a bastard to make it, that's a fact, and the Beatles are the biggest bastards on earth.

YOKO: How did you manage to keep that clean image? It's amazing.

JOHN: Everybody wants the image to carry on. You want to carry on. The press around, too, because they want the free drinks and the free whores and the fun; everybody wants to keep on the bandwagon. We were the Caesars; who was going to knock us, when there were a million pounds to be made? All the handouts, the bribery, the police, all the fucking hype. Everybody wanted in, that's why some of them are still trying to cling on to this: Don't take Rome from us, not a portable Rome where we can all have our houses and our cars and our lovers and our wives and office girls and parties and drink and drugs, don't take it from us, otherwise you're mad, John, you're crazy, silly John wants to take this all away.

Would you take it all back?

What?

Being a Beatle?

If I could be a fuckin' fisherman, I would. If I had the capabilities of being something other than I am, I would. It's no fun being an artist. You know what it's like, writing, it's torture. I read about Van Gogh, Beethoven, any of the fuckers. If they had psychiatrists, we wouldn't have had Gauguin's great pictures. These bastards are just socking us to death; that's about all that we can do, is do it like circus animals.

I resent being an artist, in that respect; I resent performing for fucking idiots who don't know anything. They can't feel. I'm the one that's feeling because I'm the one that is expressing. They live vicariously through me and other artists, and we are the ones...even with the boxers—when Oscar comes in the ring, they're booing the shit out of him; he only hits Clay once and they're all cheering him. I'd sooner be in the audience, really, but I'm not capable of it.

One of my big things is that I wish to be a fisherman. I know it sounds silly—and I'd sooner be rich than poor, and all the rest of that shit—but I wish the pain was ignorance or bliss or something. If you don't know, man, then there's no pain; that's how I express it.

What do you think the effect was of the Beatles on the history of Britain?

I don't know about the "history"; the people who are in control and in power, and the class system and the whole bullshit bourgeoisie is exactly the same, except there is a lot of fag middle-class kids with long, long hair walking around London in trendy clothes, and Kenneth Tynan is making a fortune out of the word "fuck." Apart from that, nothing happened. We all dressed up, the same bastards are in control, the same people are runnin' everything. It is exactly the same.

We've grown up a little, all of us, there has been a change, and we're all a bit freer and all that, but it's the same game. Shit, they're doing exactly the same thing, selling arms to South Africa, killing blacks on the street; people are living in fucking poverty, with rats crawling over them. It just makes you puke, and I woke up to *that*, too.

The dream is over. It's just the same, only I'm thirty, and a lot of people have got long hair. That's what it is, man, nothing happened except that we grew up, we did our thing—just like they were telling us. You kids—most of the so-called "now generation" are getting a job. We're a minority, you know; people like us always were, but maybe we are a slightly larger minority because of maybe something or other.

Why do you think the impact of the Beatles was so much bigger in America than it was in England?

The same reason that American stars are so much bigger in England: The grass is greener. We were really professional by the time we got to the States; we had learned the whole game. When we arrived here we knew how to handle the press; the British press were the toughest in the world, and we could handle anything. We were all right.

On the plane over, I was thinking, "Oh, we won't make it," or I said it on a film or something, but that's that side of me. We knew we would wipe you out if we could just get a grip on you. We were new.

And when we got here, you were all walking around in fuckin' Bermuda shorts, with Boston crew cuts and stuff on your teeth. Now they're telling us, they're all saying, "Beatles are passé, and this is like that, man." The chicks looked like fuckin' 1940 horses. There was no conception of dress or any of that jazz. We just thought, "What an ugly race"; it looked just disgusting. We thought how hip we were, but, of course, we weren't. It was just the five of us, us and the Stones were really the hip ones; the rest of England were just the same as they ever were.

You tend to get nationalistic, and we would really laugh at America, except for its music. It was the black music we dug, and over here even the blacks were laughing at people like Chuck Berry and the blues singers; the blacks thought it wasn't sharp to dig the really funky music, and the whites only listened to Jan and Dean and all that. We felt that we had the message which was, "Listen to this music." It was the same in Liverpool; we felt very exclusive and underground in Liverpool, listening to Richie Barret and Barrett Strong, and all those old-time records. Nobody was listening to any of them except Eric Burdon in Newcastle and Mick Jagger in London. It was that lonely, it was fantastic. When we came over here and it was the same—nobody was listening to rock & roll or to black music in America—we felt as though we were coming to the land of its origin, but nobody wanted to know about it.

What part did you ever play in the songs that are heavily identified with Paul, like "Yesterday"?

"Yesterday" I had nothing to do with.

"Eleanor Rigby"?

"Eleanor Rigby" I wrote a good half of the lyrics or more.

When did Paul show you "Yesterday"?

I don't remember—I really don't remember, it was a long time ago. I think he was...I really don't remember, it just sort of appeared.

Who wrote "Nowhere Man"?

Me, me.

Did you write that about anybody in particular?

Probably about myself. I remember I was just going through this paranoia trying to write something and nothing would come out, so I just lay down and tried to not write and then this came out, the whole thing came out in one gulp.

What songs really stick in your mind as being Lennon-McCartney songs?

"I Want to Hold Your Hand," "From Me to You," "She Loves You"—I'd have to have the list, there's so many, trillions of 'em. Those are the ones. In a rock band you have to make singles; you have to keep writing them. Plenty more. We both had our fingers in each other's pies.

A song from the 'Help' album, like "You've Got to Hide Your Love Away." How did you write that? What were the circumstances? Where were you?

I was in Kenwood, and I would just be songwriting. The period would be for songwriting, and so every day I would attempt to write a song, and it's one of those that you sort of sing a bit sadly to yourself, "Here I stand, head in hand..."

I started thinking about my own emotions—I don't know when exactly it started, like "I'm a Loser" or "Hide Your Love Away" or those kinds of things—instead of projecting myself into a situation, I would just try to express what I felt about myself, which I'd done in me books. I think it was Dylan helped me realize that—not by any discussion or anything but just by hearing his work—I had a sort of professional songwriter's attitude to writing pop songs; he would turn out a certain style of song for a single, and we would do a certain style of thing for this and the other thing. I was already a stylized songwriter on the first album. But to express myself I would write *Spaniard in the Works* or *In His Own Write*, the personal stories which were expressive of my emotions. I'd have a separate songwriting John Lennon who wrote songs for the sort of meat market, and I didn't consider them—the lyrics or anything—to have any depth at all. They were just a joke. Then I started being me about the songs, not writing them objectively, but subjectively.

What about on 'Rubber Soul,' "Norwegian Wood"?

I was trying to write about an affair without letting me wife know I was writing about an affair, so it was very gobbledygook. I was sort of writing from my experiences, girls' flats, things like that.

Where did you write that?

I wrote it at Kenwood.

When did you decide to put a sitar on it?

I think it was at the studio. George had just got his sitar and I said, "Could you play this piece?" We went through many different sort of versions of the song; it was never right, and I was getting very angry about it, it wasn't coming out like I said. They said, "Well, just do it how you want to do it," and I said, "Well, I just want to do it like this." They let me go, and I did the guitar very loudly into the mike and sang it at the same time, and then George had the sitar and I asked him could he play the piece that I'd written, you know, dee diddley dee diddley dee, that bit, and he was not sure whether he could play it yet because he hadn't done much on the sitar but he was willing to have a go, as is his wont, and he learned the bit and dubbed it on after. I think we did it in sections.

You also have a song on that album, "In My Life." When did you write that?

I wrote that in Kenwood. I used to write upstairs where I had about ten Brunell tape recorders all linked up. I still have them. I'd mastered them over the period of a year or two—I could never make a rock & roll record, but I could make some far-out stuff on it. I wrote it upstairs; that was one where I wrote the lyrics first and then sang it. That was usually the case with things like "In My Life" and "Universe" and some of the ones that stand out a bit.

Would you just record yourself and a guitar on a tape and then bring it in to the studio?

I would do that just to get an impression of what it sounded like *sung* and to hear it back for judging it—you never know till you hear the song yourself. I would double track the guitar or the voice or something on the tape. I think on "Norwegian Wood" and "In My Life" Paul helped with the middle eight, to give credit where it's due.

Let me ask you about one on the double album, "Glass Onion." You set out to write a little message to the audience.

Yeah, I was having a laugh because there'd been so much gobbledy-gook about *Pepper,* play it backwards and you stand on your head and all that. Even now, I just saw Mel Tormé on TV the other day saying that "Lucy" was written to promote drugs and so was "A Little Help from My Friends," and none of them were at all—"A Little Help from My Friends" only says get high in it; it's really about a little help from my friends, it's a sincere message. Paul had the line about "little help from my friends," I'm not sure, he had some kind of structure for it, and—we wrote it pretty well fifty-fifty, but it was based on his original idea.

"Happiness Is a Warm Gun" is a nice song.

Oh, I like that, one of my best; I had forgotten about that. Oh, I love it. I think it's a beautiful song. I like all the different things that are happening in it. Like "God," I had put together some three sections of different songs; it was meant to be—it seemed to run through all the different kinds of rock music.

It wasn't about H at all. "Lucy in the Sky" with diamonds which I swear to God, or swear to Mao, or to anybody you like, I had no idea spelled LSD—and "Happiness"—George Martin had a book on guns which he had told me about—I can't remember—or I think he showed me a cover of a magazine that said "Happiness Is a Warm Gun." It was a gun magazine, that's it: I read it, thought it was a fantastic, insane thing to say. A warm gun means that you just shot something.

You said to me, " 'Sgt. Pepper' is the one." That was the album?

Well, it was a peak. Paul and I were definitely working together, especially on "A Day in the Life," that was a real . . . The way we wrote a lot of the time: You'd write the good bit, the part that was easy, like "I read the news today" or whatever it was, then when you got stuck or whenever it got hard, instead of carrying on, you just drop it; then we would meet each other, and I would sing half, and he would be inspired to write the next bit and vice versa. He was a bit shy about it because I think he thought it's already a good song. Sometimes we wouldn't let each other interfere with a song either, because you tend to be a bit lax with someone else's stuff, you experiment a bit. So we were doing it in his room with the piano. He said, "Should we do this?" "Yeah, let's do that."

I keep saying that I always preferred the double album because *my* music is better on the double album; I don't care about the whole concept of *Pepper;* it might be better, but the music was better for me on the double album because I'm being myself on it. I think it's as simple as the new album, like "I'm So Tired" is just the guitar. I felt more at ease with that than the production. I don't like production so much. But *Pepper* was a peak, all right.

YOKO: People think that's the peak, and I'm just so amazed. . . . John's done all that Beatle stuff. But this new album of John's is a real peak; that's higher than any other thing he has done.

JOHN: Thank you, dear.

Do you think it is?

Yeah, sure. I think it's *Sgt. Lennon.* I don't really know how it will sink in, where it will lie in the spectrum of rock & roll and the generation and all the rest of it, but I know what it is. It's something else, it's another door.

Do you think the Beatles will record together again?

I record with Yoko, but I'm not going to record with another ego-maniac. There is only room for one on an album nowadays. There is no point, there is just no point at all. There was a reason to do it at one time, but there is no reason to do it anymore.

I had a group, I was the singer and the leader; I met Paul, and I made a decision whether to—and he made a decision, too—have him in the group: Was it better to have a guy who was better than the people I had in, obviously, or not? To make the group stronger or to let me be stronger? That decision was to let Paul in and make the group stronger.

Well, from that, Paul introduced me to George, and Paul and I had to make the decision, or I had to make the decision, whether to let George in. I listened to George play, and I said, "Play 'Raunchy,'" or whatever the old story is, and I let him in. I said, "Okay, you come in"; that was the three of us then. Then the rest of the group was thrown out gradually. It just happened like that; instead of going for the individual thing, we went for the strongest format, and for equals.

George is ten years younger than me, or some shit like that. I couldn't be bothered with him when he first came around. He used to follow me around like a bloody kid, hanging around all the time. I couldn't be bothered. He was a kid who played guitar, and he was a friend of Paul's, which made it all easier. It took me years to come around to him, to start considering him as an equal or anything.

We had all sorts of different drummers all the time, because people who owned drum kits were few and far between; it was an expensive item. They were usually idiots. Then we got Pete Best because we needed a drummer to go to Hamburg the next day. We passed the audition on our own with a stray drummer. There are other myths about Pete Best was the Beatles, and Stuart Sutcliffe's mother is writing in England that *he* was the Beatles.

Are you the Beatles?

No, I'm not the Beatles. I'm me. Paul isn't the Beatles. Brian Epstein wasn't the Beatles, neither is Dick James. The Beatles are the Beatles. Separately, they are separate. George was a separate individual singer, with his own group as well, before he came in with us, the Rebel Rousers. Nobody is the Beatles. How could they be? We all had our roles to play.

How would you assess George's talents?

I don't want to assess him. George has not done his best work yet. His talents have developed over the years, and he was working with two fucking brilliant songwriters, and he learned a lot from us. I wouldn't have minded being George, the invisible man, and learning what he learned. Maybe it was hard for him sometimes, because Paul and I are such egomaniacs, but that's the game.

I'm interested in concepts and philosophies. I am not interested in wallpaper, which most music is.

When did you realize that what you were doing transcended...

People like me are aware of their so-called genius at ten, eight, nine....I always wondered, "Why has nobody discovered me?" In school, didn't they see that I'm cleverer than anybody in this school? That the teachers are stupid, too? That all they had was information that I didn't need?

I got fuckin' lost in being at high school. I used to say to me auntie, "You throw my fuckin' poetry out, and you'll regret it when I'm famous," and she threw the bastard stuff out. I never forgave her for not treating me like a fuckin' genius or whatever I was, when I was a child.

It was obvious to me. Why didn't they put me in art school? Why didn't they train me? Why would they keep forcing me to be a fuckin' cowboy like the rest of them? I was different, I was always different. Why didn't anybody notice me?

A couple of teachers would notice me, encourage me to be something or other, to draw or to paint—express myself. But most of the time they were trying to beat me into being a fuckin' dentist or a teacher. And then the fuckin' fans tried to beat me into being a fuckin' Beatle or an Engelbert Humperdinck, and the critics tried to beat me into being Paul McCartney.

YOKO: So you were very deprived in a way...

JOHN: That's what makes me what I am. It comes out; the people I meet have to say it themselves, because we get fuckin' kicked. Nobody says it, so you scream it: Look at me, a genius, for fuck's sake! What do I have to do to prove to you son-of-a-bitches what I can do and who I am? Don't dare, don't you dare fuckin' criticize my work like that. You, who don't know anything about it.

Fuckin' bullshit!

I know what Zappa is going through, and a half. I'm just coming out of it. I just have been in school again. I've had teachers ticking me off and marking my work. If nobody can recognize what I am, then fuck 'em; it's the same for Yoko....

YOKO: That's why it's an amazing thing: After somebody has done something like the Beatles, they think that he's sort of satisfied, where actually the Beatles...

JOHN: The Beatles was nothing.

YOKO: It was like cutting him down to a smaller size than he is.

JOHN: I learned lots from Paul and George, in many ways, but they learned a damned sight lot from me—they learned a fucking lot from me. It's like George Martin, or anybody: Just come back in twenty years' time and see what we're doing, and see who's doing what—don't put me—don't sort of mark my papers like I'm top of the math class or did I come in number one in English Language, because I never did. Just assess me on what I am and what comes out of me mouth, and what me work is, don't mark me in the classrooms. It's like I've just left school again! I just graduated from the school of Show Biz, or whatever it was called.

What accounts for your great popularity?

Because I fuckin' did it. I copped out in that Beatle thing. I was like an artist that went off... Have you never heard of like Dylan Thomas and all them who never fuckin' wrote but just went up drinking and Brendan Behan and all of them, they died of drink...everybody that's done anything is like that. I just got meself in a party; I was an emperor, I had millions of chicks, drugs, drink, power and everybody saying how great I was. How could I get out of it? It was just like being in a fuckin' train. I couldn't get out.

I couldn't create, either. I created a little; it came out, but I was in the party and you don't get out of a thing like that. It was fantastic! I came out of the sticks; I didn't hear about anything—Van Gogh was the most far-out thing I had ever heard of. Even London was something we used to dream of, and London's nothing. I came out of the fuckin' sticks to take over the world, it seemed to me. I was enjoying it, and I was trapped in it, too. I couldn't do anything about it; I was just going along for the ride. I was hooked, just like a junkie.

What did being from Liverpool have to do with your art?

It was a port. That means it was less hick than someone in the English Midlands, like the American Midwest or whatever you call it. We were a port, the second biggest port in England, between Manchester and Liverpool. The North is where the money was made in the eighteen hundreds; that was where all the brass and the heavy people were, and that's where the despised people were.

We were the ones that were looked down upon as animals by the Southerners, the Londoners. The Northerners in the States think that people are pigs down South, and the people in New York think West Coast is hick. So we were hicksville.

We were a great amount of Irish descent and blacks and China-men, all sorts there. It was like San Francisco, you know. That San Francisco is something else! Why do you think Haight-Ashbury and all that happened there? It didn't happen in Los Angeles, it happened in San Francisco, where people are going. L.A. you pass through and get a hamburger.

There was nothing big in Liverpool; it wasn't American. It was going poor, a very poor city, and tough. But people have a sense of humor because they are in so much pain, so they are always cracking jokes. They are very witty, and it's an Irish place. It is where the Irish came when they ran out of potatoes, and it's where black people were left or worked as slaves or whatever.

It is cosmopolitan, and it's where the sailors would come home with the blues records from America on the ships. There is the big-gest country & western following in England in Liverpool, besides London—always besides London, because there is more of it there.

I heard country & western music in Liverpool before I heard rock & roll. The people there—the Irish in Ireland are the same—they take their country & western music very seriously. There's a big, heavy fol-lowing of it. There were established folk, blues and country & western clubs in Liverpool before rock & roll, and we were like the new kids coming out.

I remember the first guitar I ever saw. It belonged to a guy in a cowboy suit in a province of Liverpool, with stars, and a cowboy hat and a big dobro. They were real cowboys, and they took it seriously. There had been cowboys long before there was rock & roll.

What do you think of America?

I love it, and I hate it. America is where it's at. I should have been born in New York, I should have been born in the Village, that's where I belong. Why wasn't I born there? Paris was it in the eighteenth century, London I don't think has ever been it except literarywise when Wilde and Shaw and all of them were there. New York was it.

I regret profoundly that I was not an American and not born in Greenwich Village. That's where I should have been. It never works that way. Everybody heads toward the center; that's why I'm here now. I'm here just to breathe it. It might be dying and there might be a lot of dirt in the air that you breathe, but this is where it's happening. You go to Europe to rest, like in the country. It's so overpowering, America, and I'm such a fuckin' cripple that I can't take much of it, it's too much for me.

YOKO: He's very New York, you know.

JOHN: I'm frightened of it. People are so aggressive, I can't take all that. I need to go home; I need to have a look at the grass. I'm always writing about my English garden. I need the trees and the grass; I need to go into the country because I can't stand too much people.

You're going back to London; what's a rough picture of your immediate future, say the next three months?

I'd like to just vanish a bit. It wore me out, New York. I love it. I'm just sort of fascinated by it, like a fucking monster. Doing the films was a nice way of meeting a lot of people. I think we've both said and done enough for a few months, especially with this article. I'd like to get out of the way and wait till they all . . .

Do you have a rough picture of the next few years?

Oh, no, I couldn't think of the next few years; it's abysmal thinking of how many years there are to go, millions of them. I just play it by the week. I don't think much ahead of a week.

Do you have a picture of "when I'm sixty-four"?

No, no. I hope we're a nice old couple living off the coast of Ireland or something like that—looking at our scrapbook of madness.

RAY CHARLES

by Ben Fong-Torres

January 18, 1973

You lost your sight at five.

It didn't happen like one day I could see a hundred miles and the next day I couldn't see an inch. Each day for two years my sight was less and less. My mother was always real with me, and bein' poor, you got to pretty much be honest with your children. We couldn't afford no specialists. I was lucky I could get a doctor—that's a *specialist*.

When you were losing your sight, did you try to take in as much as possible, to remember things?

I guess I was too small to really care that much. I knew there were things I liked to watch. I used to love to look at the sun. That's a bad thing for my eyes, but I liked that. I used to love to look at the moon at night. I would go out in the backyard and stare at it. It just fascinated the hell out of me. And another thing that fascinated me that would scare most people is lightnin'. When I was a kid, I thought that was pretty. Anything like brightness, any kind of lights. I probably would've been a firebug or somethin'.

And there were colors. I was crazy about red. Always thought it was a beautiful color. I remember the basic colors. I don't know nothin' about chartreuse and all—I don't know what the *hell* that is. But I know the black, green, yellow, brown and stuff like that. And naturally

I remember my mother, who was pretty. God, she was pretty. She was a little woman. She must have been about four feet eleven, I guess, and when I was twelve or thirteen, I was taller and bigger than my mother, and she had this long pretty black hair, used to come way down her back. Pretty good-lookin' chick, man [*laughs*].

A lot of people have asked you to define soul. I'd like to get a definition of beauty.

If you're talkin' about physical beauty, I would have to say that to me beauty is probably about the same thing that it means to most people. You look at them and the structure of their face, the way their skin is, and say like, a woman, the contour of her body, you know what I mean? The same way as I would walk out and feel the car. Put my hands on the lines of a car, and I'd know whether I'd like it or not from the way the designs of the lines are. As I said, I was fortunate enough to see until I was about seven, and I remember the things that I heard people calling beautiful.

How about beauty in music?

I guess you could call me a sentimentalist, man, really. I like Chopin or Sibelius. People who write softness, you know, and although Beethoven to me was quite heavy, he wrote some really touching songs, and I think that *Moonlight Sonata*—in spite of the fact that it wound up being very popular—it's somethin' about that, man, you could just feel the pain that this man was goin' through. Somethin' had to be happenin' in that man. You know, he was very, very lonesome when he wrote that. From a technical point of view, I think Bach, if you really want to learn technique, that was the cat, 'cause he had all them fugues and things, your hands doin' all kinda different things. Personally, outside of technique, I didn't care for Bach.

Did you try to catch up with high school or college after you left school?

No. When I left school, I had to get out and really tough it, as you know, because my mother passed away when I was fifteen. I didn't have no brothers or sisters. But my mama always taught me, "Look, you got to learn how to get along by yourself," and she's always tellin' me, "Son, one of these days I'm gonna be dead, and you're gonna need to know how to survive, because even your best friends, although they may want to do things for you; after all, they will have their own lives." So at that point I started tryin' to help myself. So what do I do to help myself? The thing I can do best, or figure I can do best, anyway. And that is sing or play the piano or both.

What else did they teach you in school that could have been applied to a career?

Well, I don't know where I would have used it, but I can probably type as fast as any secretary. Well, not *any*. I can type about sixty to sixty-five words a minute, somethin' like that, when I wanna. Then I can make all kinds of things with my hands. I can make chairs and brooms and mops and rugs and pocketbooks and belts and all kinds of things like that. So guess if I had to, I would go and buy me some leather. I love to work with my hands, and I'm sure that's what I would do had I not played music, you see, because it's the kind of a thing that you can use plenty of imagination in it, you know what I mean? And so I know how to do various kinds of stitchin'. Mexican stitchin' and regular stitchin' overlappin' it and stuff. So I guess I would have—although it would have been a very meek livin', I suppose. You can't turn out a lot by hand.

Music was a meek living for a long time, too.

Yeah, it was really crawlin'. I became very ill a couple times. I suffered from malnutrition, you know. I was really messed up because I wasn't eatin' nothin', and I wouldn't beg. Two things you don't do, you don't beg and you don't steal. That's right.

What kind of music education did you have in Florida?

They taught you how to read the music, and I had to play Chopin, Beethoven, you know, the normal thing. Just music lessons. Not really theory. I don't know what that *is*. It's just, they taught me how to read music, and naturally how to use correct fingerin', and once you've learned that you go from the exercises into little composi-tions into things like Chopin. That's the way it went, although I was tryin' to play boogie-woogie, man, 'cause I could always just about play anything I heard. My ear was always pretty good, but I did have a few music teachers, and so I do know music quite well, if you don't mind my saying so. I was never taught to write music, but when I was twelve years old I was writing arrangements for a big band. Hell, if you can read music, you can write it, and I think certainly what helped me is that I'm a piano player, so I know chords. Naturally, I can hear chords, and I could always play just about anything I could hear. It was just a question of learning how to put it down on paper. I just studied how to write for horns on my own. Like, understanding that the saxophone is in different keys, and also, when I was goin' to school I took up clarinet. See, I was a great fan of Artie Shaw. I used to think, "Man, ooh, he had the prettiest sound," and he had so much feelin' in his playin', I always felt that, still feel it today.

Where were you hearing this boogie-woogie?

We lived next door for some years to a little general store in Greens-ville, Florida, where the kids could come in and buy soda pop and candy and the people could buy kerosene for their lamps, you know. And they had a jukebox in there. And the guy who owned it also had a piano. Wylie Pittman is the guy. Even when I was three and four years old, if I was out in the yard playin', and if he started playin' that piano, I would stop playin' and run in there and jump on the stool. Normally, you figure a kid run in there like that and jump on the stool and start bangin' on the piano, the guy would throw him off. "Say, get away from here, don't you see me"...but he didn't do that, I always loved that man for that. I was about five years old, and on my birthday he had some people there. He said, "RC"—this is what they called me then—"look, I want you to get up on the stool, and I want you to play for these people." Now, let's face it. I was five years old. They know damn well I wasn't playin'. I'm just bangin' on the keys, you understand. But that was encouragement that got me like that, and I think that the man felt that anytime a child is willin' to stop playin', you know, out in the yard and havin' fun, to come in and hear somebody play the piano, evidently this child has music in his bones, you know. And he didn't discourage me, which he could have, you know what I mean? Maybe I wouldn't have been a musician at all, because I didn't have a musical family, now remember that.

You were also able to hear 'The Grand Ole Opry' when you were a kid?

Yep, yeah, I always—every Saturday night, I never did miss it. I don't know why I liked the music. I really thought that it was somethin' about country music, even as a youngster—I couldn't figure out what it was then, but I know what it is now. But then I don't know why I liked it and I used to just love to hear Minnie Pearl, because I thought she was so funny.

How old were you then?

Oh, I guess I was about seven, eight, and I remember Roy Acuff and Gene Austin. Although I was bred in and around the blues, I always did have interest in other music, and I felt it was the closest music, really, to the blues—they'd make them steel guitars cry and whine, and it really attracted me. I don't know what it is. Gospel and the blues are really, if you break it down, almost the same thing. It's just a question of whether you're talkin' about a woman or God. I come out of the Baptist Church, and naturally whatever happened to me in that church is gonna spill over. So I think the blues and gospel music is quite synonymous to each other.

Big Bill Broonzy once said that "Ray Charles has got the blues he's cryin' sanctified. He's mixin' the blues with the spirituals. . . . He should be singin' in a church."

I personally feel that it was not a question of mixing gospel with the blues. It was a question of singin' the only way I knew how to sing. This was not a thing where I was tryin' to take the church music and make the blues out of it or vice versa. All I was tryin' to do was sing the only way I knew how, period. I was raised in the church. I went to the Sunday school. I went to the morning service, and that's where they had the young people doin' their performin', and I went to night service, and I went to all the revival meetings. My parents said, "You *will* go to *church*." I mean they ain't no *if* about *that*. So singin' in the church and hearin' this good singin' in the church and also hearin' the blues, I guess this was the only way I *could* sing, outside of loving Nat Cole so well, and I tried to imitate him very much. When I was starting out, I loved the man so much that's why I can understand a lot of other artists who come up and try to imitate me. You know, when you love somebody so much and you feel what they're doin' is close to what you feel, some of that rubs off on you—so *I* did that.

We were talking about when you started out. You played what was called cocktail music, playing piano and singing songs like "If I Give You My Love." But were you always looking to form your own big band?

Well, when I was doing what you're talkin' about right now, my only thing, my goal was, "Wow, if I could only just get to make records, too." That's why, in 1948, when they had the union ban on musicians so they weren't allowed to record, I recorded anyway—first of all, I didn't know about the ban, and, of course, later I had to pay a fine for it—I didn't care. I was only about seventeen or somethin' like that. I was workin' in Seattle, then, and a fellow came up from Los Angeles, Jack Lauderdale, and he had a little record company [Swing Time], and I was workin' at the Rockin' Chair. He came and one night he was in there and heard me playing and he said to me, "Listen, I have a record company. I would like to record you." Man, I was so glad, I didn't ask him how much money I was gonna get. I didn't *care*. I would have done it for nothin'. So he said, "Look, I'm gonna take you down to Los Angeles." And wow, Los Angeles, you know. Ooh, yeah, yeah. And I'm gonna be *recorded*, man. You know, *wow*, my own voice on a record [*laughs*].

I went down there and we made a song called "Confession Blues." That was my first record. Sold *pretty* good. Then, about a year later, 1949, we made a song called "Baby Let Me Hold Your Hand." Now that really was a big hit. "Confession Blues" sold mediocre—it sold well enough to suit me, because I was hearing it where I went. But when I was out on the road workin' with Lowell Fulsom, he had a big record called "Every Day I Have the Blues." We were on the same label. I had "Baby Let Me Hold Your Hand," and he was singin' "Every Day I Have the Blues," and we were packin' 'em in. This is really where I started touring the country.

When you left Florida, why did you choose to go to the other corner of the country?

It was just—New York I was frightful of, 'cause I just couldn't imagine myself goin' to New York or Chicago or even Los Angeles. They sounded so big, man. I guess I always felt that I was pretty good, but I wasn't sure of myself to want to jump out into a big city like New York. I was too scared for that. So what I wanted to do was pick a town that was far away from Florida, but not huge, and Seattle really was about as far away as I could get. All across the U.S., and, of course, it wasn't a huge town, half a million people or somethin' like that.

How long did you stay with Swing Time?

I was there until Atlantic bought the contract. I think it was '51 or so. About three or four years.

That was Ahmet [Ertegun] and Herb Abramson, I think, at that time. I don't know how that was done. I met with the people at Atlantic, and they said, "Well, we'd like to record you," so I said, "Well, I'm under contract to somebody." They said, "Well, look, we'll buy the contract." So I said, "Fine, buy it." And that's it. Finished.

Why did you leave Atlantic? Jerry Wexler told me it was a "shock" to him.

Well, you know the people at Atlantic—Jerry, Ahmet, Nesuhi…I love *all* the people over there. It was the kind of thing where ABC came up with a contract. I think they were trying to lure somebody there, and I hate to say this, because it makes me sound like I'm blowin' my own horn, but you know, I was with Atlantic and we had this big hit, "What'd I Say," and a couple other things, so they came up with a contract and I let Jerry and them know about it. The contract was so unreal. I mean, the thing was that, well, if ABC was really seriously going to do it, Atlantic just couldn't match it, based on the original contract I had with them. But I let them know, because, you know that Jerry and I are the best of friends because I didn't do anything sneaky, in the dark, or nothin' like that. They knew the whole bit, and my thing was, look, I'm not asking you to *better* ABC's deal, I'm just saying if you can *match* it, I'll stay with you. And it was the kind of thing where they said, "Look, Ray, it's *awfully* heavy for us."

You gotta understand, ABC at the time was offering me the kind of a contract that, believe me, in those days, in 1959, was unheard of. I don't even think that they *figured* that I would do as *well*. What they were after was the *name* and to stimulate *other* names.

To sign with ABC.

Right. And so I was like a pawn, but as it turned out we were so lucky, because right after I went with ABC, we came up with "Georgia," and then the country-western stuff, see? But I did a country-western song with Atlantic before I went to ABC, but the other side of it sold, the song "I Believe to My Soul." Well, on the back of that was a song called "I'm Movin' On."

Hank Snow.

That's right. There's where I first get the idea. But it just turned out that once I changed contracts, I followed that idea. Now, with

ABC we had people saying, "Hey, man, gee whiz, Ray, you got all these fans, you can't do no country-western things. Your fans — you gonna lose all your fans." Well, I said, "For Christ's sake, I'll do it anyway." I didn't want to be a country-western singer. I just wanted to take country-western songs. When I sing "I Can't Stop Loving You," I'm not singin' it *country-western*. I'm singin' it like *me*. But I think the words to country songs are very earthy like the blues, see, very *down*. They're not as dressed up, and the people are very honest and say, "Look, I miss you, darlin', so I went out and I got drunk in this bar." That's the way you say it. Wherein Tin Pan Alley will say, "Oh, I missed you, darling, so I went to this restaurant and I sat down and I had dinner for one." That's cleaned up now, you see? But country songs and the blues is like it is.

I did two albums of country-western, you gotta remember I did volume one, and hell, if you get an album to sell well over a million, you almost gotta do — that's almost forcing you to do one more. But that's all I did with country-western was two albums.

Atlantic gave you musical independence and built a reputation for R&B and jazz. ABC, on the other hand, wasn't known for a sound. Did you have a feeling of trepidation about moving from one to the other?

No, 'cause my thing was that it was a record company, and I thought I could sell records for ABC as well as I could sell records for Atlantic or anybody else. Plus, after all, you gotta understand, man, I had been workin' a long time, strugglin' a mighty long time with nothin', and this was a helluva chance for me to really better myself; if I really had any kind of luck, I really was gonna wind up bein' all right. I made an awful lot of money fast, real fast.

What was the production deal?

I was producin' myself, you see? In other words, it was a contract within a contract. I got paid the regular top artist scale as an artist, but also the producin' end of it was where the extra money came from. That was where, out of every dime I got seven and a half cents, and that's pretty damn good, man. That's besides the artist contract, you know.

Did your involvement in drugs almost knock you out in music?

No. No. No. Nope. I can't say that.

Heights in music were reached during that stage?

Exactly. So I mean, obviously, I couldn't say that, could I? You know, like I say, I ain't never gonna lie to you. It didn't knock me out or wasn't about to knock me out. My thing was that when my kids started growin' up—I remember one day my oldest son, he was one of the baseball players, they were havin' a little reception Thursday night and they were giving out these little trophies, and I was supposed to go, and what happened, I had a recordin' session that night. I was doing the sound track for *The Cincinnati Kid,* and I did the singin' on that, as you remember, but what I did, I went by there with him to this banquet, and I had to leave before the thing was over, and he cried. And that hurt me. I started thinkin', here's a child. It means so much to him for his father to be at this banquet. And I started thinkin' that suppose that somethin' happened, I get put in jail and somebody comes along and says, "Oh, your daddy's a jailbird." Remember now, he's gettin' up there in age, now. He's a little man, you know, and he gonna cry about that. I figure the next thing he'll do is haul up and knock hell out of 'em, and now he's gonna be in trouble all over me. And I said, okay, I've had enough—it's a risky business, it's a dangerous business, anybody knockin' on your door, you gotta double-check to see who it is.

That all came to a head right around '65 [when Charles was arrested for heroin possession]?

That's right. Right then. I just felt that it was a bad scene, and really it just was a bad scene. I got involved in it—my situation is, I was young.

I was about maybe seventeen, eighteen years old or somethin' like that, it was a thing where I wanted to be among the big fellas, like cats in the band, and these guys would always go and leave the kid "till we come back," you know. And I wanted to be a part, so I begged and pleaded until somebody said, "Okay, man, goddamn it, come on, all right." And they took me, and there I was, so they were doin' it and I wanted to belong, you know. I mean, this is really how it started, and once it started, there it was, you know. But I never got so involved in it to the point where I was out of my mind or didn't know what the hell I was doin', you know. Like, I heard of people havin' habits of sixty dollars a day or one hundred dollars a day. I never had nothin' like that.

How much did you take per day?

Oh, I probably spent about twenty dollars. Never got above that.

What did you learn through the Viennese psychoanalyst?

Who?

The psychoanalyst that you were supposed to have seen for a couple of years?

What did we talk about? Nothin'. Like, and he's not a psychoanalyst. I mean, what he was, was a psychiatrist. He had no influence, say, as far as my doing or not doing anything. I went there and said, "First of all we're gonna get one thing straight. You don't have to convince me not to do anything. I've already made up my mind, I ain't gonna do it, and it's finished." And so, when we saw each other we just talked in general about just whatever popped up, and hell, I think I probably talked to him more about his practice, what the hell he was doin', than about myself.

Was that year off hard for you?

I'm basically a lazy person. It's never hard for me to relax. But I do enjoy doin' things. The work I'm doin' is not work to me. It's fun.

See, it's like a hobby that I'm gettin' paid for and truly is part of my relaxation. This is really it for me.

Then why did you take a year off?

Well, I felt that I should do it just because I wanted to. Now, it was necessary, of course. I hired a psychiatrist so that when we went into court, I thought it might be beneficial. You tell a judge somethin' like a cat been usin' somethin' for fifteen years, and he, all of a sudden the man say he ain't gonna do it no more, and the cat gonna say, "Sure, come on now, let's get down to the facts." But if a psychiatrist says it, for some reason, at least the judge will kinda lean towards believin' the cat. So that was the whole purpose of the whole thing. Because, let's face it, man, if a guy doesn't want to stop doin' somethin', the judge, the psychiatrist, the jailer, ain't nobody gonna—the people stay in jail five years and come out on the street one day right back at it.

I believe—I'll tell you somethin', now, I had the psychiatrist, and the man had a legal right to what you call trim me down a little less each day until I got down to nothin'. I didn't do that. The doctor didn't believe this himself, that I have never in all my years, I've never seen nothin' like this in my life. They even tested me, man. They thought somebody must be slippin' me somethin'. So they cut my visitation off, just to make sure, and I still was the same way, so they said, no, it can't be that. Not only was I not doing anything, but they try to say do you want anything to help you sleep? You want any sleepin' pills? I said, well, I ain't been takin' sleepin' pills. I don't figure I need to take 'em now. So and that was kind of a shocker. Because the hospital didn't believe it, the doctor didn't believe it. And man, they tested me two or three times, the usual testin' that they do on you. They sent me up here to McLean Hospital in Boston, because this was ordered by the court. Like, they called me up one day and I'm workin' like hell, you know? Doin' my concerts, and they called me up one day and said, "Hey, we want you to go to McLean's Hospital and check in tomorrow." Not only did they send me there, but what they did, they waited until the weather got kinda cool. Now, they know if you usin' any kinda drugs, you can't stand that cold. You just can't take it. So, man, they cut off the heat on me. Made me mad as hell. I went up and told the nurse I'm gonna sue the goddamn hospital if I catch cold. I know what y'all been doin'. I want some heat put back in my room. I mean, I'm not stupid. But, I'm literally freezin'. So you put the heat back in there. I guess the woman must have said they can't be nothin' wrong with this man, after all the testin' we done and everything else, and all he can do is get mad, you know. So after a while they got to believe me, but it took an awful lot of doin', because it was unusual, quite unusual.

This came after your stay at St. Francis Hospital in Lynwood, California?

Yeah, well, this was somethin' ordered by the court. This was part of my thing. They didn't tell me I couldn't work or nothin', they just said, look, any day we might call you, you know, and say this to you. What they did, they watched my schedule and knew I was workin', so they knew of a day when I wasn't workin'. They knew my schedule better than me, and all of a sudden they just, bam—you just got to go, man. So they did test me a couple of times just to make sure.

I didn't have a wind-down program. I just *stopped,* period. You hear about people who bite the sheets and eat up the pillow, and I didn't do none of that. So that worried people. They took all my clothes. They searched them. And they came in my room one day, they looked under the mattress, shit. I said, "I don't know what the hell you all lookin' for, but they ain't any way in the world I can get anything. Nobody's comin' here, and I don't know where I could find it." And you know, they watched me like a hawk.

You were once asked about the messages in your songs; or, rather, the lack of messages.

No, it was a matter of getting material I could handle. Remember, I got to first feel the music, do somethin' with the song. And that's why you have a song like "America." I wasn't tryin' to just say the country is all bad because it ain't all bad. I love this country, man. And I wouldn't live in no place else. You understand. My family was born here. My great-grandparents were born here. I think I got as much roots in this country as anybody else. So I think when somethin's wrong, it's up to me to try to change it. I was sayin' that America is a beautiful country. It's just some of our policies that people don't dig.

You said onstage that "I Gotta Do Wrong" is "the story of my life," that "I gotta do wrong before they notice me."

Well, I kind of think that what I meant was is that it seems that out of all the pleading that a people can do, all the crying out and all the conversations, you know, we've had that for years and years and years, and nothin' really happened. They said, well, those people are happy, and they're smiling and dancing, and so they must be cool. And nobody paid them the mind, until the people began to do wrong things. And, of course, what I was really saying is not that this was anything to be proud about. I was saying that it's something to be ashamed of, that you got to do wrong before a country as rich as we are — we're the richest country in the world. We got more money and we got more of everything. I don't care what any other country's got for the most part, we got that, and the chances are, nine times out of ten, we got more of it on top of it. And it's a shame that in order for our leaders to really pay us some attention, we gotta go and burn this down, and we gotta go and break into this, and we gotta go and picket this, and we gotta go and stand on this lawn — that's pitiful.

Everybody who's in power — unfortunately, it doesn't seem like they want to do anything unless they're *forced* to it, unless they are made to feel *shame* about it. And when I sing this song — I gotta do wrong before people notice me — I'm not braggin' about that. I'm saying that that's a pity. It is, it's sad, man.

TRUMAN CAPOTE

by Andy Warhol

April 12, 1973

In 1972, *Rolling Stone* asked Truman Capote to cover the Rolling Stones' *Exile on Main St.* tour. But months later, Capote was unable to produce a story. The magazine asked Andy Warhol to interview Capote, and the resulting cover story was billed as "an audio documentary," with small talk and numbers from the tape recorder's counter included.

631

[Leaving the Oak Room. Outside — Central Park South]

000

TRUMAN: Why don't we go for a walk in the park? We'll go visit the yak. In *Breakfast at Tiffany's* that's all Holly Golightly ever used to do, every time she got what she used to call "the mean reds." She used to go to visit the yak in the zoo....

060

[They pass the horse-drawn carriages lined up on the periphery of the park.]

TRUMAN: Somehow, I could never bring myself to ride in one of those because I identify with the horse...Do you identify with animals, Andy? I know you identify with cats, because you used to keep twenty....

[Truman sees a newspaper.]

Tim Leary's going to Vacaville. Vacaville is maximum security, but it's the best-run prison and the nicest —

ANDY: Do you know that I just saw him in St. Moritz? The zoo's that way. I saw Leary Christmas Eve. Isn't that nutty?...The zoo's over there. Isn't that the zoo right over there?

TRUMAN: No, no.

ANDY: No, no. The zoo's over there...But it was so strange to go to somebody's house and there's Timothy Leary.

TRUMAN: I thought he was on his way to Afghanistan.

ANDY: Dig. No. He was with a pretty beautiful girl who's really in love with him.

TRUMAN: He was just like Meyer Lansky without money. The man did escape from prison in California, rightfully or wrongfully for whatever his offense may have been. But the point is, he really did have a marvelous run for his money. He went through Algeria, he fell out with Eldridge Cleaver...Didn't Eldridge Cleaver put him in prison? It'll be interesting to see what happens when they finally catch Eldridge Cleaver. He's going to have to come back because Algeria is absolutely fed up with him. Where can he go?

BOB [Colacello, editor of *Interview*]: He can go to any African country or any Communist country. Cuba would be delighted to have him.

ANDY: Well, then why wouldn't Cuba take Tim Leary?

TRUMAN: Well, he applied there. The Algerian government very much wants Cleaver out of there, I understand. They consider him a terrific troublemaker. On top of which—you know that plane they hijacked and sent to Algeria, and they got the $750,000 ransom. It was all done for Eldridge Cleaver.

ANDY: Oh.

133

ANDY: You're going to the gorilla? Oh, we're going to the deer.

TRUMAN: The yak's right along in here—somewhere...

ANDY: The hippie look is really gone. Everybody's gone back to beautiful clothes. Isn't it great?...Did you ever want someone to call you Daddy?

TRUMAN: Call me Daddy?

ANDY: Yes.

TRUMAN: No. Nor the other way around, either.

ANDY: You mean you don't want to call somebody Daddy.

TRUMAN: Oh, no.

ANDY: But isn't "Daddy" nice? "Daddy"..."Dad"...It sounds so nice...

TRUMAN: I've always been a highly independent person. Strictly on my own.

154

TRUMAN: You said something to me that really startled me when you came to the house today.

ANDY: What?

TRUMAN: You said that my mother telephoned you. I was absolutely startled. Really startled.

ANDY: You were? Why?

TRUMAN: Because my mother really was an alcoholic —

ANDY: But I met your mother.

TRUMAN: I know you met my mother. But my mother was very ill woman, and a total alcoholic.

ANDY: Really? When I met her, she wasn't —

TRUMAN: Yes, she was an alcoholic when you met her. She had been an alcoholic since I was sixteen, so she was an alcoholic when you met her...

ANDY: I never knew that.

TRUMAN: You didn't realize it?

ANDY: No. She was really sweet.

TRUMAN: Well, she had this sort of sweet thing, and then suddenly she'd — Well, you know, she committed suicide.

ANDY: She did? Oh, I didn't know that. I thought she just got sick.

TRUMAN: No, no, no, no. She committed suicide. She had this extraordinary sweet quality, but then she was one of those people who would have two drinks...

* * *

ANDY: I guess you have to be different to be able to be something else.

TRUMAN: One thing I'll say about Mick Jagger. He's fascinating in the sense that he's one of the most total actors that I've ever seen. He has this remarkable quality of being absolutely able to be totally extroverted. Very few people can be entirely, absolutely, altogether

extroverted. It's a rare, delicate, strange thing. Just to pull yourself
out and go— *Whamm!* This he can do to a remarkable degree. But
what makes it more remarkable is that the moment it's done, it's
over. And he reverts to quite a private, sensible, and a more emotionally mature person than most actors and intellectuals are capable of being. He's one of the few people I've seen who's able to do
that extrovert thing, and then revert into another person almost
instantly. And so, in that sense, he's really an extraordinary actor.
And that's exactly what he is because: (a) he can't sing; (b) he can't
dance; (c) he doesn't know a damn thing about music. But he does
know about coming on and being a great showman. And putting
on a fantastic act, of which the vital element is energy. Don't you
think?

Tell me what you think. You think he can sing?

BOB: Who are you talking about?

TRUMAN: Mick Jagger. Well, he can't sing compared to, say, Billie
Holiday. He can't sing compared to Lee Wiley. He can't sing compared to...

ANDY: Al Green.

TRUMAN: He can't compared to Frank Sinatra. I know you think
we're talking about things in separate categories, but we're not. You
know? It's not that it's...Sound amplification—rock—is carrying
a thing forward. The beat thing. *But!* It's got nothing to do with
the ability of the vocalist actually carrying the thing. Because Mick
does not carry the thing. He carries it as performer with his energy,
drive and thrust.

I listen to the records quite a lot. I'm in no way trying to discredit
him as a performer, because I think he's an extraordinary performer.
But what I think's amazing about him is that there is no single thing
of all the things he does that he's really good at. He's not—he really
can't dance, and, in fact, he really can't move. He's moving in the
most awkward kind of curious parody between an American majorette girl...and Fred Astaire. It's like he got these two weird people

combined together. On the one hand, it's the majorette strut, and on the other hand, it's got to be à la Astaire. But, somehow, the combination works. Or at least it works for most people....

ANDY: Did you like traveling around with them?

TRUMAN: Oh, I enjoyed it. I just didn't want to write about it, because it didn't interest me creatively. You know? But I enjoyed it as an experience. I thought it was amusing...I like the Rolling Stones individually, one by one, but the one thing I didn't like was that they had—and especially the people around them—had such a disrespect for the audience. That used to really gripe me. It was like, "Who the fuck cares about them?" Well, these kids have merely stood in line for twenty-seven hours, you know, and whatnot to go to their concert—they adore them and love them....

ANDY: Why don't we go and sit in a bar? Get a drink?

TRUMAN: I found the *real* backstage people nice. The ones who were really doing work. It's those little fakes like the press agent. There's a wretched little press agent whose name...something...who was a great friend of Charlie Manson's, and who recorded three albums of Charlie Manson's records, and he believed Charlie Manson was Jesus Christ—this was before Charlie Manson was going. *He* was a press agent on the rock & roll tour! I mean they had some beauties... Marshall Chess...

504

ANDY: Why don't we go to a bar and I can ask you the six questions that *Rolling Stone* wants me to ask.

TRUMAN: Okay. My fingers are frozen.

000

[*At the Hotel Carlyle Bar*]

TRUMAN: Whose questions are these? Jann Wenner's?

ANDY: Yes. The first question is —

TRUMAN: Wait. I want to order something before you do this.

091

TRUMAN: I'll have a J&B on the rocks with a glass of water on the side, please?

ANDY: I'll have a Grand Marnier.

TRUMAN: Well, that was a nice walk. I think the nice thing about walking through the zoo in New York is...I used to go to school here for two years. I went to a private school here, and I skipped school almost every day. I mean literally, almost every day. At least every other day. I just couldn't bear to go to school. I was about twelve years old. And I used to spend more time walking in that park around the zoo to use up the time between nine o'clock when I was supposed to go to school and two-thirty when I was supposed to get out.

Finally, I found three things to do. One was, I'd go for a walk in the park if it was a nice day. Two, I'd go to the New York Society Library. It was there I met Willa Cather, and she became this great friend of mine, when I was, you know...only a kid. She took a great interest in me. And the third thing was, believe it or not, going to Radio City Music Hall and sitting through the entire production, starting with the movie at nine, and I'd see two stage shows and the movie.

Even so I didn't get my diploma.

291

ANDY: The first question was "problems."
  [*Truman laughs*]

ANDY: Jann wanted to know your problem. With writing the article.

TRUMAN: Why I couldn't write the article?

ANDY: Yes.

TRUMAN: The reason was—twofold. One: As the thing progressed, I saw more and more trash written about the entire tour, and ordinarily that sort of thing doesn't bother me: I mean, for instance, I could cover a trial that's being covered by seventeen or eighteen newspapers at the time, and it doesn't faze me in the least because I know it has nothing to do with what my own insight is.

But my trouble with this was that especially in journalistic writing...*au reportage*...there has to be some element of *mystery* to me about it. And the problem with me with this piece was that there was no mystery. There was not a thing about it that set some mystery going into my mind as to why this should be or that should be, because it was all so perfectly timed...staged—I mean psychologically—I'm not talking about the performance itself. Just the whole combination of the thing was so perfectly obvious. The people were so obvious, and so they really had no dimension beyond their own. I mean, Mick Jagger has a certain mystery to him, but simply because he's a bit of a doppelganger. I mean, he's a highly trained performer, and on the other hand, he's a businessman par excellence. And the whole thing is perfectly obvious, and so it had no mystery to it. Since there was nothing to "find out," I just couldn't be bothered writing it. Does that make sense to you?

ANDY: Backstage people. You sort of talked about it before.

TRUMAN: The only thing I have to say about it is Marshall Chess [the president of Rolling Stones Records] and all those people have themselves confused as being one of the Stones. I mean, they're always up on the stage sort of edging nearer and dearer into the spotlight. It's always been conceded that just something *barely* is restraining them from rushing onstage, grabbing the microphone from Mick and starting to really strut...Also, they're very cantankerous and jealous of each other, and they're so jealous of their relationship with the Stones, with who's closer, who's nearer, who's more...this sort of thing. I mean it's really sort of pathetic. Well, not "sort of." It is pathetic.

ANDY: Then the next question was, "The Plane Fuck."

TRUMAN: They had this doctor on the plane who was a young doctor from San Francisco, about twenty-eight years old, rather good-looking. He would pass through the plane with a great big plate of pills, every kind you could imagine, everything from vitamin C to vitamin coke...I couldn't really quite figure out why. He had just started practice in San Francisco, and this seemed sort of a dramatic thing to be doing, traveling with, uh...I mean, especially since he wasn't particularly, as I could figure out, a great fan of theirs.

It developed that he had a super-Lolita complex. I mean thirteen-, fourteen-year-old kids. He would arrive at whatever city we would arrive at, and there would always be these hordes of kids outside and he would walk around, you know, like a little super-fuck and say, "You know I'm Mick Jagger's personal physician. How would you like to see the show from backstage?" And they'd go, "Oooo! Wigawigawigawa!" He would get quite a collection of them. Backstage, you know, he would have them spread out, and every now and then he would bring one back to the plane. Usually someone slightly older.

The one I remember the most was a girl who said she'd come to the Rolling Stones thing to get a story for her high school newspaper, and wasn't this wonderful how she'd met Dr. Feelgood and got backstage...Anyway, she got on the plane, and she sure got a story, all right [*laughs*], because they fitted up the back of the plane for this. You know Robert Frank? He was on the tour. Robert Frank got out all of his lights, the plane was flying along and there was Dr. Feelgood screwing this girl in every conceivable position while Robert Frank was filming, and as the plane was flying back to Washington it was flying at some really strange angle. And the stewardess kept saying, "Would you please mind moving forward?" [*Laughs*] And then the plane landed and they always brought these authorities on board for checkout, and Dr. Feelgood had a terribly hard time getting his trousers on. And in the end he had to come off the plane holding his trousers in his hand…with Robert Frank photographing it all. I mean the whole thing had rather a belle epoque quality.

ANDY: Well, but how long was the fuck?

TRUMAN: It was a very short flight. About thirty-five minutes. Everybody kept switching and changing camera angles. Robert Frank was photographing for a movie he's making about the tour, and said, "Well, I hope you're going to leave that in."

ANDY: Did the girl know that she was being photographed?

TRUMAN: Of course! They had lights up and everything. She was enjoying it! I said to her, "Well, you came to get a story for your high school newspaper and you're sure getting one." She got off at the next stop. I must say they were always very nice about these kids.

ANDY: You mean there were more instances like this?

TRUMAN: Well, it was going on continuously, day and night. And not just girls, but boys. The girls *and* boys, flocks of them went off with…There were, uh…mmm…a lot of people connected with the tour that used to do that. Um, went off with the boys. Very attractive sort of college kids that showed up, they'd get out there, get involved with everything from an electrician to, mmmm, to—They would go with *anybody* who was connected with the tour. A carpenter. A lightman. Anyone connected with the tour, no matter who it was. They didn't care. Boys, women, dogs, fire hydrants. I mean, the most extraordinary things you've ever seen.

ANDY: Mostly outside New York, right? Not in New York. Because I didn't see any of it happening.…

TRUMAN: The things that went on in Texas. I've never seen anything equal to it.

There's sort of all-night partying. One night…in Texas—I

mean I never did it, because in my own mind I was working at the moment, even though subconsciously I knew I was not going to do it. But they would come off and be wagged up, and one night about four o'clock in the morning when I was in bed but wasn't asleep (and I guess in a way this is the key to first question about why I didn't do it), Keith Richards came and he knocked on my door, and I said, "Yes?" and he said, "It's Keith," and I said, "Yes, Keith." He said, "Oh, come out, we're having a terrific party upstairs."

"I'm tired. I've had a long day and so have you and I think you should go to bed."

"Aw, come out and see what a rock group's really like."

"I know what a rock group's really like, Keith. I don't have to come upstairs to see." And apparently he had a bottle of ketchup in his hand—he had a hamburger and a bottle of ketchup—and he just threw it all over the door of my room. [*Laughs*]

ANDY: It sounds like fun. Oh, I've gotten to like ketchup so much! I just can really eat it.

TRUMAN: What?

ANDY: Ketchup.

TRUMAN: Oh, ketchup.

ANDY: But it seems like there's just so much material on that trip, and the way you describe things is wonderful.

TRUMAN: Yes, there's material, but it's just that. Material. It's just that. It doesn't have any echo. It isn't that you want to forget about it because of any unpleasantness; it's just because it doesn't have any echo. Nowhere in this whole story of the Rolling Stones could I find anything sympathetic except the naïveté of the kids…which wasn't—maybe in itself—true, either. Maybe it was just sentimentality.

There was this thing about the Stones that I hated. Which was that the kids would be staying there—they'd end the performance.… [Lighting director] Chip Monck would say, "Thank you, ladies and

89

gentlemen. The Rolling Stones—" And the lights would go up—or had been up actually—and the kids are standing there and they're just—breaking their hearts applauding...And there they are in this dreary Mobile, Alabama, ghastly—Fort Worth, Texas. I mean, they waited months and months for this thing. They wanted it, you know...for such a long time. And then , the Rolling Stones—Not only have they left, not only have they no intention of giving an encore, they are already on their airplane up in the sky while the kids are down there applauding and applauding and pleading, say-ing, "Please come back, please come back!" and everybody knowing that they've long since gone their way...Twice I didn't go on the plane because I wanted to watch this phenomenon. It was heart-breaking. I mean, they would stay for half an hour, and nobody would come out and tell them that they aren't going to come back. And then they would finally drift out...

That was the one thing in it...But, you see, I wrote this thing about these kids in Fort Worth virtually realizing that they weren't going to come back and that the big moment was over and the whole thing, and then they're drifting out into this ghastly July heat, gradually fading away into these dark nights with a street lamp on every other street.

ANDY: Well, who is like the number one person? How does it go down there? Is Mick really considered the whole thing?

TRUMAN: Mm. Hmm.

ANDY: He is?

TRUMAN: Yes. Mick and Keith Richard. I mean, they *are* the Rolling Stones....

ANDY: But the other kids are really nice. I mean, Charlie Watts is really nice....

TRUMAN: Oh, he couldn't be nicer, yes. But that's not the point. When you get right down to it, the two people who really are run-ning the show...

ANDY: But then it goes back to your idea when you were saying that you felt sorry for the audience, because when the Stones left them, it was negative stuff. Well, the audience wants that.

TRUMAN: The audience wants to hear the music. The audience wanted to keep on feeling good. The audience wanted to keep on dancing and huggin', shakin', rockin', rollin'...

ANDY: But they did it themselves on stereo while they were gone.

TRUMAN: But it's ridiculous. I think Mick's one of those people who has that peculiar androgynous quality, like Marlon or Garbo, transferred into a rock & roll thing, but it's quite genuine. I mean, there's nothing transvestite about it—it's just an androgynous quality. And it has something that's very sexy and amusing about it, and it appeals to both boys and girls in the audience, aside from just natural talent. It's a very special sort of quality. Brando has it par excellence. And Garbo always had it—it was always the secret of her great success. And in his own strange way, I don't know, Montgomery Clift had it. He just has it. There's something totally asexual about it. But it doesn't offend the boys in the audience or even excite them, to some degree, and it turns on the girls to a great degree, and it's part of the whole unisex syndrome. Don't you think?

ANDY: Yes. Does it have morbidity?

TRUMAN: Not for me. I just don't know where it goes from here, because I don't know where the Rolling Stones go from here. I don't know if that particular group and the particular thing that they do can go on for more than a year or two. I think Mick's whole career depends on whether he can do something else. I'm sure he'll go on. I just don't know in what area.

ANDY: Why did you go on the tour in the first place?

TRUMAN: I was talked into it...ohhh, I don't know...Jann Wenner kept sending me these telegrams about it. And then I just sort of thought, "Oh, well..." And then I just got kind of caught up in it. And then about halfway through, I knew I wasn't going to do it, and from that point on it was just sort of gradually phasing it out.

I think they have a fantastic drive and professionality that holds up in its way. I've always liked, basically, rock & roll per se, and of a certain kind of band, they're the best. Now everybody says, "Oh, they're over the hill," and this and that, and I don't agree with that. How much can you say? The Rolling Stones are first-rate. I personally prefer them on records to the performances....

ANDY: Jann wants to know, "What do you see as the predominant themes running through the recent albums?"

TRUMAN: Well, I don't see any themes running through their songs. It's just like you — taking Polaroid photographs all night long, or...I think when they're good, it's really by accident, even though everything about them is rehearsed down to the last degree. The Beatles' songs very often made *some* sense, but I can't think of a single Rolling Stones song that, from beginning to end, made absolutely logical sense. It's all in the sound.

ANDY: "Did you have a good time on the tour?"

TRUMAN: Yes. I did. Because I'm a highly curious person. It was a new world — the mechanics of it. The frantic atmosphere in which it was conducted. I really enjoyed it. I wasn't bored. I had a good time.

ANDY: Did you feel guilty about not finishing the article?

TRUMAN: Not in the least. When I make up my mind about something, I never feel guilty. That's it. No artist should feel guilty. If you start a painting and you don't like it, you don't finish it.

ANDY: Why did you take so long to tell him?

TRUMAN: Well, because I hadn't really made up my mind. I had all of the material there, and it was sitting there, and it was bothering me, and I kept thinking, "Well, it would be so easy, really, to do it."

Finally, the time came that I just made up my mind that I wasn't going to do it. And I just told him. They voted me Rookie Reporter of the Year [*laughs*].

I just have my own ideas about things, like anybody else....It wasn't something that I really wanted to do, and there were other things that I really wanted to do, which I really wanted to pull together. Which I have since pulled together, so....

A LADY: Excuse me, Mr. Capote. The next time you have a party, have your friends wear these.

TRUMAN: Oh, aren't you sweet....

ANDY: What's that?

TRUMAN: Who knows?

JOHNNY CASH
by Robert Hilburn

March 1, 1973

Music seems to have been an important part of your life from the beginning. What was the first time you remember listening to music?

The first I remember was my mother playing the guitar. Before I started school. I was four or five years old, but I remember singing with her. Carter family songs, a lot of them. I don't remember any of them in particular, but I know they were gospel songs, church songs.

Besides listening to music you had to work on the farm when you were a kid. Was that an important part of your character building?

Hard work? I don't know. Chopping cotton and picking cotton is drudgery. I don't know how much good it ever did me. I don't know how much good drudgery does anybody.

But I get the feeling, though, that you have empathy with people who work hard, that you want to reassure them in your music that their life has meaning.

Yeah. I got a lot of respect for a man that's not afraid to work. I don't think a man can be happy unless he's working. And I work hard on my music. I put in a lot of thought. I lose a lot of sleep, a lot of nights, because I'm laying awake thinking about my songs and about what's right and wrong with my music. I worry about whether that last record was worth releasing, whether I could have done it better. Sometimes I feel that the last record was exactly like the one I released fourteen years ago. I wonder if I'm just spinning my wheels sometimes. I wonder if I'm progressing, if I'm growing musically, artistically. I guess I've quoted Bob Dylan a million times, his line, "He who is not busy being born is busy dying." I've always believed that.

Going back to your childhood, what was the next step — musically?

I started writing songs myself when I was about twelve. I started writing some poems and then made some music up to go along with them. They were love songs, sad songs. I think the death of my brother Jack, when I was twelve, had a lot to do with it. My poems were awfully sad at the time. My brother and I were very, very close.

Did you sing the songs to your family? What was the reaction?

Oh well, you know how families are. My dad would pat me on the head and say that was pretty good, but you'd better think about something that will buy you something to eat someday. My mother was a hundred percent for my music. When I was sixteen she wanted me to take piano and voice lessons. She even took in washing to get the money. I think I had one voice lesson. The teacher told me not to take any more because it might affect my delivery.

What was the first time you sang in public?

I guess it was at high school commencement. I sang Joyce Kilmer's "Trees." I had a high voice, a tenor when I was a teenager. I had just piano accompaniment. I was pretty scared. I didn't do anything else until after I got out of the Air Force.

Did you have a feeling at that time, when you went into the Air Force, that you were ever going to really get into music?

Yeah, I always knew. I really did. I always knew. I remember writing my brother when I was in the Air Force telling him that I'd be recording within a year after I was discharged. I wrote "Folsom Prison Blues" while I was in the air force in Germany. I wrote it one night after seeing a movie called *Inside the Walls of Folsom*. I also wrote "Belshazzar" and "Hey Porter" in the air force.

When you got back to Memphis, how did you get into the music business?

I found out about Sun Records in Memphis. They were getting pretty hot with Elvis about that time, so I called about an audition. I remember how scared I was the first time I walked into Sun. It was Sam Phillips and his secretary, Miss McGinnis. They didn't even remember I had an appointment to record. I got the first of seven "come back laters." I told Phillips that I wrote gospel songs. I thought "Belshazzar" was the best song I had to show him. He said, "Well, the market is not too good for gospel songs. Come back sometime when you feel like you've got something else."

But we eventually got together, and I believe we recorded "Hey Porter" the same day. The first session was really something. Luther Perkins had a little secondhand Sears amplifier with a six-inch speaker. Marshall Grant had a bass that was held together with masking tape. I had a $4.80 guitar that I had brought back from Germany. Phillips had to be a genius to get anything out of that conglomeration.

Not long after "Hey Porter" was released, I was back in the studio recording everything I had written and some songs that I hadn't written. It was exciting, things were happening so fast. I remember one day going into the studio and Elvis and Jerry Lee Lewis were both there. Carl Perkins came in a few minutes later, and the four of us stood around the piano singing hymns.

I think we sang for a couple of hours; and I understand Sam had the recorder on and there is something like ten hymns recorded by that "quartet."

How did you get together with Luther Perkins and Marshall Grant?

We met at a garage where my brother worked. They were mechanics. They had just been fooling around with music. Roy told me they were both guitar players. Marshall had never touched a bass at that time. So, here we were: three guitar players. We tried to get Marshall to start playing the bass, and Luther agreed to try the electric guitar. We felt we needed the instruments to round out the sound.

How did you work out the arrangements?

I just had it all in my head. I'd show Luther the notes on the guitar, and he'd play it over and over until he learned it.

How did the Johnny Cash sound come about?

That boom-chick-a-boom sound? Luther took the metal plate off the Fender guitar and muted the strings because he said he played it so ragged that he was ashamed of it and he was trying to cover up the sound.

What did Phillips say when he heard the sound?

He thought it was really commercial. He just flipped over it.

How did you feel when you had the first record in your hand? It must have been a big day for you.

It was the most fantastic feeling I ever had in my life. I remember signing the recording contract the day the record was released.

I had both the contract and "Hey Porter" in my hand when I left Sun that day. And I had fifteen cents in my pocket. I remember coming out of the studio and there was a bum on the street. I gave him the fifteen cents. That's true. Then I took the record to the radio station, holding it like it was an old master painting. And the disc jockey *dropped it* and *it broke*. By accident. It was the next day till I could get another one. That was really heartbreaking. But the record went on to get a lot of airplay, especially in the South. Presley's first manager, Bob Neal, called me and wanted me to do some concerts with Elvis. The first place I played was Overton Park in Memphis. I did "Hey Porter" and "Cry, Cry, Cry" and the reaction was good, very good.

"I Walk the Line" was the big record for you. Did you have a special feeling about it when you finished it?

I thought it was a very good song, but I wasn't sure about the record. I was in Florida when I first heard it on the radio, and I called Phillips and begged him not to send any more copies out. I thought it was so bad. I thought it was a horrible record. And he said let's give it a chance and see. But I didn't want to. I wanted it stopped right then. I got upset with him over it. I thought it sounded so bad. Still sounds bad.

Your voice or the arrangement?

The arrangement. And I didn't like the sound, the modulation and all. But that's what turned out to be the most commercial part of it. Sam was right about it.

What made you eventually leave Sun?

There were also some business matters that we didn't see eye to eye on. He had me on a beginner's rate after three years, and I didn't feel right about it. But, mainly I knew that I could do different kinds of things with a larger label. I could record an album of hymns for Columbia, for instance, and that was important to me at the time.

What was it like returning home to Arkansas after you had become famous?

Well, I was still the country boy to those people. I mean I wasn't anything special to them. A lot of places I'd go in those days made you feel like the big radio star that I had wanted to be, and it felt good. I really ate it up. But at home all the old people would come up and say, "Boy, I remember when you used to bring me buttermilk every other Thursday" or something.

Was there a point that you ever lost touch with those people? During the bad years? Was there a point where you really didn't think of them as friends anymore?

Yes, right. I felt like I didn't belong, and for about seven years I didn't go back. I didn't go back around those people. I didn't want any of them to see me.

That was the bad time for you, the pills and all.

Yeah, not too long after I moved to California. I still don't know why I ever moved to California. I liked it there, had worked out there quite a bit and thought I'd love living there. But I didn't really belong out there. I never really felt at home there. I tried to, but I just didn't. I got into the habit of amphetamines. I took them for seven years. I just liked the feel of them.

Was it the lift?

Yes, it lifts you, and under certain conditions it intensifies all your senses—makes you think you're the greatest writer in the world. You just write songs all night long and just really groove on what you're doing, digging yourself, and keep on taking the pills. Then, when you sober up later, you realize it wasn't so good. When I run across some of the stuff I wrote, it always makes me sick…wild, impossible, ridiculous ramblings you wouldn't believe.

You took more pills to cover up the guilt feelings. And I got to playing one against the other, the uppers against the downers, and it got to be a vicious, vicious circle. And they got to pulling me down. On top of that, I thought I was made of steel and nothing could hurt me. I wrecked every car, every truck, every jeep I ever drove during that seven years. I counted the broken bones in my body once. I think I have seventeen. It's the grace of God that one of those bones wasn't my neck.

Over a period of time, though, you get to realizing that amphetamines are slowly burning you up, and burning you up is the truth—because they are hot after a while. Then you get paranoid, you think everybody is out to do you in. You don't trust anybody—even the ones who love you the most. It's like a bad dream now.

Was there a point in your life that you think you hit bottom? Like the time in Georgia when you woke up in jail?

Yeah, that was in '67. That's when things started turning. But that was just one of the many awakenings I had. You know, that one has been written up in a lot of books and magazines, but that was just one of dozens or hundreds of times that I started reawakening and realizing that there was something good that was going to happen to me, that I had to pull myself out, that life was going to take a turn for the better.

I'd had seven years of roughing it and I felt I had seven years of good times and good life coming. I really felt in 1967 that there were seven big years ahead.

How did you start pulling out of those bad times?

Well, it really started about the time June and I got married. The growth of love in my life and the spiritual strengthening came at about the same time. Religion's got a lot to do with it. Religion, love, it's all one and the same as far as I'm concerned, because that's what religion means to me. It's love. About the time I married June, we started growing in spiritual strength together. And it shows up onstage.

You can't fool the audience. You can't fool yourself. If you're not yourself onstage, it shows. I'm really happy now. But that's not the same as being content. I still want to grow more as a performer, as an artist, as a person. So, I'm still working hard at it. I never go on that stage when I'm not scared. There's always that fear that somebody's going to throw eggs at you or something.

How would you get yourself up physically and emotionally for a recording session during those troubled years?

I missed a lot of sessions. I'd come into the studio with a fog over my head, not really caring what condition I was in. Just go in on sheer guts and give it a try. It showed up on a lot of my recordings.

What was it about Dylan that attracted you?

I thought he was one of the best country singers I had ever heard. I really did. I dug the way he did the things with such a country flavor and the country sounds. "World War III Talkin' Blues" and all those things in the *Freewheelin'* album. I didn't think you could get much more country than that. Of course, his lyrics knocked me out, and we started writing each other. We wrote each other letters for about a year before we ever met.

I was playing here in Las Vegas the first time I heard one of his albums. I played it backstage, in the dressing room, and I wrote him a letter telling him how much I liked his songs, and he answered it and in so many words told me the same thing. He had remembered me from the days of "I Walk the Line" when he was living in Hibbing, Minnesota. I invited him to come see me in California, but when he came to California later he couldn't find my house.

I got another letter that was written in Carmel and by the time I answered it, he'd already gone back to New York. When I was in New York not long after that John Hammond told me that Bob was in town. So he came up and we met at Columbia Records. We spent a few hours together, talking about songs, swappin' songs and he invited me up to his house in Woodstock. After the Newport Folk Festival, he invited me to his house again.

Some people say that Dylan is aloof or withdrawn, that he is hard to talk to. Did you find him that way?

We never did really talk all that much. There's a mutual understanding between us. I never did try to dig into his personal life and he didn't try to dig into mine. If he's aloof and hard to get to, I can understand why. I don't blame him. So many people have taken advantage of him, tried to do him in when they did get to him, that I wouldn't blame him for being aloof and hard to get to. Everybody tells him what he should write, how to think, what to sing. But that's really his business.

Let's talk about your own songs. Do you have any special memories about them?

Sure, most of my songs bring back memories. Things like how I happened to write them, where I was when they were released and so forth.

"Train of Love"—I remember writing that in 1955 when I was on the *Louisiana Hayride* show in Shreveport. Sam Phillips happened to be there. And I called him into the dressing room and asked him what he thought about the song. He really liked it. We recorded it on the next session.

I wrote "Give My Love to Rose" about ten blocks from San Quentin prison. I was playing a club there one night in '56, the first time I came to California. And an ole boy came backstage, an ex-con, to talk to me about Shreveport. He was from there. And I'm not sure his wife was named Rose, but his wife was in Shreveport and he said something about "giving my love to my wife if you get back to Shreveport before I do." He had just gotten out of prison. I wrote the song that night.

"Big River"—I wrote it as a real slow bluesy thing. I remember sitting in the backseat of the car going through White Plains, New York, singing... "I ta—ught the wee—ping wil—low how to cry." Real slow and bluesy.

I wrote "Hey Porter" when I was overseas. That was my home-sick song for the South. "So Doggone Lonesome" was written with Ernest Tubb in mind. A lot of times I'd write songs with some singer in mind, never really intending to even let them hear it, but with them in mind. After I recorded "So Doggone Lonesome," Tubb heard it and did record it.

I wrote "Get Rhythm" for Elvis. But I never did let him hear it before I recorded it. "Come in Stranger" was just my life-on-the-road song.

Didn't you give Carl Perkins the idea for "Blue Suede Shoes"?

I remember the guys in the Air Force saying, "Don't step on my blue suede shoes." I thought it was a good line and told Carl he should put it into a song. But he wrote it all. It's his song.

Do you think about the future much?

I just feel it as it goes. I do whatever I feel is right for me at the time. I don't try to get the jump on anybody or anything.

Are you an optimistic person?

Oh, yeah. I sure am. I've had seventeen years of nothing but good times as far as my music has gone. It's all been good for me. All the years have been good for me. And I see nothing but growth as far as the music business is concerned. I'm really optimistic about that, the fact that the best talents will be making it. Good talent will always be heard. There's nothing going to take the place of the human being. They can get all the Moog synthesizers that they want but nothing will take the place of the human heart.

NEIL YOUNG

by Cameron Crowe

August 14, 1975

Why is it that you've finally decided to talk now? For the past five years journalists requesting Neil Young interviews were told you had nothing to say.

There's a lot I have to say. I never did interviews because they always got me in trouble. Always. They never came out right. I just don't like them. As a matter of fact, the more I didn't do them the more they wanted them, the more I said by not saying anything. But things change, you know. I feel very free now. I don't have an old lady anymore [Young had recently been divorced]. I relate it a lot to that. I'm back living in Southern California. I feel more open than I have in a long while. I'm coming out and speaking to a lot of people. I feel like something new is happening in my life.

I'm really turned on by the new music I'm making now, back with Crazy Horse. Today, even as I'm talking, the songs are running through my head. I'm excited. I think everything I've done is valid or else I wouldn't have released it, but I do realize the last three albums have been a certain way. I know I've gotten a lot of bad publicity for them. Somehow I feel like I've surfaced out of some kind of murk. And the proof will be in my next album. *Tonight's the Night,* I would say, is the final chapter of a period I went through.

Why the murky period?

Oh, I don't know. Danny's death probably tripped it off [Danny Whitten, leader of Crazy Horse and Young's rhythm guitarist/second vocalist]. It happened right before the *Time Fades Away* tour. He was supposed to be in the group. We [Ben Keith, steel guitar; Jack Nitzsche, piano; Tim Drummond, bass; Kenny Buttrey, drums; and Young] were rehearsing with him, and he just couldn't cut it. He couldn't remember anything. He was too out of it. Too far gone. I had to tell him to go back to L.A. "It's not happening, man. You're not together enough." He just said, "I've got nowhere else to go, man. How am I gonna tell my friends?" And he split. That *night* the coroner called me from L.A. and told me he'd OD'd. That blew my mind. Fucking blew my mind. I loved Danny. I felt responsible. And from there, I had to go right out on this huge tour of huge arenas. I was very nervous and...insecure.

Why, then, did you release a live album?

I thought it was valid. *Time Fades Away* was a very nervous album. And that's exactly where I was at on the tour. If you ever sat down and listened to all my records, there'd be a place for it in there. Not that you'd go there every time you wanted to enjoy some music, but if you're on the trip it's important. Every one of my records, to me, is like an ongoing autobiography. I can't write the same book every time. There are artists that can. They put out three or four albums every year, and everything fucking sounds the same. That's great. Somebody's trying to communicate to a lot of people and give them the kind of music that they know they want to hear. That isn't my trip.

You gotta keep changing. Shirts, old ladies, whatever. I'd rather keep changing and lose a lot of people along the way. If that's the price, I'll pay it. I don't give a shit if my audience is a hundred or a hundred million. It doesn't make any difference to me. I'm convinced that what sells and what I do are two completely different things. If they meet, it's coincidence. I just appreciate the freedom to put out an album like *Tonight's the Night* if I want to.

You sound pretty drunk on that album.

I would have to say that's the most liquid album I've ever made [*laughs*]. You almost need a life preserver to get through that one. We were all leaning on the ol' cactus...and, again, I think that it's something people should hear. They should hear what the artist sounds like under all circumstances if they want to get a complete portrait. Everybody gets fucked up, man. Everybody gets fucked up sooner or later. You're just pretending if you don't let your music get just as liquid as you are when you're really high.

Is that the point of the album?

No. No. That's the means to an end. *Tonight's the Night* is like an OD letter. The whole thing is about life, dope and death. When we [Nils Lofgren, guitars and piano; Talbot, Molina and Young] played that music we were all thinking of Danny Whitten and Bruce Berry, two close members of our unit lost to junk overdoses. The *Tonight's the Night* sessions were the first time what was left of Crazy Horse had gotten together since Danny died. It was up to us to get the strength together among us to fill the hole he left. The other OD, Bruce Berry, was CSNY's roadie for a long time. His brother Ken runs Studio Instrument Rentals, where we recorded the album. So we had a lot of vibes going for us. There was a lot of spirit in the music we made. It's funny, I remember the whole experience in black and white. We'd go down to S.I.R. about five in the afternoon and start getting high, drinking tequila and playing pool. About midnight, we'd start playing. And we played Bruce and Danny on their way all through the night. I'm not a junkie, and I won't even try it out to check out what it's like...but we all got high enough, right out there on the edge where we felt wide open to the whole mood. It was spooky. I probably *feel* this album more than anything else I've ever done.

Why did you wait until now to release 'Tonight's the Night'? Isn't it almost two years old?

I never finished it. I only had nine songs, so I set the whole thing aside and did *On the Beach* instead. It took Elliot [manager Elliot Roberts] to finish *Tonight's the Night*. You see, a while back there were some people who were gonna make a Broadway show out of the story of Bruce Berry and everything. They even had a script written. We were putting together a tape for them, and in the process of listening back on the old tracks, Elliot found three even older songs that related to the trip, "Lookout Joe," "Borrowed Tune" and "Come on Baby Let's Go Downtown," a live track from when I played the Fillmore East with Crazy Horse. Danny even sings lead on that one. Elliot added those songs to the original nine and sequenced them all into a cohesive story. But I still had no plans whatsoever to release it. I already had another new album called *Homegrown* in the can. The cover was finished and everything [*laughs*]. Ah, but they'll never hear that one.

Okay. Why not?

I'll tell you the whole story. I had a playback party for *Homegrown* for me and about ten friends. We were out of our minds. We all listened to the album, and *Tonight's the Night* happened to be on the same reel. So we listened to that, too, just for laughs. No comparison.

So you released 'Tonight's the Night.' Just like that?

Not because *Homegrown* wasn't as good. A lot of people would probably say that it's better. I know the first time I listened back on

Tonight's the Night, it was the most out-of-tune thing I'd ever heard. Everyone's off-key. I couldn't hack it. But by listening to those two albums back-to-back at the party, I started to see the weaknesses in *Homegrown.* I took *Tonight's the Night* because of its overall strength in performance and feeling. The theme may be a little depressing, but the general feeling is much more elevating than *Homegrown.* Putting this album out is almost an experiment.

You didn't come from a musical family....

Well, my father played a little ukulele [*laughs*]. It just happened. I felt it. I couldn't stop thinking about it. All of a sudden I wanted a guitar, and that was it. I started playing around the Winnipeg community clubs, high school dances. I played as much as I could.

With a band?

Oh, yeah, always with a band. I never tried it solo until I was nineteen. Eighteen or nineteen.

Were you writing at the time?

I started off writing instrumentals. Words came much later. My idol at the time was Hank B. Marvin, Cliff Richard's guitar player in the Shadows. He was the hero of all the guitar players around Winnipeg at the time. Randy Bachman, too; he was around then, playing the same circuit. He had a great sound. Used to use a tape repeat.

When did you start singing?

I remember singing Beatles tunes...the first song I ever sang in front of people was "It Won't Be Long" and then "Money (That's What I Want)." That was in the Calvin High School cafeteria. My big moment.

Did you know Joni Mitchell in those days?

I've known Joni since I was eighteen. I met her in one of the coffee-houses. She was beautiful. That was my first impression. She was real frail and wispy-looking. And her cheekbones were so beautifully shaped. She'd always wear light satins and silks. I remember thinking that if you blew hard enough, you could probably knock her over. She could hold up a Martin D18 pretty well, though. What an incredible talent she is. She writes about her relationships so much more vividly than I do. I use...I guess I put more of a veil over what I'm talking about. I've written a few songs that were as stark as hers. Songs like "Pardon My Heart," "Home Fires," "Love Art Blues"...almost all of *Homegrown*. I've never released any of those. And I probably never will. I think I'd be too embarrassed to put them out. They're a little *too* real.

How do you look back on the whole Buffalo Springfield experience?

Great experience. Those were really good days. Great people. Everybody in that group was a fucking genius at what they did. That was a great group, man. There'll never be another Buffalo Springfield. Never. Everybody's gone such separate ways now, I don't know. If everybody showed up in one place at one time with all the amps and everything, I'd love it. But I'd sure as hell hate to have to get it together. I'd love to play with that band again, just to see if the buzz was still there.

There's a few stock Springfield myths I should ask you about. How about the old hearse story?

True. Bruce Palmer and I were tooling around L.A. in my hearse. I loved the hearse. Six people could be getting high in the front and back, and nobody would be able to see in because of the curtains. The heater was great. And the tray...the tray was dynamite. You open the side door, and the tray whips right out onto the sidewalk.

What could be cooler than that? What a way to make your entrance. Pull up to a gig and just wheel out all your stuff on the tray. Anyway, Bruce Palmer and I were taking in California. The Promised Land. We were heading up to San Francisco. Stephen and Richie Furay, who were in town putting together a band, just happened to be driving around, too. Stephen Stills had met me before and remembered I had a hearse. As soon as he saw the Ontario plates, he knew it was me. So they stopped us. I was happy to see fucking *anybody* I knew. And it seemed very logical to us that we form a band. We picked up Dewey Martin for the drums, which was my idea, four or five days later. Stephen was really pulling for Billy Munday at the time. He's say, "Yeah, yeah, yeah. Dewey's good, but *Jesus*...he talks too fucking much." I was right, though. Dewey was fucking good.

Why did you leave the band?

I just couldn't handle it toward the end. My nerves couldn't handle the trip. It wasn't me scheming on a solo career, it wasn't anything but my nerves. Everything started to go too fucking fast, I can tell that now. I was going crazy, you know, joining and quitting, and joining again. I began to feel like I didn't have to answer or obey anyone. I needed more space. That was a big problem in my head. So I'd quit, then I'd come back 'cause it sounded so good. It was a constant problem. I just wasn't mature enough to deal with it. I was very young.

What was your life like after the Springfield?

It was all right. I needed to get out to the sticks for a while and just relax. I headed for Topanga Canyon and got myself together. I bought a big house that overlooked the whole canyon. I eventually got out of that house because I couldn't handle all the people who kept coming up all the time. Sure was a comfortable fucking place...that was '69, about when I started living with my first wife, Susan. Beautiful woman.

Was your first solo album a love song for her?

No. Very few of my albums are love songs to anyone. Music is so big, man, it just takes up a lot of room. I've dedicated my life to my music so far. And every time I've let it slip and gotten somewhere else, it's showed. Music lasts...a lot longer than relationships do. My first album was very much a first album. I wanted to prove to myself that I could do it. And I did, thanks to the wonder of modern machinery. That first album was overdub city. It's still one of my favorites, though. *Everybody Knows This Is Nowhere* is probably my best. Everything I've ever done with Crazy Horse has been incredible. Just for the *feeling*, if nothing else.

Why did you join CSNY, then? You were already working steadily with Crazy Horse.

Stephen. I love playing with the other guys, but playing with Stephen is special. David is an excellent rhythm guitarist, and Graham sings so great... shit, I don't have to tell anybody those guys are phenomenal. I knew it would be fun. I didn't have to be out front. I could lay back. It didn't have to be me all the time. They were a big group, and it was easy for me. I could still work double time with Crazy Horse. With CSNY, I was basically just an instrumentalist that sang a couple of songs with them. It was easy. And the music was great. CSNY, I think, has always been a lot bigger thing to everybody else than it is to us. People always refer to me as Neil Young of CSNY, right? It's not my main trip. It's something that I do every once in a while. I've constantly been working on my own trip all along. And now that Crazy Horse is back in shape, I'm even more self-involved.

How much of your own solo success, though, was due to CSNY?

For sure CSNY put my name out there. They gave me a lot of publicity. But, in all modesty, *After the Gold Rush,* which was kind of the turning point, was a strong album. I really think it was. A lot of hard work went into it. Everything was there. The picture it painted was a strong one. *After the Gold Rush* was the spirit of Topanga Canyon. It seemed like I realized that I'd gotten somewhere. I joined CSNY and was still working a lot with Crazy Horse...I was playing all the time. And having a great time. Right after that album, I left the house. It was a good coda.

How did you cope with your first real blast of superstardom after that?

The first thing I did was a long tour of small halls. Just me and a guitar. I loved it. It was real personal. Very much a one-on-one thing with the crowd. It was later, after *Harvest,* that I hid myself away. I tried to stay away from it all. I thought the record [*Harvest*] was good, but I also knew that something else was dying. I became very reclusive. I didn't want to come out much.

Why? Were you depressed? Scared?

I think I was pretty happy. In spite of everything, I had my old lady and moved to the ranch. A lot of it was my back. I was in and out of hospitals for the two years between *After the Gold Rush* and *Harvest.* I have one weak side, and all the muscles slipped on me. My discs slipped. I couldn't hold my guitar up. That's why I sat down on my whole solo tour. I couldn't move around too well, so I laid low for a long time on the ranch and just didn't have any contact, you know. I wore a brace. Crosby would come up to see how I was; we'd go for a walk, and it took me forty-five minutes to get to the studio, which is only 400 yards from the house. I could only stand up four hours a day. I recorded most of *Harvest* in the brace. That's a lot of the reason it's such a mellow album. I couldn't physically play an electric guitar. "Are You Ready for the Country," "Alabama" and "Words" were all done after I had the operation. The doctors were starting to talk about wheelchairs and shit, so I had some discs removed.

But for the most part, I spent two years flat on my back. I had a lot of time to think about what had happened to me.

Have you ever been in analysis?

You mean have I ever been to a psychiatrist? No [*laughs*]. They're all real interested in me, though. They always ask a lot of questions when I'm around them.

What do they ask?

Well, I had some seizures. They used to ask me a lot of questions about how I felt, stuff like that. I told them all the thoughts I have and the images I see if I, you know, faint or fall down or something. That's not real important, though.

Do you still have seizures?

Yeah, I still do. I wish I didn't. I thought I had it licked.

Is it a physical or mental . . .

I don't know. Epilepsy is something nobody knows much about. It's just part of me. Part of my head, part of what's happening in there. Sometimes something in my brain triggers it off. Sometimes when I get really high, it's a very psychedelic experience to have a seizure. You slip into some other world. Your body's flapping around and you're biting your tongue and batting your head on the ground, but your mind is off somewhere else. The only scary thing about it is not going or being there; it's realizing you're totally comfortable in this . . . *void.* And that shocks you back into reality. It's a very disorienting experience. It's difficult to get a grip on yourself. The last time it happened, it took about an hour and a half of just walking around the ranch with two of my friends to get it together.

Has it ever happened onstage?

No. Never has. I felt like it was a couple times, and I've always left the stage. I get too high or something. It's just pressure from around, you know. That's why I don't like crowds too much.

Why did you leave the ranch? [He had moved from Northern California to Malibu.]

It just got to be too big of a trip. There was too much going on the last couple of years. None of it had anything to do with music. I just had too many fucking people hanging around who don't really know me. They were parasites, whether they intended to be or not. They lived off me, used my money to buy things, used my telephone to make their calls. General leeching. It hurt my feelings a lot when I reached that realization. I didn't want to believe I was being taken advantage of. I didn't like having to be boss, and I don't like having to say, "Get the fuck out." That's why I have different houses now. When people gather around me, I just split now. I mean, my ranch is more beautiful and lasting than ever. It's strong without me. I just don't feel like it's the only place I can be and be safe anymore. I feel much stronger now.

Have you got a name for the new album?

I think I'll call it *My Old Neighborhood*. Either that or *Ride My Llama*. It's weird, I've got all these songs about Peru, the Aztecs and the Incas. Time travel stuff. We've got one song called "Marlon Brando, John Ehrlichman, Pocahontas and Me." I'm playing a lot of electric guitar, and that's what I like best. Two guitars, bass and drums. And it's really flying off the ground, too. Fucking unbelievable. I've got a bet with Elliot that it'll be out before the end of September. After that we'll probably go out on a fall tour of 3,000 seaters. Me and

Crazy Horse again. I couldn't be happier. That, combined with the bachelor life . . . I feel magnificent. Now is the first time I can remember coming out of a relationship, definitely not wanting to get into another one. I'm just not looking. I'm so happy with the space I'm in right now. It's like spring [*laughs*]. I'll sell you two bottles of it for a dollar fifty.

ORIANA FALLACI
by Jonathan Cott

June 17, 1976

*It wasn't so long ago that advice-to-the-lovelorn columnists and love advo-
cates in Hollywood movies used to suggest that all a woman had to do to get
a man interested in her was to cajole him into talking about himself all evening, thereby flattering him and bolstering his sense of self-importance. In
your interviews you seem, almost unconsciously, to have taken this piece of
folk wisdom and pushed it very far down the line, using it in order to expose
your grandiloquent subjects for what they really are.*

I've never thought of that. Neither in my private nor my public life have
I ever thought in terms of "seducing" somebody, using what are called
the "feminine arts"—it makes me vomit just to think of it. Ever since
I was a child—and way before the recent feminist resurgence—I've
never conceived of... I'm very surprised by what you say. There might
be some truth here, but you've really caught me by surprise.

What you're talking about implies a kind of psychological violence which I never commit when I interview someone. I never
force a person to talk to me. If he doesn't want to talk, or if he talks
without pleasure, I just walk out; I've done that many times. There's
no courting or seducing involved. The main secret of my interviews
lies in the fact that there's no trick whatsoever. None.

You know there are many students who write about my interviews—
in Italy, France and America, too. And they always ask me how I go
about it and if I could teach them to do it. But it's impossible, for these

interviews are what they are, good or bad, because they're made by me, with this face, with this voice. They have to do with my personality, and I bring too much of myself into them to teach them.

I was struck by a moving moment during your interview with Mrs. Gandhi where you talked about "the solitude that oppresses women intent on defending their own destinies." You mention that Mrs. Gandhi, like Golda Meir, had to sacrifice her marriage for her career. And I got the feeling that here you were somehow also talking about your sense of yourself.

The first difference between me and them is that I never give up. Marriage is an expression that to me suggests "giving up," an expression of sacrifice and regret. I never wanted to get married, so I didn't make that sacrifice—it was a victory for me. The solitude I was referring to wasn't a physical solitude. Nor was it, for instance, for Indira Gandhi, because everybody knows that at the time I interviewed her she wasn't alone at all. She likes men, thank God, and she makes use of that. It was an internal solitude that comes about from the fact of being a woman—and a woman with responsibilities in a world of men.

That kind of solitude is a victory for me, and I've been searching for it. Today, you are interviewing me in 1976. If you had interviewed me in '74 or '73 or '65, I would probably have answered a little differently— but not too much. Like a photograph, an interview has to crystallize the moment in which it takes place. Today, I need that kind of solitude so much—since it is what moves me, intellectually speaking—that sometimes I feel the need to be physically alone. When I'm with my companion, there are moments when we are two too many. I never get bored when I'm alone, and I get easily bored when I'm with others. And women who, like Indira and like Golda, have had the guts to accept that solitude are the women who have achieved something.

You must also consider that, in terms of the kind of solitude we've been talking about, women like Golda and Indira are more representative because they are old. A person of my generation and, even more so, a woman younger than myself, really *wants* that solitude.

Golda and Indira were victimized by it, since they belonged to a generation in which people didn't think as we do today. They were probably hurt, and I don't know how much they pitied themselves. Golda cried at a certain moment during the interview. When she spoke of her husband, she was regretting something.

As far as myself, in the past I felt less happy about this subject. It was still something to fight about inside myself, trying to understand it better. But today I'm completely free of it, the problem doesn't exist anymore. And I don't even gloat over the fact that what could have been considered a sacrifice yesterday is today an achievement. We must thank the feminists for this, because they've helped not only me but everybody, all women. And young people, both men and women, understand this very much.

Golda spoke of having lost the family as a *great* sacrifice—she was crying then. But to me, the worst curse that could happen to a person is to *have* a family.

That's not a very Italian attitude, is it?

You'd be surprised. We know about marriage Italian-style. But people in Italy today are getting married less and less. We have an unbelievable tax law that makes two persons who are married and who both work pay more taxes than they would if they were single. So they get separated or divorced. And there's nothing "romantic" or "Italian" about this. No, the family, at least morally and psychologically, is disappearing in Italy, as well as all over Europe.

What should exist in its place?

Free individuals.

But no community.

You ask me too much. If I could answer you I would have resolved the problem. If you said to me: "All right, socialism as it's been applied until now hasn't worked. Capitalism doesn't work. What should we do?" I'd have to respond: "My dear, if I could answer these questions, I'd be the philosopher of my time."

In the introduction to your interview with Golda Meir, you comment on the resemblances you noticed between Meir and your own mother, writing: "My mother too has the same gray curly hair, that tired and wrinkled face, that heavy body supported on swollen, unsteady, leaden legs. My mother too has that sweet and energetic look about her, the look of a housewife obsessed with cleanliness. They are a breed of women, you see, that has gone out of style and whose wealth consists in a disarming simplicity, an irritating modesty, a wisdom that comes from having toiled all their lives in the pain, discomfort and trouble that leave no time for the superfluous."

And in the introduction to your interview with Henry Kissinger, you tell how you were immediately reminded of an old teacher of yours "who enjoyed frightening me by staring at me ironically from behind his spectacles. Kissinger even had the same baritone, or rather guttural, voice as this teacher, and the same way of leaning back in the armchair with his right arm outstretched, the gesture of crossing his legs, while his jacket was so tight over his stomach that it looked as though the buttons might pop." It's at special moments like these in your book that I get the sense of a little girl looking at the world so clearly because she remembers so much—a sense one usually finds in the best literature and films, but also never in interviews.

Do you understand now why I can't teach someone how to make these interviews? Do you understand now why they are what they are because I do them? Kissinger was sitting on this raised armchair, having asked me to sit down on the sofa. So he was up there and I was down here, and it was like seeing…Manchinelli was his name, that professor of physics and mathematics. He was a real bastard who used to sit up high and mighty at his podium like God, judging us instead of teaching us, and from there cursing and reproaching us, making us suffer. He made me suffer particularly because I was the only one who answered him back. Oh, I was terrible in school. Poor people, poor professors, I made them suffer so much. Because I was very clever, I was always the first of my class, but I was terrible. Because if they said something wrong, I didn't keep my mouth shut. Anyway, when I saw Kissinger sitting like that—poor man, he wasn't aware of it, of course, and he didn't do it on purpose; he is what he is and was showing what he is—I said: "Oh, God. Here we go with this Manchinelli again."

I associated the two things, and I always do. I always go back to childhood. But do you know why I make these comparisons? Not only because they come spontaneously to me but because I like to be simple when I write, I want to be understood, as I used to say, by my mother when I write about politics. How can my mother understand me? And my audience is made up mostly of people who have not been to university. So in order to simplify things, I use everyday facts, "human" facts—that word is overused, but I'll use it here again. So you associate Kissinger with a nasty old professor, or Golda with your mother, the same wrinkles, the same irritating modesty. And then people understand. My use of associations is a result both of spontaneity and tactics.

I didn't start writing about politics until fairly recently—until Vietnam, in fact. But I've always been a very politicized person because of the family I was born into—I'll come back to this in a minute—and because of my experiences. I was a little girl during the Resistance—and a member of the Liberal Socialist party—and I spoke in public the first time when I was fifteen at a political rally. I'll always remember—I had pigtails and was trembling: *"People of Florence... a young comrade speaks to you..."*

And I kept saying to my editors: "I want to write about politics, I want to interview politicians in the same way that I interview actors. Because it's boring when we read politics, it must be done in another way." But they didn't let me do it because I was a woman. (There we go again.) And only when I demonstrated that I could be a good war correspondent in Vietnam did they allow me to do interviews with politicians in the same way that I'd done them with astronauts, soldiers and actors.

Do you think that your forceful way of doing interviews was in any way determined by the humiliation and contemptuousness you might have felt being a girl growing up in a world of political men?

Absolutely not. I can't complain too much about men because, number one, I had the luck to be born into a feminist family—they didn't know it, but indeed they were. To begin with: my father. He always believed in women. He had three daughters, and when he adopted the fourth child, he chose a girl—my youngest sister—because...he trusts women. And my parents educated me with the attitude of: you *must* do it because you are a woman. It was, for sure, a challenge, which implies the recognition of a certain reality. But they never thought that I couldn't do it.

In the beginning I wanted to become either a surgeon or a journalist. And the only reason why I didn't choose medicine was because we were too poor to afford six years of medical school. So then it seemed obvious for me to get a job as a reporter when I was sixteen. I gave up medicine because I was poor, not because I was a woman. What I never forget is that I was *poor*. And this is probably at the roots of my moralistic attitude that we were speaking about before. Not the fact that I was a woman.

I noticed that you dedicated your book to your mother. Was she a strong influence on you?

She pushed me. She pushed all of us. But my father did, too. I dedicated it to her more than to him because she's dying from cancer, but I should have dedicated it to both of them, because the person who gave me my political ideas was my father. I've changed my mind about many things, but not about my belief in freedom, social justice and socialism—*that* came from him. And when we get to this point, it doesn't matter whether one is a man or a woman.

We were speaking before of Golda and Indira. The feminists are wrong to say: "Ha-ha! Indira behaves the way she does because she lives in a society of men." No, sir. She does it simply because she's a person of power who wanted more power. She wasn't ready to give it up and she acted as a man would have acted. At that point, it was the moment of truth—*el momento de la verdad,* as the Spanish call it. She could have said goodbye, sir, thank you very much. *That* means democracy to me. But instead she became a dictator, she demonstrated that being a woman makes no difference, she was no better because she was a woman...

I want to return to something I spoke to you about earlier—about my obsession with the fascist problem and how it relates to my family experiences. I've just said that I come from an antifascist family, and this was important for me because, to me, being fascistic means making *anti*politics, not *politics.* The fascist—as I once told an interviewer—is someone who resigns, who obeys, who doesn't talk or who imposes himself with violence and avoids the problematic. The antifascist, on the contrary, is a naturally political person. Because being antifascist means to fight though a problem by means of a discussion that involves everybody in civil disobedience. And this atmosphere of disobedience...I've breathed it since I was a little girl. My mother's father was an anarchist—one of those who wore a black ribbon and the big hat. He was a deserter in World War I, and I remember my mother proudly saying: "My father was a deserter in the Great War"—as if he had won some kind of medal. In fact, he was condemned to death because he was a deserter, but they couldn't catch him. And my father's father was a Republican follower of Mazzini, when being that meant one was an extreme leftist. And my father was a leader in the Resistance. It's really in the family.

What you're saying reaffirms what I find most inspiring in your work—the fact that you stand on the side of those who have been abused and humiliated. As you state it so movingly in the introduction to your book: "I have always looked on disobedience toward the overbearing as the only way to use the miracle of having been born."

That's socialism, Jonathan. Being a socialist, or wanting socialism, doesn't mean just the distribution of wealth. It *should* work, but it doesn't in the so-called socialist countries. And for sure not in the capitalistic regimes. Socialism means much more to me. One of the great victories has been what we call the *spirit of socialism* with its sense of equality. When I was a little girl, the reality of hierarchy was so strong — the teacher above the pupil, the rich above the less rich, the bourgeoisie above the proletariat. In Europe we had it, we still have it, but we have it much less. And this was brought about by socialists and is why, for me, socialism is synonymous with freedom.

Socialism *is* freedom. When I say this, I imagine that if I were a peasant of Chianti and you were a landowner, I'd look at you like this [*skeptical and fearful look*] because of my belief in socialism, in freedom. And this spirit has such deep roots in me that when I go to interview a person of power, the more this person has — would you believe me? — the more I intimidate him. And inevitably, this personal attitude of mine is transferred mentally and technically in the interview. So I undress them. I say: "Come on, come on, maybe you're better than you look, or maybe you're worse."

This is interesting: I've noticed that when a person goes to interview someone, he often sees himself in a position of inferiority. It's a nuance, it's very subtle, it's difficult to explain. And this feeling increases when this someone being interviewed is a person of power. If you're observant, you can see the eyes tremble and something in the face and voice changing. That's never happened to me. *Never.* I'm tense, I'm worried because it's a boxing match. Oh ho! I'm climbing, I'm going into the ring. I'm nervous. My God, who's going to win? But no inferiority complex, no fear of the person. When someone starts acting superior, then I become nasty.

In the preface to your book, you regret that no one had tape recorders during the time of Jesus, in order to "capture his voice, his ideas, his words." Were you being hyperbolic or serious? And if serious, what would you have asked Jesus if you had had the chance to interview him?

I meant it seriously. For sure! Today we think and speak of Jesus as he's been told to us. So now, after 2,000 years, I'd like to know how important he was at the time or find out how much he was built up. Of course, I reject the concept of Jesus as God, Christ/God. I don't even pay attention to that for one second. But as a leader, was he that important? You know, he might very well have been a little Che Guevara.

And a deeply enlightened person.

He might have been, but not the only one. Because many of those people were crucified just as he was. We all make this fuss about him, but it would be like saying: "Jesus Christ has been executed by Franco!" What about the others? For Christ's sake, how many people have been executed in Spain? *La garotta!* What about Paredez Manot, called Txiki—one of the five Basques who was executed in the fall of 1975 in the cemetery of Barcelona, in front of his brother Miguel. He's the one who died singing, "Free, free the country of the Basques," smiling all the time and singing, then waving goodbye to Miguel. And that was Txiki. But there were four others who were executed, and hundreds of others all these years. So I don't know if Christ was that important later on.

One of the first things I would have asked him was: "Where have you been all those years, where have you been? Did you go to India?" Ooh-la-la! That would have been the first question. Then I would have asked if he really behaved chastely or if he had women, if he slept with women, if he went to bed with Mary Magdalene, if he loved her as a sister or as a woman. I would have asked that. And I would have loved to have found the grave of Jesus Christ—that would have been good reportage. And those who had stolen the corpse and reported he had flown to heaven: "Who told you to do that? For *whom* did you do that?"

That might have ended Christianity then and there.

It might have been a good thing.

I imagine that you'd have one question to ask the Virgin Mary.

[*Laughing*] Certainly one.

This is getting a bit sacrilegious.

Well, why be scared of that?

Don't you think it's possible that Jesus was an avatar?

Listen, I don't know how much about Jesus is just the image created by Mark, Luke, Matthew and John. They were so damn intelligent, those four. And I'm afraid . . . listen, Jonathan, do you know how many times I make people more interesting than they are? So what if Mark or Matthew did the same thing with Christ, huh? What about if Jesus Christ was much less than Luke or John? I have no serious evidence, I have no tapes. . . .

You'd be the first person I'd chose to interview the first being we met from outer space.

And I would do it like a *child*. That's the secret. . . . I'll tell you something. During the first moon shot, there was a press conference just before the launch. There was a group of Very Important American Journalists there, and, thank God, there was also my dear friend Walter Cronkite among them. And Cronkite sent me a note—we were in the same room because the press was interviewing the astronauts via TV—asking me if I wanted to ask them a question. "Put a question to them? Thank you." And I wrote down my little question—three words—and sent it to Cronkite.

The other questions went on and on . . . about the fuel and not the fuel, about the gas and the starter and the trajectory . . . I didn't understand anything being said. You know, I wrote a book about the conquest of the moon and I still don't know how and why a rocket goes up. I'm very proud of that. And I didn't understand the questions of the journalists, who were extremely pompous. Everybody was pompous. And then Cronkite said: "I have a question here from Oriana Fallaci." Pause. And he didn't ask the question. (*He was marvelous, he was a real actor.*) Then, dramatically: "The question is: *Are you scared?*"

Well, after discussing it with Aldrin and Collins, Neil Armstrong was elected to take the walk. "Well," he hesitated, "you know, the adrenaline goes up." "Ah, bullshit. Say you're scared!" I yelled out loud to everybody in the press room. "Who cares about the adrenaline? Tell me, tell me, fear, *fear!* Walter, ask them about *fear!*"

And that was the question of the child. If you asked my youngest sister to put a question to the astronauts, she'd say: "Are you afraid of going to the moon?" Of course. That's what she'd want to know.

BRIAN WILSON

by David Felton

November 4, 1976

Right now there's the new album, '15 Big Ones,' the tour [Wilson's first with the Beach Boys in five years] and the TV special. Why all this burst of energy at this time?

I can only consider how *my* energy has bursted. I have refrained from sexual experience. I'm trying out this yoga—I read a book. It showed how if you repress sexual desire, not your kundalini but a similar type of energy is released when you don't have sex. It's been a couple months now I haven't had any sex. That's just a personal answer.

Very personal, I'd say.

Yes. Also because it was spring. To tell you the very truth, it was springtime. It's just like they always say, in spring you start hopping, and we started hopping a little before the first of spring—we got our album and stuff.

This is the first spring in a long time, though.

Yeah, right. Well, we started hopping a few springs ago but we really hadn't been serious about it like we were this time.

Maybe it was the combination of spring and the sexual repression.

Yes, I think that that was probably it.

Do you find it difficult to get into writing?

Yeah. Lately I have found it difficult as heck to finish a song. It's a funny thing. Probably not much of a song left in me, you know, if any, because I've written so many, some 250 songs or 300 or whatever it is. And it just doesn't seem as vast [*yawn*], the creativity doesn't seem as vast. That's why we did a lot of oldies but goodies this time on our album. That got us going, as a matter of fact.

I haven't yet heard this album. Are you going into some new areas?

Not that I can think of. The only areas would be into Transcendental Meditation, using that as a base. We believe in it, so [*yawn*] we feel it's our responsibility, partially, to carry the Maharishi message into the world. Which I think is a great message. I think the meditation is a great thing.

You've just recently become more involved in that yourself, haven't you?

Yeah. I meditate and I also *think* about meditation. Which is funny. I think about Maharishi, about just the *idea* of meditating. It gives me something.

Do you think that might help you write more?

Oh, yeah, I think that's gonna be the answer. As it progresses, I think that I'm going to gather more peace of mind, I'll be able to gather my thoughts a little easier. I won't be as jangled in the nerves. I think it's going to aid in my creativity.

This difficulty in writing songs—would you describe it as a writing block?

Well, I have a writing block right now. Even today I started to sit down to write a song, and there was a block there. God knows what that is. Unless it's *supposed* to be there. I mean, it's not something you just kick away and say, "Come on, let's go, let's get a song writ." If the block is there, it's there.

Another thing, too, is that I used to write on pills. I used to take uppers and write, and I used to like that effect. In fact, I'd like to take uppers now and write because they give me, you know, a certain lift and a certain outlook. And it's not an unnatural thing. I mean the pill might be unnatural and the energy, but the song itself doesn't turn out unnatural on the uppers. The creativity flows through.

Well, why don't you do that?

I'm thinking of asking the doctor if I can go back to those, yeah.

But you believe writers really do run out of material.

I believe that writers run out of material, I really do. I believe very strongly in the fact that when the natural time is up, writers actually do run out of material [*yawn*]. To me it's black and white. When there's a song there's a song, when there's not there's not. Of *course* you run out, maybe not indefinitely, but everybody runs out of some material that writes for a while. And it's a very frightening experience. It's an awesome thing to think, "Oh my God, the only thing that's ever supplied me with any success or made us money, I'm running out of." So right there there's an insecurity that sets in. This is why I'm going through these different experiments, sexually and all, to see what can happen, to see if there's anything waiting in there that I haven't found.

Is there much else you could do if you didn't write songs?

No, not really. I'm not cut out to do very much at all.

* * *

Why don't we talk a bit about "Good Vibrations"?

That would be a good place to begin. "Good Vibrations" took six months to make. We recorded the very first part of it at Gold Star Recording Studio, then we took it to a place called Western, then we went to Sunset Sound, then we went to Columbia.

So it took quite a while. There's a story behind this record that I tell everybody. My mother used to tell me about vibrations. I didn't really understand too much of what that meant when I was just a boy. It scared me, the word "vibrations." To think that invisible feelings, invisible vibrations existed, scared me to death. But she told about dogs that would bark at people and then not bark at others, that a dog would pick up vibrations from these people that you can't see, but you can feel. And the same existed with people.

And so it came to pass that we talked about good vibrations. We went ahead and experimented with the song and the idea, and we decided that on the one hand you could say, "I love the colorful clothes she wears and the way the sunlight plays upon her hair. I hear the sound of a gentle word on the wind that lifts her perfume through the air." Those are sensual things. And then you go, "I'm pickin' up good vibrations," which is a contrast against all the sensual — there's what you call the extrasensory perception which we have. And this is what we're really talking about.

But you also set out to do something new musically. Why this particular song?

Because we wanted to explain that concept, plus we wanted to do something that was R&B but had a taste of modern, avant-garde R&B to it. "Good Vibrations" was advanced rhythm & blues music.

You took a risk.

Oh yeah, we took a great risk. As a matter of fact, I didn't think it was going to make it because of its complexity, but apparently people accepted it very well. They felt that it had a naturalness to it, it flowed. It was a little pocket symphony.

How come you used four different studios?

Because we wanted to experiment with combining studio sounds. Every studio has its own marked sound. Using the four different studios had a lot to do with the way the final record sounded.

Did everybody support what you were trying to do?

No, not everybody. There was a lot of "oh, you can't do this, that's too modern" or "that's going to be too long a record." I said no, it's not going to be too long a record, it's going to be just right.

Who resisted you? Your manager? The record company?

No, people in the group, but I can't tell ya who. We just had resisting ideas. They didn't quite understand what this jumping from studio to studio was all about. And they couldn't conceive of the record as I did. I saw the record as a totality piece.

Do you remember the time you realized you finally had it?

I remember the time that we had it. It was at Columbia. I remember I had it right in the sack. I could just feel it when I dubbed it down, made the final mix from the 16-track down to mono. It was a feeling of power, it was a rush. A feeling of exaltation. Artistic beauty. It was everything.

Do you remember saying anything?

I remember saying, "Oh, my God. Sit back and listen to *this!*"

At that time did you feel it was your most important song? Did you think in terms like that—reaching a new plateau in music?

Yes, I felt that it was a plateau. First of all, it felt very arty and it sounded arty. Second of all, it was the first utilization of a cello in rock & roll music to that extent—using it as an up-front instrument, as a rock instrument.

Not to mention the theremin.

It was also the first use of a theremin in rock & roll.

By the time you did "Good Vibrations" you had matured your artistic concept far beyond the sort of thing you were doing, say, in "Surfin'." Was there any particular time period when you realized that you now were totally into creating music on your own terms?

Yes. *Pet Sounds* would be that period when I figured that I was into my own...via the Phil Spector approach. Now, the Phil Spector approach is utilizing many instruments to combine for a single form or a single sound. Like combining clarinets, trombones and saxophones to give you a certain sound, rather than hearing that arrangement as "oh, those are piccolos, oh, those are trombones."

How much was Spector an influence on you, artistically and competitively?

Well, I didn't feel I was competing as much as I was emulating, emulating the greatness of his style in my music. We have a high degree of art in our group. We've come to regard Phil Spector as the greatest, the most avant-garde producer in the business.

Yet he's not really a composer of songs.

Well, I'm a firm believer that he wrote those songs and gave the others credit. In order to produce them the way he did, he had to write them.

Mike Love mentioned the time you composed "The Warmth of the Sun" within hours of the John F. Kennedy assassination and how it illustrated that even during a very negative time you could come up with a very positive feeling.

Yeah, it's a strange thing, but I think we were always spiritually minded and we wrote music to give strength to people. I always feel holy when it comes to recording. Even during "Surfer Girl," even then I felt a bit spiritual.

What's the nature of your spiritual outlook today? Does it present you with a kind of attitude toward the world?

No, not really. I'm not as aware of the world as I could be.

Is that necessarily a bad thing?

Yeah, because I think if I became more aware, I could structure my lyrics to be a little more in tune with people.

Are you working on that process right now?

Yes, I'm working on that right now, I'm working with people who I know know where it's at. Like Van Dyke Parks—he's a guy who's a link to where it's at for me. He keeps me very current on what's happening.

At one time you and he were working on a revolutionary album called 'Smile,' which you never released.

Yeah, we didn't finish it because we had a lot of problems, inner group problems. We had time commitments we couldn't keep. So we stopped. Plus, for instance, we did a thing called the "fire track." We cut a song called "Fire" and we used fire helmets on the musicians and we put a bucket with fire burning in it in the studio so we could smell smoke while we cut. And about a day later a building down the street burned down. We thought maybe it was witchcraft or something, we didn't know *what* we were into. So we decided not to finish it.

Plus I got into drugs and I began doing things that were over my head. It was too fancy for the public. I got too fancy and arty and was doing things that were just not Beach Boys at all. They were made for me.

Ever consider doing an album just on your own?

No, I haven't considered that because I didn't think it would be commercial if I did.

Well, so what?

Well, maybe I could do that then. I think I might.

What's this program with Dr. Landy [Wilson's therapist] and his team designed to do?

Well, it's basically designed to correct me from taking drugs.

You've had a problem with that?

Yeah, I had a problem taking drugs. Up until four months ago I was taking a lot of cocaine. And these doctors came in and showed me a way to stop doing it, which is having bodyguards with you all the time so you can't get to it.

What do you think of that approach?

That approach works because there's someone right there all the time — it keeps you on the spot. They catch you when you're ready to do something you shouldn't do. It works until you have finally reached the stage where you don't need it anymore.

Why did you consent to this program?

Because my wife called the doctors and legally she had the right to call them.

In addition to guarding you all the time, what else do Dr. Landy's people do for you?

They teach me socialization, how to socialize. They're just teaching me different social graces, like manners.

Didn't you at one time know those?

I did, but I lost them. Drugs took 'em away.

How could that be?

It just was. Drugs took 'em all away. I got real paranoid, I couldn't do anything.

Were you unhappy then?

I was unhappy as all heck. I knew I was screwing myself up, and I couldn't do anything about it. I was a useless little vegetable. I made everybody very angry at me because I wasn't able to work, to get off my butt. Coke every day. Goin' over to parties. Just havin' bags of snow around, just snortin' it down like crazy.

But aren't drugs just a symptom? There must be something else. Carl said that at some point you looked at the world and it was so messed up that you just couldn't take it.

I couldn't.

But the world is messed up. How do you deal with it?

The way I deal with it is I go jogging in the morning. I goddamn get out of bed and I jog, and I make sure I stay in shape. That's how I do it. And so far the only way I've been keeping from drugs is with those bodyguards, and the only way I've been going jogging is those bodyguards have been taking me jogging.

So in one sense you're not yet fully committed to the idea.

It's just that once you've had a taste of drugs, you like 'em and you want 'em. Do you take drugs yourself?

Yeah, I experiment.

Do ya? Do ya snort?

Sure.

That's what I thought. Do you have any with ya?

No.

That's the problem. Do you have any uppers?

I have nothin' on me.

Nothing? Not a thing, no uppers?

I wouldn't lie to you. I wish I had 'em, but I don't.

Do you have any at home? Do you know where you can get some?

See, now I guess you gotta get to the point in the program where you're not going to ask me questions like that.

That's right. You just saw my weakness coming out. Which I don't understand. I just do it anyway. I used to drink my head off too, that's another thing. They've been keeping me from drinkin', taking pills and taking coke. And I'm jogging every morning.

Had your wife not gone to see Dr. Landy and got him to work on you...

I'd have been a goner, I'd have been in the hospital by now.

GEORGE LUCAS

by Paul Scanlon

August 25, 1977

So how does it feel? Did you really expect that 'Star Wars' was going to take off like this?

No way. I expected *American Graffiti* to be a semi-successful film and make maybe $10 million—which would be classified in Hollywood as a success—and then I went through the roof when it became this big, huge blockbuster. And they said, well, gee, how are you going to top that? And I said, yeah, it was a one-shot and I was really lucky. I never really expected that to happen again. After *Graffiti*, in fact, I was really just dead broke. I was so far in debt to everyone that I made even less money on *Graffiti* than I had on [his first film] *THX 1138*. Between those two movies it was like four and a half to five years of my life, and after taxes and everything I was living on $9,000 a year. It was really fortunate that my wife was working as an editor's assistant. That was the only thing that got us through. Then I finally got a deal for very little money to develop *Star Wars*.

How many studios had turned it down?

Two.

And then Fox took it?

Fox took it, and it was close because there wasn't any other place I wanted to take it. I don't know what I would have done, maybe take a job. But the last desperate thing is to "take a job." I really wanted to hold on to my own integrity. Right after *Graffiti* I was getting this fan mail from kids that said the film changed their life, and something inside me said, do a children's film. And everybody said, "What are you talking about? You're crazy."

I had done *Graffiti* as a challenge. All I had ever done to that point was crazy, avant-garde, abstract movies. Francis [Ford Coppola, *American Graffiti*'s producer] really challenged me on that. "Do something warm," he said, "everyone thinks you're a cold fish; all you do is science fiction." So I did *Graffiti* and then I thought I had more of a chance of getting *Star Wars* off the ground. I had gone around to all the studios with *Apocalypse Now* for the tenth time and then they said no, no, no. So I took this other project, this children's film. I thought: We all know what a terrible mess we have made of the world, we all know how wrong we were in Vietnam. We also know, as every movie made in the last ten years points out, how terrible we are, how we have ruined the world and what schmucks we are and how rotten everything is. And I said, what we really need is something more positive. Because *Graffiti* pointed out that kids had forgot what being a teenager was, which is being dumb and chasing girls, doing the things—you know, at least I did when I was a kid.

Before I became a film major, I was very heavily into social science, I had done a lot of sociology, anthropology, and I was playing in what I call social psychology, which is sort of an offshoot of anthropology/sociology—looking at a culture as a living organism, why it does what it does. Anyway, I became very aware of the fact that the kids were really lost, the sort of heritage we built up since the war had been wiped out in the Sixties and it wasn't groovy to act that way anymore, now you just sort of sat there and got stoned. I wanted to preserve what a certain generation of Americans thought being a teenager was really about—in a strong sense from about

1945 to 1962, that generation. There was a certain car culture, a certain mating ritual going on, and it was something that I'd lived through and really loved.

So when I got done with *Graffiti,* I said, "Look, you know something else has happened, and I began to stretch it down to younger people, ten- to twelve-year-olds, who have lost something even *more* significant than the teenager. I saw that kids today don't have any fantasy life the way we had—they don't have westerns, they don't have pirate movies, they don't have that stupid serial fantasy life that we used to believe in. It wasn't that we really believed in it....

But we loved it.

Look, what would happen if there had never been John Wayne movies and Errol Flynn movies and all that stuff that we got to see all the time. I mean, you could go into a theater, not just watch it on television on Saturday morning, actually go into a theater, sit down and watch an incredible adventure. Not a stupid adventure, not a dumb adventure for children and stuff but a real Errol Flynn, John Wayne—*gosh*—kind of an adventure.

Or 'The Crimson Pirate' with Burt Lancaster or 'The Magnificent Seven.'

Yeah, but there aren't any. There's nothing but cop movies, and a few films like *Planet of the Apes,* Ray Harryhausen films, but there isn't anything that you can really dig your teeth into. I realized a more destructive element in the culture would be a whole generation of kids growing up without that thing, because I had also done a study on, I don't know what you call it, I call it the fairy tale or the myth. It is a children's story in history and you go back to the *Odyssey* or the stories that are told for the kid in all of us. I can see the little kids sitting there and just being enthralled with Ulysses. Plus the myths which existed in high adventure, and an exotic far-off land which was always that place over the hill, Camelot, Robin Hood,

Treasure Island. That sort of stuff that is always big adventure out there somewhere. It came all the way down through the western.

The western?

I saw the western die. We hardly knew what happened, one day we turned around and there weren't any westerns anymore. John Ford grew up with the West, the very toe end of the West, but he was out there where there were cowboys and shootings in the streets, and that was his *American Graffiti,* I realized; that's why he was so good at it. A lot of those guys were good at it. They grew up in the Tens and Twenties when the West was for all practical purposes really dying off. But, there was still some rough-and-tumble craziness going on. And the people now, the young directors like me, can't do it because there isn't anything like that anymore.

So you do a 'Star Wars'?

I was a real fan of *Flash Gordon* and that kind of stuff, a very strong advocate of the exploration of outer space and I said, "This is a natural." One, it will give kids a fantasy life and two, maybe it will make someone a young Einstein and people will say, "Why?" What we really need to do is to colonize the next galaxy, get away from the hard facts of *2001* and get on the romantic side of it. Nobody is going to colonize Mars because of the technology, they are going to go because they think maybe they will be able—it is the romantic aspect of it.

You firmly establish that at the beginning of 'Star Wars' with the words: "A long, long time ago in a galaxy far, far away..."

Well, I had a real problem because I was afraid that science-fiction buffs and everybody would say things like, "You know there's no sound in outer space." I just wanted to forget science. I didn't want to make a *2001.* I wanted to make a space fantasy that was more in the genre of Edgar Rice Burroughs; that whole other end of space fantasy that was there before science took it over in the Fifties. Once the atomic bomb came, everybody got into monsters and science and what would happen with *this* and what would happen with *that*. I think speculative fiction is very valid but they forgot the fairy tales and the dragons and Tolkien and all the *real* heroes.

So that was the mainspring of your decision to make 'Star Wars.'

Right. I had done sociological research on what makes hit films. It is part of the sociological bent in me; I can't help it.

How do you explain a Wookie to a board of directors?

You can't, and how do you explain a Wookie to an audience, and how do you get the tone of the film right, so it's not a silly child's film, so it's not playing down to people, but it is still an entertaining movie and doesn't have a lot of violence and sex and hip new stuff? So it still has a vision to it—a sort of wholesome, honest vision about the way you want the world to be.

What was your actual salary for directing?

I think in the end my actual salary was $100,000, which again was still like half of what everybody else was making.

Do you have percentage points in the film?

Everybody has points, but the key is to make them pay off. I figured I was never going to see any money on my points, so what the heck. I also had a chance to give away a lot of my points, which I had done with *Graffiti*. Part of the success is the fault of the actors, composer and crew and they should share in the rewards as well, so I got my points carved down much less than what my contemporaries have.

But I never expected *Star Wars* to . . . I expected to break even on it, I still can't understand it.

Why?

I struggled through this movie. I had a terrible time; it was very unpleasant. *American Graffiti* was unpleasant because of the fact that there was no money, no time and I was compromising myself to death. But I could rationalize it because of the fact that, well, it is just a $700,000 picture—it's Roger Corman—and what do you expect? But this was a big expensive movie and the money was getting wasted and things weren't coming out right. I was running the corporation. I wasn't making movies like I'm used to doing. *American Graffiti* had like forty people on the payroll—that counts everybody but the cast. *THX* had about the same. You can control a situation like that. On *Star Wars* we had over 950 people working for us and I would tell a department head and he would tell another assistant department head, he'd tell some guy, and by the time it got down the line it was not there. I spent all my time yelling and screaming at people, and I have never had to do that before.

I've done this thing now. I've directed my large corporation and I made the movie that I wanted to make. It is not as good by a long shot as it should have been. I take half the responsibility myself and the other half is some of the unfortunate decisions I made in hiring people, but I could have written a better script, I could have done a lot of things; I could have directed it better.

When I saw you back in California last summer you were upset. You said the robots didn't look right. R2 looked like a vacuum cleaner; you could see fifty-seven separate flaws in C3PO; you didn't like the lighting—everything seemed like it wasn't coming together. Was it coming together?

Well, for one thing, by the time we got back to California I wasn't happy with the lighting on the picture. I'm a cameraman, and I like a slightly more extreme, eccentric style than I got in the movie.

It was all right, it was a very difficult movie, there were big sets to light, it was a very big problem. The robots never worked. We faked the whole thing and a lot of it was done editorially.

How?

Every time the remote-control R2 worked it turned and ran into a wall, and when Kenny Baker, the midget, was in it, the thing was so heavy he could barely move it, and he would sort of take a step and a half and be totally exhausted. I could never get him to walk across the room, so we would cut to him there and cut to a close-up, and cut back so that he would be over here. It is all really movie magic more than it was anything else.

That's why it's amazing because when I saw the film I was surprised. I couldn't see any seams. So I went again and maybe saw a couple of seams, but that was it.

I can see nothing but seams. A film is sort of binary—it either works or it doesn't work. It has nothing to do with how good a job you do. If you bring it up to an adequate level where the audience goes with the movie, then it works, that is all. It is a fusion thing and then everything else, all of the mistakes don't count anymore.

Well, the 'Star Wars' audience has no trouble suspending disbelief.

Right. If a film does *not* work, then you can do an impeccable job with making the movie. People still see the mistakes, and they get bored and it just doesn't work. And so what can you say? *THX* was about 70 percent of what I wanted it to be. I don't think you ever get to the point where it is 100 percent. *Graffiti* was about 50 percent of what I wanted it to be but I realized that the other 50 percent would have been there, if I just had a little more time and a little more money. *Star Wars* is about 25 percent of what I wanted it to be. It's really still a good movie, but it fell short of what I wanted.

The film's success should guarantee some success in the merchandising program you've launched.

One of my motivating factors for doing the film, along with all the other ones, was that I love toys and games. And so I figured, gee, I could start a kind of a store that sold comic art, and sold 78 records, or old rock & roll records that I like, and antique toys and a lot of things that I am really into; stuff that you can't buy in regular stores. I also like to create games and things, so that was part of the movie, to be able to generate toys and things. Also, I figured the merchandising along with the sequels would give me enough income over a period of time so that I could retire from professional filmmaking and go into making my own kind of movies, my own sort of abstract, weird, experimental stuff.

So now you want to sell toys and games, and make esoteric films?

Yes. The film is a success and I think the sequels will be a success. I want to be able to have a store where I can sell all the great things that I want. I'm also a diabetic and can't eat sugar and I want to have a little store that sells good hamburgers and sugarless ice cream because all the people who can't eat sugar deserve it. You need the time just to be able to retire and do those things, and you need to have an income.

'Star Wars' is sci-fi that taps into an epic and heroic tradition.

It has always been the same thing and it is the most significant kind of fiction as far as I am concerned. It's too bad that it has gotten that sleazy comic-book reputation, which I think we outgrew a long time ago. I think science fiction still has a tendency to react against that image and try to make itself so pious and serious, which is what I tried to knock out in making *Star Wars*. Buck Rogers is just as valid as Arthur C. Clarke in his own way; I mean, they are both sides of the same thing. Kubrick did the strongest thing in film in terms of the rational side of things, and I've tried to do the most in the irrational side of things because I think we need it. Again we are going to go with Stanley's ships but hopefully we are going to be carrying my laser sword and have the Wookie at our side.

So now you have made your bid.

So I made my bid to try to make everything a little more romantic. Jesus, I'm hoping that if the film accomplishes anything, it takes some ten-year-old kid and turns him on *so much* to outer space and the possibilities of romance and adventure. Not so much an influence that would create more Wernher von Brauns or Einsteins, but just infusing them into serious exploration of outer space and convincing them that it's important. Not for any rational reason, but a totally irrational and romantic reason.

I would feel very good if someday they colonize Mars when I am ninety-three years old or whatever, and the leader of the first colony says: "I really did it because I was hoping there would be a Wookie up here."

JOHNNY CARSON
by Timothy White

March 22, 1979

I think that one of the things that is the most innovative about 'The Tonight Show' is the way that you work with the camera. The camera and, as a result, the audience become accomplices or conspirators with you, to where we feel a sense of intimacy.

Well, television is an intimate medium. I'm not conscious when I use the camera. I know it's there. I use it like another person and do a reaction at it—lift an eyebrow or shrug or whatever. I'm conscious of it, but I'm not conscious of it.

There is a real sense of... naturalness in the way you work with the camera that makes the air of intimacy so convincing.

The Tonight Show is one of the few places on television where one can see stars, prominent people, and you'll get a glimpse behind their public personas.

Sometimes you cannot penetrate them. You know they will do what *they* want to do. You try to break through and get them maybe a little off guard and have some fun, because otherwise it becomes [*stiffly*], "Tell us about your latest movie," and all of those obligatory questions you have to ask occasionally.

It's easy to be socially relevant. I could go in at five tonight and say, "Give me four guests, give me the heads of the prisons of California and give me a politician and give me some psychiatrists and we'll just discuss what happened in Guyana." And you can sit there and discuss people in cults and get very heavy, and everybody will say, "Oh, that's very socially relevant."

That's a talk show, but that's not what I do. I'm an entertainer, and I *always* look at myself as an entertainer. So it has bothered me for a while when we would get a little flak from the critics saying we're not doing anything "deep." *That's not the idea.*

Yet, there is a topicality to your show. You'll come up with witty jokes — not gags — about Watergate, Camp David, drugs, changing sexual mores...

I think some of the material we've done on political things is some of the best material on the air. And it does get a strong reaction — especially in the political arena. We sense the mood of the country very quickly.

For example, I remember when Agnew was first selected as vice president, it was easy to do jokes about him; nobody knew who he was, and he was good fodder for material. Then, when Agnew became the voice of so-called Middle America, all of a sudden the jokes were not particularly funny. When he fell into disfavor, then again you found out that the people would buy the caustic material. Same thing with Nixon.

Has there ever been a joke you felt uncomfortable doing, either at the time or in retrospect?

NBC used to come to me years ago. They wanted to see the monologue before the show, and I said, "No, I can't do that." I can't have somebody sitting up in an office and making capricious judgments on what he thinks is funny or not funny. I said, "You're going to have to trust my judgment," and they have. And nobody sees the monologue outside of the writers and myself; they give me the stuff, and I add to it or edit it, and put it together. *Nobody* sees it until it's done. And I don't think in seventeen years there have been more than one or two instances where something might have been cut.

You've always had a kind of iconoclastic flair in your humor, even going back to when you were working on the radio in Omaha. In Kenneth Tynan's [1978] piece in the 'New Yorker,' he wrote about these formatted, prerecorded interviews you would receive at the station and then mischievously distort.

I know what you're talking about, and I loved that. In the old radio days, the record companies would send out these prepared interviews and they would send you a script so you could interview the recording artist. You'd play the Patti Page tape and say, "Gee, it's nice to have you here today, Patti," and she'd say, "Thank you for inviting me tonight; it's nice to be here." Then the next question would be, "When did you first start singing?" And the taped reply would be, "Well, I think I was about ten years old, and I was in a church play or something."

So I just wrote my own questions, and I'd say, "I understand that you hit the juice pretty good and you've been known to really get drunk pretty often. When did that start?" Then they'd play the cut, and she'd say, "Well, I think I was about ten years old, and I was in a church play…" and it was wonderful. Just these insane, wild, provocative questions, and then the engineer would play this innocent track with the prerecorded reply. They quit sending them to us very soon. I've always liked irreverence.

You've talked to me in the past about "pure television." What is pure television?

To me, it's still the *performance* on TV that is most important. The personality is more important than all of the dance numbers and the big production things. I always thought those things have been kind of lost on television, because they ignore the automatic *focus* that TV provides.

But I got the feeling, even if you take all that glitter away and pare it down to a spare sitcom or variety format, it's still not the kind of pure television that you were talking about.

Well, pure television to me is also immediacy. That's why I don't like to do *The Tonight Show* a week or two in advance, like a lot of shows do. I like to be able to go out tonight and talk about what's happening *today*. So the immediacy of doing this kind of show, I think, has a certain value in it. People *know* it's happening right now.

Sure, we're delayed on tape, but we don't edit the show; we don't shoot two hours and edit it down. When *Saturday Night Live* says, "Live, from New York!" it's live in the East but it's not live out here. Doing it the same day on tape is exactly the same thing as doing it live.

In both programs there's also the element of risk.

And I think that's a part of pure television. We don't know on any given night how it's going to go. You get an immediate feedback from the audience on what you've done, and if it all falls together, it's a great feeling. If you've had troubles, you say, "Okay, there's tomorrow night." Every night cannot be a winner.

You don't stop the tape even when people are being off-color or whatever. You might bleep it out, but people can see that things were getting out of hand.

Yeah, I think there's that aura of "What's going to happen? How are they going to get out of this? This is not going well." That, to me, is what television started out to be. Now, mainly, it's a device for screening movies or situation comedies with canned laughter. And *The Tonight Show,* or shows like it, I think—if they all went off the air, it would be too bad for television.

Critics have said that you have a schoolboy quality, a puckishness that isn't seen too often on TV.

[*Intrigued*] I suppose that's only because of the face. I've never had a particularly old-looking face. Even when I was thirty or thirty-five, I looked like I was twenty-five. That may be changing rapidly now. But if I looked different, you probably wouldn't have that attitude. Or maybe it's because I was born in the Midwest; you know, Mel Brooks calls me "SuperGentile," "SuperWASP," and maybe it's that particular look, but that's just what I am.

You have become — and this is just a fact — so much a part of this culture. If you weren't there, I suspect there would be a real gap.

[*Long pause*] That's flattering. I think one of the things is that we're about the only show that does day-to-day humor. There's no other show that does it. *Saturday Night Live* is on three times a month; they do sketches. The monologue, for example, to me is a very integral part of the show. Being out there every night, it's the only show that I know of on television where anybody is commenting on what's going on in the country every single day.

But why do you think people feel so comfortable with you?

I can't analyze that. I really can't. I just do what I do. People ask me, "How do you analyze that you've stayed on seventeen years and the competition has dropped off?" See, either way you answer that, you end up sounding like a schmuck.

If you say, "Well, obviously I do a much better job than they do," or say, "I'm more talented," then people say, "You egotistical bastard!"

If, on the other hand, you play Harry Humble and say, "Gee, I don't know," then that sounds idiotic, too. So no matter what you say, people say, "Aw, come on now."

I don't try to shoot for an average audience. I do the things I like to do, and I think I've learned what people will accept from me. That's just an intuitive thing.

There's an axiom that most comedians—a variation on the sad clown thing—are very intense and self-absorbed.

There's a certain amount of truth in that. A lot of comedians are introspective, not the "sad clown" syndrome exactly; it's more like the myth "to be funny, you must have suffered." You must have been raised on the Lower East Side, and you must have fought your way out of this deprivation to be funny. That's not really true. Do you have to starve, be deprived, to be a great writer?

But I think there's a certain thing in creative people—and I'm not a psychiatrist—but I have found that people who are in the creative end of entertainment are not normal by most standards, whatever "normal" means. That is, as Margaret Sullavan said, "It's not normal to walk out and bare your soul to a bunch of strangers, that's not a normal thing for someone to do." Most people find that very awkward, and entertainers do it. I find that most comedians are a little cynical, as well they should be.

And I *am* cynical about certain things. And people sometimes mistake the cynicism for being abrupt or cold. I think it's just the way you perceive things around you. You've seen the silliness, the absurdity, the craziness that goes on in the world and you jump on that and expand it. You look at things in a different light. That's what makes comedy.

Comedians are highly competitive, many of them. I think it was Lenny Bruce who said, "Comedians hate to see other comedians get laughs." There are certain guys who really suffer when they see other comedians really scoring. I don't. But I know a lot of guys where the competition among them is just ferocious. They talk about friendship and so forth, but a lot of them would kill each other. There's something bizarre about guys who do comedy.

I find an intensity there.

[*Nodding*] And a certain amount of hostility.

In a book called 'The Human Comedy' by William Saroyan, he writes about how people make transitions in their lives; you just presume everything is there and will take care of itself, and then there's that transitional period in everyone's life when they realize if they are going to be happy for the rest of their lives, if they're going to enjoy life and fight off the boredom that's probably the big enemy of life, they are going to have to make a conscious effort to make themselves happy. I've wondered if there was a certain point in your life, a certain moment of self-esteem and self-worth upon which you built every other experience.

I know what Saroyan's saying. There comes a time or a moment, I don't know whether you can say it precisely, when you know in which direction you're going to go. Even when you're young. But you don't know *why* exactly. I know it happened to me when I was quite young.

You go through those phases — "I'll be a doctor or I'll be..." — the standard things. But I think it's when you find out, at least for me, that you can get in front of an audience and be in control. I think that probably happened in grade school, fifth or sixth grade, where I could get attention by being different, by getting up in front of an audience or even a group of kids and calling the attention to myself by what I did or said or how I acted. And I said, "Hey, I like that feeling."

When I was a kid, I was shy. And I think I did that because it was a device to get attention. And to get that reaction is a strange feeling, it is a high that I don't think you can get from drugs. I don't think you could get it from anything else. The mind starts to do things that you didn't even realize it could do. It's hard to explain.

And you walk off and you're just, everything is such a high, and it's a great feeling, and that's why many performers have big highs and very big lows. Most of them that I know. I know I do.

People don't understand that. They put you down as being stand-offish or cool or so forth. It's *not* that.

I suppose it's the manipulation, I suppose it's the sense of power, the center of attention and the me-ism. And performers have to have that. You see, that's one of the things that goes against the grain of being brought up; you should be modest, you should be humble, you shouldn't draw attention to yourself. Well, to be an entertainer, you *must.*

You gotta be a little gutsy, a little egotistical, so you have to pull back sometimes when people say, "Well, he's stuck-up." "Stuck-up" is only another word for self-conscious. You aren't stuck-up. You are aloof, because you aren't very comfortable so you put up this barrier.

Do you recall the specific moment—a spelling bee or a class recitation or a play or something—when you crossed over that barrier?

I think it was in a play. A Christmas play, as a matter of fact—Dickens' *A Christmas Carol.* My classmate Dorothy Ward played the Ghost of Christmas Present. I played the little boy who went to fetch the turkey, and this man, Scrooge, gave me a shilling to do it. And I realized that I was the center of attention. I realized that people were saying, "Hey, look, he's in a play." That makes you different right off, you see. You're stepping out of *here,* and you're stepping into a make-believe world, and all of a sudden people are looking at you. You like that, but at the same time, you find that you have an ambivalent feeling.

So you had a shyness and an awkwardness that you had to conquer?

[*Sheepish*] Yeah, oh yeah. I just felt uncomfortable. I still feel uncomfortable in large groups of people. Not audiences, mind you. With audiences, I'm fine. I can go out in front of 20,000 people because I'm in charge. See, most entertainers feel that way. When you walk into a large group of people, you're not in charge, and all of a sudden I sometimes feel uncomfortable.

155

It's hard to find a focus.

That's right. You see, when you're on the stage all the focus comes here. They're watching you and you're in control. Now you walk into a reception or a cocktail party full of two hundred people, I find that unsettling. I know a lot of people who are entertainers, they, you know, get up against the wall at these times or sit in a corner. If they're up in front, they're fine. So there are two ambivalent things at work there. David Susskind's favorite word, "dichotomy"; which he loves to use — there is that in performers.

I think people who are creative, in the arts, also seem to have larger appetites for life than most people, to excess usually. Whether it be drinking, whether it be sex, whether it be anything, the appetites seem to be larger. I don't know why, but they seem to be that way. And with writers too — most of them don't seem to be terribly happy people, whatever that means. Because I guess you are always in a way trying to prove yourself, and as an entertainer, you're always in front of an audience. People say you're only as good as your last performance.

JONI MITCHELL

by Cameron Crowe

July 26, 1979

Looking back, how well did you prepare for your own success?

I never thought that far ahead. I never expected to have this degree of success.

Never? Not even practicing in front of your mirror?

No. It was a hobby that mushroomed. I was grateful to make one record. All I knew was, whatever it was that I felt was the weak link in the previous project gave me my inspiration for the next one. I wrote poetry and I painted all my life. I always wanted to play music and dabbled with it, but I never thought of putting them all together. It never occurred to me. It wasn't until Dylan began to write poetic songs that it occurred to me you could actually sing those poems.

Is that when you started to sing?

I guess I really started singing when I had polio. Neil [Young] and I both got polio in the same Canadian epidemic. I was nine, and they put me in a polio ward over Christmas. They said I might not walk again, and that I would not be able to go home for Christmas. I wouldn't go for it. So I started to sing Christmas carols and

I used to sing them real loud. When the nurse came into the room I would sing *louder*. The boy in the bed next to me, you know, used to complain. And I discovered I was a ham. That was the first time I started to sing for people.

Do you remember the first record you bought?

The first record I bought was a piece of classical music. I saw a movie called *The Story of Three Loves,* and the theme was [*she hums the entire melody*] by Rachmaninoff, I think. Every time it used to come onto the radio it would drive me *crazy*. It was a 78. I mean, I had *Alice in Wonderland* and *Tubby the Tuba,* but the first one that I loved and had to buy? "The Story of Three Loves."

How about pop music?

You see, pop music was something else in that time. We're talking about the Fifties now. When I was thirteen, *The Hit Parade* was one hour a day — four o'clock to five o'clock. On the weekends they'd do the Top Twenty. But the rest of the radio was Mantovani, country & western, a lot of radio journalism. Mostly country & western, which I wasn't crazy about. To me it was simplistic. Even as a child I liked more complex melody.

In my teens I loved to dance. That was my thing. I instigated a Wednesday night dance 'cause I could hardly make it to the weekends. For dancing, I loved Chuck Berry, Ray Charles. "What I'd Say." I like Elvis Presley. I liked the Everly Brothers. But then this thing happened. Rock & roll went through a really *dumb* vanilla period. And during that period, folk music came in to fill the hole. At that point, I had friends who'd have parties and sit around and sing Kingston Trio songs. That's when I started to sing again. That's why I bought an instrument. To sing at those parties. It was no more ambitious than that. I was planning all the time to go to art school.

What kind of student were you?

I was a bad student. I finally flunked out in the twelfth grade. I went back a year later and picked up the subjects that I lost. I do have my high-school diploma—I figured I needed that much, just in case. College was not too interesting to me. The way I saw the educational system from an early age was that it taught you what to think, not how to think. There was no liberty, really, for freethinking. You were being trained to fit into a society where freethinking was a nuisance. I liked some of my teachers very much, but I had no interest in their subjects. So I would appease them—I think they perceived that I was not a dummy, although my report card didn't look like it. I would line the math room with ink drawings and portraits of the mathematicians. I did a tree of life for my biology teacher. I was always staying late at the school, down on my knees painting something.

How do you think the other students viewed you?

I'm not sure I have a clear picture of myself. My identity, since it wasn't through the grade system, was that I was a good dancer and an artist. And also, I was very well dressed. I made a lot of my own clothes. I worked in ladies' wear and I modeled. I had access to sample clothes that were too fashionable for our community, and I could buy them cheaply. I would go hang out on the streets dressed to the T, even in hat and gloves. I hung out downtown with the Ukrainians and the Indians; they were more emotionally honest and they were better dancers.

When I went back to my own neighborhood, I found that I had a provocative image. They thought I was loose because I always like rowdies. I thought the way the kids danced at my school was kind of, you know, *funny*. I remember a recurring statement on my report card—"Joan does not relate well." I know that I was aloof. Perhaps some people thought I was a snob.

There came a split when I rejected sororities and that whole thing. I didn't go for that. But here also came a stage when my friends who were juvenile delinquents suddenly became criminals. They could go into very dull jobs or they could go into crime. Crime is very romantic in your youth. I suddenly thought, "Here's where the romance ends. I don't see myself in jail..."

So you went to art school, and at the end of your first year decided to go to Toronto to become a folksinger.

I was only a folksinger for about two years, and that was several years before I actually made a record. By that time, it wasn't really folk music anymore. It was some new American phenomenon. Later, they called it singer/songwriters. Or art songs, which I liked best. Some people got nervous about that word. Art. They think it's a pretentious word from the giddyap. To me, words are only symbols, and the word "art" has never lost its vitality. It still has meaning to me. Love lost its meaning to me. God lost its meaning to me. But art never lost its meaning. I always knew what I meant by art. Now I've got all three of them back [*laughs*].

You and Neil Young have always been close. How did you first meet?

I was married to Chuck Mitchell at the time. We came to Winnipeg, playing this Fourth Dimension [folk] circuit. We were there over Christmas. I remember putting up this Christmas tree in our hotel room. Neil, you know, was this rock & roller who was coming around to folk music through Bob Dylan. Of course. Anyway, Neil came out to the club and we liked him immediately. He was the same way he is now—this offhanded, dry wit. And you know what his ambition was at the time? He wanted a *hearse,* and a chicken farm. And when you think of it, what he's done with his dream is not that far off. He just added a few buffalo. And a fleet of antique cars. He's always been pretty true to his vision.

But none of us had any grandiose ideas about the kind of success that we received. In those days it was *really* a long shot. Especially for a Canadian. I remember my mother talking to a neighbor who asked,

"Where is Joan living?" And she said, "In New York: she's a musician." And they went "Ooh, you poor woman." It was hard for them to relate.

Later, you know, Neil abandoned his rock & roll band and came out to Toronto. I didn't know him very well at the time we were there. I was just leaving for Detroit. We didn't connect then. It was years later, when I got to California—Elliot [Roberts, her manager] and I came out as strangers in a strange land—and we went to a Buffalo Springfield session to see Neil. He was the only other person I knew. That's where I met everybody else. And the scene started to come together.

By this time, David Crosby "discovered" you singing in a club in Coconut Grove, Florida. What was he like back then?

He was tanned. He was straight. He was clearing out his boat, and it was going to be the beginning of a new life for him. He was paranoid about his hair, I remember. Having long hair in a short hair society. He had a wonderful sense of humor. Crosby has enthusiasm like no one else. He can make you feel like a million bucks. Or he can bring you down with the same force. Crosby, in producing that first album, did me an incredible service, which I will never forget. He used his success and name to make sure my songs weren't tampered with to suit the folk-rock trend.

I had just come back from London. That was during the Twiggy-Viva era, and I remember I wore a lot of makeup. I think I even had on false eyelashes at the time. And Crosby was from this scrub-faced California culture, so one of his first projects in our relationship was to encourage me to let go of all of this elaborate war paint [*laughs*]. It was a great liberation, to get up in the morning and wash your face . . . and not have to do anything else.

Is there a moment you can look back on when you realized that you were no longer a child, that you had grown up?

There's a moment I can think of—although I'm still a child. Sometimes I feel seven years old. I'll be standing in the kitchen and all of a sudden my body wants to jump around. For no reason at all. You've seen kids that suddenly just get a burst of energy? That part of my child is still alive. I don't repress those urges, except in certain company.

My artwork, at the time I made the first album, was still very concerned with childhood. It was full of the remnants of fairy tales and fantasia. My songs still make references to fairy tales. They referred to kings and queens. Mind you, that was also part of the times, and I pay colonial allegiance to Queen Lizzy. But suddenly I realized that I was preoccupied with the things of my girlhood and I was twenty-four years old. I remember being at the Philadelphia Folk Festival and having this *sensation*. It was like falling to earth. It was about the time of my second album. It felt almost as if I'd had my head in the clouds long enough. And then there was a plummeting into the earth, tinged with a little bit of apprehension and fear. Shortly after that, everything began to change. There were fewer adjectives to my poetry. Fewer curlicues to my drawing. Everything began to get more bold. And solid in a way.

By the time of my fourth album [*Blue,* 1971], I came to another point—that terrible opportunity that people are given in their lives. The day that they discover to the tips of their toes that they're assholes [*solemn moment, than a gale of laughter*]. And you have to work from there. And decide what your values are. Which parts of you are no longer really necessary. They belong to childhood's end. *Blue* really was a turning point in a lot of ways. As *Court and Spark* was a turning point later on. In the state that I was at in my inquiry about life and direction and relationships, I perceived a lot of hate in my heart. You know, "I hate you some, I hate you some, I love you some, I love you when I forget about me" ["All I Want"]. I perceived my inability to love at that point. And it horrified me. It's something still that I...I hate to say I'm *working* on, because the idea of work implies effort, and effort implies you'll never get there. But it's something I'm noticing.

Joni Mitchell

How aware were you that your songs were being scrutinized for the relation-
ships they could be about? Even 'Rolling Stone' drew a diagram of your
supposed brokenhearted lovers and also called you Old Lady of the Year.

I never saw it. The people that were involved in it called up to con-
sole me. My victims called first [*laughs*]. That took some of the sting
out of it. It was ludicrous. I mean, even when they were drawing all
these brokenhearted lines out of my life and my ability to love well, I
wasn't so unique. There was a lot of affection in those relationships.
The fact that I couldn't stay in them for one reason or another was
painful to me. The men involved are good people. I'm fond of them
to this day. We have a mutual affection, even though we've gone on
to new relationships. Certainly there are pockets of hurt that come.
You come a little battered out of a relationship that doesn't go on
forever. I don't live in bitterness.

I'm a confronter by nature. I have a tendency to confront my
relationships much more often than people would care. I'm always
being told that I talk too much. It's not that I like to, but I habitu-
ally confront before I escape. Rather than go out and try to drown
my sorrows or something, I'll wallow and muddle through them.
My friends thought for a long time that this was done out of some
act of masochism. I began to believe it myself. But at this time in
my life, I would say that it has paid some dividend. Be confronting
those things and thinking them through as deeply as my limited
intelligence would allow, there's a certain richness that comes in
time. Even psychiatrists, mind whores for the most part, don't have
a healthy attitude toward depression. They get bored with it. I think
their problem is they need to be *deeply* depressed.

My relationship with Graham [Nash] is a great, enduring one.
We lived together for some time—we were married, you might
say. The time Graham and I were together was a highly productive
period for me as an artist. I painted a great deal, and the bulk of
my best drawings were done in '69 and '70 when we were together.
To contend with this hyperactive woman, Graham tried his hand at

several things. Painting. Stained glass. And finally he came to the camera. I feel he's not just a good photographer, he's a great one. His work is so lyrical. Some of his pictures *are* worth a thousand words. Even after we broke, Graham made a gift of a very fine camera and a book of Cartier-Bresson photographs. I became an avid photographer myself. He gave the gift back to me. Even though the romance ended, the creative aspect of our relationship has continued to branch out.

This is the thing that *Rolling Stone,* when it made a diagram of broken hearts, was being very simplistic about. It was an easy target to slam me for my romantic alliances. That's human nature. That hurt, but not nearly so much as when they began to tear apart *The Hissing of Summer Lawns.* Ignorantly. I couldn't get together, in any way; it being human nature to take the attacks that were given certain projects. I got very frustrated at the turning point, when the press began to turn against me.

When did you first meet Bob Dylan?

The first official meeting was the *Johnny Cash Show* in 1969. We played that together. Afterward Johnny had a party at his house. So we met briefly there.

Over the years there were a series of brief encounters. Tests. Little art games. I always had affection for him. At one point, we were at a concert—whose concert was that? [*Shrugs*] How soon we forget. Anyway, we're backstage at this concert. Bobby and [Dylan's friend] Louie Kemp were holding up the conversation with painting. At that point, I had an idea for a canvas that I wanted to do. I'd just come from New Mexico, and the color of the land there was still very much with me. I'd seen color combinations that had never occurred to me before. Lavender and wheat, like old-fashioned licorice, you know, when you bite into it and there's this peculiar, rich green-and-brown color? The soil was like that, and the foliage coming out of it was vivid in the context of this color of earth. Anyway, I was describing something like that, really getting carried away with all of the colors. And Bobby says to me [*an inspired imitation*]: "When you paint, do you use *white*?" And I said, "Of course." He said, " 'Cause if you don't use white, your paint gets muddy." I thought, "Aha, the boy's been taking art lessons."

The next time we had a brief conversation was when Paul McCartney had a party on the *Queen Mary,* and everybody left the table and Bobby and I were sitting there. After a long silence he said, "If you were gonna paint this room, what would you paint?" I said, "Well, let me think. I'd paint the mirrored ball spinning, I'd paint the women in the washroom, the band..." Later all the stuff came back to me as part of a dream that became the song "Paprika Plains." I said, "What would *you* paint?" He said, "I'd paint this coffee cup." Later he wrote "One More Cup of Coffee."

Is it true that you once played Dylan a just-finished tape of 'Court and Spark' and he fell asleep?

This is true.

What does this do to your confidence when Bob Dylan falls asleep in the middle of your album?

Let me see, there was Louis Kemp and a girlfriend of his and David Geffen [then president of Elektra/Asylum Records] and Dylan. There was all this fussing over Bobby's project, 'cause he was new to the label, and *Court and Spark,* which was a big breakthrough for me, was being entirely and almost rudely dismissed. Geffen's excuse was, since I was living in a room in his house at the time, that he had heard it through all of its stages, and it was no longer any surprise to him. Dylan played his album [*Planet Waves*], and everybody went, "Oh, *wow.*" I played mine, and everybody talked and Bobby fell asleep. [*Laughs*] I said, "Wait a minute, you guys, this is some different kind of music for me, check it out." I knew it was good. I think Bobby was just being cute [*laughs*].

Prior to 'Court and Spark,' your albums were mostly kept to sparse interpretations. Had you always heard arrangements like that in your head?

Not really. I had attempted to play my music with rock & roll players, but they couldn't grasp the subtlety of the form. I've never studied music, so I'd always be talking in abstractions. And they'd laugh, "Aww, isn't that cute? She's trying to tell us how to play." Never negatively, but *appeasingly,* you know. And finally it was Russ Kunkel who said, "Joni, you'd better get yourself a jazz drummer."

One night, I went down to the Baked Potato [an L.A. jazz club] to hear the L.A. Express play. I knew Tom Scott, I'd done some work on *For the Roses* with him. When I heard the band, I was very enthusiastic, and I asked them to play on my next session.

When they got in the studio, it was the same problem. They didn't really know how heavy to play, and I was used to being the whole orchestra. Many nights I would be very discouraged. But one night we suddenly overcame the obstacles. The next thing we knew, we were all aware we were making something quite unique.

Do you think you've achieved greatness?

[*Long pause*] Greatness is a point of view. There is great rock & roll. But great rock & roll within the context of music, historically, is slight. I think that I am growing as a painter. I'm growing as a musician. I'm growing as a communicator, a poet, all the time. But growth implies that if you look back, there was improvement. I don't see necessarily that this album is any, to use your word, "greater" than the *Blue* album. This has a lot more *sophistication,* but it's very difficult to define what greatness is. Honesty? Genius? The *Blue* album, there's hardly a dishonest note in the vocals. At that period of my life, I had no personal defenses. I felt like a cellophane wrapper on a pack of cigarettes. I felt like I had absolutely no secrets from the world and I couldn't pretend in my life to be strong. Or to be happy. But the advantage of it in the music was that there were no defenses there either.

What do you think of the theory that great art comes from hunger and pain? You seem now to be living a very comfortable life.

Pain has very little to do with environment. You can be sitting at the most beautiful place in the world, which doesn't necessarily have to be private property, and not be able to see it for pain. So no. Misery knows no rent bracket [*laughs*]. At this time in my life, I've confronted a lot of my devils. A lot of them were pretty silly, but they were incredibly real at the time.

I don't feel guilty for my success or my lifestyle. I feel that sometimes having a lot of acquisitions leads to a responsibility that is more time-consuming than the art. That's probably one of the reasons why people feel the artist should remain in poverty. My most important possession is my pool—it's one luxury I really don't question.

Last question. What would you have listed, as Woody Allen did at the end of 'Manhattan,' as your reasons why life is worth living?

It would be very similar to his. I would name different musicians, but it might finally be a beautiful face that would make me put the microphone down. I would just be thinking fondly of someone who I love, you know. And just dreaming off…Basically, if you want to say it in one word? Happiness?

It's a funny thing about happiness. You can strive and strive and *strive* to be happy, but happiness will sneak up on you in the most peculiar ways. I feel happy suddenly, I don't know why. Some days, the way the light strikes things. Or for some beautifully immature reason like finding myself some *toast*. Happiness comes to me even on a bad day. In very, very strange ways. I'm very happy in my life right now.

FRANCIS COPPOLA
by Greil Marcus

November 1, 1979

Would you do it all again? [Referring to 'Apocalypse Now,' a complication-plagued project]

I'm tempted to say no. I really think there's a limit to what you ought to give a project you're working on. It's not worth it, it's really not worth it. I don't know that I would be able to avoid doing it again, but I'm forty years old instead of thirty-six. My leg hurts, my back hurts, my front hurts, my head hurts. I've got nothing but problems. I mean, I could be the head of KQED [San Francisco's public television station] and do interesting little experimental things and not be such a wreck.

There were times when I wished I was working for someone else so I could quit—but I don't think I ever thought of cutting my losses and coming home. There were a lot of troubles. Marty's [Martin Sheen] heart attack [which delayed filming even further]...severely traumatized my nervous system. We didn't know if he was going to make it. If he'd gone home to the U.S. for treatment, he might not have come back—his family might not have let him. I was scared shitless. The shooting was three-quarters done; it was all him, what was left.

Firing my [original] lead actor [Harvey Keitel]—that was bad. It's a terrible, terrible thing to do: sure, it jeopardizes the production, but it can also ruin an actor's career, to be fired like that. It was a very, very hard decision. But I just pulled the plunger—I did that a lot on this movie. Still do it. I've done it before with people — but that's another form of saying you're going to really try to get it right.

Did making this movie change your idea of what it means to be a filmmaker?

It changed every idea I have on anything I might not do or be. It enlarged my mind in terms of possibilities. It would be very hard for me to go and direct the new Paddy Chayefsky screenplay now. After *Apocalypse Now* and the *Godfather* pictures, especially the two of them together, I began to think in terms of the kind of movie that is impossible: movies that are ... fourteen hours long, that really cover a piece of material in a way that justifies it, shown in some kind of format that makes sense.

Ten years ago, John Milius wrote a script: 'Apocalypse Now.' You still share script credit with him. How has the movie changed?

I think the script, as I remember it, took a more comic-strip Vietnam War and moved it through a series of events that were also comic strip: a political comic strip. The events had points to them — I don't say comic strip to denigrate them. The film continued through comic-strip episode and comic-strip episode until it came to a comic-strip resolution. Attila the Hun [i.e., Kurtz] with two bands of machine-gun bullets around him, taking the hero [Willard] by the hand, saying, "Yes, yes, here! I *have the power in my loins!*" Willard converts to Kurtz' side; in the end, he's firing up at the helicopters that are coming to get him, crying out crazily. A movie comic.

I've read the comic.

Have you?

Well, I've read comics like that one, sure.

That was the tone and the *resolution.* The first thing that happened, after my involvement, was the psychologization of Willard — which

I worked on desperately. Willard in the original script was literally zero, nobody. I didn't have a handle: that's why I cast him with Steve McQueen at first. I thought, well, God, McQueen will give him a personality. But I began to delve more into Willard. I took Willard through many, many instances in which I tried to position him as a *witness* going on this trip—and yet give him some sort of personality you could feel comfortable with, and still believe he was there.

Marty approached an impossible character: he had to be an observer, a watcher. A lot of reading dossiers, a totally introspective character. In no way could he get in the way of the audience's view of what was happening, of Vietnam. That wasn't going to work for Keitel. His stock in trade is a series of tics—ways to make people look at *him*.

The first scene of the movie—Willard is in his Saigon hotel room, waiting for a mission, drunk, losing control, finally attacking a mirror and cutting his hand open—is described in your wife's book ('Notes') almost as a breakdown on Sheen's part, certainly not action that was planned.

Marty's character is coming across as too bland; I tried to break through it. I always look for other levels, hidden levels, in the actor's personality and in the personality of the character he plays. I conceived this all-night drunk; we'd see another side of that guy. So Marty got drunk. And I found that sometimes, when he gets drunk, a *lot* comes out. He began to dance, he took off his clothes—this was ten minutes of the most incredible stuff—and then I asked him to look in the mirror. It was a way of focusing him on himself—to bring out the personality by creating a sense of *vanity*. And that's what he punched: his vanity. I didn't tell him to smash his hand into the mirror.

Many of the best things in the movie—the helicopter attack, the surfing motifs—are from Milius. The Do Lung Bridge sequence—which came partly from one of Michael Herr's *Esquire* articles—was from Milius. Many things were changed. The concept that the guys on the boat would *get killed*—that was new. From the bridge on, it's pretty much *Heart of Darkness* and me.

Was the film based on 'Heart of Darkness' in Milius' script?

Very vaguely, then: A man was going up a river to find a man called Kurtz. There were few specific references beyond that. I decided to take the script much more strongly in the direction of *Heart of Darkness*—which was, I know, opening a Pandora's box.

Michael Herr was brought in after the shooting in the Philippines was completed. Did he write all of the narration?

He dominated it; he dominated the tone. The hipster voice Willard is given—that's Michael.

Was it from 'Dispatches,' in which Herr makes such a point of Vietnam as "a rock & roll war," that the idea came to use the Doors' "The End"?

No. I knew Jim Morrison, in film school; he came to my house once—this was before he'd had a record out—with some acetates, demos, asking if I could help. I tried; I didn't get anywhere. But the idea of using the Doors came from "Light My Fire." That was from Milius: Kurtz' people would play "Light My Fire" through their loud-speakers, to jazz themselves up. In the end, there's a battle, and the North Vietnamese regulars come charging in to "Light My Fire." I went to the Philippines with *that* ending!

How did the characterization of Kurtz evolve?

Marlon arrived; he was terribly fat. As my wife says in her book, he hadn't read the copy of *Heart of Darkness* I'd sent him; I gave him another copy, he read it, and we began to talk. There were a lot of notes that we compiled together. I'd give him some—he'd write a lot himself. I shot Marlon in a couple of weeks and then he left; everything else was shot around that footage, and what we had shot with Marlon wasn't like a scene. It was hours and hours of him talking.

We had an idea: Kurtz as a Gauguin figure, with mangoes and babies, a guy who'd really gone all the *way*. It would have been great; Marlon wouldn't go for it at all.

Marlon's first idea—which almost made me vomit—was to play Kurtz as a Daniel Berrigan: in black pajamas, in VC clothes. It would be all about the *guilt* [Kurtz] felt at what we'd done. I said, "Hey, Marlon, I may not know everything about this movie—but one thing I know it's not about is *'our guilt'*!" Yet Marlon has one of the finest minds around: Thinking is what he does. To sit and talk with him about life and death—he'll think about that stuff all day long.

Finally, he shaved his head—and that did it. We'd go for it—we'd get there. That terrible face. I think it's wonderful that in this movie, the most terrifying moment is that image: just his face.

There seems to be no conventional suspense in the movie. Even in the scene where Willard kills Kurtz; that's an orchestrated scene, full of crosscutting and metaphors, like the killings that end 'The Godfather.' Is that the way you wanted to make the movie?

Maybe I'm stupid, but I always wanted the film to be graceful. My very first notion when I began to think of the *style* of the film—of course, style was going to be the whole movie—I wanted to sweep, not go *chaaa! chaaa!* I wanted it to have grace. I chose Vittorio Storaro [Bernardo Bertolucci's cinematographer in *The Conformist*, *Last Tango in Paris* and *1900*] because I wanted the camera to just *float* across the boat. That is always shot handheld, because there's no building dolly tracks in the water. The music would be Tomita-like [a Japanese synthesizer composer] for that reason.

I don't understand what you mean when you say that style was going to be the whole movie.

When I first thought of doing *Apocalypse Now*, and I read Milius' script, I was looking for a clue as to what kind of movie this was going to be.

I was very concerned about style, because I knew it wouldn't be a realistic style—I knew it would have some sort of what I'll call extension to it, but I didn't know what. People used to ask me, well, what's this movie gonna be like? I said, well, it's gonna be very stylized. And they said, well, like what? Like what director? And I would say, like Ken Russell. I wanted the movie to go as far as it would go. I was prepared to have to make an unusual, surrealist movie, and I even wanted to.

But you didn't.

Well, surrealist. What do you call or what do you not call surrealist?

Watching the movie, I never had the feeling that I was partner to a dream—and that's how I would define the experience of surrealism.

Well, then, what would you call the desire to extend the action so that it had another, different reality—or an extended reality, from just pure reality—that made use of *what was going on?*

The emergence of a different reality is raised as something that could happen—that could take over Willard, suck him in. There's an interesting shot in Kurtz' temple, a copy of 'The Golden Bough'—a book about ancient myth and practice of ritual regicide. A man became king; after a year, if anyone could kill him, he became king. After Willard kills Kurtz, he emerges from the temple. Kurtz' whole community is gathered there, and Willard is carrying two symbols of kingship—this is how I saw it—the book, Kurtz' memoirs, and the scepter, the weapon he throws down when he refuses the kingship. The community kneels before him, and it's clear that if Willard wanted to take over, he could have. And then he consciously rejects that choice. If he had not, then he, and maybe we, would have been swallowed by the extended realities you're talking about. But he rejects that. That seemed very clear. Is that not what you meant?

No…when I finally got there, the best I could come up with was this: I've got this guy who's gone up the river, he's gonna go kill this other guy who's been the head of all this. Life and death. Well, I have a friend, Dennis Jakob, we were talking—what to do?—and he said to me, "What about the myth of the Fisher King?" And I said, "What's that?" He said, "It's *The Golden Bough*." The Fisher King—I went and got the book, and I said, of course, that's what I meant. That's what was meant by the animal sacrifices [that occur among Kurtz' people as Willard murders Kurtz]. I had seen a real animal sacrifice, by the headhunters we had hired. I looked at the blood shoot up in the air, and I'm thinking—this is about something very basic. I've gone up this whole river trying to figure out this movie, and I don't know what's the matter: What do I have to express, what do I have to show to really show this war? There are millions of things you have to show. But what it really all comes down to is some sort of acceptance of the truth, or the *struggle* to accept the truth. And the truth has to do with good and evil, and life and death—and don't forget that we see these things as opposites, or we want to see them as opposites, but they are *one*. It's not so easy to define them—as good or evil. You must accept that you have the whole.

Kurtz is consciously participating in the myth of the Golden Bough; he's prepared that role for Willard, for him to take his place.

He wants Willard to kill him. So Willard thinks about this: he says, "Everyone wanted him dead. The army...and ultimately even the jungle; that's where he took his orders from, anyway." The notion is that Willard is moved to do it, to go once more into that primitive state, to go and kill.

He goes into the temple, and he goes through a quasi-ritual experience, and he kills the king. The native people there were acting out in dance what was happening. They understood, and they were acting out, with their icons, the ritual of life and death. Willard goes in, and he kills Kurtz, and as he comes out he flirts with the notion of being king, but something...does not lure him. He goes, he takes the kid back, and then he goes away and there's the image of the green stone face again [the face of an ancient Cambodian goddess from Kurtz' temple complex]. He starts to go away, and then the moment when he flirted with being king is superimposed. And that's the moment when we use "the horror, the horror."

How do you see what Willard is going through at Kurtz' compound?

I always tried to have it be implied in the movie that the notion of Willard going up the river to meet Kurtz was perhaps also a man looking at another aspect or projection of himself. I always had the idea of Willard and Kurtz being the same man—in terms of how I made my decisions as to do whatever we did. And I feel that Willard arriving at the compound to meet Kurtz is like coming to the place that you don't want to go—because it's all *your* ghosts and all *your* demons.

Willard's a murderer, an assassin, and no doubt when he's alone in the bathroom, he's had some moral thoughts about whether that's good: to go kill people you don't even know. So I'm thinking Willard has been involved—as maybe *Kurtz* has—on a moral quest, which is to say, "Is what I have done, or what I am doing, moral? Is it okay?" So when Willard gets to Kurtz' place, it's his nightmare. It's his nightmare in that it's the extreme of the issue that he has to deal with—bodies and heads—and Kurtz is the extreme of him, because Willard's a killer. Here, now, Kurtz—who has gone mad—has become the horror, the whole thing, which is no more than an extension of the horror that we're looking at on every level. Willard has to come to terms with this—and what Brando really tells him, the way I see it, is, I finally saw something so horrible…and then at the same time realized that the fact that it was so horrible was what made it wonderful…and I went to some other place in my mind, in which I became Kurtz, who is nuts.

And pathetic. One of the most beautiful lines in Michael Herr's narration is when he says, "Kurtz had driven himself so far away from his people at home"—the idea that you could go so far that you couldn't get back, even if you wanted to get back.

That's what I was trying to do with Willard in that last section. I always had this image, over and over again, of being able to stare at the something that was the truth and say, "Yes, that is the truth." Somehow a face was always important to me, and that's why I liked just looking at Brando's face for ten minutes or whatever. Remember *Portrait of Dorian Gray*? I mean, it was like ripping back the curtain—*ahhhhh!* There it is. And that's the way I felt about Vietnam. You just look at it, you open your eyes and you look at it, and you accept it if it's the truth. And then you get past it.

One line that seems to be coming out, following the L.A. screening in May and the Cannes screenings—and I'm speaking of the American press, since that's all I've seen—is "The movie is terrific for the first hour or so: it's so exciting, it's well done, spectacular, it looks as if it were worth the money that was spent, you can see the money on the screen." And then, "When the picture get to Kurtz, it becomes muddled and philosophical and pretentious—it falls apart." That line is remarkably consistent. (And has remained so in most of the reviews that have appeared since the film was officially released.)

Audiences, and therefore certain writers, really know the rules of the different kinds of movies—and whether they want to admit it, in the first hour and a half of this movie, they're locked into a formula. It's a formula movie; you just get locked into the slot and it'll take you up the river. And then, at a certain point, it doesn't develop into the action adventure that it had set you up for. In my mind, the movie had made a turn I wouldn't alter—it *curved* up the river. I chose to go with a stylized treatment, up the river into primitive times—and I *eliminated* everything in the script that *didn't* take you there. It now takes you into various difficult areas, which you have to engage with a little. They're riding down a big sled on a very formula movie, and they want it to resolve, and kick 'em off, just like movies are supposed to do, and it doesn't do it. It's like someone takes them off the slide and says, okay, now walk up the steps, and they don't want to do it.

I'm not saying they are wrong in feeling that. I think some do and some don't. But they would have preferred that it just went easy, without any difficulties—let the movie *do it all*. And I couldn't do it in the end.

Couldn't, or wouldn't?

I couldn't, I don't think—I tried. I mean, I couldn't give them an ending better than I did. I tried, and I've been trying and trying and trying. And if I could ever imagine how to do it, I would get out the goddamn film and I'd do it.

I think we live our lives hoping—impatient—for a time when things are resolved. I think that time will never come for any of us—and that's part of the irony, even in this movie. Although there seems to be a resolution of some kind: that the healthy devour the sickly, and there is some sort of life/death, night-becomes-morning cycle taking place—to me the irony is that we stand on the edge, on the razor blade, all the time, and that's why Willard looks to the left, looks to the right, and you hear, "The horror, the horror." "The horror, the horror" is precisely that we are never really comfortable understanding what we should do, what is right and what is wrong, what is rational behavior, what is irrational: that we're always on the brink.

"The horror, the horror" at the end, the fact that I wanted to end it on choice, because I think that's the truthful ending—We hope for some sort of moral resolution about Vietnam and about our part in it, our participation in it. At the [true] end, you don't have a resolution. You're in a choice, still, between deciding to be powerful or to be weak. In a way, that's how wars start. The United States chose: It wanted to be powerful, wanted to be Kurtz, in Southeast Asia. It chose not to stay home. But choice was just the only way I thought it could end.

Heart of Darkness ends with a lie. After Kurtz' death, Marlow goes to Kurtz' girlfriend, the intended, and she says, "What did he say before he died?" And Marlow says, "He mentioned your name," when in fact what Kurtz said was, "The horror, the horror." So I feel all lousy because I think the ending I had on the movie was the truth, but this ending that I'm going to put on it now is a lie—and I justify it to myself because Conrad would have ended with a lie, too.

TOM WOLFE

by Chet Flippo

August 21, 1980

Probably the most striking thing about 'The Right Stuff' is that it has made you very respectable. You're no longer the hit man who literary people fear and hate. Now you're eminently respectable.

Most of the things I have done have *not* been send-ups or zaps, but those things are remembered somehow. People love a little merciless mockery. So they'll tend to remember something like *Radical Chic,* particularly, or *The Painted Word,* since, if you even make *gentle* fun of people who inhabit the world that you and I live in or the world of the arts, or anything having to do with expression, they *scream* like *murder.* And of course they have the equipment to bite back, so the fight starts. Everyone kind of enjoys it whether they're paying any attention or not. But *The Electric Kool-Aid Acid Test* was not a send-up, was not mockery or satire.

It was not necessarily a subject the literary world understood or endorsed.

Well, the literary world certainly doesn't endorse the subject of astronauts; it hasn't been a very popular subject. As a matter of fact, one of the things that interested me most was not the space program but military life. I could see that the military, particularly the officer corps, had really been a vacant lot in the literary sense. Serious writers stopped looking at the military around 1919—in any sympathetic way or even empathetic way. It's around then that you start finding the fashion of dealing with the military in a way in which the only acceptable protagonist is the GI, the dog soldier, the grunt, the doughboy, who's presented as a *victim,* not as a *warrior,* a victim of the same forces as civilians.

I would think the astronauts weren't eager to talk to you, some weirdo saying, I'm from 'Rolling Stone' and I want to investigate your private life. Obviously you didn't say that; how did you go about it?

They weren't all that tough. By that time, some had left the astronaut corps. They were a lot looser about the whole thing, they were no longer under the *Life* magazine contract. I think many had become rather bored with the way astronauts had been described. They tended to be pretty open if they agreed to talk at all. A few wouldn't be interviewed. Alan Shepard told me that he only cooperated in documentary ventures that had a scientific purpose . . . later on he indicated that he had read the *Rolling Stone* pieces and didn't particularly like what was there; I don't know why. Neil Armstrong said he had a policy of not giving interviews and didn't see any reason why he should change it. I think he had hopes, and perhaps still does, of writing his own book. All the Mercury astronauts who were still alive — [Gus] Grissom was dead — were willing to talk and were cooperative.

Was John Glenn open?

Very open. I spent a day with him when he was campaigning for the Senate in 1974, the year he finally won the primary against Howard Metzenbaum, who had beaten him just a few years before. Then I spent an afternoon with Glenn after he won; he was actually pretty generous with his time, as senators go, and he was very helpful.

I've been surprised by the number of reviews that found my picture of John Glenn negative. I wasn't trying to send him valentines, but in my mind he came off as an exceptional and rather courageous figure. He did a lot of unpopular things. He told off a lot of people, and he almost lost his flight by telling the administrator of NASA and everybody else that Lyndon Johnson couldn't go into his house, that he and his wife didn't want him in there. That took a lot of courage.

When did the notion first strike you—of course it should have been obvious to everyone—that the original astronauts were not the Boy Scouts who were presented to America?

I guess from the first conversation that I ever had with any of them. It's not that they bragged about their exploits or talked about things like driving these wild races on the highway. At the same time I was starting this thing, in late 1972, there had been reports in the press indicating trouble in paradise among the astronauts. Buzz Aldrin's nervous breakdown had been revealed. That was the same year there was a stamp scandal, which wasn't really much of a scandal, but nevertheless it made people stop and ask, "What, astronauts took a cut of some stamp sales?" One of the astronauts had just become an evangelist. Two or three had been photographed with long hair, and this was immediately interpreted by newspapers and magazines as a sign that there were astronauts who were turned into hippies, which never happened as far as I can tell.

Perhaps because the general whitewash of the astronauts' flaws had gone to such an extreme at the beginning, the least little crack was overinterpreted. To this day, so many people think that most of the astronauts who went to the moon have suffered breakdowns or become alcoholics. It just isn't true.

For a while there was the assumption that this voyage was traumatic because it removed them from all familiar environments, and that this just had devastating effects on these simple men who weren't prepared for it. The truth was, they had had such sophisticated simulations that there was very little new to see when they reached the moon. By the time Armstrong got there, he had had probably 500 simulated missions in replicas of the Apollo command module, with moving pictures of the moon, based on films that had been brought back by manned and unmanned vehicles. I think it was false for Armstrong to have delivered some apostrophe to the gods or some statement of poetic awe about what he had seen, 'cause he had already seen it all simulated in such high fidelity, how the hell could he pretend there was something startling about it? So he said it's "a small step for man, a giant leap for mankind." When I asked him about it, he said, "Sure, I worked on it for a couple of weeks."

How did you get the notion to cut this book off where you did? The idea of the end of innocence—I believe you make the point that the astronauts' parade was, in a sense, the peak of American innocence.

I think that was the last great national outpouring of patriotism. There was some of that with Gordon Cooper's flight, but it was much bigger in the case of Glenn. By the time Cooper flew in 1963, there were many signs that the United States and the Soviet Union were reaching some sort of rapprochement, so that there wasn't the tension about the flight. The cold war was still a big thing at the time of Glenn's flight.

I liked your characterization of the press as the proper Victorian gent, that the press was reverent through all this.

I'll never forget working on the *Herald Tribune* the afternoon of John Kennedy's death. I was sent out along with a lot of other people to do man-on-the-street reactions. I started talking to some men who were just hanging out, who turned out to be Italian, and they already had it figured out that Kennedy had been killed by the Tongs, and then I realized that they were feeling hostile to the Chinese because the Chinese had begun to bust out of Chinatown and move into Little Italy. And the Chinese thought the mafia had done it, and the Ukrainians thought the Puerto Ricans had done it. And the Puerto Ricans thought the Jews had done it. Everybody had picked out a scapegoat. I came back to the *Herald Tribune* and

I typed up my stuff and turned it in to the rewrite desk. Late in the day they assigned me to do the rewrite of the man-on-the-street story. So I looked through this pile of material, and mine was missing. I figured there was some kind of mistake. I had my notes, so I typed it back into the story. The next day I picked up the *Herald Tribune* and it was *gone,* all my material was gone. In fact there's nothing in there except little old ladies collapsing in front of St. Patrick's. Then I realized that, without anybody establishing a policy, one and all had decided that this was the proper moral tone for the president's assassination. It was to be grief, horror, confusion, shock and sadness, but it was not supposed to be the occasion for any petty bickering. The press assumed the moral tone of a Victorian gentleman.

I say Victorian gentleman, because it's he who was the constant hypocrite, who insisted on public manifestations of morality that he would never insist upon privately in his own life. And I think that one tends to do that on a newspaper. Less so in a magazine. A newspaper seems to have such an immediate tie to the public. Television doesn't have it. Newspapers do. I'm not entirely sure why, but it makes newspapers fun to work for.

It also leads to these funny sorts of reactions. People *never* read editorials. All newspapers know this. And yet if you would publish a newspaper without editorials, it would be as if you had sold your soul to somebody. Everyone would ask, in effect, "Well, where are the editorials? They must have sold them. They're taking something on the side." And so newspapers are quite right to run editorials. It all has to do with this moral assumption.

Hell, to this day you can't get anything in newspapers. I think of this as the period of incredible shrinking news. I'm really convinced that there's less news covered in America now than at any time in this century. Television creates the impression that there's all this news because the press has become very incestuous and writes stories about the press, with all these marvelous phony wars about television and what it does or doesn't do. But television as a news medium has no reporting at all, really, except for some cosmetic reporting done by so-called Washington correspondents, who usually stand in front of some government building with a microphone covered in black sponge rubber, reading AP or UPI copy. In effect, every shred of news on television comes from either the wire services or from *nonevents,* to use Daniel Boorstin's phrase—the press conference, the basketball game and so on. So you then have to ask, "What are the wire services giving us?" Well, the wire services are totally creatures of local newspapers. Those big wire services just cannibalize local newspapers. Suddenly you're up against the fact that there's no competition in most parts of the country *at all.* I doubt if there are five cities where there is still newspaper competition. When this happens, the monopoly newspaper cuts back on its staff—always happens. They just stop covering local events—too expensive.

So really, what you're seeing on television via the wire services is just getting smaller and smaller. It's really very sad. I don't know how much corruption there is at the local level, but there's never been a better time in the century for there to be corruption in local government, because the press is not gonna spot it.

Television, which has the money to do the reporting, has gotten away so beautifully *without* doing it that it's not about to start. You talk to these guys and they'll say, "Well, they sent me from Beirut to Teheran, and I had forty-five minutes to get briefed on the situation." What they should say is, "I read the AP copy." Just try to think of the last major scoop, to use that old term, that was broken on television. They can do a set event. And that's what television is actually best at. In fact, it'd be a service to the country if television news operations were shut down *totally* and they only broadcast hearings, press conferences and hockey games. *That* would be television news. At least the public would not have the false impression that it's getting news coverage.

I believe it was in the 'New Republic' that Mitch Tuchman wrote that the reason you turned against liberals is that you were rejected by the white-shoe crowd at Yale.

Yeah, he wrote that after *The Painted Word*. All I ever did was write about the world we inhabit, the world of culture, with a capital *C*, and journalism and the arts and so on, with exactly the same tone that I wrote about everything else. With exactly the same reverence that the people who screamed the most would have written about life in a small American town or in the business world or in professional sports, which is to say with no reverence at all, which is as it should be. And these days, if you mock the prevailing fashion in the world of the arts or journalism, you're called a *conservative*. Which is just another term for a heretic.

Have you always been a real clothes horse, really careful about clothes?

The first time I remember being interested at all in clothes was after I saw *The Kiss of Death* [1947] with Richard Widmark as Tommy Udo. That was his first big role, he was the villain; Victor Mature was the hero. It was a gangster movie. I was at Washington and Lee, and there was a custom, I guess you'd call it, of conventional dress. It was an all-male school, and everyone had to wear a conventional jacket and tie. I guess I just wanted to put a *spin* on the custom without transgressing the rules, so I decided on these dark shirts.

Style, men's clothing, has very rigid presumptions about it, and if you really experiment, suddenly you're out of the ball game. You could certainly cut a striking figure by wearing a royal blue caftan everywhere you go, but you would remove yourself from most transactions of life. So if you want to have any fun with it, it really has to be rather marginal. But the interesting thing is that marginal things seem outrageous at first.

I also think I was the only person on campus who wore a hat. And I know I was the only person who carried an umbrella every day. When I got to my next stop, Yale graduate school, I fell into great confusion, because the grad school was full of genuinely eccentric people, and to try to be eccentric in the midst of a zoo full of eccentrics was a lost cause. The currency was debased. At the same time, it was no use trying to dress very conventionally because there was a whole campus full of undergraduates who were dressed very conventionally.

Finally, when I got to Washington, I started having clothes made because I discovered a traveling British tailor. There were actually several who advertised in the back pages of the *Manchester Guardian* air-mail edition. They would set up shop in a hotel room. The samples used to always be on top of the bureau. You'd go look at all these samples books and pick some material. They'd make you whatever you wanted.

When I came to New York I decided I should start getting clothes made in this country so I could get fittings, because there were some rather bad mistakes, though not as bad as you would get with a Hong Kong tailor. So I went to a tailor here in New York and picked out a white material to have a suit made for the summertime. Silk tweed is actually a very warm material, so I starting wearing the thing in the wintertime. This was the winter of 1962 or 1963, and the reaction of people was just astonishing.

Long hair at that time outraged people. It was a real transgression. I did a story on Phil Spector in 1964, and he had hair about as long as the Beatles'. The things that were yelled to him on the street—I mean the *hostility*—were just amazing.

The hostility for minor changes in style was just marvelous. I had a great time. I was really getting into the swing of things. I remember my friend Bill Rollins, who was one of the great figures on the *Herald Tribune* at the time. Every time I came into Bleek's or one of those places where newspaper people met, he'd say, "Here comes the man with the double-breasted underwear." I rather *liked* that.

Which brings me to one final note on style. It's still possible to have fun with clothes if you're willing to be pretentious. That still annoys people: pretension in dress. In fact, this summer I was in East Hampton visiting some people who took me to a party. I was wearing a four-button seersucker jacket that buttons up really high—I think it is actually Edwardian—with a little tiny collar and a white tie with small, far-apart black stripes, and I had on a collar pin and cuff links, white serge pants and white cap-toed shoes, which are real English banker shoes, only I had them made in white doeskin. I had on some sheer white socks with black stripes to pick up the stripes in the necktie—I'm the *only* person who would confess all this to somebody. Pretty soon I noticed that I was the only man in the room—and this was a party of maybe sixty people—who had on both a jacket and a necktie. I think everyone had an income far in excess of mine. Finally this man came over to me; he was a little drunk, but he was also angry. He asked, "What's the idea of the rig?" I asked, "What do you mean?" He said, "The *tie,* the *pin,* all this stuff." So I looked at him, and he had on a polo shirt and some kind of go-to-hell pants, and he had this big *stain* down the front of his polo shirt, right down the middle, right down to his belt line. I said, "Well, gee, I guess I can't keep up with the styles in these parts. How do you do that bright stripe down your polo shirt?" He looked down sort of in surprise and said, "That's sweat, goddamn it, that's *sweat!*" He suddenly was very proud of it. I could see that I had landed in the midst of the era of funky chic.

You know when I write certain things and it turns out that I'm correct, it amazes me, I must confess. When I wrote that thing, funky chic, I never dreamed how correct that was.

On several occasions, most recently in the Polo Lounge in Beverly Hills, I'd just be standing around and people would come up and ask me if there's a table available, because I'd have on a suit and necktie. Wear some trick outfits. If it's worth it to you.

Does it ever get in the way of your role as the observer?

No, most often the opposite has gotten in the way. In the beginning of my magazine-writing career, I used to feel it was very important to try to fit in.

To be the chameleon?

Yes, and it almost always backfired, most notably when I went to do a story on Junior Johnson, the stock-car racer, one of the first stories I did for *Esquire.* I was quite aware that he was from the hills of North Carolina. A lot of moonshine and ex-moonshine runners were involved with stock-car racing at that time, Junior being one of them. I thought I'd better try to fit in, so I very carefully picked out the clothes I'd wear. I had a knit tie, some brown suede shoes and a brown Borsalino hat with a half inch of beaver fur on it. Somehow I thought this was very casual and suitable for the races; I guess I'd been reading too many P.G. Wodehouse novels. I really thought I'd fit in until about five days after I was down there. Junior Johnson came up to me and said, "I don't like to say anything, but all these people in Ingle Hollow here are pestering me to death saying, 'Junior, do you realize there's some strange little green man following you around?'"

I realized that not only did I not fit in, but because I thought I *was* fitting in in some way, I was afraid to ask such very basic questions as, what's the difference between an eight-gauge and seven-gauge tire, or, what's a gum ball, because if you're supposed to be hip, you can't ask those questions. I also found that people really don't want you to try to fit in. They'd much rather fill you in. People like to have someone to tell their stories to. So if you're willing to be the village information gatherer, they'll often just pile material on you. My one contribution to the discipline of psychology is my theory of information compulsion. Part of the nature of the human beast is a feeling of scoring a few status points by telling other people things they don't know. So this does work in your favor.

After that, when I did *The Pump House Gang*, I scarcely could have been in a more alien world. I did the whole story in my seersucker rig. I think they enjoyed that hugely. They thought of me as very old. I was thirty-odd years old, and they thought of me as very stuffy. They kind of liked all that—this guy in a straw boater coming around asking them questions. Then it even became more extreme when I was working on *Electric Kool-Aid Acid Test*. I began to understand that it would really be a major mistake to try to fit into that world. There was a kind of creature that Kesey and the Pranksters, practically everybody in the psychedelic world, detested more than anything else, and that was the so-called weekend hipster, who was the journalist or teacher or lawyer, or somebody who was hip on the weekends but went back to his straight job during the week. Kesey had a habit of doing what he called testing people's cool. If he detected the weekend hipster, he would dream up some test of hipness, like saying, "Okay, let's everybody jump on our bikes and ride naked up Route 1." They *would* do that, and usually at that point the lawyer, who didn't want an indecent exposure charge on his life's score sheet, would drop out. Kesey explained this theory of testing people's cool, his notion that there're lots of people who want to be amoral, but very few who are up to it. And he was *right*.

How did you come across the third great awakening and the Me Decade? Was that originally a lecture that you were doing?

I think I did it for *The Critic;* I used "the third great awakening" in that.

One of the few things I learned on the lecture circuit, which I have abandoned for the most part, was the existence of these new religious movements and some insight into what they were like. I would begin to meet members of religious communes who had come to my talks in hopes of hearing about Ken Kesey and the Merry Pranksters, whom I was not talking about any longer. I would talk about art, and the first question would be, "What's Ken Kesey doing now?" And I can't tell you how many times that happened. I began to see that I was perceived as a medium who could put them in touch with the other world. And all these people were patiently listening *just* to get to the question period, or to get me alone to ask, "What's Ken Kesey doing now? What's he really like? Where can I find a commune? Are we running our commune correctly?" *God*, I used to get all these letters—I could have started a column like "Dr. Hip Pocrates, Advice for Heads."

Well, the other question that everyone asks, I recall, is how many times you'd taken acid in order to do 'Kool-Aid Acid Test,' and you said you hadn't, which disappointed everyone greatly.

Yeah, I think they really wanted me to be on the bus. In fact, I never was.

You went off in private and took acid, just to see what it was like?

Well, I actually did it once during the writing of the book; I'd started writing the book, and then I thought, well, this is one little piece of reporting I haven't done. So I did do it; it scared the hell out of me. It was like tying yourself to a railroad track to see how big the train is. It was pretty big. I would never do it again. Although at several places I went to lecture in the years that followed, people would put things in the pie that was cooked for dinner—not LSD, but a lot of hashish, marijuana baked into things, or methedrine. People would pop poppers under my nose, things of this sort. They thought they were doing me a favor. But one of the reasons I wrote *The Electric Kool-Aid Acid Test*, one of the reasons I thought it was important enough to write about, was that it was a religion; Kesey's group was a primary religious group.

And you could see how just such a group developed, as if you'd been able to have been a reporter when the early Christians were forming and then again, running into students who would tell me they had formed communes, and who were very frankly religious and would call themselves Jesus people. They said they didn't use dope, but they all *had*. In the beginning the whole Jesus movement was made up of former acidheads, and when they said they didn't use dope, in most cases they really meant they didn't use chemical dope. Anything you could grow was quite all right. That mean that marijuana was okay, peyote was okay...

... mescaline was all right, mushrooms, etc.

Yeah, if you would go to the trouble of making it. Those things were all okay. The people in the psychedelic world had been religious but had always covered it up. There was such a bad odor about being frankly religious. I mean Kesey would refer to Cosmo, meaning God; someone in the group used the word "manager." Hugh Romney [a.k.a. Wavy Gravy] used to say, "I'm in the pudding and I've met the manager." Or they'd say, if they were getting into a very religious frame of mind and began to notice a lot of—what's the word when two people pick up the same thought at the same time? Probably "coincidence" is the right word, but they had another name for it—they would begin to say, "Well, there's some real weird shit going down," or "Brothers, this is the holy moment," or anything like that.

In the early Seventies, the mood of all this began to get more and more frankly religious, and the idea that this was the third great awakening popped into my head. Because I had remembered from graduate-school days the first awakening and second great awakening, out of which came Mormonism. Then I began to read about it. I saw that the Mormons, for example, had been just like hippies and had been *seen* as such. Just *wild* kids. They were *young* when they started. You think of Mormons as being old and having big beards. They were *children*. They were in their early twenties. Joseph Smith was twenty-four years old—he was the leader of the band. And they were just *hated, more* than the hippies were hated. And Smith was lynched. He wasn't hanged, but he was in jail in Carthage, Illinois, and it was invaded by vigilantes and they shot him to death. That's why Brigham Young took the group out to the woods of Utah.

And I think that movement is growing bigger and bigger. There's such a…yearning in everybody—there always has been—for blind faith. There's no such thing, I think, as rational faith. It isn't faith. And people always want it, one way or another, me included, although I hide it from myself, as do most people who think they are really sophisticated and learned. But this is something people really *want*, because blind faith is a way of assuring yourself that the kind of life that you're either leading or *intend* to lead is inherently and absolutely the *best*. That's really what it's all about.

Now is a great time for new religions to pop up. There are people who get religious about jogging, they get religious about sex, and you talk to some of these people who are avowed swingers—they'll *bore your head off.* God, it's just *painful* to listen to them. Fifteen minutes in a roomful of these people is like turning your head into a husk. Health foods have become the basis of a religion. Let's see, ESP, of course, flying saucers, *anything* is fertile ground now. There's a new messiah born every day. That's why Jimmy Carter made such a colossal mistake in not preaching. He'd gotten away with murder as it was, getting elected as a born-again Christian. *That's* what people wanted. If he had just ranted and raved for the last three years about the depravity of the people, they would have *loved it.*

Tell me, where are you going to turn your eye next? Are you at loose ends, or casting around?

I'm doing something that I've had on my mind for a long time, which is a *Vanity Fair* book about New York, à la Thackeray. When I went to Leonard Bernstein's party [to report on *Radical Chic*], it was with the idea of gathering material for what was going to be a nonfiction book, which *could* be done, incidentally, if you could find enough events or scenes like that to move into. My impulse now, though, is to try to do it as a novel, since I've never done one, and to just see what happens. I'm also very much aware of the fact that novelists themselves hardly *touch* the city. How they can pass up the city I don't know. The city was a central—character is not a very good way to put it, but it was certainly a dominant theme—in the works of Dickens, Zola, Thackeray, Balzac. So many talented writers now duck the city as a subject. And this is one of the most remarkable periods of the cities. Who has been the great novelist of New York since the Second World War? Nobody. Or Chicago or Cleveland or Los Angeles or Newark, for that matter. My God, the story of Newark must be absolutely amazing.

So you're going to be out prowling the streets?

Well, I don't know if I'll be charging into people's houses, but I will have to do a lot of reporting. There's more good material out there than in any writer's brain. A writer always likes to think that a good piece of work he has done is the result of his genius. And that the material is just the clay, and it's ninety-eight percent genius and two percent material. I think that it's probably 70 percent–30 percent in favor of the material. This ends up putting a great burden on the reporting, and I don't think many fiction writers understand this.

JACK NICHOLSON

by Nancy Collins

March 29, 1984

Garrett Breedlove, the astronaut you played in 'Terms of Endearment,' is hardly a matinee idol. Any qualms about playing a clearly middle-aged, out-of-shape guy?

No, because I've always wanted to play older. Some of my early heroes are Walter Huston, Edward Arnold, Charles Bickford. They didn't have any problems with it. This middle-life thing has become a phobia; people think it's *got* to be a big problem, when it's simply not. I know from real life that middle-aged people are very attractive. I feel I'm beating out all those guys who stay on rigid diets. They run; they go crazy; their skin is always in fabulous shape. I feel like I'm going to scoop the pot going the other way. Besides, I've been physically dissected more than any frog in a biology class—it's my eyebrows, my eyes, my teeth. And now it's my stomach. For twenty-five years, they've been writing that I'm totally bald, and now they're all bald and—have a look [*points to his head*].

I've been overweight since I was four years old. Of course, I have all the normal defenses against it. But it's always bugged me. I don't want to overinflate my role and my job, but isn't there more to me than what I weigh?

One of the themes of 'Terms' is middle-aged sexuality and crisis. You're forty-six. Have you suffered any form of midlife crisis?

Oh, sure. You're aware of the rings in your tree. It's like when Mick Jagger says it would be terrible to be singing rock & roll at forty. Well, it's not so terrible, as he now appreciates. I'm aware that in the job I do, age is a big factor, so it's the first time in a professional way that I've accepted any limitations. I don't want to be a man who, just past a certain point of physicality, believes it when young women say they actually prefer you this way. It's an image I've always feared. I hope I'm not that vulnerable, but I could be. It's a goofy, clownish part. I don't mind acting it, but I don't want to be it.

I gather you know you have a reputation as a womanizer. Is that guilt by association, because of your friendship with Warren Beatty?

That's right, guilt by association. I mean, what night is this? Do you hear women calling me on the phone? They know I'm here, don't they? Look, that's just bullshit. I can't go around saying I'm not a womanizer, because that's silly. First of all, it's good for business if people think I'm a womanizer. Beyond that, I've no motivation to deny it, unless it begins to dominate the reality of my situation.

As a child, I had one of those scaldingly embarrassing experiences when I realized that all these other boys were lying about their sexual prowess. I always assumed they were telling the truth. I believed them when I was six through ten, and at eleven, I said, "Those guys are lying." The result of that lag is that it's very hard for me to lie about my prowess or my experience. It's apropos of my reputation that I'm a little embarrassed that people look at me that way, because they're giving me too much credit.

But your audience wants to give you that credit. Men, in particular, like living vicariously. They want to think that being a big-time movie star means having lots of women.

That I like. That part I don't mind. That's getting even [*flashes the smile*].

Are you monogamous? Could you stay faithful in order to maintain an important relationship like, for instance, yours with Anjelica [Huston, who Nicholson had been seeing for eleven years]?

By nature, I am not monogamous. But I have been monogamous, which is the only reason I'm comfortable saying this out loud. It doesn't make any difference, except in a positive way, primarily for appearances. I only believe this because of experience. Once I've had enough experience about something, I don't give a fuck about anybody else's theory. I say monogamy doesn't make any difference; women suspect you whether it's true or not.

You were raised by women: Ethel May, whom you believed to be your mother, and her two daughters, Lorraine and June, who was seventeen years your senior. Ethel May's husband, a drinker, wasn't around much, and she supported everybody by opening a beauty shop in your house in Neptune City, New Jersey. When June died in 1975, the real truth emerged! You were illegitimate. Ethel May was actually your grandmother, posing as your mother, while June, whom you thought to be your sister, was your natural mother. How did you feel about this?

I was making *The Fortune,* and someone called me on the phone—I think it was turned over by the investigative reporting for the *Time* cover story they did on me. Ultimately, I got official verification from Lorraine. I was stunned. Since I was at work, I went to Mike Nichols, the director, and said, "Now, Mike, you know I'm a big-time method actor. I just found out something—something just came through—so keep an extra eye on me. Don't let me get away with anything."

Do you know who your father was?

Only June and Ethel knew, and they never told anybody.

Who was this woman, June?

Fast-cutting? A talented seventeen-year-old child who goes to New York and Miami as an Earl Carroll dancer and progresses through the gypsy line....[Entertainer] Pinky Lee's straight lady for a while....And when the war comes, she's the Irish-American patriot, the girl in the control tower at Willow Run, the central domestic-sending center for the military in World War II. She marries the son of a wealthy Eastern brain surgeon, one of American's most glamorous test pilots....And they live a very country-club life in Stony Brook, Long Island, where I always spent my summers in this very nice upper-class atmosphere.

All the time thinking June was your sister?

Right. The marriage broke up over a drinking problem, and like all great chicks, she comes home. She commutes to New York, teaches dancing at Arthur Murray's and, taking a shot on her own, drives to California with her kids...where she works in an aircraft factory, teaching herself to be a secretary. I come out to California and veer out on my own. She becomes an assistant buyer at J.C. Penney's, gets cancer and passes on.

June and I had so much in common. We both fought hard. It didn't do her any good not to tell me, but she didn't because you never know how I would have reacted when I was younger. I got a job in Mexico when June was dying. First time with a studio, a lot of weeks. Sandra was pregnant with Jennifer, and June was in a terminal state. She looked me right in the eye and said, "Shall I wait?" In other words, "Shall I try and fight this through?" And I said no.

I'm very contra my constituency in terms of abortion because I'm positively against it. I don't have the right to any other view. My only emotion is gratitude, literally, for my life. [If June and Ethel had been] of less character, I would never have gotten to live. These women gave me the gift of life. It's a feminist narrative in the very pure form. They trained me great, those ladies. I still, to this day, have never borrowed a nickel from anybody and never felt like I couldn't take care of myself. They made the imperative of my self-sufficiency obvious.

You genuinely like women, don't you?

Yeah, I genuinely do. I prefer the company of women, and I have deep respect for them. I'm buzzed by the female mystique. I always tell young men there are three rules: They hate us, we hate them; they're stronger, they're smarter; and, most important, they don't play fair.

What attracts you to a woman? You once said you like women who are alluring but unobtainable.

It's not categorizable. The heaviest prejudice to deal with is the beautiful woman. I'd like to say, "No, it doesn't matter whether somebody's beautiful or not," but whatever I find beautiful is what I'm attracted to. As for the other, I'd like to have all the women I'm attracted to *still* with me. I don't want them unattainable. I don't even want them unavailable!

Do you think you're sexy?

I know I'm sexy to some people. In the moment-to-moment thing, I always assume that my superstructural identity is working against me with women. It helps you because they know about you, and women like to be involved with known people. But in the case of my specific fantasy, it works against me. I find myself apologizing for being a film star if I'm interested in a person socially.

You've said that in all your major relationships, you were the one who got left.

In all cases but one in my life, that's true. But, again, it's like every male: You're not sure that you're not driving them away because you don't know how to leave them.

Incidentally, have you ever been in therapy?

My therapy was Reichian, which is all sexual.

Did you do the whole Reichian shot, taking off your clothes and getting analyzed in the nude?

Uh-hum. It didn't take any rationalization. It worked with me like this [*snaps fingers*].

You once said about acting, "You have to determine, what is your sexuality in this scene? Everything else comes from that." The sexual part of acting is very important to you, isn't it?

It's the key. The total key. Actually, sex is my favorite subject. But it's scary for me to talk about because of Anjelica. It's like she says: "How would you feel if I were sitting down with some interviewer, telling him all I felt about sex and fucking. You know you'd flip out." And a certain part of me says, "You're absolutely right, I would." But that's the dichotomy. I yearn for honesty in life. As an artist, I yearn for the clear moment. I would tell anybody any living thing about me, and there's a lot of stuff that ain't great.

You realize you have a reputation as a man who indulges in a slew of drugs. Is that true?

A slew of drugs? No. And never have. Do I relate to drugs? Yes, I do. But, for instance, though I've said—forever—that I smoke marijuana, I've never told anyone that I actually do cocaine. I've never said that to anyone.

Then why do you think people believe you do cocaine?

I think it's the normal assumption to make, particularly about someone who's been candid about his privacy. I can only blame myself. I'm not so sure I should've been this candid. I thought it was a very good thing to do because, first of all, I'm for legalization, and because I know what the costs are. The costs are lying.

How would you describe your drug use?

Convivial.

What does that mean?

It means I have a good time. I don't drink, although the last couple of years, I've started to drink a little alcohol — a glass of wine, maybe two brandies at night after coffee.

Do you still smoke marijuana?

Why talk about it? I'm not helping anybody. I've no desire to conceal what I do, but I've tried not concealing it, and it has the opposite effect. People love to have a reason to level you. They don't have to deal with me as directly because they have this disqualifying clause in their perception of me. It's hard for me to think I live in a world where it's not good for you to be candid about something that, in your heart, there's nothing wrong with.

Would you be willing to say you don't use cocaine?

Would I say? I really have decided I have nothing further to say about this that's of any use to me or anyone else.

Some people seem to be more worried about your health than your morals, in terms of your alleged drug use.

Doctor, cure yourself. I feel that most of the time I know what I'm doing. I missed no acting classes during the twelve years I was in class, and I haven't missed a day's work from illness in thirty years.

I'll put my medical charts, my sanity charts up against anybody's. I'm not doing anything wrong. I'm not doing anything but trying to do everything right. I know what's true, who I am. I would like to say I don't care what people think, but I do. Everyone who knows me may think I'm...a tad boyish and fun-loving, but I don't think anybody thinks I have any negative momentum, corrupting philosophies or overly radical moral opinions. As a workman, I'm known as a model of professionalism. I have to put up with being falsely described because it's unhip to bridle at it. Besides, it's just like womanizing. I'm not so sure it ain't good for business.

You started out in Hollywood writing and producing as well as acting, mostly as part of the Roger Corman B-movie stable. You also directed two films, 'Drive, He Said' and 'Goin' South'—neither of which was a big hit but both got some decent reviews. Yet directing doesn't seem to be a burning ambition of yours.

It comes and goes. It's not burning because I don't like criticism. I'm not that good at it yet. If I didn't have another career, I'd be getting more encouragement to do it. I like the action. Directing is a pleasant job to me. I don't have to go through the self-doubt. So what if I showed my stomach? As a director, I'm just there to help people, and I like that. I don't have to question my own greed. I also haven't been writing much, which is one of the banes and torments of my life.

Why aren't you writing?

Can't sit down. Life is not going that way—one of the problems about having a lot of possibilities. In the early days, I was writing for my life. That was big money to get Screen Actors Guild minimum of any kind. I wrote quite a few things during that period. It was improving me as an actor. I started producing, which, again, broadened me as a filmmaker. About that time, I adopted my work credo: You're a tool in the hands of a filmmaker, and you serve the film. If I had no conventional work, I believe I could start from here and have a movie in theaters by the end of the year, doing whatever I had to do. I was the first person of my own generation to be one of those hyphenated people. It wasn't the big leagues, but the action of making a movie is the same. I improvise and write a lot of the things I do. I try to collaborate with everyone on all aspects, but I long ago stopped worrying about who got the credit for the writing.

Are you a self-confident man? What things don't you like about yourself?

Basically, I am self-confident. I don't like it if I'm not creatively free-flowing—it worries me and I wonder, is this the end? Is the well empty now? I worry about the lack of self-confidence of someone who, at times, has to get himself up or hype himself. I wonder why I think I have to do it. Sometimes I'm not able to take in the positive communication that's directed at me because I'm not sure I deserve it. The difference now is, I let all these symptoms of lack of self-confidence just be. I don't let them define me. In other words, I'm more comfortable with my lack of self-confidence, so in a way, it's more self-confidence.

Were you always sure of your talent?

I was at times surer than I am now. Nobody was ever bored with my work, even when I didn't know what I was doing. But I worried about the other side of it. I thought, "Well, anybody can fool these idiots. So where's the million dollars? Why doesn't everybody love me? Where's the ego gratification?" I talk to most good actors, and none of them know they're any good.

Does it matter to you if you win the Best Supporting Actor Oscar for 'Terms of Endearment'?

I told my betting friends before I ever met any of the people involved and read all of the script that they should bet in Las Vegas if they could get a price. That's how much I liked this part. I'll tell you another childish reason why I'd like to win. I think you gotta have nutty goals in life. I'd like to win more Oscars than Walt Disney, and I'd like to win them in every category. And I've been after this category for a while. Unstylistically, I love the Academy Awards. And I'm very Fifties Zen—all tributes are false, all is vanity—but I like seeing a Mount Rushmore of 1984 movie stars in a row for the one night, no matter what nutty ideas they've got. It's fun. Nobody gets hurt. With a couple of exceptions, I've known whether I was going to win or not because I've been following these things since I was a kid. And I've always had a better time when I know I'm not going to win, because then I'm just into the evening. I'm Mr. Hollywood. I love everybody. Of course, I've also done the opposite, gone deciding I'm going to be the worst loser in history and just say outrageous things. Even when I don't go, I love the Oscars. I sit at home and talk about the slime green dress and say, "God, if I ever had this kind of breakdown on television, I'd shoot myself."

How do you spend your money?

I run a few houses [in Aspen and Los Angeles] that are going all the time, so I piss away a lot of money on that. Paintings—but I hate to call them an investment; it's banking rather than investment. I'm not a trader or collector, but I'm aware that I don't throw $10,000 out the window. I own two tickets to the Lakers game that cost about $160 a night even though I'm not there half the year. I follow the theatrical tradition of whoever's making the most money picks up the check. And I like buying presents for people.

Are you happy nowadays?

Extremely. I would love to see a big wide avenue of tremendous productivity inevitably spread before me, but that's not the nature of the thing. Other than that, nobody's mad at me now. I'm in shape. Things are going well for my friends. But then, I've been on bonus time since I was twenty-eight. I had a great enough life for anybody who ever lived up until then, so past that, it's been a *big* bonus.

What's the secret of your appeal?

I don't know. As a teenager and in my early twenties, my friends used to call me "the Great Seducer"—even though they definitely were not sure I was attractive—because I seemed to have something invisible but unfailing.

And now, as an actor, you get paid for it. Seduction is your business.

[*Laughs*] Right. But I don't want to enforce my will on anybody. I want it to be willing. I want it the way it is, and believe me, the way it is [*flashes the killer smile*] is pretty damn good.

BILL MURRAY

by Timothy Crouse

August 16, 1984

I know that you come from Chicago, but I'd be interested to know your social background.

That's tough to call. My father was a lumber-company salesman, and he got promoted to vice president about six months before he died. He was just about to start making the dough.

When did he die?

He died December 1969, when I was seventeen. I was a junior in high school. He never made a lot of money, and we had nine kids in the family, so even a lot of money wouldn't have made much difference. I grew up in a suburb called Wilmette, and people had money there, but we weren't among them.

Did everyone work to help support the family?

Well, it wasn't like that. My father did it, really. We paid our way through high school, 'cause we all went to a Catholic school—except for two of my brothers, who were heathens and went to public school. My brothers and I, we would caddy in the summer, and my sisters would babysit.

Where do you fit into the family constellation?

Fifth. I like to say that they peaked with me, and it was all down-hill after that. I was sort of in an odd spot, but I guess everybody thought they were in an odd spot in our family. I had the misfortune of reaching adolescence at a time when the world turned upside down, and I somehow had to represent the changing society to my parents—with limited success. I was speaking for the entire culture, everyone from Tim Leary to the Airplane.

Were you a problem in school?

The schools are still standing. But I was an underachiever and a screw-off. I remember I took the National Merit Scholarship test, and I scored high enough to win, but when I got the score back, there was an asterisk next to my name, meaning I had qualified for the National Merit Scholarship but wouldn't get one because I wasn't in the top half of my class. Which was devastating, really bad news, 'cause my father would have loved to have heard somebody was going to come up with the money for college.

What was the matter with you in school?

This is the same conversation I had with my teachers then. "What's wrong, Bill? Something bothering you? Something wrong at home?" I don't know, I just didn't care for school much. Studying was boring, I was lazy. I'm still lazy. And I had no interest in getting good grades. In grade school, I was basically causing trouble all the time. But not very serious trouble. When I got to high school, I started to meet a more sophisticated kind of troublemaker. I mean, these guys were really smart—with 148 IQs—and really nuts, the first guys that got kicked out of our school for grass. They just traveled on a different plane than the general Jesuit "all right you'll study tonight, you'll crack them, you'll come in and you'll shut up" sort of attitude. I mean, you couldn't have long hair in our school, so these guys would let their hair grow long and grease it down so it looked like it was short, and you'd see them on the weekends, and you couldn't believe how much hair they had, 'cause they'd washed it. They put up with all the grief that the preppie crowd gave them for being greasers, and they didn't care. Because come the weekend, they were doing a completely different thing than the guys from Wilmette who were trying to drink beer and get high. They didn't have any interest in being part of the social scene at this preppie Catholic school. They were downtown, stoned, listening to blues.

So where were you? Were you downtown at the blues joints?

I was not. I was basically in the middle. It was all right, because I got to look at both sides. I didn't know from downtown and the blues joints, but at the same time, I didn't have enough money to really have a lot of fun. I didn't have a car; I didn't have a driver's license until God knows when. So I basically relied on friends; they were my wheels. Or I'd take a bus or hitchhike. And in the suburbs, that's really lowballing it. Everybody else's parents drove them, or they had their own car. My parents just looked at me: "Your brother hitchhiked to school, and *you'll* hitchhike to school."

Were you close to the people in your family?

I was pretty close to my sister Peggy. She was the one close to me in age.

What has she become?

She's become a parody of herself. No, she lives in the suburbs, and she's got three kids. She's an activist. She's about as active as anybody can get. She drops out of bed rolling. Gets a lot done. She always was that way. So when I went into my bad phase, in college, she had no time for me. At that point, the only decent relationship I had in the house was with the dog.

What was the dog like?

The dog was the greatest dog in the world. Cairn terrier, one of those little dogs. My mother's dog. He was one of those dogs that will play fetch forever. And he just loved to go for walks. I'd take him for walks to Evanston, about a fifteen-mile walk. His feet would be sore, but he would love it. This was my bad period. Everybody had left the house. My oldest brother was in the air force, my second oldest brother was living downtown, one sister was in the convent, another sister had moved away somewhere.

My day would basically begin around twelve or one. I'd wake up, and I'd eat like about eight fried eggs and about half a loaf of toast, and then I'd drink about half a gallon of milk, and then I'd hang around, I'd read, I'd listen to the radio, I'd make a few phone calls. And then, at about five-thirty or six, when my mother was going to come home, I'd split. And I'd come back around four or five in the morning. I'd be lying there in bed, and my mother would scream at me, "I want you here when I get back."

I'd have been downtown, hanging out with my brother Brian Doyle-Murray. Also, I had friends who went to Northwestern. I'd walk the streets of Evanston all night long. Walk home or ride home on the subway in the middle of the night. It was so cold in the winter, I would just jump in front of cars to get them to give me a ride. And they were so scared, so glad I didn't have a gun, that they'd give me a ride home.

When was the first time that you figured out that you might want to be an actor?

I was in *The Caine Mutiny* at school. I played Keefer, a sleaze guy who rats on everybody. It wasn't much of a part. The only great thing about it was that you got to get out of class for a few hours, and that was like getting a three-day leave in the army, because class was hell.

Then they had another show, *The Music Man*. I auditioned for the part of the Music Man because I could sing. I auditioned for the part with two other guys, but someone else got it. Then, we three auditioned for the barbershop quartet, and we got those parts. One day after school, I walked by the school theater, and there were girls in there, and I just walked in. It was an all-boys school, you know, so it was like, *girls*—you wanted to take your clothes off. They were attractive girls, too, and they were wearing almost no clothes, 'cause it was a dance audition. A woman turned around and said, "Now, who's going to audition to be a dancer?" I just jumped up and said, "I'm a dancer." And people were like, "Huh? What? Come on." So I went up onstage. I just wanted to sort of stand behind these girls, really, get as close as I could. I did my little audition, just clowning around, really. The woman said, "Okay, you, you, you and you," and she pointed to me, and I was in. So I told my friends, "Hey, I'm not going to be in the barbershop quartet—I'm a dancer now." They said, "What? *Why?*" I said, "I don't know, man, I don't know. It's just an instinct."

It turned out to be a good move, because the dancers rehearsed at night. The dancers rehearsed at seven-thirty, 'cause the dance instructor was a real dancing teacher, and her only time was between seven-thirty and ten at night. So it meant that I would go home, eat dinner and say, "Mom, I gotta go out." And I would leave the house, which was even better than leaving school. I would get to go out for three hours, and it turned out that the dancers were like the kind of people I was telling you about who were misfits in that school. They were slightly nuts and had different tastes in all areas. We had just incredible times. Sometimes, the dance teacher would say, "I have to leave early," and we'd go, "Oh, that's too bad; that means we just have another hour to drink gin out of Coke bottles and jive around with these girls; that's just too damn bad." And I'd come home half snookered on gin and Coke, and my mom would say, "How was it?" and I'd say, "Uh, I hurt my foot." She was thinking I was Baryshnikov or something, since I was so dedicated. I had the greatest time of my high school career doing that show, so I got hooked on show business.

What was your next step?

Well, I took one acting class in college, 'cause I thought it'd be a piece of cake and there were a lot of girls in it. I knew I could act as good as these girls could, just by seeing them around the coffee shop. And I figured if you were a man and went into a course that was mostly women, you couldn't get a worse grade than your costar. And all these girls were getting good grades because the teacher was kind of working the ropes. He was running "the artist one" by them—you know, "Oh, yes, I am an artist." But when class was over, he was lonely and so on. So long as you never looked funny at him while he was staring at a girl, you got a good grade. But I only hung in there for one semester. That was that.

So still there was no star that you were following.

Still no star I was following. And it really only happened because my brother Brian started acting, and I went and started seeing him. Brian is five years older than I am. After high school—when I was still a grade school punk—he vanished. He went to school out in California for a while and then quit and became a railroad switchman. He put a couple cars into San Francisco Bay once, but I guess all railroad men do something like that. He did a lot of weird things.

When my father died, Brian came back and was supposed to support the family. He got a good job, and if he'd stayed in it, he'd have ended up a very wealthy man. But after six months, he quit the job and went to work at Second City. He had started by taking workshops there, and then he went to work there full-time. That drove my mother completely around the bend. She couldn't believe it.

Brian lived in Old Town, where all the hippies were, and I started hanging out at his place. That's where I met Harold Ramis and John Belushi and Joe Flaherty and Del Close, who directed the show, and Bernie Sahlins, who ran Second City. They thought I was a riot—weekend hippie, you know, going back to my straight life in the 'burbs every night.

I had good friends at Northwestern, and I would drag them down there, and we would all weasel our way into the show for free and watch. After you'd seen the show a hundred times, they couldn't really expect you to pay.

Were you and Brian the family cutups?

No, everybody was a cutup. Everybody was funny.

Was your father funny?

He was real funny, and he was a very tough laugh. He was very tough to make laugh. He was very dry, very dry. He sure as hell wasn't going to laugh unless it was really funny.

My father's father was the real nut. He was crazy till the day he died. He lived to be ninety. He was the kind of guy who had the light-up bow tie. But you'd really have to beat on him to get that bow tie out there. He would do it only at the most tastefully tasteless occasions.

He was a real good man, my grandfather. He always had licorice in his pocket, and he always had a Budweiser and a Camel. He had false teeth. There was always a baby in our family, and he'd always say, "Come here, little baby." And then he'd pop out his teeth exactly like the ghost in *Ghostbusters* and just scare the hell out of the baby. My mother'd get really pissed at him. "Grandpa! How could you scare him like that?" He wouldn't say anything; he'd just drink his beer.

Is your mother funny?

Well, I didn't use to think she was funny, but now I realize she's like completely out of control, nuts. I just never noticed it. I sort of took it all seriously, you know, and acted like it was normal. Now I realize that she's funny to watch at least 60 percent of the time, like the way it's funny to watch a baby panda fall over stuff at the zoo. I finally started taping her phone calls when I worked in *Saturday Night Live*. I couldn't believe that someone could go on like that, and I realized that I'd been listening to that my whole life. I mean, you can really hear her mind work. I steal her stuff all the time.

Can you think of an example?

Well, not really. I mean, I steal so much that sometimes Brian will laugh, and he'll say, "Mother." If I'd started paying attention to my mother when I was twelve instead of trying to sneak out the door and avoid her, not only could I have handled her a little better, but I could have gotten a much better education about women and about people. But it was a fear of the unknown, I guess. Now she's become a show-business mother. She's gone around the bend. I remember when she came out to Hollywood one time, and we took her to the Polo Lounge. Brian called Doug Kenney [cofounder of the *National Lampoon* and cowriter of *National Lampoon's Animal House*] and said, "Page my mother at the Polo Lounge." So this guy who looks like a Mexican general walks through, saying "Lucille Murray, Lucille Murray" at the top of his lungs, and the entire Polo lounge is looking around for Lucille Murray, and she gets up to, like, *visual applause* from the entire crowd. And all of a sudden, she just snapped. She started talking like *Photoplay* magazine circa 1959, about Eddie Fisher and Liz Taylor and Richard Burton and all this stuff. For about six or seven weeks she was completely around the corner. She would call me up and say stuff like, "Well, they have to come to *you* now." I mean, we'd taken her into our dark little world, and now she was a show-business authority. It was insane. This was my mother, this was the woman who'd said to me, "Couldn't you be happy doing community theater?" And now she was cutting my deal for me.

When had she said that about the community theater?

Just in the beginning, after Second City. Maybe she said it to Brian, actually. She didn't see any money in acting, even though Brian had gotten good reviews in Chicago and was really great in the show. Or it may have been in the period when he'd gone out to Hollywood and tried to get different kinds of work and was starving again. She said, "This is not working. Couldn't you try community theater?" She wanted him to do anything to make some dough. "Fine, you're having a ball, but I still have an eight-year-old to feed at home." I mean, how she managed to get all the rest of the family raised is amazing. How my father did it on the money *he* made was amazing.

When did you first work with Belushi?

I might have improvised with him once or twice at Second City. But I didn't work with him until I got to New York. It was on the *National Lampoon Radio Hour.* John was one of the producers. He dragged all these people to New York—Flaherty and Harold and Brian—and got them on the radio. A lot of people stayed at his place. Then he put *The National Lampoon Show* together, and we went on tour—Philadelphia, Ontario, Toronto, Long Island. That was in 1975. Later we opened off-Broadway in a place called the New Palladium. I was Belushi's roommate on the road. We drank a lot of Rolling Rock in those days.

You mean you weren't doing coke all night long?

No, no, no. We didn't have any money to do coke. Coke wasn't a big deal anyway at that time.

Were you doing any drugs?

Oh, smoking grass. But basically we were juicers at that time. At most of these gigs, we got free drinks, so we drank. We were still starving actors, so we had to get whatever perks we could get. We drank Champa Tampas at the New Palladium, champagne and orange juice. It was a special there. And it's a great drink to work on because it's got that sugar pump, and it's nice and cold. And the air-conditioning was no good in that place, and we were just drenched with sweat. After three shows on a Saturday night, you'd literally have to wrap up your shirt in a paper bag and put it inside a plastic bag.

Everybody in the show was good: Belushi, Gilda Radner, my brother Brian, Harold Ramis, Joe Flaherty and later Richard Belzer. One night something happened and I came late, so I got to watch the scenes. And it was the funniest show I've ever seen in my life. They were the funniest people in the world. I was laughing so hard. And I'd already done the show for three and a half months.

How did you get from the Lampoon show to 'Saturday Night Live'?

Well, while we were in the stage show, they started to cast *Saturday Night Live with Howard Cosell* and *Saturday Night Live* at the same time. People from both programs would come and watch our show. We all auditioned for Lorne Michaels of *Saturday Night Live*. Things dragged on and on, and Brian and I and Belushi were going to take the job on *Saturday Night Live with Howard Cosell*, 'cause it didn't look like Michaels was going to hire us. Then Belushi got hired for *Saturday Night Live*, and Brian and Chris Guest and I took a job on *Saturday Night Live with Howard Cosell*. Everybody else was on the other show. So we were on TV, and they were on TV. But they were the show, and we were on with the Chinese acrobats and elephants and all sorts of crazy acts, and we would get cut almost every other week. And then that show got canceled, and we got a job working on a documentary that TVTV was making about the Super Bowl. Michael Shamberg was doing it, and he wanted to have funny people doing funny things with the situation.

Then Shamberg asked me if I wanted to work for him on the next couple of documentaries, so I went out to California for nine months. During which time *Saturday Night Live* kept rolling, and Chevy left the show, and they wanted somebody new, and they called me up. I'd worked with Gilda and Belushi in the Lampoon show; I'd met Danny when we were both in Second City. So they just figured I knew the styles. "We've worked with him. He's all right."

What was it like coming on as the new guy?

Well, it was tough. I had to spend about six months being the second cop, the second FBI guy. The first week I was on they gave me sort of a test. They gave me a lot of stuff to do, and I went crazy, I loved it. I roared. I was there on a look-see basis. I had a three-show deal. It was three shows, see if I can do it. After the first show, Lorne said, "Well, I guess you'll be moving to New York." So that made me feel good, but then for the next six months, I didn't have anything to do. They gave me a lot the first week, and then I realized how competitive it really was.

The hard part was, the writers made the show, and the writers didn't know me, so they'd write for who they knew. If you do a great scene one week, the next week the writers would write for you. If you blew a joke in somebody's sketch, you were history. You were invisible. I blew a joke in one of Anne Beatts' sketches, and she still hasn't forgiven me.

What was the joke, and how did you blow it?

We were four guys running clubs, and I was opening a new bar called the Not Just a Meat-Rack Bar. I blew the line. I had the office right next to hers, and she wouldn't even look at me for at least six weeks. It was like that. If you blew a joke, people didn't trust you. If you blew a joke, what you basically did was you failed to get this writer's joke to 20 million people that were watching the show. Twenty million people would have laughed if you'd said those words properly. It was very serious. I blew one of Michael O'Donoghue's jokes. It was the Burger King sketch. The counterman said, "How do you want yours? We'll make it any way you want it." And I was supposed to say, "I want mine with the blood of a Colombian *cocoi* frog on it." What happened was I went out there and for the heck of it, I wore this brand-new yellow silk baseball jacket that someone had given me. It was the most beautiful thing I've ever seen in my life. I said, "I'll wear it in the sketch. I look so damn good in it."

We'd rehearsed the sketch, done it in blocking, so on and so forth. For the real show, they put stage blood onto this Colombian-frog burger, and whoever it was sprayed blood all over this jacket. I just about went nuts. I guess I blew the first line, then they sprayed the blood all over me. This is my classic *Saturday Night Live* story. They sprayed the blood all over me, completely destroyed the jacket, I had blood all over my hands, and I had two minutes to get out of this clothing. Taking off the jacket, I got blood all over everything. I had two minutes to get on a wig, a mustache on my lips and a pillow in my stomach to look like Walter Cronkite. And all this stuff was being done while the band was playing "Contusion," by Stevie Wonder, at top volume. The makeup guys were fighting about how much gray to put in my hair. I'd blown O'Donoghue's joke, and I was now in danger of blowing myself completely out, because I had this huge pillow and it never fit; the zipper didn't close. There was blood still all over my hands and the wig and everything. The band screeched to a halt, and the guy said, "Five seconds." And I went absolutely crazy. I went absolutely hysterical. I shrieked like a banshee, and the audience started laughing. They said, "This guy's having a breakdown." But then I pulled it together, and I was really funny in the sketch, and that was really when I realized that it could be fun because it was so ridiculous. That was when I finally relaxed. But I had to blow a big joke in order to do it.

I heard that you had to agree to do 'Ghostbusters' in order to get the backing for 'The Razor's Edge.' Is that how it worked out?

What happened was, John Byrum and I had *The Razor's Edge* in a developmental stage at Columbia—they'd given us a little dough to write the screenplay, but nobody was getting into work early to find out how the rewrites were going. Then Dan Aykroyd called me up with this *Ghostbusters* idea, and I said, "Yeah, this is great." He sent me about seventy-five pages, and within an hour there was a deal. They had a producer, they had a caterer, they had a director, they had everything. But it wasn't at any particular studio yet; it was just a project floating in space. Then all of a sudden, all of the studios found out about it, and they all wanted it. So Dan said, "Well, we gotta get going on this." I said, "Well, you know, I'm really trying to get this other thing done. I'm trying to convince the studio to give us the go." And he said, "Well, tell 'em they can have *Ghostbusters* if they do *The Razor's Edge*." So, another forty-five minutes later, we had a caterer and a producer and a director for *The Razor's Edge*. We went out and shot it last summer. Columbia started getting impatient about *Ghostbusters*. All the time we were in Ladakh we'd get these messages that were like three days old, saying, "Is Bill finished? He's supposed to be doing *Ghostbusters* on the twenty-fifth." I made the mistake of calling America from Agra, that white building—you know, the Taj Mahal. There's a phone booth at the Taj. They said, "You gotta get right back." I wanted to take ten days off. I was so tired that I couldn't even get out of the hotel room in Delhi for four or five days. I didn't really do anything except sleep. Then I found out that they were going to have the rough version of *The Razor's Edge* ready by the end of the week, so I decided to fly to London and see it. Flew to London, saw it. The next day I got on the Concorde, flew to New York and went from the airport to the set on Madison and Sixty-Second Street. I weighed about 171 pounds, I think. I'd lost 35 pounds. So I started eating right away [*laughs*]. A production assistant said, "Do you want a cup of coffee?" And I said, "Yeah, and I want a couple of doughnuts, too."

For the first few weeks, I was getting beaten to go to work. It was like, "Where's Bill?" "Oh, he's asleep." Then they'd send three sets of people to knock on the door and say, "They really want you." I'd stumble out and do something and then go back to sleep. I kept thinking to myself, "Ten days ago I was up there working with the high lamas in a *gompa,* and here I am removing ghosts from drugstores and painting slime on my body." It was kind of tough to get into it for about a month. I thought, "What the hell am I doing here?" I mean, you'd look around on the set in Ladakh, and there were thirty-five monks looking at you, just looking at you. And you realized that they were looking for a reason. It was a reminder all the time. A reminder that you're a man and you're going to die, so you'd better not waste this time here. So when I got to New York, I would be sitting there looking across the street, and there'd be the entire staff of Diana Ross Productions waving out of the window, then coming over to get autographs. That was the first day on the job. All of a sudden, it was like a whole different world. But after a while it became nice, working on the movie, and I sort of got into the rhythm of Hollywood again, as opposed to Ladakh. It was fun being with Dan and Harold Ramis. Acting-wise, they're fantastic. But also, they're very much aware of the situation, that you are just a guy, and then for thirty seconds or a minute and a half, you're a movie star, and then you're a guy again. And then you're a movie star again. They know the difference, and they see the hilarious things that are happening all around, while you're supposedly being a movie star.

Had you had time to think about your part in 'Ghostbusters' at all? I mean, there you were, wham, off the 'Concorde' onto the set.

Not a bit. I just did it. Harold and Dan wrote the script. Wherever there wasn't a line, they'd say, "Well, we gotta have a line here." We just made stuff up. When I saw the movie the other night, I realized more of it was improvised than I thought. Especially the action stuff.

I'd never worked on a movie where the script was good. *Stripes* and *Meatballs,* we rewrote the script every single day. I think most movie actors change their lines nowadays. I didn't use to think so. Then I worked for Dustin Hoffman [in *Tootsie*]. Dustin changed all his lines a lot of the time. He gave a different performance every single take. He shot five different movies. Even if he didn't change the lines, he would change the meaning. How they cut that movie, I don't know. I think it's the only way to work. I don't believe that you can give the same performance every take. It's physically impossible, so why bother? If you don't do what is happening at that moment, then it's not real. Then you're holding something back.

Are you fed up with comedy?

I think all the comedies that we all do, they all get better. And even though they're not perfect or maybe silly to some people, we learn each time about how to do it. People don't expect master carpenters to get it right after they do six chairs, and we've only done six movies. You've got to do a lot of them, and it takes time, there's just so much pressure because the money is so big. There's only so many movies made a week. I mean, in the old days, I would have made fifty-five movies by now, and I'd have worked with a lot of people and learned a lot. As it is, I've worked with six directors, seven directors, eight directors, something like that. You know, that's peanuts compared to what the old guys did. And I'd like to work with a lot more actors, too, though it's the directors that really teach you something, and cinematographers. Those are the guys that know. There's like a pure knowledge there; there's no clowning around. They either know it or they don't. You can't lie about it.

Are you expecting to do more serious parts in the future? Does that depend on whether 'The Razor's Edge' is a success?

Well, to a certain extent, it does depend on whether *The Razor's Edge* is a success or a failure, because if directors see it and they say, "That guy can act a little," then I'll get offered jobs from serious directors. As it is now, I'm in the phone book under *K* for Komedy.

CLINT EASTWOOD
by Tim Cahill

July 4, 1985

You are, by some accounts, the world's most popular movie star. Do you sometimes wake up in the morning, look in the mirror and say, "Can that possibly be me?" I mean, does it surprise you?

If I thought about it enough, it might. Yeah, I guess so. I guess you'd look back and say, "How did a kid from Oakland get this far?" I'm sure other people do that to some degree. It's like waking up with a hooker—how the hell did I get here?

Let's start with 'A Fistful of Dollars.' How did that come about?

Well, at that time I'd done *Rawhide* for about five years. The agency called and asked if I was interested in doing a western in Italy and Spain. I said, "Not particularly." I was pretty westerned out on the series. They said, "Why don't you give the script a quick look?" Well, I was curious, so I read it, and I recognized it right away as *Yojimbo*, a Kurosawa film I had liked a lot. When I'd seen it years before, I thought, "Hey, this film is really a western." Nobody in the States had the nerve to make it, though, and when I saw that someone somewhere did have the nerve, I thought, "Great."

Sergio [Leone] had only directed one other picture, but they told me he had a good sense of humor, and I liked the way he interpreted the *Yojimbo* script. And I had nothing to lose, because I had the series to go back to as soon as the hiatus was over. So I felt, "Why not?" I'd never been to Europe. That was reason enough to go.

You've said that in the original script, the Man with No Name shot off his mouth more than his gun.

The script was very expository, yea. It was an outrageous story, and I thought there should be much more mystery to the person. I kept telling Sergio, "In a real A picture, you let the audience think along with the movie; in a B picture, you explain everything." That was my way of selling my point. For instance, there was a scene where he decides to save the woman and the child. She says, "Why are you doing this?" In the script he just goes on forever. He talks about his mother, all kinds of subplots that come out of nowhere, and it goes on and on and on. I thought that was not essential, so I just rewrote the scene the night before we shot it.

Okay, the woman asks, "Why are you doing this?" and he says...

"Because I knew someone like you once and there was nobody there to help."

So you managed to express ten pages of dialogue in a single sentence.

We left it oblique and let the audience wonder: "Now wait a minute, what happened?" You try to let people reach into the story, find things in it, choice little items that they enjoy. It's like finding something you've worked and hunted for, and it's much more enjoyable than having some explanation slapped into your face like a wet fish.

So you have a lot of faith in your audience.

You have to. You don't play down to people, you don't say, "I'd better make this a little simpler, a little more expository." For instance, in

Josey Wales, when he rides off at the end of the picture, the editor and I had wanted to superimpose the girl's face over him. He said, "We want the audience to know that he's going back to her." Well, we all know he's going back. If he rides off on the other side of town, the audience will say, "Well, he's gonna turn left." It's really looking down on an audience to tell them something they already know. Or tell them something they can draw in because it arises out of the story. I try to make that part of their job.

To...

To think about it a little bit.

You did two more of the Italian westerns with Leone: 'For a Few Dollars More' and "The Good, the Bad and the Ugly."

Yeah. The other two, the productions were glossier, more refined. The stories didn't mean a whole lot. They were just a lot of vignettes all shuffled together. I enjoyed them, they were fun to do. Escapism. And the American western at that point was in a dull period. But when Sergio approached me about being in some of the subsequent westerns, I thought it would be going too far. So I came back to Hollywood and did *Hang 'Em High.* Sergio was interested in expanding the size and scope of his films, and I was more interested in the people and the story line. I guess, selfishly, because I am an actor, I wanted to do something with more character study.

You've described yourself as introverted. Do you think that's because you moved around so much as a kid?

Maybe, yes. We moved around California a lot. We lived in Redding, Sacramento, Hayward. My parents were married around 1929, right at the beginning of the Depression. It was a tough period for everybody, and especially a young guy like my dad who was just starting out. In those days, people struggled for jobs. Sometimes jobs didn't pan out, or they couldn't afford to keep you. We drove around in an old Pontiac, or something like that, towing a one-wheel trailer. We weren't itinerant. It wasn't *The Grapes of Wrath,* but it wasn't uptown either.

It gives you a sort of conservative background, being raised in an area when everything was scarce. Once, I remember, we moved from Sacramento to Pacific Palisades because my father had gotten a gas-station attendant's job. It's still there, the station. It's at Highway 101 and Sunset Boulevard.

Were you involved in any school activities?

Yeah. I played a little basketball. Some football in junior high. I didn't really get involved in team sports, because we moved so much. I did some competitive swimming, and one of the schools I went to had a great gymnastics program, so I diddled with that for a while. I wasn't particularly suited for it, because I was so tall, but I liked it.

I suppose one of the biggest things when I was a kid—I always liked jazz. A wide spectrum of jazz. Back in the Forties and Fifties I listened to Brubeck and Mulligan. And I loved Ellington and Basie. I'd get books on everybody: Bix Beiderbecke, King Oliver, Buddy Bolden. I used to be very knowledgeable.

Then, up through the Forties, I used to go to these Jazz at the Philharmonic things. One time, they had Coleman Hawkins, Lester Young, Charlie Parker and a whole group of classic players. In fact, nowadays, when I talk to composers that are maybe ten years younger than I am, they're all jealous about that concert: "You saw those guys live!"

You play some jazz piano yourself.

Yeah, when I was a kid, I played. Fooled around with some other instruments, but I was lazy. I didn't really go for it. I just started again in the last few years. I've been diddling around with composition.

Five or six things. I used one as my daughter's theme in *Tightrope*, and I also did the theme for the young girl in *Pale Rider*.

I have some regrets that I didn't follow up on music, especially when I hear people who play decently. I played on one cut of the album for *City Heat*. After the session, Pete Jolly and Mike Lang and I were all talking about how we started out playing piano. We all started the exact same way, only those guys went on to really play. We began by playing blues: blues figures at parties. I was such a backward kid at that age, but I could sit down at a party and play the blues. And the gals would come around the piano, and all of a sudden you had a date.

You had a country hit, "Barroom Buddies," a duet with Merle Haggard. When did you get interested in country music?

Well, I think you can say that Merle Haggard had a hit and sort of dragged me along. I was never terribly knowledgeable about country music. The first real good taste of it I got was when I was eighteen or nineteen, working in a pulp mill in Springfield, Oregon. It was always wet, really depressing. Wintertime. Dank. I really didn't know anyone, and someone told me to go out to this place where there was a lot of country music. I wasn't very interested, but this guy told me there were a lot of girls there. So I went. I saw Bob Wills and the Texas Playboys. Unlike most country bands, they had brass and reeds and they played country swing. They were good. It surprised me a little bit, how good they were. Also, there were a lot of girls there, which didn't surprise me at all. So I guess you could say that lust expanded my musical horizons.

Why didn't you follow up on the music?

I was going to. I tried to enroll in Seattle University, where they had a good music program. I got my draft notice before I got there, though, and ended up at Fort Ord [California]. And I guess I just failed away from music.

I served my two years and went down to L.A. City College, where I enrolled in business administration. In the service I had met some guys who were actors—Martin Milner, David Janssen—and when we got out, a cinematographer got me a screen test. I got an offer to go under contract with Universal, seventy-five bucks a week to start. They threw me out a year and a half later. But it was a pretty good deal for a young guy. We had acting classes every day.

Is that when you realized that being introverted could be an asset for an actor? That you could play on it?

I don't know if I played on it consciously. I know that for many years before I became known for the way I act now, I played characters that were not terribly talkative. Economical characters. Some books—even Stanislavsky's people—discuss the fact that sometimes less can be best. Sometimes you can tell more with economy than you can with excess gyration.

The *Rawhide* series was a great training ground. All of a sudden, everything you ever studied about being an actor you could put into play every day. It's one thing to work for a week in a Francis the Talking Mule picture—which was how it had been going for me—and another thing to be doing it all day for eight years.

It's like the story of the great classical trumpet player they found one day playing in a baseball orchestra at Wrigley Field. Somebody recognized him and said, "My God, Maestro, what is the greatest classical trumpet player in the world doing playing in a baseball band?" He said, "You must play every day."

In *Rawhide,* I got to play every day. It taught me how to pick up and run, how to make things up, wing things in there.

The 'New York Review of Books' recently ran an article about you that said, "What is most distinctive about Eastwood . . . is how effectively he struggles against absorption into mere genre, mere style, even while appearing, with his long-boned casualness and hypnotic presence, to be nothing but style." Do you want to comment on that?

Well, yeah, style. Take guys like Kirk Douglas and Burt Lancaster. They're terrific actors, but their style is more aggressive. Both of them did some marvelous things and some films that weren't big hits but were great all the same: Douglas in *Lonely Are the Brave* and *Paths of Glory;* Lancaster in *Trapeze*. But their style was a little different than, say, Gary Cooper's or Henry Fonda's, because those guys were more laid-back, more introverted, and you were always leaning forward, wondering what they were thinking. With the Lancaster-Douglas school, there was never any doubt. Fonda or Cooper: you were never quite sure with them. They had a mysterioso quality.

Which is something you strive for: that little taste of ambiguity.

Exactly.

Let's go over a few of your films. 'Dirty Harry.'

There was something there I felt some people missed. One critic said Dirty Harry shot the guy at the end with such glee that he enjoyed it. There was no glee about it at all, there was a sadness about it. Watch the film again and you'll see that.

'Every Which Way but Loose.'

All of a sudden Norman Mailer comes out and says he likes this film, and because he's such a well-thought-of writer, people think, "Wait a second, maybe that wasn't such a bad movie after all." I thought it was kind of a hip script myself when I read it. Here's a guy pouring his heart out to an ape, and losing the girl. I like the correlation with some of my westerns, too. The guy purposely loses the big fight at the end because he doesn't want to go around being the fastest gun in the West.

'Bronco Billy.'

It's about the American Dream, and Billy's dream that he fought so hard for. And it's all in the context of this outdated Wild West show that has absolutely no chance of being a hit. But it's sweet. It's pure.

In the pivotal scene, Billy allows himself to be humiliated by the sheriff rather than allow his friend to be arrested. That played so against your established image, it must have been fun to do.

Really fun. It was suggested that Billy come back at the end and punch this guy out. That would have ruined the picture, the whole theme of loyalty. Billy doesn't approve of this kid being a deserter, and he doesn't know enough to intellectualize what his friend's feelings were about the war in Vietnam. He just knows he doesn't approve but he's going to stick by his friend. Now if Billy had come back and kicked the crap out of the sheriff at the end, it would have wrecked all that.

There's no real excuse for being successful enough as an actor to do what you want and then selling out. You do it pure. You don't try to adapt it, make it commercial. It's not *Dirty Bronco Billy*.

'Honkytonk Man.'

Red Stovall is based a bit on some self-destructive people I've known. He's wild and funny, but he's been a coward in his time. He won't face up to his ambitions. He's not that great a singer, but he writes some interesting things. When he gets his moments, he's already destroyed himself.

And the studio suggested that it might be a good idea if Red didn't die in the end?

I resisted that.

Your new one, 'Pale Rider.'

It's a western. One of the earliest films in America was a western: *The Great Train Robbery*. If you consider film an art form, as some people do, then the western would be a truly American art form, much as jazz is. In the Sixties, American westerns were stale, probably because the great directors—Anthony Mann, Raoul Walsh, John Ford—were no longer working a lot. Then the Italian western came along, and we did very well with those; they died of natural causes. Now I think it's time to analyze the classic western. You can still talk about sweat and hard work, about the spirit, about the love for the land and ecology. And I think you can say all these things in the western, in the classic mythological form.

You're not generally credited with having any sense of humor, yet certain of your films get big laughs in all the right places. The first half of 'Honkytonk Man,' for instance, was very funny.

That's the way it was designed: a humorous story that becomes a tragedy. A lot of the humor is not in what you say but in how you react. Comedians are expert at that. Jackie Gleason in *The Honeymooners:* Alice zaps him, and his reaction—just look at his face—cracks you up. Jack Benny could do that. Comedy isn't necessarily all dialogue. Think of Buster Keaton: the poker face and all this chaos going on all around him. Sometimes it's a question of timing, of the proper rhythm.

You have a reputation for shooting your films quickly and bringing them in under budget. Do you think that this has anything to do with having grown up in the Depression?

I would like to say it's just good business, but it may be that. It may be a background of not wanting to see waste.

There's a rumor that people work quickly on your sets because you don't provide chairs.

That rumor derived from some comment I made. Someone asked why I like shooting on location as opposed to in the studio. I said,

"In the studio, everyone's looking around for a chair. On location, everyone's working." But there are chairs on the set and on location.

You also have a reputation for bringing in bright or underappreciated talent. 'Thunderbolt and Lightfoot,' for instance, was Michael Cimino's first film. Some people might say that you do that because you get these folks cheap.

Nothing's cheap, and I don't think I'd cut off my nose to spite my face. I don't think I'd get somebody cheap just because I thought he was cheap. I think I'd want the film to be the best possible. Otherwise you're selling yourself short. An awful lot of directors are expensive, but you don't know how they got to be that way. Sometimes it's just a matter of salesmanship and agenting.

I haven't worked with a lot of big-name directors, but I came up during an era when they were all beginning to retire. I never worked with Hitchcock or Wyler or Stevens or Capra or Hawks or Walsh. I missed all that.

I suppose the most expensive director I've worked with is Don Siegel. I think I learned more about directing from him than from anybody else. He taught me to put myself on the line. He shoots lean, and he shoots what he wants. He knew when he had it, and he doesn't need to cover his ass with a dozen different angles.

I learned that you have to trust your instincts. There's a moment when an actor has it, and he knows it. Behind the camera you can feel that moment even more clearly. And once you've got it, once you feel it, you can't second-guess yourself. If I would go around and ask everyone on the set how it looked, eventually someone would say, "Well, gee, I don't know, there was a fly 600 feet back." Somebody's always going to find a flaw, and pretty soon that flaw gets magnified and you're all back to another take. Meanwhile, everyone's forgotten that there's certain focus on things, and no one's going to see that fly, because you're using a 100-mm lens. But that's what you can do. You can talk yourself in or out of anything. You can find a million reasons why something didn't work. But if it feels right, and it looks right, it works.

Without sounding like a pseudointellectual dipshit, it's my responsibility to be true to myself. If it works for me, it's right. When I start choosing wrong, I'll step back and let someone else do it for me.

ERIC CLAPTON

by Robert Palmer

June 20, 1985

Since we're starting at the beginning, why don't you tell me a bit about the town of Ripley, where you grew up.

It's only about thirty miles outside of London, but it's very country—Ripley is not even a town, it's a village with farms all around it. And very few people ever leave there. They usually stay, get jobs, get married.

What kind of music did you hear when you were growing up?

Pop music, first. Mostly songs that were still hanging over from wartime; "We'll Meet Again," that sort of thing, melodic pop music.

There was a funny Saturday-morning radio program for children, with this strange person, Uncle Mac. He was a very old man with one leg and a strange little penchant for children. He'd play things like "Mule Train," and then every week he'd slip in something like a Buddy Holly record or a Chuck Berry record. And the first blues I ever heard was on that program; it was a song by Sonny Terry and Brownie McGhee, with Sonny Terry howling and playing the harmonica. It blew me away. I was ten or eleven.

When was the first time you actually saw a guitar?

Hmmm...I remember the first rock & roll I ever saw on TV was Jerry Lee Lewis doing "Great Balls of Fire." And that threw me; it was like seeing someone from outer space. And I realized suddenly that here I was in this village that was never going to change, yet there on TV was something out of the future. And I wanted to go there! Actually, he didn't have a guitarist, but he had a bass player, playing a Fender Precision bass, and I said, "That's a guitar." I didn't know it was a bass guitar, I just knew it was a guitar, and again I thought, "That's the future. And that's what I want." After that I started to build one, tried to carve a Stratocaster out of a block of wood, but I didn't know what to do when I got to the neck and frets and things.

I was living with my grandparents, who raised me, and since I was the only child in the family, they used to spoil me something terrible. So I badgered them until they bought me a plastic Elvis Presley guitar. Of course, it could never stay in tune, but I could put on a Gene Vincent record, look in the mirror and mime.

When I was fourteen or fifteen, they gave me a real guitar, an acoustic, but it was so hard to play, I actually didn't even try for a while. And pretty soon the neck began to warp. But I did invent chords. I invented E, and I invented A. I thought I had discovered something incredible. And then I put it down again, in my later teens, because I started to become interested in being an artist. The bohemian existence beckoned; actually, the good-life part of it beckoned more than the work. And at that point, when I was about sixteen, I started making weekend trips to London.

From hanging around in coffee bars and so on, I met a certain crowd of people, some of whom played guitar. One was Long John Baldry, who was then playing a twelve-string, doing folk and blues. Every Friday night, there would be a meeting at someone's house, and people would turn up with the latest imported records from the States. And shortly, someone showed up with that Chess album, *The Best of Muddy Waters,* and something by Howlin' Wolf. And that was it for me. Then I sort of took a step back, discovered Robert Johnson and made the connection to Muddy. For me, it was very serious, what I heard. And I began to realize that I could only listen to this music with people who were equally serious about it.

Did getting involved with this music send you back to the guitar?

Yeah, Baldry and these other people would just sit in a corner, playing folk and blues while everyone else was drinking and getting stoned. And I saw that it was possible to actually, if you like, get on with it—to just sit in the corner playing and not have everyone looking at you. I saw that it wasn't something to be frightened of or shy in doing. So I started doing it myself.

Playing what, folk blues?

Yeah, things by Big Bill Broonzy and Ramblin' Jack Elliott, "Railroad Bill," "Cocaine." But then I was drawn more and more toward electric blues, along with a few friends, a select few people. And, of course, then we had to be purists and seriously dislike other things.

When I was about seventeen, I got booted out of art school, and I did manual labor for about a year for pocket money. And during that time, I met up with a guy, Tom McGuinness, who was going to get involved with a band, and I knew just about enough to be able to play and keep up that end of it. So I got involved in that band, the Roosters, and that was a good feeling.

What kind of music did the Roosters play?

We did "Boom Boom" and a couple of other John Lee Hooker things, "Hoochie Coochie Man" and some others by Muddy, I think. We did whatever we could get on records, really, on up to rock & roll things like "Slow Down" by Larry Williams, because you had to have the odd rock & roll number in there.

Then Tom McGuinness brought in "Hideaway" by Freddie King,

and the B side was "I Love the Woman," which is still one of the greatest. And that's the first time I heard that electric-lead-guitar style, with the bent notes—T-Bone Walker, B.B. and Freddie King, that style of playing. Hearing that Freddie King single was what started me on my path.

According to rock historian Pete Frame's family tree of your various bands, the Roosters only lasted from January to August 1963.

Yeah, some of the people had day jobs that were more important to them than the band. Practical considerations brought the band down. But by that time, I had no other interests at all. I practiced a lot.

After the Roosters, I got a job with Tom McGuinness in another band, Casey Jones and the Engineers. That folded pretty soon, too, and then I heard the Yardbirds had started up.

The Stones had been playing at the Crawdaddy Club, and when they moved on, the next band in was the Yardbirds. I had met two guys from the Yardbirds at some bohemian parties, and at that time they were playing music by Django Reinhardt, "Nuages" and so on. We became friends. I went down to hear them at the Crawdaddy and was fairly critical of them, especially the guitarist they had. And I don't really remember how it came about, but I replaced him. I was watching one week and playing the next.

Were you really listening to nothing but the blues?

No, I listened to some modern jazz. I would put on a John Coltrane album after a John Lee Hooker album. I don't think I understood Coltrane, but I listened to him a lot. I loved his tone, the feel of it.

Were the Yardbirds' gigs with Sonny Boy Williamson the first chance you had to play with an American bluesman?

Yes, and I think that's when I first realized that we weren't really being true to the music—when Sonny Boy came over and we didn't know how to back him up. It was frightening, really, because this man was real and we weren't. He wasn't very tolerant, either. He did take a shine to us after a while, but before that he put us through some bloody hard paces. In the first place, he expected us to know his tunes. He'd say, "We're going to do 'Don't Start Me to Talkin''' or 'Fattening Frogs for Snakes,'" and then he'd kick it off, and of course, some of the members of this particular band had never heard these songs.

There was a certain attitude in the band, a kind of pride in being English and white and being able to whip up a crowd on our own, and there was a sort of resistance toward what we were being asked to do—why should we have to study this man's records? Even I felt a little bit like that, because we were coming face-to-face with the reality of this thing, and it was a lot different from buying a record that you could take off when you felt like it. So we were all terrified of him, me most of all I think, because I was really making an attempt. Years later, Robbie Robertson of the Band told me that Sonny Boy had gone back to the South and hung out with them and had said he'd just been over playing with these white guys who didn't know how to play anything at all.

Yeah, Robertson once told me that Sonny Boy had said, "Those Englishmen want to play the blues so bad—and they play it so bad!"

Right. At the time, I thought we'd done pretty well. But by that time, the momentum of the band was toward becoming a pop group, and this man arrived and took it all back down to the basic blues. And I had to almost relearn how to play. It taught me a lot; it taught me the value of that music, which I still feel.

What caused you to leave the Yardbirds just when they were on the brink of success? You're supposed to have been grossed out by that first pop hit, "For Your Love."

Yeah. At a certain point we started getting package tours, with the Ronettes, Billy J. Kramer, the Kinks, the Small Faces, lots of others, and we lost our following in the clubs. We decided to get suits, and I actually designed suits for us all. Then we did the Beatles' Christmas show, and at that point we really began to *feel* the lack of a hit. We'd be on for twenty minutes or half an hour, and either you were *very* entertaining or you did your hits. A lot of times the raveup bit got us through, and a lot of times it didn't. It became very clear that if the group was going to survive and make money, it would have to be on a popular basis. We couldn't go back to the clubs, because everyone had got that taste and seen what fun it would be to be famous.

So a lot of songs were bandied about, and Giorgio [Gromelsky, Yardbirds manager] came up with a song by Otis Redding. I thought that would make a great single because it was still R&B and soul, and we could do it really funky. Then Paul [Samwell-Smith, Yardbirds bassist] got the "For Your Love" demo, and he heard it with harpsichord. Whoa, harpsichord. Where does that leave me? Twelve-string guitar, I suppose. So we went in the studio to do both songs, but we did "For Your Love" first. Everyone was so bowled over by the obvious commerciality of it that we didn't even get to do the Otis Redding song, and I was very disappointed, *disillusioned* by that. So my attitude within the group got really sour, and it was kind of hinted that it would be better for me to leave. 'Cause they'd already been to see Jeff Beck play, and at the time he was far more adaptable than I was. I was withdrawing into myself, becoming intolerable, really, dogmatic. So they kind of asked me to leave, and I left and felt a lot better for it.

Is this the time when you did nothing but practice every day for a year? Or is that story apocryphal?

Well, it wasn't a year, it was only a few months. I had never really practiced seriously, just practiced as I worked, until I got edged out of the Yardbirds. Then I went up to Oxford to stay with Ben Palmer, who had played piano in the Roosters and was a close friend, and during that time I began to think seriously about playing blues. And then while I was there, I got a call from John Mayall, who'd heard I was serious, if you like, and not money orientated or popularity orientated, and he asked me to come and audition, or just come around and play. I got the job, and I actually got to feel like I was a key member of that band from the minute I walked in. Right away, I was choosing material for the band to do.

And Mayall went along with this? He has a reputation for being kind of autocratic.

Well, I think in me he met a soul mate who liked the same things. With the guitarist he'd had before, he hadn't been able to do certain numbers he wanted to do — the Otis Rush songs, for example, which I really wanted to do. We were really together on that.

Otis Rush is very intense. What did you think when you first heard him?

I always liked the wilder guys. I liked Buddy Guy, Freddie King and Otis Rush because they sounded like they were *really on the edge,* like they were barely in control and at any time they could hit a really bad note and the whole thing would fall apart — but, of course, they didn't. I liked that a lot more than B.B. I got into B.B. later, when I realized that polish was something, too.

You were with Mayall for a while and then, before making the 'Bluesbreakers' album, you left to go to Greece. What was that all about?

I was living in a place with some pretty mad people — great people, really. We were just drinking wine all day long and listening to jazz and blues, and we decided to pool our money, buy an estate wagon and take off round the world. The job with Mayall had become a job, and I wanted to go have some fun as well. So we ended up in Greece, playing blues, a couple of Rolling Stones songs, anything to get by. We met this club proprietor who hired us to open for a Greek band that played Beatles songs.

I was stuck there, with this Greek band. A couple of weeks of that, and I escaped somehow, headed back up here.

When I got back with Mayall, Jack Bruce was on bass, and we hit it off really well. Then he left to go with Manfred Mann, and Mayall got John McVie back. I decided that playing with Jack was more exciting. There was something creative there. Most of what we were doing with Mayall was imitating the records we got, but Jack had something else — he had no reverence for what we were doing, and so he was composing new parts as he went along playing. I literally had never heard that before, and it took me someplace else. I thought, well, if he could do that, and I could, and we could get a drummer...I could be Buddy Guy with a composing bass player. And that's how Cream came about.

But before that happened, you made the 'Bluesbreakers' album, which really has become a classic. How do you feel about it now?

At the time, I just thought it was a record of what we were doing every night in the clubs, with a few contrived tiffs we made up kind of as afterthoughts, to fill out some of the things. It isn't any great achievement. It wasn't until I realized that the album was actually turning people on that I began to look at it differently.

Were you already thinking about starting Cream, or at least starting a band with Jack Bruce?

Well, after I had the experience of meeting and playing with Jack, the next thing that happened was that Ginger Baker came to this John Mayall gig. We'd worked the same circuits as the band Ginger was in, the Graham Bond Organisation, and I'd liked their music, except it was too jazzy for me — the jazz side of Ray Charles, Cannonball Adderley, that's what they were playing. But then Ginger came backstage after this Mayall gig and said to me, "We're thinking of breaking up, and I like the way you play. Would you like to start a band?" I said, "Yeah, but I'd have to have Jack Bruce as well," and he kind of backed

off that. It turned out that he and Jack were really chemically opposite, they were just *polarized,* always getting into fights. But we talked
some more, and then we had a meeting at Ginger's house, where he
and Jack immediately had an argument. I had no foresight whatsoever; I didn't think it was really serious. I left Mayall pretty soon after
that.

*What were your original ideas for Cream? You became known for those long
jams, but on your first album, 'Fresh Cream,' there was a lot of country blues
and other songs, all of them pretty compact.*

I think our ideas about what we were supposed to be were pretty
abstract. At first, I was throwing in Skip James and Robert Johnson
songs, Jack was composing and Ginger was composing. The American thing with "flower power" was filtering over, and I started seeing us as the London version of all that. I had an idea of how we
could look good as well as be a good band. We were just scrambling
for the forefront, and we didn't get much feedback until we played
in front of an audience. That was when we realized that they actually wanted to go off somewhere. And we had the power to take
them.

*I heard Cream play one night at the Cafe Au Go Go in Greenwich Village,
on your first trip over to the U.S. It was really loud — big stacks of amps in
this little room! And you'd go off into these twenty-minute jams. I wasn't
really aware that Jack and Ginger had such strong jazz backgrounds, but it
did seem like they were going off into a much freer thing and sort of playing
around your blues, which was like the music's backbone. Were you comfortable in that role?*

Very occasionally, when my purist side got the better of me, I might
get a little insecure. But if you think about it, if I had formed a trio,
say, with a blues drummer and a blues bass player, we would have
gone on imitating, as I had been doing with John Mayall. I would
never have learned how to play anything of my own. In Cream, I

was forced to try and improvise; whether I made a good job of it a lot of the time is debatable.

The three of us were on the road all the time, trusting one another, living in one another's hearts, and I found I was *giving*, you know, more than I had ever done before, and having faith in them. Jack is such a musical genius, there was no way he could be wrong about anything. I had to trust these people, so I did, I went with it. Of course, when we got back to our hotel rooms, we would all be listening to something different. And then I would sometimes have doubts, because a part of me still wanted to duplicate. That's the fear, you know, the fear of actually expressing and being naked.

There seems to have been a change in your listening tastes between the recording of 'Fresh Cream' and the second album, 'Disraeli Gears.' You started using some effects, like wah-wah, and you must have been very impressed by Albert King, because your solos on "Strange Brew" and several other songs were really pure Albert.

The big change was that Hendrix had arrived. Cream was playing at London Polytechnic, a college, and a friend brought this guy who was dressed up really freaky. This was Jimi. He spent a lot of time combing his hair in the mirror. Very cute but at the same time very genuine and very shy. I took to him straightaway, just as a man. Then he asked if he could jam, and he came up and did "Killing Floor," the Howlin' Wolf tune. And it blew me away. I was floored by his technique and his choice of notes, of sounds. Ginger and Jack didn't take to it kindly. They thought he was trying to upstage me. But I fell in love, straightaway. He became a soul mate for me and, musically, what I wanted to hear.

We were hanging out in some London clubs not long after that, and we started listening to the singles Stax was putting out by Albert King. We were both very, very attracted by that.

Even after you'd been hanging out with Hendrix, your playing and his were still really different.

He was the leader of his band, and that was that. What I felt with Cream was that I owed it to the other two not to try and dominate too much, even though I did. Apart from that, I didn't—and still don't—like to rely on effects that I can't create myself. It's what you're going to *play* that matters.

This was the period when you ascended to godhood.

All during Cream I was riding high on the "Clapton is God" myth that had been started up. I was flying high on an ego trip; I was pretty sure I was the best thing happening that was popular. Then we got our first kind of bad review, which, funnily enough, was in *Rolling Stone* [RS 10, May 11, 1968, by Jon Landau]. The magazine ran an interview with us in which we were really praising ourselves, and it was followed by a review that said how boring and repetitious our performance had been. And it was true! The ring of truth just knocked me backward; I was in a restaurant and I fainted. And after I woke up, I immediately decided that that was the end of the band.

There toward the end, we'd been flying with blinkers for so long, we weren't aware of the changes that were taking place musically. New people were coming up and growing, and we were repeating ourselves, living on legend, a year or two years out of date.

We didn't really have a *band* with Cream. We rarely played as an ensemble; we were three virtuosos, all of us soloing all the time.

You must have been in an acid phase toward the end of Cream. Some of the playing had that sort of . . . flavor.

Yeah, we did a lot of acid, took a lot of trips, in our spare time. And we did play on acid a couple of times.

There are still plenty of people around who think Cream was rock's absolute zenith. A lot of what's now called heavy metal came out of stuff you were doing, by way of Led Zeppelin. What can you say to those people?

You have to move on.

I know you haven't had much good to say about Blind Faith, but I actually think the album holds up really well.

Well, there was a lack of direction in Blind Faith, or a reticence to actually declare among ourselves where we were going. Because it seemed to be enough just to be making the money, and that wasn't good; the record company and the management had taken over. I felt that it was too soon for Steve [Winwood]. He was feeling uncomfortable, and since it had originally been my idea, I was uncomfortable. I started looking for somewhere else to go, an alternative, and I found that Delaney and Bonnie [Bramlett] were a godsend. After the Blind Faith tour, I lived with Delaney for a while.

The first night we met, we were in New York, and we went down to Steve Paul's club, the Scene, and we took acid. From there we went to see Mac Rebennack [Dr. John] and hung out in his hotel room, and then we went back to our hotel, to one of the rooms, his or mine. And Delaney looked straight into my eyes and told me I had a gift to *sing* and that if I *didn't* sing, God would take it away. I said, "No, man, I can't sing." But he said, "Yes, you can. Hit this note: *Ahhhh...*" And it was suddenly like the most impossible thing I could do was to hit that note, because of the acid. So it quavered, but I did hit it, and I started to feel that if I was to gain his respect, I ought to really pursue this. That night we started talking about me making a solo album, with his band.

Didn't you sing back when you were playing folk blues for the beatniks?

Yeah, I started singing in the pubs, but I had a very weak voice. I still have a small voice, 'cause I have no diaphragm to speak of. Then I sang a couple of backup things with the Yardbirds, but that was it. Most of the time, I concentrated on the guitar. Which is a shame, 'cause maybe I'd have been better if I'd managed to balance out the singing and playing at an earlier stage of my career.

Sounds like Delaney, being from Mississippi, got into a Baptist-preacher bit to get you singing again. So what happened after the Blind Faith tour? Did you start working on the solo album?

No, first of all we did a tour of England and Europe, as Delaney and Bonnie and Friends with Eric Clapton. And having got me to sing, Delaney started trying to get me to compose, as well. So we were writing a lot. And that was great. He'd start something off, and when I came up with the next bit, he'd say, "Look what you can do." Some of the time I think it was so he could get fifty percent of the songwriting, but it was also inspiring me. By the end of that tour, I was ready to make the album and felt very sure of myself.

Why did you go to Miami to record 'Layla'?

The attraction was Tom Dowd. I'd worked with him in Cream, and he was to me—and still is—the ideal recording man.

Yeah, he engineered all those great early Atlantic R&B and soul sessions and practically invented stereo.

Right. And he can guide you in a very constructive way. So we got there, we were doing a lot of dope and drinking a lot and just party-ing. It was great times. After about a week of jamming, I wanted to go hear the Allman Brothers, who were playing nearby, because I'd heard Duane Allman on Wilson Pickett's "Hey Jude," and he blew me away with that. After the concert I invited him back to the stu-dio, and he stayed. We fell in love, and the album took off from there.

The first time I ran into you was during those sessions at Criteria Record-ing Studios. There was a lot of dope around, especially heroin, and when I showed up, everyone was just spread out on the carpet, nodded out. Then you appeared in the doorway in an old brown leather jacket, with your hair slicked back like a greaser's, looking like you hadn't slept in days. You just looked around at the wreckage and said, to nobody in particular, "The boy stood on the burning deck/Whence all but he had fled." And then you split.

Yeah. We were staying in this hotel on the beach, and whatever drug you wanted, you could get it at the newsstand; the girl would just take your orders. We were on the up and the down, the girl and the boy, and the drink was usually Ripple or Gallo. Very heavy stuff. I remember Ahmet [Ertegun, chairman of Atlantic Records] arriving at some point, taking me aside and crying, saying he'd been through this shit with Ray [Charles], and he knew where this was gonna end, and could I stop now. I said, "I don't know what you're talking about, man. This is no problem." And, of course, he was dead right.

I guess you have to work that stuff out for yourself.

I don't know about that. When I started using [heroin], George [Harrison] and Leon [Russell] asked me, "What are you doing? What is your intention?" And I said, "I want to make a journey through the dark, on my own, to find out what it's like in there. And then come out the other end." But that was easy for me to say, because I had a craft, music, that I could turn to. For people who don't have that, there's a lot of danger; if you haven't got something to hold on to, you're gone. It's no good just saying, "Well, that per-son is gonna go through it, no matter what." You've actually got to stop them and try to make them think.

The music you and Duane got into on 'Layla' was really special, a once-in-a-lifetime thing. Did you tour after you finished recording?

Not with Duane, of course, but the Dominos did a very big tour of America. We copped a lot of dope in Miami—a *lot* of dope—and that went with us. Then I met up with this preacher from New York who was married to one of the Ronettes, and he asked if he could come along on part of the tour. The spiritual part of me was attracted to this man, but he immediately started giving me a very hard time about the dope. I felt very bad about this, and after the first week on the road I put everything I had in a sack and flushed it down the loo. Then, of course, I was going to the other guys, trying to score off them.

By the end of the tour, the band was getting very, very loaded, doing way too much. Then we went back to England, tried to make a second album, and it broke down halfway through because of the paranoia and the tension. And the band just...dissolved. I remember to this day being in my house, feeling totally lost and hearing Bobby Whitlock pull up in the driveway outside and *scream* for me to come out. He sat in his car outside all day, and I hid. And that's when I went on my journey into the smack. I basically stayed in the house with my girlfriend for about two and a half years, and although we weren't using any needles, we got very strung out. All that time, though, I was running a cassette machine and playing; I had that to hold on to. At the end of that period I found I had boxes full of playing, as if there was something struggling to survive.

I guess that's what kept you alive.

I had no care for the consequences; the idea of dying didn't bother me. Dying from drugs didn't seem to me then to be a terrible thing. When Jimi died, I cried all day because he'd left me behind. But as I grow older, as I live more, death becomes more of a reality, something I don't choose to step toward too soon.

So then, in January 1973, Pete Townshend organized a concert for you at the Rainbow in London, with Ron Wood, Steve Winwood and others.

I did that very much against my will. I wasn't even really there. It was purely Townshend's idea, and I didn't know what I'd done to earn it. It's simply that he's a great humanitarian and cannot stand to see people throw their lives away. It didn't matter to him if I was willing or unwilling; he was making the effort so that I would realize, someday, that someone cared. I'm always indebted to him for that.

If that didn't draw you out, what did?

Carl Radle sent me a tape of him playing with Dick Sims and Jamie Oldaker in Tulsa. I listened to it and played along with it, and it was great. So I sent him a telegram saying, "Maintain loose posture, stay in touch." And at some point after that, I started to get straight.

Then you made '461 Ocean Boulevard,' your resurrection album. Are you happy with that record?

Yeah, very. I'd wanted to do "Willie and the Hand Jive" since my childhood, and the Robert Johnson song ["Steady Rollin' Man"] and "Motherless Children" for almost as long. George Terry was there [in Miami], and when we were hanging out before the band arrived from Tulsa, he played me this Bob Marley album, *Burnin'*, and "I Shot the Sheriff" was on there. I loved it, and we did it, but at the time, I didn't think it should go on the album, let alone be a single. I didn't think it was fair to Bob Marley, and I thought we'd done it with too much of a white feel or something. Shows what I know. When I went to Jamaica after that, a lot of people were very friendly because of the light it had thrown on Bob Marley, and Marley himself was very friendly to me as well.

Your Tulsa band could play everything from reggae to blues to pop. What happened to that band?

Toward the end of that particular band, we were gettin' out of it again, and I was in the lead. I started to get straight, but I was drinking maybe two bottles a day of whatever hard stuff I could get my hands on. And there was real bad tension in the band that was aimed at me. Then I hired Albert Lee. We became friends, and there was a division between these two Englishmen and the Tulsa boys. And at the end of this particular tour, I think it was in '78, I fired everybody. Not only that, I didn't even tell them—I fired them by telegram. And I never saw Carl again. He'd saved me at one point, sending me that tape, and I turned my back on him. And Carl died. It was, I think, drugs, but I hold myself responsible for a lot of that. And I live with it.

Bobby Whitlock is a songwriter in Nashville, right? And I read recently that Jim Gordon had been convicted of murdering his mother [RS 449]. I heard that you were among the few people from his past who got in touch and tried to help.

I did try. When I was last in L.A., I kept making inquiries about how to get in to see him. But then I spoke to [drummer] Jim Keltner about it, and Keltner said it probably wouldn't be a good idea, that they had him on so much Thorazine he didn't really know what was going on.

I remember your coming to America in 1981 for a tour and landing in the hospital about eight days into the tour. Was that when your drinking started to come to an end?

Not quite. But it was pointed out to me while I was in hospital that I had a drink problem, and I think that was the first time anyone had ever said something like that to me. But I was still happy drinking and actually quite terrified of not drinking. I had to go further down that road to complete insanity before I stopped. It wasn't until it finally hit me in the head that I was killing other people around me, *as well as* killing myself and going insane, that I decided to stop.

What is the lure there, the attraction, of addictive behavior, whether it's using dope or booze?

It's obsessive. Part of my character is made up of an obsession to push something to the limit. It can be of great use if my obsession is channeled into constructive thought or creativity, but it can also be mentally or physically or spiritually destructive. I think what happens to an artist is, when he feels the mood swings that we all suffer from if we're creative, instead of facing the reality that this is an opportunity to create, he will turn to something that will stop that mood, stop that irritant. And that would be drink or heroin or whatever. He won't want to face that creative urge, because he knows the self-exploration that must be undertaken, the pain that must be faced. This happens most, or very painfully, to artists. Unless they realize what it is that is doing that to them, they'll always be dabbling in something or other to kill it.

TINA TURNER

by Nancy Collins

October 23, 1986

You've come a long way in life, Tina. You must feel very satisfied in how you've pulled yourself together in the last ten years since leaving Ike.

I don't have one debt at the moment. I have a home now. I always wanted a home, but I didn't have one because my parents broke up. I was determined to have that foundation. So I bought my mother a house, and now we all go there — my sons, my sister, her daughter. I'm reliving something I wanted when I was a child. The principal's daughters had homes, and now I have a home. I've made that dream a reality.

I'm self-made. I always wanted to make myself a better person, because I was not educated. But that was my dream — to have class. My role model was always Jacqueline Kennedy Onassis. Now, you're talking about high stuff, right? [*Laughs*] My taste was high. So when it came to role models, I looked at presidents' wives. Of course, you're talking about a farm girl who stood in the fields, dreaming, years ago, wishing she was that kind of person. But if I had been that kind of person, do you think I could sing with the emotions I do? You sing with those emotions because you've had pain in your heart. The bloodline of my family didn't come from that kind of royalty. Why I relate to it, I don't know. That's the class I wanted to be.

Basically, your family were sharecroppers. Do you feel you were middle-class?

We were well-to-do farmers—that's as close as I can get to explaining it. To me, it seemed as if we lived well. My sister and I had our own room. Each season we'd get new clothes, and I was always fresh and neat, especially compared to a lot of other people around me. We were never hungry. Of course, we knew the difference between our family and, say, the daughters of schoolteachers—those people were educated. My parents weren't, per se, but they had a lot of common sense and spoke well. We weren't low-class people. In fact, my parents were church people; my father was a deacon in the church.

Both of your parents deserted you at different points in your childhood. Didn't they have a tumultuous marriage?

My mother and father didn't love each other, so they were always fighting.

Your mother left when you were ten. Did you have any idea that she was going to leave?

No, but when she was gone, I knew she was gone. She'd left before, but then she'd always taken us with her, because she would go to her mother's. Daddy would come and talk her into coming back home. But this time he knew she was really gone. He knew it was the end. I thought she was going to send for me, but she never did. She didn't have the money to take my sister and me with her, because she was going to St. Louis, where she'd have to live with people herself.

How old were you when your father left you?

I was thirteen. But Daddy and I weren't that close, so that was fine. I didn't mind. I was a little bit afraid of him. He wasn't friendly. He was friendly with everybody else but not with me.

My parents weren't mine, and I wasn't theirs, really, so when they left, it was as if they had always been gone as far as I was concerned.

Although you've said you were surrounded by white people, you attended all-black schools. Do you recall the first time you felt any prejudice because of race?

No. The only thing I remember is the first time I ever felt like I wanted to be white. There was this pretty little white girl whose name was Puddin'. She had short blond hair and wore a ballerina skirt and shoes. I was in the fourth grade and a tomboy. Suddenly, here comes this golden little fairy, bouncing along, looking pretty, and I thought, "That's what I'd like to look like." It was the first time I remember ever thinking about race. Of course, when we went into town, we'd have to use the back door at many places, but you really didn't want to go into a place where you had to use the back door, because you felt the presence of not being wanted.

It hurts to be a minority. I am looked down upon because I'm black. It's forever. It's like a curse on you. We're moving out of it, of course. We can stand now, but it's still there—it's a memory, because you are branded. It's wishing that we, as a black people, had had a chance to be as fantastic as we were before being knocked down and made slaves. It goes way back, this thing of wanting to be proud, wanting not to feel second-class.

After your parents left, you started working for a white family, the Hendersons, doing babysitting and housework, did you not?

Yes, I was finally being taught. I would sit with them, and she'd teach me manners. She was young, but she almost felt like my mother. And I saw love in the Henderson household. They were very affectionate. They were always just like a couple who were really in love. It was a perfect marriage scene: the house, the baby, the car. And they never fought. Mrs. Henderson was my role model. I took every mannerism she had.

But there were times I was put in my place. One time—when it was very hot—I took the child walking. I stopped, knocked on a door and asked for a glass of water from the lady who answered. She slammed the door in my face. Suddenly, I remembered, "Don't get that comfortable. You can't just stop at someone's door and ask for water." But in the Hendersons' house, I didn't feel any discrimination at all.

You were left by not one parent but two. I'm surprised that that didn't leave you more disillusioned, even bitter.

I never allowed that to happen. I was never that person. I made a world for myself. I searched for what I wanted, and when I found it, I patterned myself after another class. When I went to school, I didn't observe the misfortunate ones, I observed the fortunate ones, people with manners, educated people. So I never became what I was. It's the same thing that I did with Ike. I never did the drugs, never drank, never stooped to his level. No one, even now, can get me to stoop to be anything I don't want. I've always held my head high. I might not have dressed as nice as the principal's daughters, but what I had I kept neat and clean. Once at school, I was being naughty, and the principal called me over. He said, "I'm surprised at you. You're different. You should know better." I didn't know what he meant, but I felt it was a compliment. I was very happy that he saw something different.

Were you a good student?

No, I was a dumb girl. I wasn't interested in school. I'm sure there was some psychological factor about my home life. Without knowing it, I was afraid and embarrassed, which is why I wasn't as good in school as I wanted to be. But I was always promoted, because I had manners and personality and I tried. I turned in my homework, even though it was most times wrong. I took hard stuff, like French — anything that would make me a better person. But what I did was the common-sense thing — that's surviving [*laughs*]. I was always worried I wouldn't pass, but I felt I had to graduate, because that was the respectable thing to do.

That's very admirable, since you must have known that if you did drop out, no one would really have cared.

Except me. I was the only one who saw my report cards. I knew the difference between the girls who got A's and B's and me. And it hurt. I did get the occasional A in drama and gym, and those were wonderful! I also worked through high school, for the Hendersons. I had planned to move into the city, I had already found a house, but then I went to St. Louis to live with my mother.

What was she doing at this point?

She was doing day work — cleaning. She came home for her mother's funeral, and I decided to go back with her. My mother and I didn't get along, but I went because it was my way out of the South.

Once I got to St. Louis, I still had to stay away from our house a lot because we argued so much. I had become rebellious. Plus, she was taking care of me, and I didn't like that because I had gotten used to taking care of myself.

It was in St. Louis, while you were still in high school, that you met Ike Turner, wasn't it?

Yeah. I started going to clubs with my sister, Alline. She was a barmaid, and one of the tops. My sister was really pretty. I was skinny, with long legs, and not really attractive. To be attractive with black men, you had to be heavier... sexier looking. Alline had big boobs, black, black skin and the same features as mine, but smaller. She had a lot of style. She always wore stilettos and black stockings with a seam. Her hair was soft, while my hair was very full and thick. Alline was really sexy.

Do you recall the first time you laid eyes on Ike?

I thought he was terribly ugly. There had been such a buildup about him because he had the hottest band around. When I first saw him, I remember thinking that I had never seen anyone that skinny. He was immaculately dressed, real clean and all sculptured—the bones and the hair. He wore his hair processed. I didn't like processed hair, so I didn't like his hairdo. But when he walked out, he did have a great presence...although you have to realize that I was a school-girl looking at a man. I was used to boys in jeans and short-sleeved shirts. But, boy, could he play that music. The place just started rocking. I wanted to get up there and sing *sooooo* bad. But that took an entire year.

One day [during one of the band's breaks], the drummer came up and set the microphone down in front of me, and I started singing. Well, when Ike heard me, he rushed over to me and said, "Girl, I didn't know you could sing!" The band came back, and I kept singing, and everybody came around to see who it was. Everybody was real happy for me because they knew I was Alline's little sister who wanted to sing. I was a star. Ike went out and bought me all these clothes. I had a fur and rings and [*motions to elbow*] gloves up to here. I was driving a Cadillac and I was still in school. I started dating one of the boys in the band, named Raymond. We didn't fool around right away, because I was so unsophisticated.

But eventually you got pregnant. Did it occur to you to have an abortion?

I didn't know about abortion, and I wanted the baby. After my mother found out, I went to stay with Raymond. I did feel ashamed and afraid, because I didn't think my mother would help me. But she did. Raymond broke his foot when I was living with him and had to go home to his family, so she said I could come home. So then I took care of her house, did all the cleaning, washing and cooking for the family.

How did you plan on taking care of your baby?

Well, I went to a city hospital for unwed mothers, so there wasn't a hospital bill. My mother and sister supported us for a while, so I was taken care of in my early stages. But I didn't plan on hanging around; I planned on getting a job—which I did, in a hospital. I found a babysitter, and I did all right. At the time, I wasn't a show person. I was planning on going to school to be a practical nurse, because the club thing was still a bit shaky. Then Ike lost his singer and asked me if I would sing.

When was the turning point, professionally speaking?

Ike recorded a demo, and I sang on it. He wasn't trying to sell my voice; he was trying to sell stuff as a producer. The record company said, "Why don't you record it with the girl's voice?" As a result, I became, officially, a professional performer. I was twenty, and my kid was about two. Ike said, "Now we have to make up a name." And that's when Ike and Tina started. He wanted his name there because he'd always produced people, only to have them get record deals and leave.

When did your sexual relationship with Ike begin?

He had broken up with the mother of his two sons, who I ended up raising. He was without a girlfriend. One of the musicians said he was going to come to my room and have sex with me. I couldn't lock the door, so I went to sleep with Ike, thinking he would protect me. Shit! [*Laughs*] It happened then, but I thought, "Well, okay, I'll just do it once." [*Laughs*] I didn't really know what to do because I wasn't turned on to him, even though [*laughs*] it was good. I did enjoy the physical part, but I didn't love him, and I didn't like it because of that. But I didn't know how to handle it because I also didn't want to lose my job. I knew he wasn't right for me. He was a man, he did serious things, like going to clubs and talking business. I was still used to going to movies and playing basketball. I had a kid, but I was still hanging out with high school friends.

Who was the Ike Turner whom you knew?

Ike was the son of a preacher and a seamstress. He didn't like school, so he wasn't an educated person. I don't think he even finished grade school. He had a complex about how he spoke. A lot of his fight came because he was embarrassed about his manners and not being educated. So Ike had a built-in anger. And the drugs just magnified that.

I always knew that Ike had talent and was a great musician. He was not a great songwriter, though, because all of his songs were about pain or women—that was his life dilemma. I hated those songs. I knew he was writing about other women. Psychologically, you have to try and make yourself think you like a song when you sing it. When he sensed I was delivering it poorly, he blamed me for not getting involved in the work. He said he couldn't make hit records because of my lack of involvement. All the blame was put on me. It was all this suppressed anger he had.

Did Ike have lots of other women?

He always did; he never stopped that. I didn't like it, but I was trapped. We had a hit record ["A Fool in Love," 1960], and I was the star, so he just grabbed on because he was afraid of losing me. The success and the fear came almost hand in hand. When I finally went to tell him that I didn't want to go on . . . that's when he got the shoe stretcher.

And beat you for the first time?

Yeah. I said, "I cannot travel with you, I cannot sing these songs." So he said, "Okay, we'll make some allowances, give you a certain amount of money," and I said okay. That was the trick. So we started traveling, and that's when I got involved. I didn't plan it, because he said he was going to pay me, and when he didn't, I was afraid to ask for the money because I was living with him. I got involved before I knew what to do about it.

That, of course, began sixteen years of beatings. You were a battered wife, controlled by fear.

It was a thoroughly unhappy situation I was in, but I was too far gone. I was trapped into really caring about Ike. If I left him, what was he going to do? Go back to St. Louis? I didn't want to let him down. As horrible as he treated me, I still felt responsible for letting him down. That was a mental problem I had at the time. And I was afraid to leave. I knew I had no place to hide, because he knew where my people were. My mother was actually living in Ike's house in St. Louis. My sister was living in an apartment basically rented by Ike.

It's hard to explain. This man was beating me—I always had a black eye or something, and he had women all over the place, and he wouldn't give me any money—and yet, I didn't leave. I felt sorry for him.

There were many terrible things that Ike did to you, but none more incomprehensible than beating you and then making you have sex with him afterward.

He acted as if that was a normal part of a relationship. But the part that was really torture were the wire hangers. I am so embarrassed that people know that's what I had to go through. I didn't want an ugly life, and I got myself trapped into one. I never stopped praying…that was my tool. Psychologically, I was protecting myself, which is why I didn't do drugs and didn't drink. I had to stay in control. So I just kept searching, spiritually, for the answer.

Did you ever actually try to leave him?

Yeah, a few times, but he always caught me before I left. And that scared me. I knew if I got caught, I was going to get the hanger. The first time he used the hanger I had run off. I borrowed money from the people around me — they always helped me because they knew what was going on — and I took a bus. I fell asleep, and when I woke up, I looked right into his face. "Get off, you motherfucker," he said. It scared the shit out of me. Ike got to my destination before I did.

He had a gun at the time. He always made me feel that at any moment he might put it to my head. Anyway, we went back to the hotel, and he kept playing with the gun. He knew what he was doing. There was a hanger lying there, and suddenly he grabbed it and started turning it in his hand. I couldn't believe what was happening. He had such control of it, he must have used it on somebody else before.

It finally got so bad that you attempted suicide by taking an overdose of Valium.

Because I didn't know how to get out. You've got to think, you've got to use your head, and when I started chanting is when I started using my head. I started thinking, "I'm not going to kill myself, there's nothing here for me. This person doesn't realize that I am helping him, that I have tried to be good and kind." So that's when I actually went to the spiritual side of myself for help. And I got it.

When you left him, in July 1976, you left with no money, right?

I had nothing. I didn't even know how to get money. I had a girl working for me who had worked for Ike, because she knew about ways of getting money. I didn't know how to do any of that stuff. Ike didn't think I'd be able to find a house, but I did. He sent over the kids, and money for my first rent, because he thought I'd have to come back when that ran out. We slept on the floor the first night. I rented furniture. I had some Blue Chip stamps that I had the kids bring, and I got dishes. Then my sister helped me with food. We also used food stamps—yeah, food stamps. I was doing *Hollywood Squares* and some of these television shows.

When was the last time you saw Ike?

I haven't seen him since my divorce. It was in court.

Where is he now?

In California someplace. He still sends telegrams asking for money.

How do you feel about men today? Did your experience with Ike embitter you?

It's very hard to say what I think about guys. I'm not biased about men. And I am looking for a great relationship when it comes, but I'm not foolish enough to jump onto every Tom, Dick and Harry simply because I don't, now, have a man in my life. All men are not violent. All men don't fight. The point is, you've got to find your equal.

You are an exquisite-looking woman. Do you think you're beautiful?

I'm nowhere near beautiful. Ethiopian women are beautiful: their sculptured faces, their noses, their hairline. And Scandinavian women are beautiful. I love that complete blond hairline. They almost glisten, they're so white. I don't have a great figure, but I know how to dress my body. My legs are nice, and I know the right shoes to wear to make my legs look pretty. I know how to make myself look good, but I'm not a pretty woman. I'm in the class with folks who are "all right."

You do understand that a lot of men might be put off or intimidated by the Tina Turner they see onstage—that sexy, smoldering, leather-clad woman in net stockings and miniskirt.

That's so funny, because everything I've done for my act has really been so practical. I started wearing net stockings because the other stockings ran. I didn't stop to think whether guys would like them or not. I don't feel that I dress for men. The short dresses work for me onstage because I've got a short torso and because there's a lot of dancing and sweating. My legs are nice, but you see so much of them because my body is short. It's not as if I put them out there on display because I'm trying to advertise. I never advertise myself for men. I always work to the women, because if you've got the girls on your side, you've got the guys. Black women can very easily become jealous. And I didn't want them to dislike me onstage, so I started working to them years ago. I knew I had the image of being sexy. I didn't want the guys to think that I was performing for them, so I looked at the women, because I felt less embarrassed. A woman knows I'm having fun and not trying to catch a guy. I'm there for a performance. The leather came because I was looking for a material that didn't show perspiration. I get drenched onstage, and if I wore regular jeans, the perspiration would show. Dirt doesn't show on leather, and it's good for traveling. It doesn't wrinkle, and it's durable. When I wore it, I didn't think people were going to think I was hot or tough.

Also, onstage, you never see me grouch. I smile. My songs are a little bit of everybody's lives who are watching me. You gotta sing what they can relate to. And there are some raunchy people out there. The world is not perfect. And all of that is in my performance; I play with it. That's why I prefer acting to singing, because with acting you are forgiven for playing a certain role. When you play that same role every night, people think that you are it. They don't think you're acting.

That is the scar of what I've given myself with my career. And I've accepted that. I don't hate myself anymore. I used to hate my work, hated that sexy image, hated those pictures of me onstage, hated that big raunchy person. Onstage, I'm acting the whole time I'm there. As soon as I get out of those songs, I'm Tina again.

ROBIN WILLIAMS
by Bill Zehme

February 25, 1988

Do you recognize this guy? [Hands Williams a Mork doll.]

[*In a geriatric warble*] Oh, *look,* from the *old* days! Here, let me check the nose to see if there's anything up his nostrils! [*Inspects doll*] This way we'll know if it's authentic. This is amazing. This is the doll that had the bad voice backpack where you pull the string and hear garbled sentences. Some people sued because some dolls in the Midwest actually said, "Go fuck yourself."

Strangely enough, its body is dated 1973 and the head 1979.

Oh, that's scary. Then the body is obviously from an old G.I. Joe or maybe a Ken or a Barbie. Yes, it's probably from a *Barbie* doll. "*Mommy, look, Mork has tits!*" It's very strange to see this again. It was also strange to see them dismembered after the show was canceled. You'd see 'em hanging out of garbage cans, burned. It's so weird.

I don't know whether I'm experiencing nostalgia or nausea looking at this. It's like a combination of both. But that's a great way to start an interview. "I handed him a Mork doll." Well. Let's put this away for now, shall we?

All right. Do you think Mork complicated your progress in Hollywood?

Hardly. You can't say that something that took you from zero to a hundred was damaging your progress. It certainly wasn't a hindrance economically, either. And no matter what happened on the TV series, I always had the other image: the nightclub comedian. If I'd just done Mork and nothing else, it might've been dangerous. But I always had a total other outlet beyond that character. I thank God for cable TV. Without it, I think it would be death for comedians.

Did you ever find the transition from TV to films unwieldy? It seemed in some ways like bringing a Tasmanian devil into captivity.

Some of the reviews have indicated that. I've had an odd habit of choosing projects that were the opposite of me, sometimes to the detriment. People are now saying about *Good Morning, Vietnam,* "This film is basically you and what you do best. So why did you wait eight years?" Well, I made other choices. I wanted to go against what I was doing on TV—not just with *Mork & Mindy* but the cable stuff as well. I was saying, in effect, "I'll *act*. I'll show you *I can act.*"

The real Adrian Cronauer wasn't exactly the radio desperado you portrayed him as in 'Good Morning, Vietnam.'

No, he's a very straight guy. He looks like Judge Bork. In real life he never did anything outrageous. He did witness a bombing in Saigon. He wanted to report it—he was overruled, but he said okay. He didn't want to buck the system, because you can get court-martialed for that shit. So, yes, we took some dramatic license.

But he did play rock & roll, he did do characters to introduce standard army announcements, and "*Goooood* morning, Vietnam" really was his signature line. He says he learned whenever soldiers in the field heard his sign-on line, they'd shout back at their radios, "*Gehhhhht* fucked, Cronauer!"

I heard you improvised several characters on mike that we never saw in the movie. Do you remember any?

We left out a lot of stuff because the jokes just took too long to set up. Some other stuff might have been too rough. I was trying a riff on booby traps and said [*as black GI*], "Now, if it was a pussy trap, people would line up to get in." Armed Forces Radio used to give out winning bingo numbers, so I tried this: "Our lucky bingo winners are 14, 12 and 35. If you've been with any of these girls, call your medic immediately!"

Do you think Bob Hope approved of you moving in on his territory? It looked like he gave you the cold shoulder on the Carson show a few weeks ago.

[*As Hope*] "Yeah, *wiiiiild*, isn't he?" I don't know. Certainly, there's that line about him in the film: "Bob Hope doesn't play police actions. Bob likes a *big room*." I think Hope knew about that, because he leaned over to me at one point and said, "You know, I was there in '65, but they didn't want to get all the guys in one place." At one point he was talking about the Persian Gulf, and I said, "I'll go if you like." He said, "Yeah, *right*." Translated: "I'd no sooner have you there than a third testicle."

For the first time ever you're seeing a therapist. People around you are saying you're saner than ever.

[*Grinning*] Yeah, they bought it.

Has inner peace been difficult to achieve?

Oh, I don't have inner peace. I don't think I'll ever be the type that goes, "I am now at one with myself." Then you're fucking *dead*, okay? You're out of your body. I do feel much calmer. And therapy helps a little.... I mean, it helps *a lot*. It makes you reexamine everything: your life, how you relate to people, how far you can push the "like me" desire before there's nothing left of you to like. It makes you face your limitations, what I can and can't do.

Sounds like Robin Williams has grown up.

[*Facetiously*] Yeah, right. [*As Freudian analyst*] "But you still talk about your dick a lot, though, don't you?" It's been a tough year with the death of my father, the separation from my wife, dealing with life, with business, with myself. Someone said I should send out Buddhist thank-you cards, since Buddhists believe that anything that challenges you makes you pull yourself together.

You used to refer to your father as Lord Posh — he was an uncommonly elegant man, a powerful automobile executive. Did you see him any differently at the end?

I got to know another side of him in the last few years. I saw that he was funkier, that he had a darker side that made the other side work. He was much older than me; he died at eighty-one. Up until four or five years ago, I kept distance out of respect. Then we made a connection. It's a wonderful feeling when your father becomes not a god but a man to you — when he comes down from the mountain and you see he's this man with weaknesses. And you live him as a whole being, not a figurehead.

Were you with him when he died?

I was here in San Francisco, and he died at home, out in Tiburon [a nearby suburb]. So I was close. He'd had operations and chemotherapy. It's weird. Everyone always thinks of their dad as invincible, and in the end, here's this little, tiny creature, almost all bone. You have to say goodbye to him as this very frail being.

At least he was home and died very peacefully in his sleep. My mother thought he was still asleep. She came downstairs and kept trying to shake him. She called me that morning and said [*calmly and evenly*], "Robin, your father's dead." She was a little in shock, but she sounded happy in a certain way, if only because he went without pain.

Is it true that you scattered his ashes?

[*Chuckles*] Yeah, it was amazing. It was sad but also cathartic and wonderful in the sense that it brought my two half brothers and me together. It kind of melded us closer as a family than we've ever been before. We've always been very separate.

That day we gathered right on the sea in front of where my parents live. It was funny. At one point I had poured the ashes out, and they're floating off into this mist, seagulls flying overhead. A truly serene moment. Then I looked into the urn and said to my brother, "There's still some ashes left, Todd. What do I do?" He said, "It's Dad—he's holding on!" I thought, "Yeah, you're right, he's hanging on." He was an amazing man who had the courage not to impose limitations upon his sons, to literally say, "I see you have something you want to do—do it."

What has fatherhood taught you about yourself?

That most of your actions have consequences with the child. And I've learned to have the security not to worry that he will love me—as long as I keep the connection strong enough. I've learned not to try to force the love. You can't. All you can do is try to set up a world for him that's safe and stable enough to make him happy. I want to protect him and shield him from public sight. I want him to have his own life.

Do you find yourself performing for him?

Yeah, and sometimes he'll love it. I did a Señor Wences thing for him. I dressed my fist in a napkin and was Mother Teresa. I played her drunk and made her drink water, which I'd spill down my arm. He liked that.

The hard part is when you really have to back off and provide him with the time to play alone. Children are a drug. I used to say they beat the shit out of cocaine: You're paranoid, you're awake, and you smell bad. It's this constant metamorphosis. This is a precious time. Some of those lines in *Garp* ring true. I never thought I would literally sit and watch a child sleep. But you can. I never thought that would be real.

You've been drug free for how long now?

Five years. Six months before Zach was born I basically stopped everything.

Do you remember the last time you were on the cover of 'Rolling Stone,' in 1982?

Wasn't the basic premise that I'd cleaned up my act?

The headline was "Robin Williams Comes Clean." Was that honestly the end of the self-abusive chapter in your life?

There was no going back. I realized that the reason I did cocaine was so I wouldn't have to talk to anybody. Cocaine made me so paranoid: If I was doing this interview on cocaine, I would be looking out the window, thinking that somebody might be crawling up fourteen floors to bust me or kick down the door. Then I wouldn't have to talk. Some people might have the metabolism where cocaine stimulates them, but I would literally almost get sleepy. For me, it was like a sedative, a way of pulling back from people and from a world that I was afraid of.

Going from zero to a hundred on the American fame-o-meter, I take it, was a bit harrowing.

I was twenty-six or twenty-seven, and then, *bang*, there's all this money, and there are magazine covers. Between the drugs and the women and all that stuff, it's all coming at you, and you're swallowed whole. It's like *"Whooooaaa!"* Even Gandhi would have been kind of hard-pressed to handle it well. [*As Gandhi on cocaine*] "Just one line, if you pleeeze. I'll just do a little and save *the world*—fuck India!"

Talking about your marriage five years ago, Valerie said, "If I had said, 'Don't cross this line,' he would have been long gone." In retrospect, was she too tolerant of your indulgences?

Maybe. I don't think I would have been long gone. I think I was crying out for someone to say, "Enough." In the end I had to make my own line. Anybody who finally kicks himself in the ass and wants to clean up makes his own line. You realize the final line is the edge.

Is the failure of your marriage a great disappointment to you?

It's not disappointing. That's why therapy helps a lot. It forces you to look at your life and figure out what's functioning and what isn't. You don't have to beat your brains against a wall if it's not working. That's why you choose to be separated rather than to call each other an asshole every day. Ultimately, things went astray. We changed, and then with me wandering off again a little bit, then coming back and saying, "Wait, I need help"—it just got terribly painful.

Would you admit you're tough to live with, even cleaned up?

Oh, God, yes. I'm no great shakes. It's the "love me" syndrome combined with the "fuck you" syndrome. Like the great joke about the woman who comes up to the comic after a show and says, "God, I really love what you do. I want to fuck your brains out!" And the comic says, "Did you see the first show or the second show?" One hand is reaching out and the other is motioning to get back.

Couldn't you have gotten therapy sooner and circumvented a lot of trouble? Were you afraid of it?

A little bit. My mother is a Christian Scientist, whose tenets maintain that you can always heal yourself. So I said, "Well, I'll fix myself." But there are certain things you can't fix in yourself. You can get yourself healthy. I kicked drugs alone—I never went to a hospital.

You may be the only celebrity who beat dependency without the benefit of the Betty Ford clinic. What's your secret?

With alcohol it was decompression. The same way I started drinking, I stopped. You work your way down the ladder from Jack Daniel's to mixed drinks to wine to wine coolers and finally to Perrier. With cocaine, there is no way to gently decompress yourself. It took a few months. Someone said you finally realize you've kicked cocaine when you no longer talk about it. Then it's gone. It's like pulling away and seeing Pittsburgh from the air. People come up to you with twitching Howdy Doody jaws, and you think, "Hmmm, I looked like that." You realize that if you saw by daylight the people you'd been hanging out with at night, they'd scare the shit out of you. There are bugs that look better than that.

How much money do you think you ultimately spent supporting your drug habit?

The weird thing about the drug habit was that I didn't have to pay for it very often. Most people give you cocaine when you're famous. It gives them a certain control over you; you're at least socially indebted to them. And it's also the old thing of perfect advertising. They can claim, "I got Robin Williams fucked up." "You did? Lemme buy a gram, then." The more fucked up you get, the more they can work you around. You're being led around by your nostril. I went to one doctor and asked, "Do I have a cocaine problem?" He said, "How much do you do?" I said, "Two grams a day." He said, "No, you don't have a problem." I said, "Okay."

A few years ago, you ended one of your cable shows with a vignette about Albert Einstein. You quoted him, saying, "My sense of God is my sense of wonder about the universe." What do those words mean to you?

It's like Mel Brooks' great line as the 2,000-year-old man [*in a Yiddish accent*]: "There's something bigger than *Phil.*" You can't help but see it when you deal with nature in the extreme. Like when you're bodysurfing on Maui and a storm suddenly makes a ten-foot wave come at you. It gives you a sense of your mortality. Or it's when you see something incredibly beautiful. I get it when I see Zachary changing. Here's this being who is you but *not* you slowly growing and forming opinions of his own.

It stems, too, from a sense of horror at things that go on in the world. The planet's climate is changing at such a drastic rate, causing the worst blizzards and droughts in history. Now there is an incredibly large hole in the ozone layer. Like Shakespeare said, this place is such a delicate, fragile firmament. It's a one-in-a-billion crapshoot. And we're fucking it up.

Einstein is your idol, isn't he?

Yeah. Good old Al. [*Chuckles*] Imagine Al doing stand-up. [*As Einstein*] "So, it's *relative.* Does that mean I have to make love to my mother? No, I'm *keeding,* please! I gotta go.... I came back to make a bomb. *Nagasaki!* Who's there? It was a *joke!* Hey, I gotta go!" Wasn't he *wiiiiild?*

LEONARD BERNSTEIN

by Jonathan Cott

November 29, 1990

You once said: "I am a fanatic music lover. I can't live one day without hearing music, playing it, studying it or thinking about it." When did this obsession begin?

The day in 1928 that my aunt Clara, who was in the process of moving, dumped a sofa on my family—I was ten years old at the time—along with an old upright piano, which, I still remember, had a mandolin pedal: The middle pedal turned the instrument into a kind of wrinkly sounding mandolin. And I just put my hands on the keyboard and I was hooked...for life. You know what it's like to fall in love: You touch someone and that's it. From that day to this, that's what my life's been about.

At first, I started teaching myself the piano and invented my own system of harmony. But then I demanded, and got, piano lessons, at a buck a lesson, from one of our neighbor's daughters—a Miss Karp. Frieda Karp. I adored her, I was madly in love with her. She taught me beginner's pieces like "The Mountain Belle." And everything went along fine until I began to play—probably very badly—compositions that she couldn't. Miss Karp couldn't keep up with my Chopin Ballades, so she told my father that I should be sent to the New England Conservatory of Music. And there I was taught by a Miss Susan Williams, who charged three dollars an hour. And now my father started to complain: "A klezmer you want to be?" To him, a klezmer [an itinerant musician in Eastern Europe who played at weddings and bar mitzvahs] was little more than a beggar.

You see, until that time, neither my father [who was in the beauty-supply business] nor I really knew that there was a real "world of music." I remember his taking me when I was fourteen years old to a Boston Pops concert, a benefit for our synagogue, where I fell in love with Ravel's *Bolero,* and several months later to a piano recital by Sergei Rachmaninoff—both at Symphony Hall. And my father was just as astonished as I was to see thousands of people paying to hear one person play the piano!

But still he balked at three-dollar lessons for me. One dollar for lessons and quarter-a-week allowance—that's all he allotted for my music. So, I started to play in a little jazz group, and we performed at…weddings and bar mitzvahs! [*Laughs*] Klezmers! The sax player in our group had access to stock arrangements for "St. Louis Blues," "Deep Night" and lots of Irving Berlin songs; and I'd come home at night with bleeding fingers and two bucks, maybe, which went toward my piano lessons.

Now, my new teacher, Miss Williams, didn't work out—she had some kind of system, based on never showing your knuckles. Can you imagine playing a Liszt Hungarian Rhapsody like that? So I found another teacher…at six dollars an hour…and therefore I had to play more jazz, and I also started to give piano lessons to the neighborhood kids.

Meanwhile, I was going to Hebrew school after regular school; and the temple we belonged to [Temple Mishkan Tefila] also introduced me to live music. There was an organ, a sweet-voiced cantor and a choir led by a fantastic man named Professor Solomon Braslavsky from Vienna, who composed liturgical compositions that were so grand and oratorio-like—very much influenced by Mendelssohn's *Elijah,* Beethoven's *Missa Solemnis* and even Mahler.

And I used to weep just listening to the choir, cantor and organ thundering out—it was a big influence on me. I realized, many years later, that the "gang call"—the way the Jets signal to each other—in *West Side Story* was really like the call of the shofar that I used to hear blown in temple on Rosh Hashanah.

'West Side Story' is your most famous and successful work. Did you have a sense that it would be so popular when you composed it?

Not at all. In fact, everybody told us that the show was an impossible project. Steve Sondheim [who wrote the lyrics] and I auditioned it like crazy, playing piano four-hands to convey a quintet or the twelve-tone "Cool" fugue. But no one, we were told, was going to be able to sing augmented fourths—as with "Ma-ri-a" (C to F-sharp). Also, they said the score was too "rangy" for pop music: "Tonight, Tonight"—it went all over the place. Besides, who wanted to see a show in which the first-act curtain comes down on two dead bodies lying on the stage? "That's not a Broadway musical comedy."

And then we had the really tough problem of casting it, because the characters had to be able not only to sing but to dance and act and be taken for teenagers. Ultimately, some members of the cast were teenagers, some were twenty-one, some were thirty but looked sixteen. Some were wonderful singers but couldn't dance very well or vice versa. And if they could do both, they couldn't act.

Somehow it worked out. And it even saved Columbia Records financially—which at the outset didn't want to invest in or record it. Remember: It was a bad time for popular music. Bebop's appeal was limited and was practically over, and there was mostly a lot of smarmy ballads sung by people like Johnny Mathis.

Through your Young People's Concerts, television specials, books, lectures and preconcert chats, you've been giving people an education for more than forty years. You yourself once called teaching probably the "noblest...most unselfish...most honorable" profession in the world. And you once referred to "this old quasi-rabbinical instinct" you had for "teaching and explaining." It's said that in traditional Jewish society, a child, when he was six or seven years old, was carried to the schoolroom for the first time by a rabbi, where he received a clean slate on which the letters of the Hebrew alphabet had been written in honey. Licking off the slate while reciting the name of each letter, the child was thus made to think of his studies as sweet and desirable.

Though I can't prove it, deep in my heart I know that every person is born with the love of learning. Without exception. Every infant studies its toes and fingers; and a child's discovery of his or her voice is one of the most extraordinary of life's moments. I've suggested that there must be proto-syllables existing at the beginnings of all languages—like *ma* (or some variant of it), which, in almost every tongue, means "mother"—*mater, madre, mutter, mat, Ima, shi-ma, mama.* Imagine an infant lying in its cradle, purring and murmuring *mmm* to itself…and suddenly it gets hungry. So it opens its mouth for the nipple and out comes *mmaa-aa!*…and thus it learns to associate that syllable with the breast and the pleasure of being fed. *Madre* and *mar* ["mother" and "sea"] are almost the same word in Spanish; and in French, *mère* and *mer* are near homonyms. The amniotic sea is where you spend your first nine months—that great ocean in which you don't have to breathe or do anything. It all comes to you. Even after the trauma of being born—which we never get over—there's still that delight with which children first learn to say *ma!*

Then, one day, the kid says "Ma!" and the nipple does not arrive. This can happen on day five or month five of the child's life; but whenever it happens, it's an unimaginable shock. I know great big grown-up guys who have jumped—literally jumped—into the arms of their lady therapists and wept, hoping to be cradled at their breasts!

Like MAH-ler?

[*Laughs*] Why not? You know, Mahler made four appointments with Sigmund Freud, and three times he broke them because he was so scared to find out why he was impotent. His wife, Alma—who at various times carried on with [Walter] Gropius, [Oskar] Kokoschka, [Franz] Werfel and Bruno Walter, among others—sent him to see Freud. He was twenty years older than she, and she was the prettiest girl in Vienna—rich, cultured, seductive.

Didn't you yourself once meet her?

Certainly. Many years ago she was staying at the Hotel Pierre, in New York, and she invited me for "tea"—which turned out to be aquavit—then suggested we go to look at some "memorabilia" of her composer husband in her bedroom. I spent a half hour in the living room, a minute or two less in the bedroom. She was really like a wonderful Viennese operetta.

Anyway, Mahler didn't pay enough attention to her; he was busy writing his Sixth Symphony up in his little wood hut all night, and she was tossing around in bed. Mahler was terribly guilty about it all—when he gets to the Alma theme in the Scherzo of the Sixth Symphony, the margins of the score are filled with exclamations like "Almschi, Almschi, please don't hate me, I'm dancing with the devil!" [*Sings the Alma theme*]

Mahler finally met up with Freud at the University of Utrecht, where they sat on a campus bench for a couple of hours. And Freud later commented in a letter to one of his pupils, writing something to the effect of "I have analyzed the musician Mahler"—a two-hour analysis, mind you! Freud was as crazy as his patient—"and as you will notice, Mahler's mother was named Maria, all his sisters had Maria for their middle names, and his wife is named Alma Maria Schindler."

"I've just kissed a mom named Maria!"

Indeed. Freud thought that Mahler was in love with the Madonna image and was suffering from the Latin-lover dilemma—the mother versus the whore. You worship the former and fuck the latter. Anyway, Freud considered Mahler to have had this problem in spades. But back to my point about infants who are all born with the craving to learn: having experienced the birth trauma, the denial traumas and the series of other traumas—I almost forgot about gender discovery!—that cause tantrums (the terrible threes, the fearsome fours, the frightful fives). My own granddaughter, according to her mother (who is my daughter Jamie—the first fruit of my loins), made a great confession when she was two and a half years old. Until then everything had revolved around her—she was the goddess and queen, and now a new baby was expected: Enter Evan! And she went into tantrums! Jamie stroked and caressed and calmed her down until she finally admitted: "You know what, Mommy? I don't like the new baby." And just to have come out and said that will probably save her a good ten years on the couch! For each time a kid learns a new trick of manipulating a parent—"I'll scream, I won't pay attention, I won't speak when spoken to"—he or she becomes more cynical and turns off. And each manipulation and each trauma impairs the love of learning with which the infant is born.

Moreover, anybody who grows up—as those of my generation did not—taking the possibility of the immediate destruction of the planet for granted is going to gravitate all the more towards instant gratification. You don't get the nipple, so you push the TV button, you drop the acid, you snort the coke, you do the needle: "Right away, right away, yeah, man!" It doesn't matter that it makes you impotent. You've gone so high and then you pass out in the bed...and you wake up, cynical and unsatisfied and guilty and ashamed and full of manic fears and anxiety...and one thing reinforces the other.

Then, if you happen to be born into a black, single-parent family in the inner city—impoverished, disadvantaged, along with all the shocks and traumas that man is heir to—by the time you go to school, if you're not a Hasidic or Sikh child who's learned to lick the honey-coated letters (wherever the written tradition is important), you're already completely resistant to learning. And the more poverty and greed of the Reagan-Bush kind around you, the greater the attraction of the streets—the instant gratification of crack, television, fast food.

Anything of a serious nature isn't "instant"—you can't "do" the Sistine Chapel in one hour. And who has time to listen to a Mahler symphony, for God's sake?

In the introduction to your book 'The Infinite Variety of Music' [1966], you wrote: "At this moment, as of this writing, God forgive me, I have far more pleasure following the musical adventures of Simon and Garfunkel or of the Association singing 'Along Comes Mary' than I have in most of what is being written now by the whole community of 'avant-garde' composers....Pop music seems to be the only area where there is to be found unabashed vitality, the fun of invention, the feeling of fresh air." What do you think of rock music today?

Boo, hiss! I've become very disappointed with most of it. In the Sixties and Seventies there were many wonderful musicians I liked. And to me the Beatles were the best songwriters since Gershwin. Recently, though, I was at a party where there were a lot of kids in their twenties, and most of them didn't even know songs like "Can't Buy Me Love," "She's Leaving Home," "She Said She Said" or any one of ten other Beatles masterpieces. What is that? And if I hear one more metallic screech or one more horrible imitation of James Brown, I'm going to scream.

When I was in Spain several years ago, I remember watching huge rings of people in the square of a Catalonian village, joining arms and dancing *sardanas* to a type of band called a *cobla*—dances with twenty-seven counts, dances of such complexity that I couldn't learn them. Talk about innate dance and musical competence! Those people just did it. Like those drunken Greek sailors who come into a tavern and start dancing in fives or sevens...and the band doesn't know that it's playing in fives or sevens. That is extraordinary music—much more exciting than almost anything the current rock world has to offer.

I want to ask you about your refusal to accept an arts award from President Bush and to attend a dinner given by John Frohnmayer, the chairman of the National Endowment for the Arts, in response to the latter's decision to withdraw the agency's sponsorship of an exhibition about AIDS—a result of congressional legislation against government financing of supposedly "obscene" and overtly political art.

The last time I went to the White House was during Jimmy Carter's administration, when I was honored along with Agnes de Mille, James Cagney, Lynn Fontanne and Leontyne Price, among others—a good bunch. I love the White House more than any house in the world—after all, I'm a musician and a citizen of my country—but since 1980 I haven't gone there because it's had such sloppy housekeepers and caretakers.

With regard to the Jesse Helms–inspired restrictions on federal funding, the worst thing concerns the removal of politics as an acceptable subject of artistic works. Because then you'd have to forget Goya, Picasso's *Guernica,* Hemingway's *A Farewell to Arms.* Forget everything. And as for "obscenity": Almost the entire Metropolitan Museum of Art would have to come down—Mars fucking Venus, the Rubens collection of large, fleshy ladies with wet thighs and the naked ephebus from ancient Greece, Hermes with his cock up innumerable inches! And the picture of little Jesse Helms running around the Senate as if it were the boys' lavatory of a high school, showing dirty pictures to the other senators, is so disgraceful that I cannot ever forgive him.

We had eight lovely, passive, status quo, don't-make-noises years with Ronald Reagan. The fights I had with my mother! "Don't you dare say a word against our president!" she'd say to me. She's now ninety-one years old—God bless her!—and she's still bright and witty. She doesn't like the family name being dragged in the mud;

and when she saw my name in the newspaper every day regarding my refusal to attend the White House luncheon awards ceremony given by Bush (or the Frohnmayer dinner), she'd call me up to say, "You're on the front page of the *New York Times*." And I'd say, "Hold your water, baby: I was also on the front page of the *Washington Post*." And she'd exclaim, "Well, that's horrible!" So I informed her that some of my most conservative Midwestern friends sent me congratulatory messages . . . people who voted for Reagan!

We now have a black governor in Virginia, the right governor in New Jersey and Dinkins in New York City. That's terrific! In the past I've met and argued, in pessimistic fashion, with Helmut Schmidt, Ted Heath and François Mitterrand about the mindlessness, carelessness and heedlessness of the Reagans of the world. But I think there's a turnaround coming — look at what's happening around the world from Central Europe and South Africa to Haiti. And I'm looking forward to Jesse Helms being routed in the near future.

People like William Buckley Jr., William Safire and George Will think of me as a kind of "liberal" fool. Basically, a liberal is a progressive who wants to see the world change and not just remain stuck in the status quo. So, yes, I'm a liberal, but one who believes in people, not in some "thing." And I've never felt more strength and confidence.

What you call "liberal" was once termed "radical chic" by Tom Wolfe in his infamous article about the party you gave in 1970 to raise money for the Black Panthers.

Wrong on all counts! What happened is that my wife hosted a meeting in our New York City apartment for the American Civil Liberties Union in connection with its defense of thirteen Black Panthers who, at the time, were imprisoned in the Tombs without the right of due process. At our reception were one Black Panther and two pregnant Black Panther wives; and Felicia gave the reception in order to raise contributions for the ACLU defense fund and to allow invited friends of ours to ask questions. My wife had requested that the press not cover this event; and Charlotte Curtis—then the editor of the women's page of the *New York Times*—arrived (simply as an individual, we thought), accompanied by a young friend of hers in a white suit. He turned out to be Tom Wolfe. So what am I to do? You can't beat the legends. Fortunately, legends eventually die. And maybe I can help this one on its way.

SPIKE LEE

by David Breskin

July 11, 1991

As far as your image, people think of you as a hustler. Now, we know that everybody has to hustle to make it as an artist....

Do people accuse Madonna of hustling? I'm asking.

It's got a different spin with you. In other cases, it's "So-and-so is hard-working," but with you it's—

Self-promotion.

Are you conscious of that?

Look, I know there are two sets of rules. So, that's just the way it is. I just have to keep doing what I do best—and know what I have to do—and pursue that. I can't let other people dictate the agenda.

Do you still see your function as a filmmaker as one of "shedding light on problems" so they can get discussed and understood?

Not every film. It depends on the subject matter. I think we start to get in trouble if we expect the artist to have answers all the time. For instance, *School Daze* was the examination of petty, superficial differences that still keep black people apart. To me, we black people are the most ununified people on the face of the earth.

The same differentiations exist within a lot of cultures.

Yeah, but they ain't in the shape that we're in. We don't have the same liberties as other people.

There's a tension, maybe a fundamental contradiction between unification and diversity. How do you deal with that?

I think Jewish people are very diverse but they are very unified, on a lot of things. You talk about Israel: Jewish people are unified on the state of Israel.

You've never heard people argue like Jews argue about what to do about it, or how to deal with Israel.

I know Jewish people are more unified than black people, I know that.

Why do you think that is the case, historically?

I don't want to get into the whole Jewish-black thing.

I'm not asking about Jewish-black relations, I'm asking why you think Jews are more unified than blacks.

As far as America is concerned? Because I don't think Jews have ever been taught to hate themselves the way black people have. That's the whole key: self-hatred. That's not to say that Jewish people haven't been persecuted. I'm not saying that. But they haven't been taught to hate themselves to the level black people have been. When you're persecuted, it's natural for people to come together; but when you're also taught at the same time that you're the lowest form of life on earth, that you're subhuman, then why would you want to get together with other people like that? Who do you hate? Yourself.

'Joe's Bed-Stuy Barbershop: We Cut Heads,' your thesis film, brings up the problem of economic self-reliance. What kind of economic —

I don't really have a program. All I'm saying is that black people for too long haven't really thought of owning businesses. That's the key. Because when you own businesses, you have more control and you can do what you want. That was one of the key things about *Do the Right Thing*—the whole thing about Sal's Famous Pizzeria, between Sal and Buggin' Out. Buggin' Out rightfully felt that Sal should have the decency to at least have some black people up on the Wall of Fame, since all his income is derived from people in the community who are black and Hispanic. Sal had, to me, a more valid point: This is my motherfucking pizzeria, and I can do what I want to do. When you open your own restaurant, you can do what you want. Of course, now Buggin' Out countered by trying to organize a boycott of Sal's, which has always been one of our ways of fighting that type of thinking. But in the case of Buggin' Out, it didn't work.

A boycott takes patience, organization, determination —

And more than rhetoric, and that's something that Buggin' Out didn't have.

It's sad that the fight is over a symbol when the economic realities are so much more significant. You can spend all your time trying to boycott a Korean deli in Brooklyn —

Black people should have their own fruit and vegetable stands in Flatbush. I'd be crazy to spend a year out there boycotting that one Korean place! That doesn't make any sense to me.

How many people have asked you, "Does Mookie do the right thing?"

How many people are there in New York City?

And what's your answer to them?

Black people never ask that. It's only white people.

Why's that?

Because black people understand perfectly why Mookie threw the garbage can through the window. No black person has ever asked me, "Did Mookie do the right thing?" Never. Only white people. White people are like, "Oh, I like Mookie so much up to that point. He's a nice character. Why'd he have to throw the garbage can through the window?" Black people, there's no question in their minds why he does that.

Yeah, but why you do something and whether what you do is right are very different things. I know why he does it but—

But only white people want to know why he does it. I spoke at twenty-five universities last year, and that's all I ever got asked. "Did Mookie do the right thing?"

What do you tell them?

I feel at the time he did. Mookie is doing it in response to the police murdering Radio Raheem, with the infamous Michael Stewart choke hold, in front of his face—also knowing this is not the first time that something like this has happened, nor will it be the last. What people have to understand is that almost every riot that's happened here in America involving black people has happened because of some small incident like that: cops killing somebody, cops beating up a pregnant black woman. It's incidents like that that have sparked riots across America. And all we were doing was using history. Mookie cannot lash out against the police, because the police were gone. As soon as Radio Raheem was dead, they threw his ass in the back of the car and got the hell out of there so they could make up their story.

What about attacking Sal?

I think he likes Sal too much. For Mookie, in my mind, Sal's Pizzeria represents everything—and that's why he lashed out against it. It was Mayor Koch, it was the cops—everything.

That's "the power" to him?

It's the power at the moment. But when it's burnt down, he's back to square one, even worse. Look at all those riots: Black people weren't burning down downtown; they were burning down their own neighborhoods.

You end up with no place to have pizza; that's the net effect of the whole action. You haven't stopped the police, you—

That's the irony. Because that's the only way they can really fight. They felt very powerful at that moment, but it was fleeting.

Now Malcolm X said that whether you're using ballots or bullets, your aim has to be true, and you don't aim for the puppet, you aim for the puppeteer. Isn't everybody on the corner there in 'Do the Right Thing' aiming for just a puppet, and not a very powerful puppet at that?

That's true. But Mayor Koch is not in front of them. Rarely do you get a chance to actively engage the enemy, and the closest there was, was Sal's Pizzeria.

One of the disturbing things to me about the reaction to that film is that people focused on the burning of the pizzeria and not the death of Radio Raheem, and that there might be a reason for that other than just hog-calling racism.

The thing I liked about *Do the Right Thing*, especially for critics, is that it was a litmus test. I think you could really tell how people thought and who they were. And if I read a review and all it talked about was the stupidity of burning the pizzeria, the stupidity of the violence, the looting, the burning, and not one mention of the murder of Radio Raheem, I knew *exactly* where they were coming from. Because people that think like that do not put any value on black life, especially the life of young black males. They put more importance on property, white-owned property.

I'm going to assume that that's true, that those people don't put a value on black life. But let me suggest another reason why the burning of the pizzeria becomes the centerpiece of the picture and not the death of Raheem. I think there are aesthetic, as opposed to racial, reasons. Two reasons: One, Radio Raheem is not a fully drawn character—he's a caricature. He's a type, albeit a new type for many people. But the audience doesn't really develop an empathy for him.

I don't know if I agree with that. I think a life is a life.

It is, but Mookie's life would have meant more to the audience, because they knew Mookie better. The second reason is that the burning reads as the climax of the film in terms of the way it's shot and structured.

What you're saying are both good points. But I'm talking about people that don't even *think* about the death of Radio Raheem. What's important to them is that the pizzeria was burnt. For them, Sal is the cavalry. Fort Apache among savages. That's who their interest is with.

One of Malcolm X's favorite quotes was by Goethe: "Nothing is more terrible than ignorance in action." If Malcolm was watching that scene go down, would he have felt fear because it was ignorance in action?

[*Pause*] He might. But he would have perfectly understood why they were doing what they did. See, Malcolm never condemned the victim. And the people who were burning down the pizzeria were the victims.

Let's talk more about black film. You said, in the documentary on the making of 'Do the Right Thing': "The No. 1 concern is to try to be the best filmmaker you can be and not be out there bullshitting, saying you're a black filmmaker."

I think it holds true more now than when I said that.

Are there people out there bullshitting, saying, "I'm a black filmmaker, love me!"

Not "love me," but a lot of people are getting deals now, to make films, and I'm not begrudging anybody, but we'll find out the contenders from the pretenders.

Do you still want to be seen as a "black" filmmaker, or a filmmaker first, who happens to be black? It's a subtle but important distinction.

To me, I don't think there's ever going to be a time in America where a white person looks at a black person and they don't see that they're black. That day ain't coming very soon. Don't hold your breath. So that's a given. So why am I going to get blue in the face, worrying about that? For me, that's one of the most important things Malcolm X said: "What do you call a black man with a Ph.D.? Nigger." That's it. So why am I going to spend time and energy saying: "Don't call me a black filmmaker. I'm a filmmaker!" I'm not getting into that argument. I'll leave that to the other *Negroes*. [*Laughs*] The other so-called Negroes.

Do you still feel that you are writing for a black audience? Right up front you said, "Look, Woody Allen writes for intellectual New York City Jews and I write for blacks."

Yes, but that does not exclude—if you do it well—everybody else. I like Woody Allen's films, but there's stuff in those films I don't get, and the person next to me is *dying!* I don't get it. But that does not deter from my enjoyment of the film. I think the same is true of me. Black people be rolling down the aisle, and white folks don't understand it. They may not get everything—all the nuances—but they still enjoy the film. So I don't think there's any crime in writing for a specific audience.

I think people were surprised, maybe because of their own naïveté, that you would do that, that you would want to—

See, that's that whole crossover motherfucker that motherfuckers fall into. That's because anytime they see the word "black," they have a negative connotation. I wasn't raised like that. That wasn't my upbringing. So I'm never going to run from the word "black."

In 1987, in writing about racism, you wrote: "We're all tired about white-man this, white-man that. Fuck dat! It's on us." No more excuses. But if you ask white people if you had said that, given your persona, they would be surprised.

Yeah, but where are they getting their perceptions from? [*Laughs*] From TV, magazines and newspapers.

And are you coming across in a way that's not truthful to who you are?

Yeah, because the way the media portrays me is as an angry black man. The funny thing to me is when white people accuse blacks, when they see somebody black who's angry, they say, "Why are you so angry?" [*Laughs*] If they don't know why black people are angry, then there's *no hope.* I mean, it's a miracle that black Americans are as complacent and happy-go-lucky as we are. I don't think I have that much anger. I don't think I'm angrier than I have a right to be. See, that statement you read me is not a complete statement. On one hand, you cannot deny the injustices that have been committed against you as a people.

On the other hand, you cannot use as an excuse: "Well, I really would have liked to have done that, but Mr. Charlie was blocking me every single time." I think that's the more complete statement.

You've said you don't think blacks can be racist.

Right.

Are you speaking of black Americans?

In this case, I am speaking of black Americans. And then what I always say, and people never print, is that for me there's a difference between racism and prejudice. Black people can be prejudiced. But to me, racism is the *institution*. Black people have never enacted laws saying that white folks cannot own property, white folks can't intermarry, white folks can't vote. You got to have power to do that. That's what racism is — an institution.

Institutionally hindering an entire people?

Yeah. Me calling you "white motherfucker," I don't think that's racism, I think that's prejudice. That's just racial slurs. That ain't gonna hurt nobody. *Anybody* can be prejudiced. That's the complete statement. But that never gets printed.

I see racism all over the world: one tribe to another tribe, the Japanese to the Chinese, and so on. It's incredibly complicated and incredibly sad, and so I can't buy your statement, "White people invented racism."

Where did it start then?

I don't know where it started. What do you think caused it?

Because they wanted to exploit people. Colonization. Why do you think there's no Native Americans? Why do you think they're on reservations?

You think that was the beginning of racism? The 1600s?

No, way before that.

We're talking about history now, and I'm curious as to whether you've thought about what are the origins of prejudice, what are the origins of racism. "White people invented racism" makes it seem like you believe there was a grand conspiracy to deny the fruits of the planet to everybody by a group of people sitting in a room in Amsterdam in 1619.

You don't think there was a plan to wipe out the Indians?

I think that's certainly what happened, but I don't think it was drawn up like the Magna Carta.

Look, that shit had to be planned. There's no way…They saw the riches this land had and they took over. And that's what the Afrikaners did in South Africa. And before that, that's what all of Europe did when they split up Africa into colonies. I mean, [*pause*] maybe white people didn't invent the patent on racism, but they sure perfected that motherfucker! They got that shit down to a science that's being implemented now, full throttle.

You don't see any decline in it, do you?

What, racism? No. I don't smoke crack. [*Laughs*] If anything, it's on the upswing—with eight years of Reagan, and now Bush. And now this war, America's in this patriotic fever. I went to the Super Bowl, man, I wish I hadn't gone. I was nauseous with all that flag-waving and airplanes flying overhead. God bless America.

It's fascistic.

It was like being in Nazi Germany at that Super Bowl game! Instead of Leni Riefenstahl—

— You had NFL Films!

You had NFL Films and "Up With People." [*Laughs wildly*] And Whitney Houston lip-syncing the national anthem. That marred the game for me.

Do you care that some people feel you hide behind the shield of racism, that you're quick to call people racists to deflect criticism of yourself?

No. [*Yawns*] That doesn't bother me, not at all.

Let me bring up two instances, quite specifically. When you opened your shop in Brooklyn, some dude from MTV asked you, "Spike, what are you going to do with the profits from this store?" And in what didn't get bleeped out, you said you don't ask Robert De Niro what he does with the profits from his restaurant. So you were assuming that he was asking you because you're black and you were opening your own business. I won't come to his defense—because I don't know what was in his mind, asking the question—but look, Robert De Niro is not at all a political guy, but there are white artists who—

That is *bullshit*. That is complete bullshit. No white person who's opened up a motherfucking business has *ever* been asked, "What are you gonna do with your profits?"

But people like Sting and Bono, who are political—

That is bullshit, that is bullshit. You're telling me people ask Sting if his album goes triple platinum, "What are you going to do with your profits?" This is motherfucking America. When black people start to make some money, then it becomes a fucking problem. [*Very upset, yelling*] Tell me a time when a white artist was asked, "What are you going to do with your profits?"

I've asked white—

That is bullshit! No one would ever come to someone's restaurant opening or book coming out and say, "Mr. White Person, what are you going to do with your profits?" I don't care what you say, that shit don't happen.

I'm telling you, I've asked white artists who have political points of view, okay, whether it be the rain forest or the Irish problem, if they're doing something about it, I've asked them.

That is not the same thing, David. I'm talking about the first day the store is open, and he has a microphone in my face, "What are you going to do with your profits?" It was a racist question. The night the motherfucking Tribeca Grill opened, they did not ask Robert De Niro, "What are you gonna do with your profits?" It's plain and simple.

Got it. The other controversy involved kids being killed for expensive sneakers such as Air Jordans. Then you wrote in 'The National' that the criticism of you was racially motivated. Do you feel it's possible to be concerned about what's going on—kids being killed for sneakers—and not have it be racist?

I don't believe that shit. [*Jumps up, acts this out*] You go around Chicago and look for some motherfucker that wears the same size Air Jordans you have and boom...

It seems illogical to me, too, but Michael Jordan reacted in a very different way than you did. Maybe because he has a different program than you do. But I know there were black groups that actually picketed Chicago Stadium and put out leaflets—

And Operation PUSH is behind that.

—about Michael and Nike, and the creation of status symbols in the community. Your reaction to that was very defensive. I'm not blaming you. You have a right to defend yourself, but—

You don't think I should defend myself when they're saying that the blood of young black America is on my hands and Spike Lee is responsible for black kids killing each other?

No, I would hope that you would. It was the manner in which you defended yourself that suggested that anyone who cared about that problem was a racist, because they don't really care about black kids anyway. To me, if it was white kids that were getting killed and someone screamed bloody hell, that you could say was racist—the only reason they care is 'cause it's white kids getting killed; if it were black kids in the inner city, no one would care.

Wrong. Wrong. The emphasis is wrong. The emphasis should not be on the sneakers. The emphasis should not be on the sneakers or the Starter jackets. The emphasis should not be on the sheepskin coats or the gold chains. The emphasis should be on: What are the conditions among young black males that are making them put that much emphasis on material things? What is it that makes the acquisition of a pair of sneakers or a gold chain that gives them their worth in life, that makes them feel like a human being? That's where the motherfucking emphasis should be.

The causes, not the symptoms.

Exactly.

I understand that. But don't you feel, in creating those ads, that you increased the level of status attached to that particular product, Air Jordans, so that it became something more desirable? Don't you feel you increased people's desire for the product? Isn't that what a good commercial does? Makes them salivate, makes them want?

Yes, but at the same time I believe that young black Americans are not going to go kill each other over a pair of sneakers. That is my belief. I don't think a motherfucker is going to shoot somebody because he has a pair of sneakers. And if that's the case, then ... then let's not sell cars. Let's get rid of the whole capitalist system as a whole! I mean, you just can't harp on the sneakers. If people want to be so righteous, let's do away with the shit across-the-board. Just don't jump on me, Michael Jordan and [Georgetown basketball coach] John Thompson.

Are you comfortable saying you're a capitalist?

[*Pause*] Am I a capitalist? [*Pause*] We all are, over here. And I'm just trying to get the power to do what I have to do. To get that power, you have to accumulate some type of bank. And that's what I've done. I've always tried to be in an entrepreneurial mode of thinking. Ownership is what's needed amongst Afro-Americans. Ownership. Own stuff.

JERRY GARCIA

by James Henke

October 31, 1991

I heard there was a meeting recently, and you told the other band members that you weren't having fun anymore, that you weren't enjoying playing with the Dead. Did that actually happen?

Yeah. Absolutely. You see, the way we work, we don't actually have managers and stuff like that. We really manage ourselves. The band is the board of directors, and we have regular meetings with our lawyers and our accountants. And we've got it down to where it only takes about three or four hours, about every three weeks. But anyway, the last couple of times, I've been there screaming, "Hey, you guys!" Because there are times when you go onstage and it's just plain hard to do and you start to wonder, "Well, why the fuck are we doing this if it's so hard?"

And how do the other band members feel?

Well, I think I probably brought it out into the open, but everybody in the band is in the same place I am. We've been running on inertia for quite a long time. I mean, insofar as we have a huge overhead, and we have a lot of people that we're responsible for, who work for us and so forth, we're reluctant to do anything to disturb that. We don't want to take people's livelihoods away. But it's us out there, you know. And in order to keep doing it, it has to be fun.

And in order for it to be fun, it has to keep changing. And that's nothing new. But it is a setback when you've been going in a certain direction and, all of a sudden, boom! A key guy disappears.

You're talking about Brent Mydland [Grateful Dead keyboardist, 1979–1990]?

Yeah. Brent dying was a serious setback—and not just in the sense of losing a friend and all that. But now we've got a whole new band, which we haven't exploited and we haven't adjusted to yet. The music is going to have to take some turns. And we're also going to have to construct new enthusiasm for ourselves, because we're getting a little burned out. We're a little crisp around the edges. So we have to figure out how we are going to make this fun for ourselves. That's our challenge for the moment, and to me the answer is: Let's write a whole bunch of new stuff, and let's thin out the stuff we've been doing. We need a little bit of time to fall back and collect ourselves and rehearse with the new band and come up with some new material that has this band in mind.

Did you see Brent's death coming?

Yeah, as a matter of fact we did. About six or eight months earlier, he OD'd and had to go to the hospital, and they just saved his ass. Then he went through lots of counseling and stuff. But I think there was a situation coming up where he was going to have to go to jail. He was going to have to spend like three weeks in jail, for driving under the influence or one of those things, and it's like he was willing to die just to avoid that.

Brent was not a real happy person. And he wasn't like a total drug person. He was the kind of guy that went out occasionally and binged. And that's probably what killed him. Sometimes it was alcohol, and sometimes it was other stuff. When he would do that, he was one of those classic cases of a guy whose personality would change entirely, and he would just go completely out of control.

Brent had this thing that he was never able to shake, which was that thing of being the new guy. And he wasn't the new guy; I mean, he was with us for ten years! That's longer than most bands even last. And we didn't treat him like the new guy. We never did that to him. It's something he did to himself. But it's true that the Grateful Dead is tough to... I mean, we've been together so long, and we've been through so much, that it is hard to be a new person around us.

But Brent had a deeply self-destructive streak. And he didn't have much supporting him in terms of an intellectual life. I mean, I owe a lot of who I am and what I've been and what I've done to the beatniks from the Fifties and to the poetry and art and music that I've come in contact with. I feel like I'm part of a continuous line of a certain thing in American culture, of a root....My life would be miserable if I didn't have those little chunks of Dylan Thomas and T.S. Eliot. I can't even imagine life without that stuff. Those are the payoffs: the finest moments in music, the finest moments in movies. Great moments are part of what support you as an artist and a human. They're part of what make you a human. What's been great about the human race gives you a sense of how great you might get, how far you can reach. I think the rest of the guys in this band all share stuff like that. We all have those things, those pillars of greatness. And if you're lucky, you find out about them, and if you're not lucky, you don't. And in this day and age in America, a lot of people aren't lucky, and they don't find out about those things.

When it comes to drugs, I think the public perception of the Dead is that they are into pot and psychedelics — sort of fun, mind-expansion drugs. Yet Brent died of a cocaine and morphine overdose, and you also had a long struggle with heroin. It seems to run counter to the image of the band.

Yeah, well, I don't know. I've been round and round with the drug thing. People are always wanting me to take a stand on drugs, and I can't. To me, it's so relativistic, and it's also very personal. A person's relationship to drugs is like their relationship to sex. I mean, who is standing on such high ground that they can say: "You're cool. You're not."

For me, in my life, all kinds of drugs have been useful to me, and they have also definitely been a hindrance to me. So, as far as I'm concerned, the results are not in. Psychedelics showed me a whole other universe, hundreds and millions of universes. So that was an incredibly positive experience. But on the other hand, I can't take psychedelics and perform as a professional. I might go out onstage and say, "Hey, fuck this, I want to go chase butterflies!"

Does anyone in the Dead still take psychedelics?

Oh, yeah. We all touch on them here and there. Mushrooms, things like that. It's one of those things where every once in a while you want to blow out the pipes. For me, I just like to know they're available, just because I don't think there's anything else in life apart from a near-death experience that shows you how extensive the mind is.

And as far as the drugs that are dead-enders, like cocaine and heroin and so forth, if you could figure out how to do them without being strung out on them, or without having them completely dominate your personality...I mean, if drugs are making your decisions for you, they're no fucking good. I can say that unequivocally. If you're far enough into whatever your drug of choice is, then you are a slave to the drug, and the drug isn't doing you any good. That's not a good space to be in.

Was that the case when you were doing heroin?

Oh, yeah. Sure. I'm an addictive-personality kind of person. I'm sitting here smoking, you know what I mean? And with drugs, the danger is that they run you. Your soul isn't your own. That's the drug problem on a personal level.

Jerry Garcia

How long were you doing heroin?

Oh, jeez. Well, on and off, I guess, for about eight years. Long enough, you know.

Has it been difficult for you to leave heroin behind?

Sure, it's hard. Yeah, of course it is. But my real problem now is with cigarettes. I've been able to quit other drugs, but cigarettes...Smoking is one of the only things that's okay. And in a few years it won't be okay. They're closing the door on smoking. So now I'm getting down to where I can only do one or two things anymore. My friends won't let me take drugs anymore, and I don't want to scare people anymore. Plus, I definitely have no interest in being an addict. But I'm always hopeful that they're going to come up with good drugs, healthy drugs, drugs that make you feel good and make you smarter....I still have that desire to change my consciousness, and in the last four years, I've gotten real seriously into scuba diving.

Really?

Yeah. For me, that satisfies a lot of everything. It's physical, which is something I have a problem with. I can't do exercise. I can't jog. I can't ride a bicycle. I can't do any of that shit. And at this stage of my life, I have to do something that's kind of healthy. And scuba diving is like an invisible workout; you're not conscious of the work you're doing. You focus on what's out there, on the life and the beauty of things, and it's incredible. So that's what I do when the Grateful Dead aren't working — I'm in Hawaii, diving.

Your father, Joe Garcia, was a musician, wasn't he?

Yeah, that's right. I didn't get a chance to know him very well. He died when I was five years old, but it's in the genes, I guess, that thing of being attracted to music. When I was little, we used to go to the Santa Cruz Mountains in the summer, and one of my earliest memories is of having a record, an old 78, and I remember playing it over and over on this wind-up Victrola. This was before they had electricity up there, and I played this record over and over and over, until I think they took it from me and broke it or hid it or something like that. I finally drove everybody completely crazy.

What instrument did your father play?

He played woodwinds, clarinet mainly. He was a jazz musician. He had a big band—like a forty-piece orchestra—in the Thirties. The whole deal, with strings, harpist, vocalists. My father's sister says he was in a movie, some early talkie. So I've been trying to track that down, but I don't know the name of it. Maybe I'll be able to actually see my father play. I never saw him play with his band, but I remember him playing me to sleep at night. I just barely remember the sound of it. But I'm named after Jerome Kern, that's how seriously the bug bit my father.

How did he die?

He drowned. He was fishing in one of those rivers in California, like the American River. We were on vacation, and I was there on the shore. I actually watched him go under. It was horrible. I was just a little kid, and I didn't really understand what was going on, but then, of course, my life changed. It was one of those things that afflicted my childhood. I had all my bad luck back then, when I was young and could deal with it.

Like when you lost your finger?

Yeah, that happened when I was about five, too. My brother Tiff and I were chopping wood. And I would pick up the pieces of wood, take my hand away, pick up another piece, and boom! It was an accident. My brother felt perfectly awful about it.

But we were up in the mountains at the time, and my father had to drive to Santa Cruz, maybe about thirty miles, and my mother had my hand all wrapped up in a towel. And I remember it didn't hurt or anything. It was just a sort of buzzing sensation. I don't associate any pain with it. For me, the traumatic part of it was after the doctor amputated it, I had this big cast and bandages on it. And they gradually got smaller and smaller, until I was down to like one little bandage. And I thought for sure my finger was under there. I just knew it was. And that was the worst part, when the bandage came off. "Oh, my God, my finger's gone." But after that, it was okay, because as a kid, if you have a few little things that make you different, it's a good score. So I got a lot of mileage out of having a missing finger when I was a kid.

What did your mother do for a living?

She was a registered nurse, but after my father died, she took over his bar. He had this little bar right next door to the Sailors' Union of the Pacific, the merchant marines' union, right at First and Harrison, in San Francisco. It was a daytime bar, a working guy's bar, so I grew up with all these guys who were sailors. They went out and sailed to the Far East and the Persian Gulf, the Philippines and all that, and they would come and hang out in the bar all day long and talk to me when I was a kid. It was great fun for me.

I mean, that's my background. I grew up in a bar. And that was back in the days when the Orient was still the Orient, and it hadn't been completely Americanized yet. They'd bring back all these weird things. Like one guy had the world's largest private collection of photographs of square-riggers. He was an old sea captain, and he had a mint-condition 1947 Packard that he parked out front. And he had a huge wardrobe of these beautifully tailored double-breasted suits from the Thirties. And he'd tell these incredible stories. And that was one of the reasons I couldn't stay in school.

[Garcia dropped out of high school after about a year.] School was a little too boring. And these guys also gave me a glimpse into a larger universe that seemed so attractive and fun and, you know, crazy.

But there were a couple of teachers who had a big impact on you, weren't there?

I had a great third-grade teacher, Miss Simon, who was just a peach. She was the first person who made me think it was okay to draw pictures. She'd say, "Oh, that's lovely," and she'd have me draw pictures and do murals and all this stuff. As soon as she saw I had some ability, she capitalized on it. She was very encouraging, and it was the first time I heard that the idea of being a creative person was a viable possibility in life. "You mean you can spend all day drawing pictures? Wow! What a great piece of news."

She enlarged the world for me, just like the sailors did. I had another good teacher, Dwight Johnson. He's the guy that turned me into a freak. He was my seventh-grade teacher, and he was a wild guy. He had an old MG TC, you know, beautiful, man. And he also had a Vincent Black Shadow motorcycle, the fastest-accelerating motorcycle at the time. And he was out there. He opened lots and lots of doors. He's the guy that got me reading deeper than science fiction. He taught me that ideas are fun.

You turn fifty next year. How does that feel?

God, I never thought I'd make it. I didn't think I'd get to be forty, to tell you the truth. Jeez, I feel like I'm a hundred million years old. Really, it's amazing. Mostly because it puts all the things I associate with my childhood so far back. The Fifties are now like the way I used to think the Twenties were. They're like lost in time somewhere back there.

And I mean, here we are, we're getting into our fifties, and where are these people who keep coming to our shows coming from? What do they find so fascinating about these middle-aged bastards play-ing basically the same thing we've always played? I mean, what do seventeen-year-olds find fascinating about this? I can't believe it's just because they're interested in picking up on the Sixties, which they missed. Come on, hey, the Sixties were fun, but shit, it's fun being young, you know, nobody really misses out on that. So what is it about the Nineties in America? There must be a dearth of fun out there in America. Or adventure. Maybe that's it, maybe we're just one of the last adventures in America. I don't know.

AXL ROSE

by Kim Neely

April 2, 1992

What's your earliest memory?

My earliest conscious memory was of a feeling that I'd been here before and that I had a toy gun in my hand. I knew it was a toy gun, and I didn't know how I knew. That was my first memory. But I've done regression therapy all the way back, just about to the point of conception. I kind of know what was going on then.

Can you talk about what you've learned?

Just that...my mom's pregnancy wasn't a welcome thing. My mom got a lot of problems out of it, and I was aware of those problems. That would tend to make you real fucking insecure about how the world felt about your ass. My real father was a pretty fucked-up individual. I didn't care too much for him when I was born. I didn't like the way he treated my mother. I didn't like the way he treated me before I was born. So when I came out, I was just wishing the motherfucker was dead.

Talking about being conscious of things that happened before you were born might throw a few people.

I don't really care, because that's regression therapy, and if they've got a problem with it, they can go fuck themselves. It's major, and it's legit, and it all fits together in my life. Everything is stored in your mind. And part of you is aware from very early on and is storing information and reacting. Every time I realize I have a problem with something, and I can finally admit it to myself, then we go, "Okay, now what were the earliest stages?" and we start going back through it.

What have you figured out?

I blacked out most of my childhood. I used to have severe nightmares when I was a child. We had bunk beds, and I'd roll out and put my teeth right through my bottom lip—I'd be having some violent nightmare in my bed. I had these for years.

Do you remember what the nightmares were about?

No, I only remember one dream. I dreamt I was a horse. You ever see those movies of wild mustangs running and how heavy that looks? I dreamt about that. I dreamt I was caught and then put in the movies. And in some really stupid movies. And it was totally against my will, and I could not handle it, and I freaked. I didn't understand the dream. Back then, I was like, "I was a horse, they tried to put me in the movies!" You know, all I could think of at the time was Mr. Ed or Francis. But I always remembered that dream, and now I understand it real well. I didn't know what my nightmares were about. My parents had always said something really tragic and dark and ugly happened. They wouldn't say what happened—they always just freaked out whenever anything was mentioned about my real father. I wasn't told I had a real father until I was seventeen. My real father was my stepdad, as far as I knew. But I found some insurance papers, and then I found my mom's diploma, with the last name Rose. So I was never born Bill Bailey. I was born William Rose. I am W. Rose because William was an asshole.

Your mother married your biological father when she was in high school?

Yeah. My mom's eyes actually turn black whenever it's brought up how terrible this person was. And what I found out in therapy is, my mother and him weren't getting along. And he kidnapped me, because someone wasn't watching me. I remember a needle. I remember getting a shot. And I remember being sexually abused by this man and watching something horrible happen to my mother when she came to get me. I don't know all the details. But I've had the physical reactions of that happening to me. I've had problems in my legs and stuff from muscles being damaged then. And I buried it and was a man somehow, 'cause the only way to deal with it was bury the shit. I buried it then to survive—I never accepted it. I got a lot of violent, abusive thoughts toward women out of watching my mom with this man. I was two years old, very impressionable, and saw this. I figured that's how you treat a woman. And I basically put thoughts together about how sex is power and sex leaves you powerless, and picked up a lot of distorted views that I've had to live my life with. No matter what I was trying to be, there was this other thing telling me how it was, because of what I'd seen. Homophobic? I think I've got a problem, if my dad fucked me in the ass when I was two. I think I've got a problem about it.

Yeah, I would imagine so. What happened later?

After I was two, my mom remarried, and I was really upset by that. I thought I was the man in her life or something, because she got away from this man and now she was with me. You know, you're a baby.

She was yours.

Yeah. And then she married someone else, and that bothered me. And this person basically tried to control me and discipline me because of the problems he'd had in his childhood. And then my mom had a daughter. And my stepfather molested her for about twenty years. And beat us. Beat me consistently. I thought these things were normal. I didn't know my sister was molested until last year. We've been working on putting our lives together ever since and supporting each other. Now my sister works with me. She's very happy, and it's so nice to see her happy and that we get along. My dad tried to keep us at odds. And he was very successful at some points in our lives.

Where is your real father?

His brother called me right around the Stones shows, and I had my brother talk to him. I didn't talk to him, 'cause I needed to keep that separation. I haven't heard from him since. But I confronted my mom, and she finally talked to me a bit about it, and they told me that he was dead. It looks pretty much to be true that he is. He was pretty much headed for that anyway. A very unsavory character. I've had a problem with not wanting to be him. I had to be macho. I couldn't allow myself to be a real man, because men were evil, and I didn't want to be like my father. Around the Stones shows, some paper in L.A. wrote this piece about how "The truth will come out about Axl's anger," and they were making it look like I was trying to hide something. I wasn't trying to hide it. I didn't know what had happened to me. I wouldn't allow myself to know. I wouldn't have been able to handle it.

How do you deal with knowing now?

It's not about going, "Well, I can handle it, I'm a man." And it's not about going, "Well, I forgive them now." You have to reexperience it and mourn what happened to you and grieve for yourself and nurture yourself and put yourself all back together. And it's a very strange, long chain. Because you find out your mother and father had their problems, and their mother and father had problems, and it goes back through the ages.

How do you stop the cycle?

I don't know. It's finding some way to break the chain. I'm trying to fix myself and turn around and help others. You can't really save anyone. You can support them, but they have to save themselves. You know, you can live your life the way you have and just accept it, or you can try to change it. My life still has its extremes and ups and downs, but it is a lot better because of this work. I'm very interested in getting involved with child-abuse organizations. There's different methods of working with children, and I want to support the ones that I believe in.

Have you talked to anyone yet?

I've gone to one child-abuse center. When I went, the woman said that there was a little boy who wasn't able to accept things that had happened to him and to deal with it, no matter how many children were around him who'd had the same problems. And apparently he saw something about me and childhood problems, and he said, "Well, Axl had problems, and he's doing okay." He started opening up, and he's doing all right. And that's more important to me than Guns n' Roses, more important to me than anything I've done so far. Because I can relate to that more than anything. I've had such hatred for my father, for women, for...

Yourself?

Yeah. Myself. And it's just made me crazy. I'm working on getting past those things, and the world doesn't seem to be too tolerant of me doing that in public. It's like, "Oh, you got a problem? You go away and take care of it." All these relatives knew little pieces of this puzzle, and nobody helped me with shit. I'm angry about that. I can't sit and think about Uncle So-and-So and enjoy it much. And if you're talking with any of these people, they try to get you to just tolerate it and take things back to the way they were: "Let's not get it public." My family did everything they could, thinking they were doing what was right, to bury it all. My stepfather was just adamant that he was going to protect Mom and himself: "Your real father does not get brought up." And he was also trying to cover his own tracks for what he did.

Why are you talking about this publicly?

One reason is for safety's sake. My stepfather is one of the most dangerous human beings I've ever met. It's very important that he's not in my life anymore or in my sister's. We may be able to forgive, but we can't allow it to happen again. There's a lot of reasons for me to talk about it publicly. Everybody wants to know "Why is Axl so fucked up?" and where those things are coming from. There's a really good chance that by going public I'm gonna get attacked. They'll think I'm jumping on a bandwagon. But then it's just gonna be obvious who's an asshole and who's not. There are probably people that are jumping on a bandwagon. But I think it's time. Things are changing, and things are coming out.

It's only been in the last few years that people have really been talking about what constitutes abuse. I'm not talking about molestation but emotional abuse.

All parents are going to abuse their children in some way. You can't be perfect. But you can help your child heal, if he's able to talk to you. Then he can say, "You know, when I was five, I saw this." I wear a shirt onstage sometimes that says, TELL YOUR KIDS THE TRUTH. People don't really know what that's about. Up until early this year, I was denied what happened to me, who I was, where I came from. I was denied my own existence, and I've been fighting for it ever since. Not that myself is the greatest thing on earth. But you have a right to fight for yourself.

If you don't have a sense of your own identity, everything's going to seem like a losing battle.

My growth was stopped at two years old. And when they talk about Axl Rose being a screaming two-year-old, they're right. There's a screaming two-year-old who's real pissed off and hides and won't show himself that often, even to me. Because I couldn't protect him. And the world didn't protect him. And women didn't protect him and basically thought he should be put out of existence. A lot of people out there think so now. It's a real strange thing to deal with on a consistent basis. I'm around a three-year-old baby now and then, and sometimes after a few days it's just too overwhelming for me. My head is spinning because of the changes it's putting me through.

You mean Stephanie's son?

Yeah. Stephanie [Seymour, Rose's girlfriend] has been very supportive in helping me deal with all this. People write all kinds of things about our relationship, but the most important thing in our relationship is that we maintain our friendship. The romance is a plus. We want to maintain our friendship and be really protective of how our relationship affects [Seymour's son] Dylan. Dylan gets priority over us, because he could be greatly damaged, and I don't want that to happen.

You were talking about Dylan last night.

Oh, man, they jump off things and stuff. It scares me. It's like they could break at any time. It scares the shit out of me. I've been with Dylan and he'll be upset about something, and I'm trying to help him, and he gets mad at me, and I've been offended. I've thought, "The only way I can deal with this is 'Okay, he's just being a jerk right now.'" But it was pointed out to me that he's not being a jerk, he doesn't know. What he needs is love. I thought about it, and I was like, "Yeah, because I was told that, too." About my music, which is pure expression and honest emotion and feeling. I mean, I'll be singing something and know, "Man, they're not gonna like this" and "This isn't right." But it's how I feel. The way I've been attacked has been strange. The press has actually helped me get my head more together. You know, my stepfather helped me, too. I learned a lot of things. That doesn't mean he wasn't also being an asshole. It's not quite fair to bring a two-year-old into the realities of who's an asshole and who's not. There's a part of me that's still two and getting a little better every day.

That would explain a lot.

One thing I want to say is, these aren't excuses. I'm not trying to get out of something. The bottom line is, each person is responsible for what they say and what they do. And I'm responsible for everything I've said and everything I've done, whether I want to be or not. So these aren't excuses. They're just facts, and they're things I'm dealing with. And if you've got a real problem with it, don't come to the show. If you gotta be home at fucking midnight, don't bother. Do yourself a favor. I'm not telling you to come—I don't think that I'd want to. If you've got a problem with me trying to deal with my shit and doing the show the best I can, then just don't come, man. It's not a problem. Just stay the fuck away. Because you're getting something out of it, but I'm also there for myself. I've got a lot of work to do. A lot of work to do. I've done about seven years' worth of therapy in a year, but it takes a lot of energy. And Guns n' Roses takes a lot of energy. It's a weird pressure to try to deal with both at the same time. And I'm gonna do it the best I can when I can and how I can. And I'm the judge of that—not anybody in the crowd.

How do you think all of this will affect your songwriting?

I really think that the next official Guns n' Roses record, or the next thing I do, at least, will take some dramatic turns that people didn't expect and show the growth. I don't want to be the twenty-three-year-old misfit that I was. I don't want to be that person.

Who do you want to be?

I guess I like who I am now. I'd like to have a little more internal peace. I'm sure everybody would.

BRUCE SPRINGSTEEN

by James Henke

August 6, 1992

The music scene has changed a lot since you last released an album. Where do you see yourself fitting in these days?

I never kind of fit in, in a funny kind of way. In the Seventies the music I wrote was sort of romantic, and there was lots of innocence in it, and it certainly didn't feel like it was a part of that particular time. And in the Eighties, I was writing and singing about what I felt was happening to the people I was seeing around me or what direction I saw the country going in. And that really wasn't in step with the times, either.

Well, given the response to your music then, I think you fit in pretty well during the Eighties.

Well, we were popular, but that's not the same thing. All I try to do is to write music that feels meaningful to me, that has commitment and passion behind it. And I guess I feel that if what I'm writing about is real, and if there's emotion, then hey, there'll be somebody who wants to hear it. I don't know if it's a big audience or a smaller audience than I've had. But that's never been my primary inter-est. I've had a kind of story I've been telling, and I'm really only in the middle of it....I want to sing about who I am now. When I was young, I always said I didn't want to end up being forty-five or fifty and pretending I was fifteen or sixteen or twenty. That just didn't interest me. I'm a lifetime musician; I'm going to be playing music forever. I don't foresee a time when I would not be onstage some-where, playing a guitar and playing it loud, with power and passion. I look forward to being sixty or sixty-five and doing that.

You mentioned the 'Born in the U.S.A.' tour as marking the end of one phase of your career. How did the enormousness of that album and tour affect your life?

I really enjoyed the success of *Born in the U.S.A.*, but by the end of that whole thing, I just kind of felt "Bruced" out. I was like, "Whoa, enough of that." You end up creating this sort of icon, and eventu-ally it oppresses you.

What specifically are you referring to?

Well, for example, the whole image that had been created — and that I'm sure I promoted — it really always felt like, "Hey, that's not me." I mean, the macho thing, that was just never me. It might be a little more of me than I think, but when I was a kid, I was a real gentle child, and I was more in touch with those sorts of things.

It's funny, you know, what you create, but in the end, I think, the only thing you can do is destroy it. So when I wrote "Tunnel of Love," I thought I had to reintroduce myself as a songwriter, in a very non-iconic role. And it was a relief. And then I got to a place where I had to sit some more of that stuff down, and part of it was coming out here to L.A. and making some music with some differ-ent people and seeing what that's about and living in a different place for a while.

How's it been out here [in Los Angeles], compared with New Jersey?

Los Angeles provides a lot of anonymity. You're not like the big fish in the small pond. People wave to you and say hi, but you're pretty much left to go your own way. Me in New Jersey, on the other hand, was like Santa Claus at the North Pole [*laughs*].

What do you mean?

Hmm, how can I put it? It's like you're a bit of a figment of a lot of other people's imaginations. And that always takes some sorting out. But it's even worse when you see yourself as a figment of your own imagination. And in the last three or four years, that's something I've really freed myself from.

I think what happened was that when I was young, I had this idea of playing out my life like it was some movie, writing the script and making all the pieces fit. And I really did that for a long time. But you can get enslaved by your own myth or your own image, for the lack of a better word. And it's bad enough having other people seeing you that way, but seeing yourself that way is really bad. It's pathetic. And I got to a place, when Patti [Scialfa, Springsteen's second wife] and I hooked up, where I said I got to stop writing this story. It doesn't work.

And that's when I realized I needed a change, and I like the West. I like the geography. Los Angeles is a funny city. Thirty minutes and you're in the mountains, where for a hundred miles there's one store. Or you're in the desert, where for five hundred miles there's five towns.

So Patti and I came out here and put the house together and had the babies and . . . the thing is, I'd really missed a big part of my life. The only way I could describe it is that being successful in one area is illusory. People think because you're so good at one particular thing, you're good at many things. And that's almost always not the case. You're good at that particular thing, and the danger is that

that particular thing allows you the indulgence to remove yourself from the rest of your life. And as time passed, I realized that I was using my job well in many ways, but there was a fashion in which I was also abusing it. And—this began in my early thirties—I really knew that something was wrong.

That was about ten years ago?

Yeah, it started after I got back from the River tour. I'd had more success than I'd ever thought I'd have. We'd played around the world. And I thought, like, "Wow, this is it." And I decided, "Okay, I want to have a house." And I started to look for a house.

I looked for two years. Couldn't find one. I've probably been in every house in the state of New Jersey—twice. Never bought a house. Figured I just couldn't find one I liked. And then I realized that it ain't that I can't find one, I couldn't buy one. I can find one, but I can't buy one. Damn! Why is that?

And I started to pursue why that was. Why did I only feel good on the road? Why were all my characters in my songs in cars? I mean, when I was in my early twenties, I was always sort of like, "Hey, what I can put in this suitcase, that guitar case, that bus—that's all I need, now and forever." And I really believed it. And really lived it. Lived it for a long time.

In a 'Rolling Stone' cover story from 1978, Dave Marsh wrote that you were so devoted to music that it was impossible to imagine you being married or having kids or a house. . . .

A lot of people have said the same thing. But then something started ticking. It didn't feel right. It was depressing. It was like, "This is a joke. I've come a long way, and there's some dark joke here at the end."

I didn't want to be one of those guys who can write music and tell stories and have an effect on people's lives, and maybe on society in some fashion, but not be able to get into his own self. But that was pretty much my story.

I tend to be an isolationist by nature. And it's not about money or where you live or how you live. It's about psychology. My dad was certainly the same way. You don't need a ton of dough and walls around your house to be isolated. I know plenty of people who are isolated with a six-pack of beer and a television set. But that was a big part of my nature.

Then music came along, and I latched onto it as a way to combat that part of myself. It was a way that I could talk to people. It provided me with a means of communication, a means of placing myself in a social context—which I had a tendency not to want to do.

And music did those things but in an abstract fashion, ultimately. It did them for the guy with the guitar, but the guy without the guitar was pretty much the same as he had been.

Now I see that two of the best days of my life were the day I picked up the guitar and the day that I learned how to put it down. Somebody said, "Man, how did you play for so long?" I said: "That's the easy part. It's stopping that's hard."

When did you learn to put the guitar down?

Pretty recently. I had locked into what was pretty much a hectic obsession, which gave me enormous focus and energy and fire to burn, because it was coming out of pure fear and self-loathing and self-hatred. I'd get onstage and it was hard for me to stop. That's why my shows were so long. They weren't long because I had an idea or a plan that they should be that long. I couldn't stop until I felt burnt, period. Thoroughly burnt.

It's funny, because the results of the show or the music might have been positive for other people, but there was an element of it that was abusive for me. Basically, it was my drug. And so I started to follow the thread of weaning myself.

For a long time, I had been able to ignore it. When you're nineteen and you're in a truck and you're crossing the country back and forth, and then you're twenty-five and you're on tour with the band—that just fit my personality completely. That's why I was able to be good at it. But then I reached an age where I began to miss my real life—or to even know that there was another life to be lived. I mean, it was almost a surprise. First you think you are living it. You got a variety of different girlfriends, and then, "Gee, sorry, gotta go now." It was like the Groucho Marx routine—it's funny, 'cause it runs in my family a little bit, and we get into this: "Hello, I came to say I'd like to stay, but I really must be going." And that was me.

What was it that woke you up to the fact that you were missing something or had a problem?

Unhappiness. And other things, like my relationships. They always ended poorly; I didn't really know how to have a relationship with a woman. Also, I wondered how can I have this much money and not spend it? Up until the Eighties, I really didn't have any money. When we started the River tour, I had about twenty grand, I think. So, really, around 1983 was the first time I had some money in the bank. But I couldn't spend it, I couldn't have any fun. So a lot of things started to not feel logical. I realized there was some aberrational behavior going on here. And I didn't feel that good. Once out of the touring context, and out of the context of my work, I felt lost.

Did you ever go to a therapist or seek help like that?

Oh, yeah. I mean, I got really down. Really bad off for a while. And what happened was, all my rock & roll answers had fizzled out. I realized that my central idea—which, at a young age, was attacking music with a really religious type of intensity—was okay to a point. But there was a point where it turns in on itself. And you start to go down that dark path, and there is a distortion of even the best of things. And I reached a point where I felt my life was distorted. I love my music, and I wanted to just take it for what it was. I didn't want to try to distort it into being my entire life. Because that's a lie. It's not true. It's not your entire life. It never can be.

And I realized my real life is waiting to be lived. All the love and the hope and the sorrow and sadness—that's all over there, waiting to be lived. And I could ignore it and push it aside or I could say yes to it. But to say yes to part of it is to say yes to all of it. That's why people say no to all of it. Whether it's drugs or whatever. That's why people say no: I'll skip the happiness as long as I don't have to feel the pain.

So I decided to work on it. I worked hard on it. And basically, you have to start to open up to who you are. I certainly wasn't the person I thought I was. This was around the time of *Born in the U.S.A.* And I bought this big house in New Jersey, which was really quite a thing for me to do. It was a place I used to run by all the time. It was a big house, and I said, "Hey, this is a rich man's house." And I think the toughest thing was that it was in a town where I'd been spit on when I was a kid.

This was in Rumson?

Yeah. When I was sixteen or seventeen my band, from Freehold, was booked in a beach club. And we engendered some real hostile reaction. I guess we looked kind of—we had on phony snakeskin vests and had long hair. There's a picture of me in the Castiles, that's what it was. And I can remember being onstage, with guys literally spitting on it. This was before it was fashionable, when it kind of meant what it really meant.

So it was a funny decision, but I bought this house, and at first I really began to enjoy it, but then along came the *Born in the U.S.A.* tour, and I was off down the road again.

It was during this time that you met Julianne [Phillips, Springsteen's first wife]?

Yeah, we met about halfway through that tour. And we got married. And it was tough. I didn't really know how to be a husband. She was a terrific person, but I just didn't know how to do it.

Was the marriage part of your whole effort to make connections, to deal with that part of your life?

Yeah, yeah. I really needed something, and I was giving it a shot. Anybody who's been through a divorce can tell you what that's about. It's difficult, hard and painful for everybody involved. But I sort of went on.

Then Patti and I got together, on the *Tunnel of Love* tour, and I began to find my way around again. But after we came off the road in 1988, I had a bad year right away. I got home, and I wasn't very helpful to anyone.

Some of your fans seem to think along the same lines, that by moving to L.A. and buying a $14 million house, you've let them down or betrayed them.

I kept my promises. I didn't get burned out. I didn't waste myself. I didn't die. I didn't throw away my musical values. Hey, I've dug in my heels on all those things. And my music has been, for the most part, a positive, liberating, living, uplifting thing. And along the way I've made a lot of money, and I bought a big house. And I love it. Love it. It's great. It's beautiful, really beautiful. And in some ways, it's my first real home. I have pictures of my family there. And there's a place where I make music, and a place for babies, and it's like a dream.

I still love New Jersey. We go back all the time. I've been looking at a farm there that I might buy. I'd like my kids to have that, too. But I came out here, and I just felt like the guy who was born in the U.S.A. had left the bandanna behind, you know?

I've struggled with a lot of things over the past two, three years, and it's been real rewarding. I've been very, very happy, truly the happiest I've ever been in my whole life. And it's not that one-dimensional idea of "happy." It's accepting a lot of death and sorrow and mortality. It's putting the script down and letting the chips fall where they may.

What's been the toughest thing about being a father?

Engagement. Engagement. Engagement. You're afraid to love some-thing so much, you're afraid to be that in love. Because a world of fear leaps upon you, particularly in the world that we live in. But then you realize: "Oh, I see, to love something so much, as much as I love Patti and my kids, you've got to be able to accept and live with that world of fear, that world of doubt, of the future. And you've got to give it all today and not hold back." And that was my specialty; my specialty was keeping my distance so that if I lost something, it wouldn't hurt that much. And you can do that, but you're never going to have anything.

It's funny, because the night my little boy was born, it was amaz-ing. I've played onstage for hundreds of thousands of people, and I've felt my own spirit really rise some nights. But when he came out, I had this feeling of a kind of love that I hadn't experienced before. And the minute I felt it, it was terrifying. It was like, "Wow, I see. This love is here to be had and to be felt and experienced? To everybody, on a daily basis?" And I knew why you run, because it's very frightening. But it's also a window into another world. And it's the world that I want to live in right now.

DAVID LETTERMAN

by Bill Zehme

February 18, 1993

How are you sleeping at night during these heady times? [Letterman had just signed a $14 million deal to host CBS's *The Late Show*]

By and large, I sleep fitfully. And when I wake up, the sheets are drenched in perspiration. But the experts believe it's just a lack of amino acids. So we're trying to correct that with the cigars.

Has all the pressure driven you back to smoking?

For Christmas, somebody gave me a perfectly humidored twenty-five-year-old cigar, and it was so pleasant, I just thought, well, I'll try these again for a bit.

Aren't those Cuban contraband?

[*Cups cigar away from view*] Uh, these are White Owls! You can get these anywhere!

I heard you only smoked Cubans.

You got the wrong guy. You don't know what the hell you're talking about! Call the IRS. I pay my taxes.

By the way, now that you're getting the big dough, do you have any plans to acquire a better hairpiece?

[*Laughs*] By God, when they build a better hairpiece, I'll buy it!

Have you spoken to Johnny Carson lately?

Not too long ago, Peter Lassally, who came to our show as an executive producer after doing the same for Johnny, told a newspaper that Carson used to come in to work at two each afternoon and that I was coming in at ten. And so Carson read this and started calling my office at ten o'clock that day. I didn't get in till like eleven-thirty, and as soon as I got on the phone with him, he was screaming and howling: "Oh, get in at ten, huh? Where ya been? Car trouble?" The last time I saw him, at the Emmy dinner, he just seemed great and happy. He's really getting a kick out of everybody else's troubles.

Are you more comfortable in your relationship with him?

I'm more comfortable now that he doesn't have a show. I can maybe relax a little bit and try to have a more honest human exchange with him. For a whole generation, he kind of established the model of how cool guys behaved. I just had so much respect for him that, right or wrong, it was an inhibitor for me.

On the air, he was always inviting you to come over to play tennis with him. Ever go?

Yeah, I finally said to myself, "This is a living legend — you're stupid if you don't screw up the courage to go!"

And?

He beat me. He's very good. He can stand in one place, never break a sweat and run your pants off. But in my defense, how can you just go to Johnny's house? First of all, his house is like a goddamn Olympic venue. Johnny's court is like a stadium where they have the Davis Cup trials. He's got this state-of-the-art tennis surface—something NASA developed when they went to Neptune. The whole experience was unnerving. And his wife was very nice to me. But there wasn't a second I didn't fully expect to just kind of turn abruptly and destroy a $6,000 lamp or vase. I just felt, something's going to go wrong, like I'm going to kill Johnny's wife with the ball machine. "How could you have killed his wife with the ball machine!" It's just like I'm too big, I'm too dumb, I'm too clumsy.

Is it true that for years you wouldn't watch his show?

It was too depressing for me. I know what it takes to just get something on tape. Hosting this show, I always feel like, "Man, I'm struggling, I'm like a drowning man in quicksand!" And then you turn on Johnny's show and say [*daunted*], "Oh, it's fuckin' Johnny!" He's just easy, cool, funny. He looks good, he's got babes hanging on him, he's saying witty things and making fun of Ed. It so intimidated me that I couldn't watch it. But I guess like everybody else I watched him pretty much every night during the last month or so.

How did your own Johnny grief manifest itself?

I can remember watching that last show and just being woefully depressed. I couldn't sleep, I was up the whole night—which maybe tells you more about me than I would like. I know it sounds like I'm a complete ninny, but I felt a sadness for weeks after. It was sort of like a doctor telling you, "Well, we've looked at the X-rays, and your legs are perfectly healthy, but we're still going to amputate them." You think, "*Whaaa?* Why is he going?"

But as with most aspects of his career, he did this retiring thing at the right time, the right way. And I look at the mess I'm in now, and I think [*as Dumb Guy*], "What the hell am I gonna do now?" I have no clue. But Carson just figures it out and carries it off with great skill, grace and aplomb.

One week before he retired, you went on 'The Tonight Show.' At the end of the program, you said to him, "Thanks for my career."

I knew at the time it might have sounded flip, but it's certainly the case. He's the only reason I'm here. There have been a lot of people in my life who have been very helpful to me and have really done me favors and helped me in ways I'll never be able to repay. But if there's one person to whom I owe the most, it has to be him.

If you'd gotten 'The Tonight Show,' would you have dared—as did Leno—to go on the Monday following Carson's final Friday? Isn't that a no-win scenario?

No, if the circumstances had been different—by which I mean, *if they'd given me the job!* [*laughs*] —sure, I would have done it. This is not to demean what Jay accomplished, but were it I that night, it would have been handled much differently. Because you can't just turn off over one weekend that six-month period of genuine emotion and interest and care and concern. You *have* to address that, and I would have done it. Now you could be criticized for trying to make yourself look good by kissing up to Johnny. But there was so much positive feeling about this man that it would have been hard to make too big a mistake there. I'm confident that we would have done a really nice job for that first show. Now, I'm not saying the rest of the week would have been anything. It would have sped downhill immediately.

Some of your former writers are working on 'The Larry Sanders Show,' a great neurotic satire of talk-show life. Does this suggest that you are the real Larry Sanders?

Every time I watch that show I think: "Hey, wait a minute! That's me!" But I don't know if it really is me or if they have the talk-show machine so well assessed that it looks like me. During almost every episode I think, "Boy, didn't that happen here once?" They've all had an eerie effect on me.

You're famously brutal about your own performance. For instance, your recent session with Walter Cronkite—while genial to the naked eye—left you greatly unhinged.

I really felt like I had screwed that up, because I was just overwhelmed by the guy. He sits down and you think, "Oh, my God, it's Walter Cronkite!" So I just yammered all over him and just fumbled it.

Your post-show drill, then, is to come back to your office and review the tape, dwelling on the mishaps?

I have my own little ritual, yeah. But I should. If you've got men on base and you can't drive them in, how come you're getting major-league money? That's the point. At this stage, I ought to be able to do a better job. I just felt that not only did I let the show down, I let Walter Cronkite down and I let myself down.

But do you recognize you're being hard on yourself—

No! No! Why let yourself off the hook? If I fucked it up, I fucked it up. So obviously you come back the next day and try it again. Fortunately, we had Marv Albert on and got right to his blooper reel. Smooth sailing!

Do you buy the notion that awkward TV is good TV?

Yeah, if it doesn't involve you—absolutely.

To a certain degree, if a guest brings out visible discomfort in you, it's actually kind of entertaining.

I've heard people tell me that many, many, many times. And I guess if you provide yourself the luxury of some distance and a little objectivity, that couldn't be more accurate. But at the time, you just think the studio is filling up with room-temperature saliva.

Pee-wee Herman was that type of catalyst. You introduced him to the main-stream, but then he disappeared from the show.

Something about a Florida movie theater, I think. Did you hear anything about that?

Before all that. Was he banished?

No, Pee-wee Herman was always great for us. There was a very small falling-out—I think it had something to do with *The Arsenio Hall Show*. I don't know whether it was him or us or both of us.

Would you have him back?

Oh, yeah, absolutely. You know who I really miss? There's a song on the new R.E.M. CD that I listened to like six times before I finally realized, "Holy shit, this is about Andy Kaufman!" Andy would orchestrate and rehearse each of his appearances for maximum impact. And when the impact worked, good or bad, he would savor it. If we could have one guest like Andy—to me that's worth six months of new material. Steve Martin also does it for us. He comes on and actually performs. There's nobody else like that now.

The night Sonny and Cher reunited on your show, you spoke of the futility of mixing business and romantic partnerships. You were alluding, I guess, to your relationship with Merrill Markoe, with whom you created this show.

Right, right. One night I think maybe Merrill and I will get back together on the show and do a couple of songs. I'm still very fond of her, and she's one of these people to whom I owe a great debt. Sadly, I haven't talked to her in years. This is so silly, but in the time that has elapsed, Merrill's mother died, and I never knew about it. Two more years go by and her dog Stan dies. So I sent her a note of condolence over the death of Stan—completely ignorant of the fact that her mother had passed away. I somberly wrote, "I now take pen in hand..." and she must have thought: "*Yeah, but what about my mother? She's been dead for a year and a half, and you never said anything!*" But with Stan, word came to us that he'd somehow eaten an entire ham. Oh, God. [*Chuckles*] And it just killed him. Too much ham.

As I recall, your dog Bob was on the West Coast with Merrill when he died. That must have been a tough night for you to get through the show.

Yep, yep. At the time, Merrill and I were estranged. It turned out Bob was ridden with cancer. He had eaten a Presto log, and as a result, his lungs were covered with tumors. But they give off a nicely colored flame if burned—very festive for the holidays. So she called and said the vet thought we should put him to sleep. I said I'd be off the following week and would come out. But the vet said we couldn't wait. So they put him to sleep right there, which was—it was sad...But I can't—I'm not sure I would have been much good had I been there.

Merrill recently published a tell-all book about life with Bob and Stan, didn't she?

We wanted her to be on the show to promote it, but the only request we made—because of her relationship with me and the show—was that we wanted her to do our show first. It made a difference to me. But because of scheduling, it couldn't happen. She did every other show: Howard Stern, Arsenio Hall, Jay. Which is fine. She's one of the smartest people I've ever known in my life. I mean, we haven't had a good idea since she left.

Is there a downside to being in a relationship with you?

Do the words "moody drunk" mean anything to you?

Many would imagine you're every gal's dream.

Yeah, you'd think so, wouldn't you? But I'm no day at the beach, let's just say that.

Does fatherhood beckon?

Well, I get very excited about kids. A while back, all of my friends started having kids, and I was spending more time with infants than I had ever spent since I was an infant. And I found them just a wonder. It was something that I hadn't really thought about until the last two or three years. So I've decided that as soon as I get everything in my life just perfect, then I'll start having kids. I'm looking at maybe six, eight months of fine-tuning, and then we're on to the family.

Are you feeling pressure to get yourself hitched?

Well, you know, I've had that kind of pressure for as long as I can remember. In fact, the only one who didn't pressure me was the woman I was actually married to. And I think she was greatly relieved when we were no longer married.

I don't know, it seems like I've spent way too much time in my life concentrating on just one thing—the work. And the older I get, it now seems like maybe that was not necessarily *the* thing to spend all my time on. Because after almost eleven years, it's not like we've got it figured out. I think to myself, "We're doing something wrong, we've misplaced part of the instructions," because after all this time, it's still hard, and you would think at this stage of things it would be easier. I don't think Carson ever went home with his stomach in knots because Sharon Stone was in tears.

Sharon Stone was in tears?

In fairness to me, Howard Stern made her cry in the greenroom—it wasn't me. What a baby.

The Talk Show Wars were first made a gruesome spectacle when NBC fired Leno's irascible manager-producer, Helen Kushnick. Did you ever feel the effects of her hardball tactics?

It was mostly just something in the air that we'd rather have done without. We were closely tied to it because we're back-to-back on the same network and booking a lot of the same guests. But it was more of a nuisance in theory than in reality. She was just trying to do the best job she could possibly do for Jay and for the show. People operate in different ways.

Life at NBC turned especially ugly before the holidays. You labeled it "the Happy Network."

That last day it just seemed like the sky had opened up. There was all this friction—and it had little to do with me. Even if Johnny were still hosting *The Tonight Show,* I'd do myself a great disservice if I didn't explore other possibilities after ten, eleven years in one spot. The thing that's made it so dramatic is the situation with *The Tonight Show* and my alleged bitterness. But I was disappointed that I didn't get the show. I would have loved to try to follow Carson.

If you had aggressively campaigned for the job—which Jay reportedly did with NBC big shots—do you think things might have turned out differently?

Well, in regard to *The Tonight Show* when Johnny was still there, it would have hurt my feelings if he'd thought that I was politicking for his job. I mean, Carson was still sitting up and taking solid food—who am I to be sliding up and saying, "Oh, by the way, Johnny, when you step down—and we're not saying you're close, you understand—let's grease it for me to step in"? Who could be that presumptuous? So what I did was take every opportunity, if asked, to go on record as saying, "Yes, I would like to be considered for the job." I wasn't comfortable with anything more than that.

Because in essence what I would be saying was, "John, the clock is ticking, it's time to go."

Have you spoken to Jay amid all this stuff?

I speak to Jay now with the same regularity that I have always spoken to Jay. Which is not much. There's no ill will personally. If I felt I was deprived of something that was rightfully mine, if I had fantasies about being hoodwinked or misled—then there might be ill will. I'm not the kind of person that wants to see somebody else fail on television. Whatever the future holds, I'm in pretty good shape. So, no, I'm not upset with NBC, I'm not upset with Jay.

I guess a case could be made that maybe Bush is upset with Clinton, because George didn't get the job and Bill did. So what? Who among us hasn't endured disappointment in our life? But for me to be upset with Jay, you would have to suppose that he did something hurtful and awful to me by being hired as the host of *The Tonight Show*. And I would guess that you could look long and hard and not find evidence of that.

Your relationship with him has great ironic overtones in that you've credited him with being among your primary comic inspirations.

Oh, without question. As he's probably been for a whole batch of other guys who came after me. He was the best—and still is—as far as stand-up comedians go.

On the flip side, he's said repeatedly that he wouldn't be where he is if you hadn't given him a showcase on 'Late Night.'

Well, he's being gracious, because he did as much for us as we did for him—maybe more. He could have accomplished for himself what he did here on any other show. But for us, like I said earlier, to find a regular guest who could always come out and who really could deliver, jeez, that was money in the bank.

On the first day outside parties were permitted to bid for your services, you opened your monologue by saying, "I feel like a million bucks!" Just how does a million bucks feel?

Beats me. I'm just tickled by the phrase.

You're saying you've yet to feel like a million bucks during any of this?

No, no. I'm embarrassed by all the attention.

So what kind of dollar value would you place on how you feel?

I feel like a million bucks.

DAVID GEFFEN

by Patrick Goldstein

April 29, 1993

Did you always want to be in the entertainment business?

I couldn't wait to be old enough to move to California. I wanted to be where the movies are made, in that land of sunshine and Gidget and surfboards and convertibles and green lawns and beautiful houses. The day after I graduated high school, I moved to Los Angeles.

You were fascinated even as a little boy?

I remember the first time I went to Radio City Music Hall, I went out to get chocolate cigarettes, and when I came back into the theater and opened up those big doors, it was at the end of a Rockettes number, and I was walking down this aisle, and people were applauding like crazy. And I had this fantasy that I was walking down to get my Academy Award. I remember that clearly.

And were you interested in the business of show business?

I used to read everything I could get my hands on about the entertainment business. When I was nine years old, I knew what was in Hedda Hopper's column and Walter Winchell's column too. My brother used to say that I was a wealth of worthless information.

And what did you envision yourself doing?

I had an epiphany when I bought a biography of Louis B. Mayer by Bosley Crowther called *Hollywood Raja*. I read this book and I thought, "I want this job." To me, it seemed like the greatest job in the world.

But when you finally had a big job in the movie business at Warner Bros. Pictures in 1975, you hated it.

I didn't find it satisfying at all. The worst job in the world is running a movie studio. It's very hard when every piece of product costs thirty or forty million dollars, and every day you have to read two gossip-column items in the trade papers which talk about what a schmuck you are for the decisions you've made or not made.

Most studio executives seem trapped by this awful malaise.

I don't think it's malaise. I think it's fear. The operative word in Hollywood is "fear." Most people are afraid they'll make a mistake, be humiliated and lose their jobs. They want to be safe. I don't think that's true in the record business. People don't lose their jobs because they sign an artist whose record comes out and flops.

You still think the record industry is free from Hollywood's blockbuster mentality?

You just can't compare them. You can still make a record for hundreds of thousands of dollars. Today you can't make a movie for less than $18 to $25 million, so the failure of one of those movies has a profound effect on the lives of the people involved. The failure of any record doesn't have a profound effect on any record company, so there's a tremendous leeway given for failure. And I think if you don't give people the opportunity to fail, you don't give them much chance to succeed either, and so what you end up with in the film business is a lot of shitty movies.

You've been involved with a lot of artists, from David Crosby through John Lennon to Axl Rose, who lived on the edge, whether it was drugs or primal screams or throwing tantrums onstage or urinating on your A&R executives' desks. Why are creative people caught up in so many psychodramas?

Because there are lots of voices speaking in their heads, very often at the same time, and it can be very confusing. I have complete respect for the insanity of what it was like to be fifteen or sixteen or nineteen or twenty-five. I couldn't have been more fucked up myself, going through all those years. I may not have been peeing on someone's desk, but I was certainly driving myself or some other person crazy. I think it's a miracle that certain people can survive the fame they get at an early age. I mean, Axl Rose—one minute he's sleeping in doorways, a minute later he's a multimillionaire and every girl wants to fuck him. That's very hard to deal with. I think it's a miracle that people survive becoming big stars. As we well know, many don't.

Yet there's a thrill to being a celebrity. I remember seeing a wonderfully striking Annie Leibovitz photo of you, lying in bed in the morning, on the phone—and you were completely at ease. It didn't look like you had any clothes on. Do you normally sleep in the nude?

I do. The truth of the matter is I've known Annie for many years and I trust her completely. So I'll do anything. I once posed in 1971 in front of the Beverly Hills Hotel naked with a leaf in front of my dick because she dared me to do it. Jackson Browne has it framed in his living room.

What I found intriguing about the photo of you in bed was that all the books on the shelf were biographies of people from dysfunctional families. 'The Hustons,'

'The Binghams of Louisville.' You came from a complicated family yourself. Your mother fled the pogroms in Russia and never saw her family again. And when you grew up in Brooklyn, she was the real breadwinner in the family.

She was an amazing woman, one of those kinds of classic people who survived incredibly difficult lives. My father didn't have a job, so she took in sewing and ended up developing a business where she made corsets and brassieres for people in her apartment. Then she had a store and finally bought the building the store was in.

So your mother always worked?

I grew up in an odd family. When other kids came home at three p.m. for milk and cookies, my mother wasn't there. When you're a kid, you don't quite understand. You kind of wonder—is there something wrong with you? I don't know how to describe my mother except to say that I admired her, although there were times in my growing up that I wanted to kill her.

Why? Was she domineering? Overprotective?

When I was fifteen, she said: "Okay, that's it. No more allowance. You want money, you go to work." That's the way it was in our family. My mother was going to teach us to take care of ourselves. I can remember my mother ironing my shirts, and she said to me: "Come on, I'll teach you how to iron a shirt." When it was finished, she said: "Okay, that's it. I don't have to iron any of your shirts anymore. Now that you know how to do it, you do it." I wanted to kill her.

You've said your father fancied himself an intellectual. He spoke many languages, but he never really worked much.

He read a lot. He was scholarly. He traveled the world. In Yiddish there's an expression: *schvare arbiter*. Hard worker. He wasn't one of those. As a kid, it made me resentful.

Did you consider him a failure because he didn't work?

Yes. I was angry with him for what I saw as his failure in life. But he died when I was seventeen. So I never really got to resolve my relationship with him. That's always been a sad thing for me.

What made your mother a big influence on you?

No matter how badly I did in school, no matter how little faith I had in myself, my mother always said, "You have golden hands. Whatever you want to be, you'll succeed at." And I thought she was a nut, because I was a complete fuck-up and I didn't think I could do anything. But my mother's belief in me gave me a level of confidence that enabled me to succeed in life.

Michael Apted has made a series of documentaries that follow kids as they grow into adulthood, based on the maxim "Give me the child at seven, and I'll show you the man." What were you like at seven?

When I was seven, my mother had suffered a nervous breakdown and was institutionalized, and my grandmother was taking care of the family. I was confused. I didn't understand what was going on.

What happened?

When I was six, in 1949, my mother got a letter from a sister in Russia who she didn't even know was alive. They hadn't seen each other since 1917. And she told her that everyone in the family had died and that she was the only survivor. And my mother had a nervous breakdown.

Had they been killed in the Holocaust?

No, they had lived in the Ukraine. And when the Nazis were marching across Russia, the Ukrainians didn't wait for the Germans to get there. They rounded up all the Jews in the neighborhood and killed them. In the case of my mother's family, they threw everyone down their wells. Eleven people. My mother's mother and father and grandmother and grandfather and seven brothers and sisters. My mother's sister survived because she wasn't home.

And when did your mother tell you all this?

She never did. No one knew what had happened. The day after my mother died, her sister told me she had written her all about it. No one ever saw the letter. Not my father and my brother. All they knew was that Mom had gone crazy. My mother was very secretive. Before she died, she had a series of strokes, and the last stroke affected her ability to use her right hand and to speak. But she worked and worked on it, and she regained her ability to speak and the use of her hand. And the last time I spoke to her before she died, I said, "Mom, to what do you attribute this miracle?" And she said: "I have no envy. I have no jealousy. And I have no hate." And she died two days later.

What kind of advice did she give you as you grew up?

It was advice tinged with a lot of suspicion and fear, because my mother lived a life that would encourage suspicion and distrust. I learned how to be careful.

Careful in your relationships with people?

Careful in business, careful in everything. I acquired a healthy amount of my mother's suspicion.

Has that in some ways cut you off from people?

I don't think so. I'm a person who's been in therapy, analysis, Lifespring, est, Course in Miracles, for the last twenty-five years.

I've been working on myself and my demons and my nonsense and my fucked-up-ness for a long, long time. Which is not to say that I'm still not a little fucked up. I think you get better and better in tiny increments, and you die unhealed.

To use your mother's words: No envy, no jealousy and no hate. How far along the road are you to those three?

At my mother's funeral, I told [Hollywood agent] Sue Mengers, who is a good friend, what my mother had said, and Sue looked at me and said, "Well, they'll never be able to say that about us."

There's a famous story about how you got your first real job, working in the William Morris mailroom, by faking your résumé and saying you'd graduated from UCLA. And you watched the mail every morning, waiting for the letter to come saying you hadn't graduated. And when it came, you steamed it open and replaced it with a letter on fake university stationery saying you had. What does that say about your level of ambition?

It's about survival. If you want this job and the only way you can get it is to be a college graduate and you clearly aren't—I made it up. It just seemed like the practical thing to do.

And is that what it takes to get ahead in show business?

Let's not kid ourselves. I could have done that and been untalented, and I would have failed. The reason I succeeded in my life is not because I have chutzpah. I succeeded in life because I'm smart and I'm talented.

What initially made you want to launch Asylum Records [in 1971]?

I started the record company because I couldn't get a record deal for Jackson Browne. I had taken him around, and everybody had passed. Nobody wanted him. I told Ahmet Ertegun, "Listen, I'm doing you a favor." And he said: "Don't do me no favors. If he's such a big star, why don't you do it yourself?"

You once said that everywhere you went in 1970 you found somebody talented—Linda Ronstadt, Jackson Browne, Glenn Frey, Don Henley, Tom Waits, Steve Martin. It's a long list. Is it really true nobody wanted to sign them?

I could've signed twice as many people if I really had an idea of what I was doing. They'd all been around. Linda Ronstadt was on Capitol—she'd had a hit with the Stone Poneys and her career went nowhere. Jackson Browne had already been signed and dropped by Elektra without ever making a record! Don Henley and Glenn Frey had been signed by a company called Amos Records. I bought their recording contract and their music publishing rights, which were owned by Amos, for $5,000. And gave them back half their publishing. People just didn't recognize these people's talents.

What was different about the music business then? Was it more about music than about business?

I don't think so. But in those days there were lots of young entrepreneurs—Chris Blackwell had Island Records; Jerry Moss and Herb Alpert had A&M Records; Herb Cohen had Bizarre Records. Today, except for Ahmet, all the entrepreneurs are gone. All the small record companies are gone. The costs are incredible today. What it costs to make one record today by an unknown artist—$300,000—would equal the entire recording budget for Asylum Records in 1972. In those days, people were, for the most part, self-contained. Joni Mitchell performed with a guitar, Laura Nyro with a piano. Today everyone has a big band, and it's very expensive to keep that kind of organization going.

You and Joni Mitchell lived together for three years—as roommates, not as lovers. You said you two were like the Odd Couple. What did you mean?

I was doing business. Joni was painting and creating. She would try out new songs all the time. She wrote a song about me — "Free Man in Paris." I was embarrassed when she first wrote it. I felt it was an exposure of some kind. It was like "Oh, my God..." It seemed so personal. I knew exactly what she meant: "He said you just can't win. Everybody's in it for their own game." It was very deep and very right. That's why she's such a great songwriter. Her stuff is extraordinarily revealing, both about herself and about others. Of course, today I'm extraordinarily proud of it.

You don't have anyone quite like Joni Mitchell or Bob Dylan on your label today, but you do have Guns n' Roses. How did you first meet them?

Tom Zutaut had signed the band, and they were camped out in the reception room of our record company, looking like they were sleeping in the street. And I remember going upstairs and saying, "Who is that in the reception area?" And they said, "It's Guns n' Roses." And I said, "My God, these guys look like they haven't got a nickel." And Tom Zutaut said, "They don't."

So looking back, which artists' careers do you think you really had an impact on, in the sense that you helped them reach certain artistic achievements?

I felt I had a big impact on Jackson Browne's career, and Crosby, Stills, Nash and Young and Laura Nyro and Joni Mitchell. But if I didn't exist, they still would have been successful. The only thing I'm sure of is that Joni Mitchell wouldn't have written "Free Man in Paris."

KURT COBAIN

by David Fricke

January 27, 1994

Along with everything else that went wrong onstage tonight [at Chicago's Aragon Ballroom], you left without playing "Smells Like Teen Spirit." Why?

That would have been the icing on the cake [*smiles grimly*]. That would have made everything twice as worse.

I don't even remember the guitar solo on "Teen Spirit." It would take me five minutes to sit in the catering room and learn the solo. But I'm not interested in that kind of stuff. I don't know if that's so lazy that I don't care anymore or what. I still like playing "Teen Spirit," but it's almost an embarrassment to play it.

In what way? Does the enormity of its success still bug you?

Yeah. Everyone has focused on that song so much. The reason it gets a big reaction is people have seen it on MTV a million times. It's been pounded into their brains. But I think there are so many other songs that I've written that are as good, if not better, than that song, like "Drain You." That's definitely as good as "Teen Spirit." I love the lyrics, and I never get tired of playing it. Maybe if it was as big as "Teen Spirit," I wouldn't like it as much.

But I can barely, especially on a bad night like tonight, get through "Teen Spirit." I literally want to throw my guitar down and walk away. I can't pretend to have a good time playing it.

But you must have had a good time writing it.

We'd been practicing for about three months. We were waiting to sign to DGC, and Dave [Grohl] and I were living in Olympia [Washington], and Krist [Novoselic] was living in Tacoma [Washington]. We were driving up to Tacoma every night for practice, trying to write songs. I was trying to write the ultimate pop song. I was basically trying to rip off the Pixies. I have to admit it [*smiles*]. When I heard the Pixies for the first time, I connected with that band so heavily I should have been in that band—or at least in a Pixies cover band. We used their sense of dynamics, being soft and quiet and then loud and hard.

"Teen Spirit" was such a clichéd riff. It was so close to a Boston riff or "Louie, Louie." When I came up with the guitar part, Krist looked at me and said, "That is so ridiculous." I made the band play it for an hour and a half.

Where did the line "Here we are now, entertain us" come from?

That came from something I used to say every time I used to walk into a party to break the ice. A lot of times, when you're standing around with people in a room, it's really boring and uncomfortable. So it was, "Well, here we are, entertain us. You invited us here."

How did it feel to watch something you'd written in fun, in homage to one of your favorite bands, become the grunge national anthem, not to mention a defining moment in youth marketing?

Actually, we did have our own thing for a while. For a few years in Seattle, it was the Summer of Love, and it was so great. To be able to just jump out on top of the crowd with my guitar and be held up and pushed to the back of the room, and then brought back with no harm done to me—it was a celebration of something that no one could put their finger on.

But once it got into the mainstream, it was over. I'm just tired of being embarrassed by it. I'm beyond that.

This is the first U.S. tour you've done since the fall of '91, just before 'Nevermind' exploded. Why did you stay off the road for so long?

I needed time to collect my thoughts and readjust. It hit me so hard, and I was under the impression that I didn't really need to go on tour, because I was making a whole bunch of money. Millions of dollars. Eight million to 10 million records sold — that sounded like a lot of money to me. So I thought I would sit back and enjoy it.

I don't want to use this as an excuse, and it's come up so many times, but my stomach ailment has been one of the biggest barriers that stopped us from touring. I was dealing with it for a long time. But after a person experiences chronic pain for five years, by the time that fifth year ends, you're literally insane. I couldn't cope with anything. I was as schizophrenic as a wet cat that's been beaten.

How much of that physical pain do you think you channeled into your songwriting?

That's a scary question, because obviously if a person is having some kind of turmoil in their lives, it's usually reflected in the music, and sometimes it's pretty beneficial. I think it probably helped. But I would give up everything to have good health. I wanted to do this interview after we'd been on tour for a while, and so far, this has been the most enjoyable tour I've ever had. Honestly.

It has nothing to do with the larger venues or people kissing our asses more. It's just that my stomach isn't bothering me anymore. I'm eating. I ate a huge pizza last night. It was so nice to be able to do that. And it just raises my spirits. But then again, I was always afraid that if I lost the stomach problem, I wouldn't be as creative. Who knows? [*Pauses*] I don't have any new songs right now.

Every album we've done so far, we've always had one to three songs left over from the sessions. And they usually have been pretty good, ones that we really liked, so we always had something to rely on—a hit or something that was above average. So this next record is going to be really interesting, because I have absolutely nothing left. I'm starting from scratch for the first time. I don't know what we're going to do.

One of the songs that you cut from 'In Utero' at the last minute was "I Hate Myself and I Want to Die." How literally did you mean it?

As literal as a joke can be. Nothing more than a joke. And that had a bit to do with why we decided to take it off. We knew people wouldn't get it; they'd take it too seriously. It was totally satirical, making fun of ourselves. I'm thought of as this pissy, complaining, freaked-out schizophrenic who wants to kill himself all the time. "He isn't satisfied with anything." And I thought it was a funny title. I wanted it to be the title of the album for a long time. But I knew the majority of the people wouldn't understand it.

Have you ever been that consumed with distress or pain or rage that you actually wanted to kill yourself?

For five years during the time I had my stomach problem, yeah. I wanted to kill myself every day. I came very close many times. I'm sorry to be so blunt about it. It was to the point where I was on tour, lying on the floor, vomiting air because I couldn't hold down water. And then I had to play a show in twenty minutes. I would sing and cough up blood.

This is no way to live a life. I love to play music, but something was not right. So I decided to medicate myself.

Even as satire, though, a song like that can hit a nerve. There are plenty of kids out there who, for whatever reasons, really do feel suicidal.

That pretty much defines our band. It's both those contradictions. It's satirical, and it's serious at the same time.

What kind of mail do you get from your fans these days?

[*Long pause*] I used to read the mail a lot, and I used to be really involved with it. But I've been so busy with this record, the video, the tour, that I haven't even bothered to look at a single letter, and I feel really bad about it. I haven't even been able to come up with enough energy to put out our fanzine, which was one of the things we were going to do to combat all the bad press, just to be able to show a more realistic side of the band.

But it's really hard. I have to admit I've found myself doing the same things that a lot of other rock stars do or are forced to do. Which is not being able to respond to mail, not being able to keep up on current music, and I'm pretty much locked away a lot. The outside world is pretty foreign to me.

I feel very, very lucky to be able to go out to a club. Just the other night, we had a night off in Kansas City, Missouri, and Pat [Smear, Nirvana's touring guitarist] and I had no idea where we were or where to go. So we called up the local college radio station and asked them what was going on. And they didn't know! So we happened to call this bar, and the Treepeople from Seattle were playing.

And it turns out I met three really, really nice people there, totally cool kids that were in bands. I really had a good time with them, all night. I invited them back to the hotel. They stayed there. I ordered room service for them. I probably went overboard, trying to be accommodating. But it was really great to know that I can still do that, that I can still find friends.

And I didn't think that would be possible. A few years ago, we were in Detroit, playing at this club, and about ten people showed up. And next door, there was this bar, and Axl Rose came in with ten or fifteen bodyguards. It was this huge extravaganza; all these people were fawning over him. If he'd just walked in by himself, it would have been no big deal. But he wanted that. You create attention to attract attention.

Where do you stand on Pearl Jam now? There were rumors that you and Eddie Vedder were supposed to be on that 'Time' magazine cover together.

I don't want to get into that. One of the things I've learned is that slagging off people just doesn't do me any good. It's too bad, because the whole problem with the feud between Pearl Jam and Nirvana had been going on for so long and has come so close to being fixed.

It's never been entirely clear what this feud with Vedder was about.

There never was one. I slagged them off because I didn't like their band. I hadn't met Eddie at the time. It was my fault; I should have been slagging off the record company instead of them. They were marketed—not probably against their will—but without them realizing they were being pushed into the grunge bandwagon.

Don't you feel any empathy with them? They've been under the same intense follow-up-album pressure as you have.

Yeah, I do. Except I'm pretty sure that they didn't go out of their way to challenge their audience as much as we did with this record. They're a safe rock band. They're a pleasant rock band that everyone likes. [*Laughs*] God, I've had much better quotes in my head about this.

It just kind of pisses me off to know that we work really hard to make an entire album's worth of songs that are as good as we can make them. I'm gonna stroke my ego by saying that we're better than a lot of bands out there. What I've realized is that you only need a couple of catchy songs on an album, and the rest can be bullshit Bad Company rip-offs, and it doesn't matter. If I was smart, I would have saved most of the songs off *Nevermind* and spread them out over a fifteen-year period. But I can't do that. All the albums I ever liked were albums that delivered a great song, one after another:

Aerosmith's *Rocks,* the Sex Pistols' *Never Mind the Bollocks...,* *Led Zeppelin II, Back in Black,* by AC/DC.

You've also gone on record as being a big Beatles fan.

Oh, yeah. John Lennon was definitely my favorite Beatle, hands down. I don't know who wrote what parts of what Beatles songs, but Paul McCartney embarrasses me. Lennon was obviously disturbed [*laughs*]. So I could relate to that.

And from the books I've read—and I'm so skeptical of anything I read, especially in rock books—I just felt really sorry for him. To be locked up in that apartment. Although he was totally in love with Yoko and his child, his life was a prison. He was imprisoned. It's not fair. That's the crux of the problem that I've had with becoming a celebrity—the way people deal with celebrities. It needs to be changed; it really does.

No matter how hard you try, it only comes out like you're bitching about it. I can understand how a person can feel that way and almost become obsessed with it. But it's so hard to convince people to mellow out. Just take it easy, have a little bit of respect. We all shit [*laughs*].

Let's talk about your songwriting. Your best songs—"Teen Spirit," "Come As You Are," "Rape Me," "Penny Royal Tea"—all open with the verse in a low, moody style. Then the chorus comes in at full volume and nails you. So which comes first, the verse or the killer chorus?

[*Long pause, then he smiles.*] I don't know. I really don't know. I guess I start with the verse and then go into the chorus. But I'm getting so tired of that formula. And it is formula. And there's not much you can do with it. We've mastered that—for our band. We're all growing pretty tired of it.

It is a dynamic style. But I'm only using two of the dynamics. There are a lot more I could be using. Krist, Dave and I have been working on this formula—this thing of going from quiet to loud—for so long that it's literally becoming boring for us. It's like, "Okay, I have this riff. I'll play it quiet, without a distortion box, while I'm singing the verse. And now let's turn on the distortion box and hit the drums harder."

I want to learn to go in between those things, go back and forth, almost become psychedelic in a way but with a lot more structure. It's a really hard thing to do, and I don't know if we're capable of it—as musicians.

Songs like "Dumb" and "All Apologies" do suggest that you're looking for a way to get to people without resorting to the big-bang guitar effect.

Absolutely. I wish we could have written a few more songs like those on all the other albums. Even to put "About a Girl" on *Bleach* was a risk. I was heavily into pop, I really liked R.E.M., and I was into all kinds of old Sixties stuff. But there was a lot of pressure within that social scene, the underground—like the kind of thing you get in high school. And to put a jangly R.E.M. type of pop song on a grunge record, in that scene, was risky.

We have failed in showing the lighter, more dynamic side of our band. The big guitar sound is what the kids want to hear. We like playing that stuff, but I don't know how much longer I can scream at the top of my lungs every night, for an entire year on tour. Sometimes I wish I had taken the Bob Dylan route and sang songs where my voice would not go out on me every night, so I could have a career if I wanted.

In "Serve the Servants," you sing, "I tried hard to have a father/But instead I had a dad." Are you concerned about making the same mistakes as a father that might have been made when you were growing up?

No. I'm not worried about that at all. My father and I are completely different people. I know that I'm capable of showing a lot more affection than my dad was. Even if Courtney and I were to get divorced, I would never allow us to be in a situation where there are bad vibes between us in front of her. That kind of stuff can screw up a kid, but the reason those things happen is because the parents are not very bright.

I don't think Courtney and I are that fucked up. We have lacked love all our lives, and we need it so much that if there's any goal that we have, it's to give Frances as much love as we can, as much support as we can. That's the one thing that I know is not going to turn out bad.

With all of your reservations about playing "Smells Like Teen Spirit" and writing the same kind of song over and over, do you envision a time when there is no Nirvana? That you'll try to make it alone?

I don't think I could ever do a solo thing, the Kurt Cobain Project.

Doesn't have a very good ring to it, either.

No [*laughs*]. But yes, I would like to work with people who are totally, completely the opposite of what I'm doing now. Something way out there, man.

That doesn't bode well for the future of Nirvana and the kind of music you make together.

That's what I've been kind of hinting at in this whole interview. That we're almost exhausted. We've gone to the point where things are becoming repetitious. There's not something you can move up toward, there's not something you can look forward to.

The best times that we ever had were right when *Nevermind* was coming out and we went on that American tour where we were play-ing clubs. They were totally sold out, and the record was breaking big, and there was this massive feeling in the air, this vibe of energy. Something really special was happening.

I hate to actually even say it, but I can't see this band lasting more than a couple more albums, unless we really work hard on experimenting. I mean, let's face it. When the same people are together doing the same job, they're limited. I'm really interested in studying different things, and I know Krist and Dave are as well. But I don't know if we are capable of doing it together. I don't want to put out another record that sounds like the last three records.

I know we're gonna put out one more record, at least, and I have a pretty good idea what it's going to sound like: pretty ethereal, acoustic, like R.E.M.'s last album. If I could write just a couple of songs as good as what they've written...I don't know how that band does what they do. God, they're the greatest. They've dealt with their success like saints, and they keep delivering great music.

That's what I'd really like to see this band do. Because we are stuck in such a rut. We have been labeled. R.E.M. is what? College rock? That doesn't really stick. Grunge is as potent a term as New Wave. You can't get out of it. It's going to be passé. You have to take a chance and hope that either a totally different audience accepts you or the same audience grows with you.

And what if the kids just say, "We don't dig it, get lost"?

Oh, well. [*Laughs*] Fuck 'em.

COURTNEY LOVE

by David Fricke

December 15, 1994

After everything that has happened to you this year, does it feel weird—or right—to be on tour playing rock & roll?

It was easier than staying home. I prefer this. I would like to think that I'm not getting the sympathy vote, and the only way to do that is to prove that what I've got is real. That was the whole point of *Live Through This.*

It feels normal to me. You just put one foot in front of the other. I don't think about all the stuff that's happened all the time. I don't even know if I'm supposed to think about it—or if I'm not—or what I'm supposed to do. There's no rule book or guide to what I'm supposed to do.

What goes through your mind when you're onstage?

When the lights are blue and there are two of them in front of me, often they will symbolize Kurt's eyes to me. That happens a lot. That happened to me when I used to strip. I had a friend who died, and he had almost-lavender eyes. There'd be these lights on, and I'd see that when the big purple lights came on.

So there's that. The energy is reaching in. I know that wherever he is—whatever is left, whether it's part of one egoless divinity or what—his energy is concentrated on me and on Frances. And it's also concentrated on the cause and effect he's had on the world.

Do you feel vulnerable in front of an audience, especially now?

I had this theory that the persona people project onstage is the exact opposite of who they are. In Kurt's case, it was "Fuck you!" And ultimately his largest problem in life was not being able to say, "Fuck you." "Fuck you, Courtney. Fuck you, Gold Mountain [Nirvana's management firm]. Fuck you, Geffen—and I'm gonna do what I want."

My thing is "Don't fuck with me." In real life, real real life, I'm supersensitive. But people tend to think I'm not vulnerable because I don't act vulnerable.

It has been a year, almost to the day, since I interviewed Kurt. At the time, he told me he was happier than he'd ever been. And frankly, I believed him.

He probably was—at that moment. But his whole thing was "I'm only alive because of Frances and you." Look at his interviews in your magazine alone. And everything in between. In each and every one he mentions blowing his head off.

He brought a gun to the hospital the day after our daughter was born. He was going to Reading [the Reading Festival, in England] the next morning. I was like, "I'll go first. I can't have you do it first. I go first." I held this thing in my hand. And I felt that thing that they said in *Schindler's List*: I'm never going to know what happens to me. And what about Frances? Sort of rude. "Oh, your parents died the day after you were born."

I just started talking him out of it. And he said, "Fuck you, you can't chicken out. I'm gonna do it." But I made him give me the gun, and I had Eric [Erlandson, Hole guitarist] take it away. I don't know what he did with it. Then Kurt went to some hospital room; he had some dealer come. In hospital, he almost died. The dealer said she'd never seen someone so, dead. I said, "Why didn't you get a nurse? There's nurses all over the place."

And yet Kurt never lost faith in his ability to make music, even during the week before he died.

I never really heard him put that down. That was the one area that he wouldn't touch like that. I got to sit and listen to this man serenade me. He told me the Meat Puppets' second record was great. I couldn't stand it. Then he played it to me — in his voice, his cadence, his timing. And I realized he was right.

The only time I asked him for a riff for one of my songs, he was in the closet. We had this huge closet, and I heard him in there working on "Heart-Shaped Box." He did that in five minutes. Knock, knock, knock. "What?" "Do you need that riff?" "Fuck you!" Slam. [*Laughs*] He was trying to be so sneaky. I could hear that one from downstairs.

What kind of mood was he in on the European tour before he overdosed in Rome? Was that a genuine suicide attempt?

He hated everything, everybody. Hated, hated, hated. He called me from Spain, crying. I was gone forty days. I was doing my thing with my band for the first time since forever.

Kurt had gone all out for me when I got there [Rome]. He'd gotten me roses. He'd gotten a piece of the Colosseum, because he knows I love Roman history. I had some champagne, took a Valium, we made out, I fell asleep. The rejection he must have felt after all that anticipation — I mean, for Kurt to be that Mr. Romance was pretty intense.

I turned over about three or four in the morning to make love, and he was gone. He was at the end of the bed with a thousand dollars in his pocket and a note saying, "You don't love me anymore. I'd rather die than go through a divorce." It was all in his head.

I'd been away from him during our relationship maybe sixty days. Ever. I needed to be on tour. I had to do my thing.

I can see how it happened. He took fifty fucking pills. He probably forgot how many he took. But there was a definite suicidal urge, to be gobbling and gobbling and gobbling. Goddamn, man. Even if I wasn't in the mood, I should have just laid there for him. All he needed was to get laid. He would have been fine. But with Kurt you had to give yourself to him. He was psychic. He could tell if you were not all the way there. Sex, to him, was incredibly sacred. He found commitment to be an aphrodisiac.

Yeah, he definitely left a note in the room. I was told to shut up about it. And what could the media have done to help him?

What happened after he came out of the coma and returned to Seattle?

The reason I flipped out on the 18th of March [Love summoned the police to the house after Cobain locked himself in a room with a gun] was because it had been six days since we came back from Rome, and I couldn't take it anymore. When he came home from Rome high, I flipped out. If there's one thing in my whole life I could take back, it would be that. Getting mad at him for coming home high. I wish to God I hadn't. I wish I'd just been the way I always was, just tolerant of it. It made him feel so worthless when I got mad at him.

The only thing I can call it was a downward spiral from there. I got angry, and it was the first time I ever had. And I'm sorry— wherever the hell he is. And when people say, "Where was she, where was she?" I was in L.A. because the interventionist said I had to leave. Interventionist walks into the house: "Dominant female, get rid of her." I did not even kiss or get to say goodbye to my husband. I wish to God . . .

[*Long pause*] Kurt thought I was on their side because I had gone along with them. I wasn't. I was afraid. "It was in the L.A. *Times* that you're not going to do Lollapalooza. Everybody thinks you're going to die. Could you just go to rehab for a week?" "I just want to see Michael [Stipe]. You think I'm going to do dope in front of Michael? No, I won't."

I should have just left there, flown up to him. Peter Buck lives next door. Stephanie [Dorgan, Buck's girlfriend] had the tickets [to Atlanta]. I wish I'd just drove him to the airport. Let him go. He worshiped Michael.

Guns were a big issue in the arguments you had with Kurt, and the police were constantly taking them away. Yet when I pointedly asked him about guns in our interview, he started talking about target practice.

He totally fucking lied to you. He never went shooting in his life. One time he said, "I'm going shooting." Yeah. Shooting what? He never even made it to the range.

Yeah, it was an issue in the house. I liked having a revolver for protection. But when he bought the Uzi thing... "Hey, is that a toy, Kurt?" Yeah, it's dangerous when you're dealing with two volatile people — one is clinically depressed and the other one is suicidal at moments and definitely codependent.

Did Kurt's suicide note make any sense to you — that he'd found any kind of peace in what he was going to do?

He wrote me a letter other than his suicide note. It's kind of long. I put it in a safe-deposit box. I might show it to Frances — maybe. It's very fucked-up writing. "You know I love you, I love Frances, I'm so sorry. Please don't follow me." It's long because he repeats himself. "I'm sorry, I'm sorry, I'm sorry. I'll be there, I'll protect you. I don't know where I'm going. I just can't be here anymore."

There's definitely a narcissism in what he did, too. It was very snotty of him. When we decided we were in love at the Beverly Garland Hotel, we found this dead bird. Took out three feathers. And he said, "This is for you, this is for me, and this is for our baby we're gonna have." And he took one of the feathers away.

What about Frances? On the tour bus today she seemed like a happy, bouncy, normal toddler. But how much does she really know about where her father is?

I don't know. On some nights she cries out for him, and it freaks me out. And I thought she didn't know anything. [*Long pause*] So every couple of days I mention him. But it's when she's gonna be six and seven.... People are gonna make fun of her, make fun of her dad, and she's gonna feel like she's not good enough for him, and she'll probably feel ugly.

He thought he was doing the right thing. How could he fucking think that? In his condition he was so fucked up to think that. If I could have just spoken two words to him . . .

And then he would have OD'd when he was about thirty-four or thirty-five. But at least he would have had those seven years to make his decision to be a heroin addict forever. Or whatever the hell it is he wanted.

Let's go back to your life before Kurt. On the tour bus today you were talking about Frances growing up on the road, how she thinks everybody plays in a band. What do you remember about your childhood environment?

Guys in stripy pants in a circle around me, and my mother telling me to act like spring. Then to be summer and fall. Interpretive dancing.

People in tents with wild eyes, painting my face. I remember a really big house in San Francisco and all my real father's exotic girl-friends. We'd drive down Lombard Street in a Porsche my father probably borrowed from the Dead.

We went to Oregon pretty quick, and I was in Montessori school. Then things got a little more straightened out. Mother remarried and went to college in Eugene [Oregon].

What was your relationship with your mother like?

A lot of it was—I believe in my heart—a projection that my mother made on me because of a repulsion she felt for my father, for which

I don't blame her. But it is something she denies to the death. If I had a child, and I was repulsed by the father, I would have a difficult time. Knowing the history of my father, I don't know if I would try and make up for it.

There is some irony in the fact that given your own very public problems, your mother is a well-known therapist.

When *Newsweek* found out she was my mother in the middle of the Katherine Ann Power thing, she was just mortified. Because people have met me who were her clients: "If that's your product, my friend…" The only advice she ever gave me in my life was "Don't wear tight sweaters. They make you look cheap."

But I'm not out to make a public forum of my relationship with my mother. It is what it is. She didn't have an abortion, and that's what counts. I'm here. I've survived.

Where was the picture of you as a barefoot young girl on the back cover of 'Live Through This' taken?

It was taken in Springfield, Oregon, when I was living in a tepee in a communal environment. There was an outhouse. And I had to go to school just like that that day. I know it's very Freudian narcissism to use pictures of yourself. But my purpose was to say, "Well, that's who I am."

When I talk about being introverted, I was diagnosed autistic. At an early age, I would not speak. Then I simply bloomed. My first visit to a psychiatrist was when I was, like, three. Observational therapy. TM for tots. You name it, I've been there.

Who were your early musical inspirations?

I recall growing up with Leonard Cohen records and going, "I wish that was me he was writing about." I wanted to be Suzanne, I wanted to live down by the river. Not being old enough to know what I wanted to do, I just wanted to be the girl in the Leonard Cohen song. Or the girl in [Bob Dylan's] "Leopard-Skin Pill-Box Hat." Or the girl in "Sad-Eyed Lady of the Lowlands." All these girls riding the Jersey highway in a Bruce Springsteen song.

And then I came around. "No, no, no. I don't want to be the girl. I want to be Leonard Cohen!" We had *Blue,* the Joni Mitchell album, when I was growing up. That was very helpful. Once I was on PCH [Pacific Coast Highway], and Joni was smoking Newports in front of me, getting a protein pickup at the 7-Eleven in Malibu [California]. I was just like [*her jaw drops*]. I didn't say anything. I was just, "Oh, my God!"

What happened once you got turned on to punk rock?

My grand plan was to write this intensely primal record—go into my room and learn *Led Zeppelin I* through *V,* play all those things perfectly, and then come out and make the perfect rock record. That was my plan, if I'd been alone, utterly masculine and totally oriented.

I was into Brian Jones, the type of person who would start a band and kick everyone's butt. But all through the Eighties, it was a goddamn nightmare, hearing things from other women like, "Well, I can borrow my boyfriend's bass. We can open for my boyfriend's band. I can't make practice tonight because I have to meet my boyfriend." Ugh!

How much of your early music with Hole, especially that version of Mitchell's "Both Sides Now" [a.k.a. "Clouds"] on 'Pretty on the Inside,' was your revenge against dysfunctional hippie parents?

It is interesting that you've picked up on "Both Sides Now." Because we used to be forced to sing that in the fucking Volvo in unison. I felt so humiliated by it. It was a major dis at my mother, as much as I love Joni Mitchell.

But just like the baby boomers had to grow up with Dean Martin touting booze, we had to grow up with this idealization that was never going to fucking come true, and it turned us into a bunch of cynics—or a bunch of drug addicts. None of my parents' friends ever died from acid overdoses or marijuana overdoses. But the popularity now of IV drug use—it's something that my generation does. And to become an icon of it is something I fear. And it was something Kurt feared most.

He called me from Spain. He was in Madrid, and he'd walked through the audience. The kids were smoking heroin off of tinfoil, and the kids were going, "Kurt! Smack!" and giving him the thumbs up. He called me, crying. That's why he would tell people, "No, I'm not on it." Because he did not want to become a junkie icon. And now he is.

How free of drugs are you at this point?

I take Valiums. Percodan. Don't like heroin. It turns me into a cunt. Makes me ugly. Never liked it. Hate needles. When I did do it, it was like [*holds out her arm and turns her head*]. I have used heroin—after Kurt died.

You've been doing one of Kurt's unrecorded songs during the encore on this tour. How many of those songs exist?

There are three completed, finished songs. And there are ten others, and then there's all the riffing. There's one song called "Opinions" that was a couple of years old. It was from the era when he was in Olympia, Washington, between *Bleach* and *Nevermind*. The other one goes, "Talk to me/In your own language, please" [*she sings the lyric and guitar riff*]. The third one, I can't sing. It's too fucking good. Every part of it is really catchy. He was calling it "Dough, Ray and Me." I thought it was a little corny.

It was the last thing he wrote on our bed. The chorus was "Dough, Ray and me/Dough, Ray and me," and then it was "Me and my IV." I had asked him after Rome to freeze his sperm. So there's this whole thing about freezing your uterus.

Then there's a song called "Clean Up Before She Comes," which is classic, formula Nirvana. There's the one we're going to play tonight. Melissa sings my part, and the part I'm singing is Kurt's part. I just call it "Drunk in Rio."

I recorded a whole slew of stuff in Rio that was just me and Kurt. It was when Nirvana did that Hollywood Rock Festival in Rio [in January 1993]. Patty [Schemel, Hole bassist] and me went down there, so we recorded. There's these beautiful harmonizings with me and Kurt. Of course, I can't release the shit. No matter how aesthetically right it would be to do. "Fuck it, fuck what people say." No, I can't. I have to do this on my own. And no matter how normal it seems, the contribution of your husband or wife to your art, our case and circumstances were different. And now it would even be grosser.

Yet one of the most provocative images in the video for "Doll Parts" is the young blond Kurt-like boy.

Because it was my right to reference it. And I wanted to reference it. It happened. My husband was taken away. It was tasteful. I had this gorgeous little boy with me; we had a real fun time with him.

I have this real obsession with grace. That's the number one thing I look for in a person in the physiological realm. But part of grace is not speaking—like the silent ballerina. I've wondered, after everything that's happened, "You can change your persona. You can be the silent widow." But I cannot kill the thing inside of me. That has to be kept alive. Or I will die.

MICK JAGGER

by Jann S. Wenner

December 14, 1995

When did you first realize you were a performer, that what you did onstage was affecting people?

When I was eighteen or so. The Rolling Stones were just starting to play some clubs around London, and I realized I was getting a lot of girl action when normally I hadn't gotten much. I was very unsophisticated then.

It was the attention of the girls that made you realize you were doing something onstage that was special?

You realize that these girls are going, either quietly or loudly, sort of crazy. And you're going, "Well, this is good. You know, this is something else." At that age you're just so impressed, especially if you've been rather shy before.

There's two parts of all this, at least. There's this great fascination for music and this love of playing blues — not only blues, just rock & roll generally. There's this great love of that.

But there's this other thing that's performing, which is something that children have or they haven't got. In the slightly post-Edwardian, pretelevision days, everybody had to do a turn at family gatherings. You might recite poetry, and Uncle Whatever would play the piano and sing, and you all had something to do. And I was just one of those kids [who loved it].

You were going to the London School of Economics and just getting started playing with the Stones. How did you decide which you were going to do?

Well, I started to do both, really. The Stones thing was weekends, and college was in the week. God, the Rolling Stones had so little work—it was like one gig a month. So it wasn't really that difficult.

How committed to the group were you then?

Well, I wasn't totally committed; it was a good, fun thing to do, but Keith [Richards] and Brian [Jones] didn't have anything else to do, so they wanted to rehearse all the time. I liked to rehearse once a week and do a show Saturday. The show that we did was three or four numbers, so there wasn't a tremendous amount of rehearsal needed.

Were you torn about the decision to drop out of school?

It was very, very difficult because my parents obviously didn't want me to do it. My father was furious with me, absolutely furious. I'm sure he wouldn't have been so mad if I'd have volunteered to join the army. Anything but this. He couldn't believe it. I agree with him: It wasn't a viable career opportunity. It was totally stupid. But I didn't really like being at college. It wasn't like it was Oxford and had been the most wonderful time of my life. It was really a dull, boring course I was stuck on.

Tell me about meeting Keith.

I can't remember when I didn't know him. We lived one street away; his mother knew my mother, and we were at primary school together from [ages] seven to eleven. We used to play together, and we weren't the closest friends, but we were friends.

Keith and I went to different schools when we were eleven, but he went to a school which was really near where I used to live. But I always knew where he lived, because my mother would never lose contact with anybody, and she knew where they'd moved. I used to see him coming home from his school, which was less than a mile away from where I lived. And then—this is a true story—we met at the train station. And I had these rhythm & blues records, which were very prized possessions because they weren't available in England then. And he said, "Oh, yeah, these are really interesting." That kind of did it. That's how it started, really.

We started to go to each other's house and play these records. And then we started to go to other people's houses to play other records. You know, it's the time in your life when you're almost stamp-collecting this stuff. I can't quite remember how all this worked. Keith always played the guitar, from even when he was five. And he was keen on country music, cowboys. But obviously at some point, Keith, he had this guitar with this electric-guitar pickup. And he played it for me. So I said, "Well, I sing, you know? And you play the guitar." Very obvious stuff.

I used to play Saturday night shows with all these different little groups. If I could get a show, I would do it. I used to do mad things—you know, I used to go and do these shows and go on my knees and roll on the ground—when I was fifteen, sixteen years old. And my parents were extremely disapproving of it all. Because it was just not done. This was for very low-class people, remember. Rock & roll singers weren't educated people.

What did you think was going on inside you at fifteen years old that you wanted to go out and roll around on a stage?

I didn't have any inhibitions. I saw Elvis and Gene Vincent, and I thought, "Well, I can do this." And I liked doing it. It's a real buzz, even in front of twenty people, to make a complete fool of yourself.

But people seemed to like it. And the thing is, if people started throwing tomatoes at me, I wouldn't have gone on with it. But they all liked it, and it always seemed to be a success, and people were shocked. I could see it in their faces.

Shocked by you?

Yeah. They could see it was a bit wild for what was going on at the time in these little places in the suburbs. Parents were not always very tolerant, but Keith's mum was very tolerant of him playing. Keith was an only child, and she didn't have a lot of other distractions, whereas my parents were like, "Get on your homework." It was a real hard time for me. So I used to go and play with Keith, and then we used to go and play with Dick Taylor [who was later in the Pretty Things]. His parents were very tolerant, so we used to go round to his house, where we could play louder.

What was it like to be such a success at such a young age?

It was very exciting. The first time we got our picture in the music paper called the *Record Mirror*—to be on the front page of this thing that probably sold about 20,000 copies—was so exciting, you couldn't believe it. And this glowing review: There we were in this club in Richmond, being written up in these rather nice terms. And then to go from the music-oriented press to national press and national television, and everyone seeing you in the world of two television channels, and then being recognized by everyone from builders and people working in shops and so on. It goes to your head—very champagne-feeling.

I recently listened to the very early albums, the first four or five you did, and they're all pretty much the same. You were doing blues and covers, but one song stood out: "Tell Me (You're Coming Back)," your first U.S. hit and your first composition together with Keith. It's the first one that has the seeds of the modern Stones in it.

Keith was playing twelve-string and singing harmonies into the same microphone as the twelve-string. We recorded it in this tiny studio in the West End of London called Regent Sound, which was a demo studio. I think the whole of that album was recorded in there. But it's very different from doing those R&B covers or Marvin Gaye covers and all that. There's a definite feel about it. It's a very pop song, as opposed to all the blues songs and the Motown covers, which everyone did at the time.

The first full album that really kind of jumps out is 'Out of Our Heads.'

What's on there? [*Laughter*] I have no idea. I'm awfully sorry.

"Cry to Me," "The Under Assistant West Coast Promotion Man," "Play With Fire," "I'm All Right," "That's How Strong My Love Is"...

Yeah. A lot of covers, still.

But it had a unity of sound to it.

Most of that was recorded in RCA Studios, in Hollywood, and the people working on it, the engineers, were much better. They knew how to get really good sounds. That really affects your performance, because you can hear the nuances, and that inspires you.

And your singing is different here for the first time. You sound like you're singing more like soul music.

Yeah, well, it is obviously soul influenced, which was the goal at the time. Otis Redding and Solomon Burke. "Play With Fire" sounds amazing—when I heard it last. I mean, it's a very in-your-face kind of sound and very clearly done. You can hear all the vocal stuff on it. And I'm playing the tambourines, the vocal line. You know, it's very pretty.

Who wrote that?

Keith and me. I mean, it just came out.

A full collaboration?

Yeah.

That's the first song you wrote that starts to address the lifestyle you were leading in England and, of course, class consciousness.

No one had really done that. The Beatles, to some extent, were doing it, though they weren't really doing it at this period as much as they did later. The Kinks were kind of doing it—Ray Davies and I were in the same boat. One of the first things that, in that very naive way, you attempted to deal with were the kind of funny, swinging, London-type things that were going on. I didn't even realize I was doing it at the time. But it became an interesting source for material. Songwriting had only dealt in clichés and borrowed stuff, you know, from previous records or ideas. "I want to hold your hand," things like that. But these songs were really more from experience and then embroidered to make them more interesting.

Where does that come from in you? I mean, you're writing about "Your mother, she's an heiress/Owns a block in St. John's Wood," but she's sleeping with the milkman, or something.

Yeah, yeah. Well, it was just kind of rich girls' families—society as you saw it. It's painted in this naive way in these songs.

But at the time to write about stuff like that must have been somewhat daring.

I don't know if it was daring. It just hadn't been done. Obviously there had been lyric writers that had written stuff much more interesting and sophisticated—say, Noël Coward, who I didn't really know about. He was someone that your parents knew.

The lyricist who was really good at the time was Bob Dylan. Everyone looked up to him as being a kind of guru of lyrics. It's hard to think of the absolute garbage that pop music really was at the time. And even if you lifted your game by a marginal amount, it really was a lot different from most everything else that had gone before in the ten years previously.

A lot of it was perhaps not as good as we thought, but at the time it was fantastic. "Gates of Eden" and all these Mexican-type songs, even the nonsense ones: "Everybody Must Get Stoned" and "Like a Rolling Stone," "Positively 4th Street."

Then you did 'December's Children (and Everybody's).' Does that title mean anything particular?

No. It was our manager's [Andrew Loog Oldham] idea of hip, Beat poetry.

That record features "Get Off My Cloud."

That was Keith's melody and my lyrics.

This is decidedly not a love song or "I Want to Hold Your Hand."

Yeah. It's a stop-bugging-me, post-teenage-alienation song. The grown-up world was a very ordered society in the early Sixties, and I was coming out of it. America was even more ordered than anywhere else. I found it was a very restrictive society in thought and behavior and dress.

Based on your coming to the States in '64?

Sixty-four, '65, yeah. And touring outside of New York. New York was wonderful and so on, and L.A. was also kind of interesting. But outside of that we found it the most repressive society, very prejudiced in every way. There was still segregation. And the attitudes were fantastically old-fashioned. Americans shocked me by their behavior and their narrow-mindedness.

It's changed fantastically over the last thirty years. But so has everything else [*laughs*].

Is there anything more to say about "(I Can't Get No) Satisfaction" than has already been said on the record? Written sitting by a pool in Florida...

Keith didn't want it to come out as a single.

Is there anything special to you about that song, looking back at it after all these years?

People get very blasé about their big hit. It was the song that really made the Rolling Stones, changed us from just another band into a huge, monster band. You always need one song. We weren't American, and America was a big thing, and we always wanted to make it here. It was very impressive the way that song and the popularity of the band became a worldwide thing. You know, we went to play in Singapore. The Beatles really opened all that up. But to do that you needed the song; otherwise you were just a picture in the newspaper, and you had these little hits.

Was "Satisfaction" a great, classic piece of work?

Well, it's a signature tune, really, rather than a great, classic painting, 'cause it's only like one thing—a kind of signature that everyone knows.

Why? What are the ingredients?

It has a very catchy title. It has a very catchy guitar riff. It has a great guitar sound, which was original at that time. And it captures a spirit of the times, which is very important in those kind of songs.

Which was?

Which was alienation. Or it's a bit more than that, maybe, but a kind of sexual alienation. Alienation's not quite the right word, but it's one word that would do.

Isn't that a stage of youth?

Yeah, it's being in your twenties, isn't it? Teenage guys can't often formulate this stuff—when you're that young.

Who wrote "Satisfaction"?

Well, Keith wrote the lick. I think he had this lyric, "I can't get no satisfaction," which, actually, is a line in a Chuck Berry song called "30 Days."

Which is "I can't get no satisfaction"?

"I can't get no satisfaction from the judge."

Did you know that when you wrote it?

No, I didn't know it, but Keith might have heard it back then, because it's not any way an English person would express it. I'm not saying that he purposely nicked anything, but we played those records a lot.

So it just could have stuck in the back of your head.

Yeah, that was just one little line. And then I wrote the rest of it. There was no melody, really.

What about your relationship with Keith? Does it bug you, having Keith as your primary musical partner? Does it bug you having a partner at all?

No, I think it's essential. You don't have to have a partner for every-thing you do. But having partners sometimes helps you and some-times hinders you. You have good times and bad times with them. It's just the nature of it.

People also like partnerships because they can identify with the drama of two people in partnership. They can feed off a partner-ship, and that keeps people entertained. Besides, if you have a suc-cessful partnership, it's self-sustaining.

You have maybe the longest-running songwriting-performing partnership in our times. Why do you think you and Keith survived, unlike John Len-non and Paul McCartney?

That's hard to make even a stab at, because I don't know John and Paul well enough. I know them slightly, same as you, probably, and maybe you knew John better at the end. I can hazard a guess that they were both rather strong personalities, and both felt they were totally independent. They seemed to be very competitive over lead-ership of the band. The thing in leadership is, you can have times when one person is more at the center than the other, but there can't be too much arguing about it all the time. Because if you're always at loggerheads, you just have to go, "Okay, if I can't have a say in this and this, then fuck it. What am I doing here?" So you sort of agree what your roles are. Whereas John and Paul felt they were too strong and they wanted to be in charge. If there are ten things, they both wanted to be in charge of nine of them. You're not gonna make a relationship like that work, are you?

Why do you and Keith keep the joint-songwriting partnership?

We just agreed to do that, and that seemed the easiest way to do it. I think in the end it all balances out.

How was it when Keith was taking heroin all the time? How did you handle that?

I don't find it easy to talk about other people's drug problems. If he wants to talk about it, fine, he can talk about it all he wants. Elton John talks about his bulimia on television. But I don't want to talk about his bulimia, and I don't want to talk about Keith's drug problems.

How did I handle it? Oh, with difficulty. It's never easy. I don't find it easy dealing with people with drug problems. It helps if you're all taking drugs, all the same drugs. But anyone taking heroin is thinking about taking heroin more than they're thinking about anything else. That's the general rule about most drugs. If you're really on some heavily addictive drug, you think about the drug and everything else is secondary. You try and make everything work, but the drug comes first.

How did his drug use affect the band?

I think that people taking drugs occasionally are great. I think there's nothing wrong with it. But if you do it the whole time, you don't produce as good things as you could. It sounds like a puritanical statement, but it's based on experience. You can produce many good things, but they take an awfully long time.

You obviously developed a certain relationship based on him as a drug addict, part of which was you running the band. So when he cleaned up, how did that affect the band? Drug addicts are basically incompetent to run anything.

Yeah, it's all they can do to turn up. And people have different personalities when they're drunk or take heroin, or whatever drugs. When Keith was taking heroin, it was very difficult to work. He still was creative, but it took a long time. And everyone else was taking drugs and drinking a tremendous amount, too. And it affected everyone in certain ways. But I've never really talked to Keith about this stuff. So I have no idea what he feels.

You never talked about the drug stuff with him?

No. So I'm always second-guessing. I tell you something, I probably read it in *Rolling Stone.*

What's your relationship with him now?

We have a very good relationship at the moment. But it's a different relationship to what we had when we were five and different to what we had when we were twenty and a different relationship than when we were thirty. We see each other every day, talk to each other every day, play every day. But it's not the same as when we were twenty and shared rooms.

Charlie says, "Mick is better with Keith Richards than he is with any other guitar players. I mean even a technically better guitar player—he's better with Keith." Do you feel that?

Well, yeah, up to a certain point. I do enjoy working with other kinds of guitar players, because Keith is a very definite kind of guitar player. He's obviously very rhythmic and so on, and that works very well with Charlie and myself. Though I do like performing or working with guitar players that also work around lead lines a lot—like Eric [Clapton] or Mick Taylor or Joe Satriani. Whether it's better or not, it's completely different working with them. We made records with just Mick Taylor, which are very good and everyone loves, where Keith wasn't there for whatever reasons.

Which ones?

People don't know that Keith wasn't there making it. All the stuff like "Moonlight Mile," "Sway." These tracks are a bit obscure, but they are liked by people that like the Rolling Stones. It's me and [Mick] playing off each other—another feeling completely, because he's following my vocal lines and then extemporizing on them during the solos. That's something Jeff Beck, to a certain extent, can do: a guitar player that just plays very careful lead lines and listens to what his vocalist is doing.

In the mid-Eighties, when the Stones were not working together, did you and Keith talk?

Hardly at all.

A little while ago, Keith described your relationship like this to me: "We can't even get divorced. I wanted to kill him." Did you feel you were trapped in this marriage?

No. You're not trapped. We were friends before we were in a band, so it's more complicated, but I don't see it as a marriage. They're quite different, a band and a marriage.

How did you patch it up?

What actually happened was, we had a meeting to plan the tour, and as far as I was concerned, it was very easy. At the time [1989], everyone was asking [whispers], "Wow, what was it like? What happened? How did it all work?" It was a nonevent. What could have been a lot of name-calling, wasn't. I think everyone just decided that we'd done all that. Of course, we had to work out what the modus vivendi was for everybody, because we were planning a very different kind of tour. Everyone had to realize that they were in a new kind of world. We had to invent new rules. It was bigger business, more efficient than previous tours, than the Seventies drug tours. We were all gonna be on time at the shows. Everyone realized they had to pull their weight, and everyone had a role to play, and they were all up for doing it.

Can you describe the time you spent in Barbados with Keith, deciding if you could put this together?

Keith and I and [financial adviser] Rupert [Lowenstein] had a small meeting first and talked about business. We were in a hotel with the sea crashing outside and the sun shining and drinks, talking about all the money we're gonna get and how great it was gonna be, and then we bring everyone else in and talk about it.

So that was your reconciliation with Keith? Was there any talk of putting your heads together and airing issues?

No, and I'm glad we didn't do that, because it could have gone on for weeks. It was better that we just get on with the job. Of course, we had to revisit things afterward.

Charlie said to me, "I don't think you can come between Mick and Keith — they're family. You can only go so far, and then you hit an invisible wall. They don't want anyone in there."

Well, it sounds like one of the wives talking, doesn't it? I remember Bianca [Jagger] saying a very similar thing. But if that's what he thinks, that's what he thinks. It's funny he thinks that. I don't know why he should say that. I think people are afraid to express their opinions half the time.

In front of you and Keith?

Or just in front of me. They think they're gonna go back to a period where people would jump down their throats for having an opinion. Drug use makes you snappy, and you get very bad-tempered and have terrible hangovers.

One more quote. Keith says, "Mick clams up all the time. He keeps a lot inside. It was the way he was brought up. Just being Mick Jagger at eighteen or nineteen, a star, gives him reason to protect what space is left."

I think it's very important that you have at least some sort of inner thing you don't talk about. That's why I find it distasteful when all these pop stars talk about their habits. But if that's what they need to do to get rid of them, fine. But I always found it boring. For some people it's real therapy to talk to journalists about their private lives and inner thoughts. But I would rather keep something to myself.

It's wearing. You're on all the time. As much as I love talking to you today, I'd rather be having one day where I don't have to think about me. With all this attention, you become a child. It's awful to be at the center of attention. You can't talk about anything apart from your own experience, your own dopey life. I'd rather do something that can get me out of the center of attention. It's very dangerous. But there's no way, really, to avoid that.

PATTI SMITH

by David Fricke

July 11, 1996

How did you meet [your husband] Fred?

It was March 9th, 1976. The band was in Detroit for the first time. Arista Records had a little party for us at one of those hot-dog places. I'm not one much for parties, so I wanted to get out of there. I was going out the back door—there was a white radiator, I remember. I was standing there with Lenny [Kaye, Patti Smith Group guitarist]; I happened to look up, and this guy is standing there as I was leaving. Lenny introduced me to him: "This is Fred 'Sonic' Smith, the legendary guitar player for the MC5," and that was it. Changed my life.

As far as your fans and the music business were concerned, you literally disappeared during the 1980s. How did you and Fred spend those missing years?

That was a great period for me. Until [her son] Jackson had to go to school, Fred and I spent a lot of time traveling through America, living in cheap motels by the sea. We'd get a little motel with a kitchenette, get a monthly rate. Fred would find a little airport and get pilot lessons. He studied aviation; I'd write and take care of Jackson. I had a typewriter and a couple of books. It was a simple, nomadic, sparse life.

Was there a period of adjustment for you, going from rock & roll stardom to almost complete anonymity?

Only in terms of missing the camaraderie of my band. And I certainly missed New York City. I missed the bookstores; I missed the warmth of the city. I've always found New York City extremely warm and loving.

But I was actually living a beautiful life. I often spent my days with my notebooks, watching Jackson gather shells or make a sand castle. Then we'd come back to the motel. Jackson would be asleep, and Fred and I would talk about how things went with his piloting and what I was working on.

Because people don't see you or see what you're doing doesn't mean you don't exist. When [photographer] Robert [Mapplethorpe] and I spent the end of the Sixties in Brooklyn working on our art and poetry, no one knew who we were. Nobody knew our names. But we worked like demons. And no one really cared about Fred and I during the Eighties. But our self-concept had to come from the work we were doing, from our communication, not from outside sources.

What did you live on financially?

We had some money, some royalties. We experienced difficult times. Sometimes we'd have windfalls—Bruce Springsteen recorded "Because the Night" [on *Live, 1975–1985*]. I might complain about that song because I get sick of it [*laughs*], but I've been really grateful for it. That song has bailed us out a few times. [The MC5's] "Kick Out the Jams" bailed us out, too.

But we learned to live really frugally. And when we could no longer live like that, we did *Dream of Life*. That's why we were getting ready to record the summer before Fred died—it was time to finance our next few years.

How far along were the two of you in planning the new album before he died?

He had the title, *Gone Again*. That was going to be the title cut, although he had a different concept for the lyric. And he wanted it to be a rock album. He was competitive—for me. He actually seemed to have more ambition for me than I had for myself.

What was his original concept for the song "Gone Again"?

He wanted it to have an American Indian spirit, because that was part of his heritage. I was to be the woman of the tribe who lived in the mountains, and in times of hardship, when things got really rough—they had a heavy snow, crops failed, warriors died—she would come down and recount the history of the tribe. There was famine and drought, and then the rains came and the corn grew high. The warriors died, but then a baby was born. It was a song of renewal. And that was the last music he wrote.

I hadn't written the lyrics yet. It was the last song I recorded, and when I was finally ready, it took a different turn. Instead, I paid homage to the warrior—the warrior who fell.

You also pay tribute to Kurt Cobain in "About a Boy." What was it about his life and music that touched you?

When Nirvana came out, I was really excited. Not so much for myself—my time had passed for putting so much passion into music and pinning my faith on a band. I'd had the Rolling Stones. I was happy for the kids to have [Nirvana]. I didn't know anything about his torments or personal life. I saw the work and the energy, and I was excited by that.

So it was a tremendous shock—quite a blow to me—when he died. I remember being upstairs taking care of the kids. I came down, and Fred told me to sit down at the table. When he did it a certain way, I knew it was serious. He sat me down and said, "Your boy is dead." And when he told me how...

That day, we went to a record store for something, some Beethoven thing Fred wanted. And I remember kids were outside crying. They didn't seem to know what to do with themselves. I felt a little like Captain Picard: I couldn't mess with the Prime Directive. It was not my place to say anything. These kids didn't know anything about me. But I really wanted to comfort them, tell them it was all right, that his choice was a very rare choice. I started writing "About a Boy" right after that.

What did you want to say in the song about his choice?

He had the song "About a Girl," and I got the title from that. Initially I had two parallel things I wanted to express in the double meaning of the chorus ["About a boy/Beyond it all"]. When I was a kid, the ones who were beyond it all were the ones who felt they were beyond responsibility. But I was also shifting it to mean beyond it all in terms of earthly things—and hopefully beyond all earthly pain, to some better place. Nirvana. [*Smiles*]

But I have to admit, originally it was written with a little more frustration and anger. In 1988–89, I watched my best friend die—slowly. Robert Mapplethorpe, in that time period, did every single thing he could to hold on to his life force. He let himself be a guinea pig for every type of drug. He met with mystics; he met with priests. Any scientist he could find. He was fighting to live even in his last hours. He was in a coma, but his breathing was so hard the room reverberated.

When you watch someone you care for fight so hard to hold on to their life, then see another person just throw their life away, I guess I had less patience for that. You want to take a person by the scruff of the neck and say, "Okay. You're suffering? This is suffering. Check it out."

I don't say any of these things with any kind of judgment. It's just frustration, concern for how something like that affects young people. I am aware that I am somewhat estranged and out of touch, maybe even a little out of time. But I'm not so out of time that I can't see that young people feel even worse than I ever did. I remember the early Fifties and fallout shelters. But still, life in general seemed pretty safe. Now kids must look around—there are viral conditions, pollution, still the threat of nuclear war, AIDS. Drugs are so plentiful and scary.

How hard has it been for you as a mother to navigate your own children through that minefield?

I was lucky because they had a father who was continually involved in their growth process. We were never separated from our children—ever. They knew what our philosophies were, and I know they felt protected.

What was also important was to tell them about God, to say prayers with them. I never promoted any religion to them because I don't believe in that. But the concept of God, or a Creator, has always been alive in our household. My mother taught me to pray when I was a little girl, and I'll always be grateful to her. Because in that way I never felt completely alone.

I know that Jackson perceives the world around him as completely mad. He studies CNN and the Weather Channel to check the state of the world. And I can see the admonishment in his eyes: "What have all you people done?" I see him walking around shaking his head. I'm glad he has Stevie Ray Vaughn to guide him right now [*laughs*]. He can find some abstract joy or guidance in music—music being an inspiring and somewhat safe haven.

In a 1971 issue of 'Rolling Stone,' you reviewed an album by the German actress and singer Lotte Lenya, and at the end you wrote, "It was hard for me to face up to being a girl. I thought girls were dumb. But Lotte Lenya showed me how high and low-down you can shoot being a woman."

She was pretty tough. I only saw rare footage of her doing "Pirate Jenny," but she was pretty strong. And when I was a teenager, I listened to Nina Simone, another strong female. But in terms of women I could relate to, there weren't too many. I related to Lotte Lenya, but I related more to Bob Dylan. I loved Billie Holiday, but as a performer I related more to Mick Jagger.

What were some of your seminal rock & roll epiphanies?

I grew up with the whole history of rock & roll. I was a little girl when Little Richard hit the scene. I remember the first time I heard Jim Morrison on the radio: "Riders on the Storm." We were in a car, me and a friend of mine. We stopped the car—we couldn't go on: "What is this? What are we hearing?" I remember that sense of wonder.

When "Like a Rolling Stone" came out, I was in college—I think I was a freshman. It was so overwhelming that nobody went to class. We were just roaming around, talking about this song. I didn't know what Dylan was talking about in the song. But it didn't matter. It needed no translation. It just made you feel like you weren't alone—that someone was speaking your language.

What was your vision—musically, lyrically, spiritually—at the time you recorded 'Horses'? It was a pivotal album in its time but does not sound at all dated today.

Part of that is because it came out of five years' work. The opening lines—"Jesus died for somebody's sins, but not mine"—I wrote in 1970. "Redondo Beach" was an early poem. The process of doing a record happened organically from years of improvising, gaining a voice and gathering my ideas.

But the early intention, right from my first performance with Lenny at St. Mark's Church [in New York] in February of '71, was merely to kick a little life into what I perceived as a dead poetry scene. It seemed self-absorbed and cliquish. It didn't make me feel expansive or beautiful or intoxicated or elevated at all. I was trying to kick poetry in the ass.

People felt that I was stepping on hallowed ground, being irreverent. But I didn't care because the people who were supportive were cool. What do you care when 80 percent of the poets in America were against you but you have William Burroughs on your side?

Did you read at rock & roll shows in the early days?

Sometimes I'd get jobs opening up for other acts. The New York Dolls would play with three or four other bands you never heard of, and I'd have to open the whole night. Nobody wanted to see me. I had no microphone. I'd just yell my poetry. And these guys would yell, "Get a job! Get back in the kitchen!" I just shot it back at them. But as I started developing with Lenny and Richard [Sohl, Patti Smith Group bassist], we got sturdier, and our thing started to get more defined.

I seriously worried that I was seeing the decline of rock & roll. It was stadium rock and glitter bands. It was getting square from Peter Frampton on up. So I started aggressively pursuing what we were doing. But still not self-motivated—I don't care if anybody believes me or not. My design was to shake things up, to motivate people and bring a different type of work ethic back into rock & roll.

Was there a defining moment when you sensed that real change was imminent?

Seeing Television. On Easter of 1974, Lenny and I were invited to the premiere of *Ladies and Gentlemen, the Rolling Stones*. It was such an exciting night. I had my *Horses* clothes on; I looked like Baudelaire. I was so thrilled to be asked to see the premiere of a movie. I'd never been to one.

After the movie, Lenny told me he had promised to go down to CBGB to see this new group. It was about midnight, and there were like fourteen people there. We saw Television, and I thought they were great. I really felt that was it, what I was hoping for: to see people approach things in a different way with a street ethic but also their full mental faculties. Of course, Tom Verlaine and Richard Hell—he was in the group at the time—were both poets.

Then we started working together. They opened for us at Max's Kansas City; I think we did eight weeks together at CBGB. They were really heightened nights. Sometimes I see 8 mm footage that somebody took and think, "God, did I have guts!" Because I wasn't much of a singer. But I had bravado, and I could improvise.

What is it like for you to perform "Piss Factory" [her 1974 debut single] now, twenty-two years after you recorded it? Even though you wrote it as an expression of your own adolescent frustration, the poem still has a potent, contemporary resonance.

It's important for people to remember the crap they had to go through. Teenagehood, to me, is the toughest thing in life. Maybe some people loved their teenage years; I found them really difficult.

But it's not a negative piece. It's not about the factory or those people in it. They're all minor characters. What it's really about is the human spirit. I was saying that as a young person, I still had desire—desire to do well. Perhaps some of these people in the factory lost all desire. I can understand how that can happen. It can be a rough life. But I also know that it is possible, as long as a person has a breath in their body, to feel alive. What "Piss Factory" is about is: someone who in the midst of the dead felt alive.

As I read it now, it doesn't matter whether I relate or don't relate to the whole scenario, which happened a long time ago. I'm still a human being with desires, hopes and dreams. In that respect, I haven't changed much.

What did they make in this factory besides piss?

They made baby buggies. I was a baby-buggy bumper-beeper inspector. [*Laughs*] You know those beepers on the buggies? I had to beep them to make sure they worked. But I kept getting demoted. I actually liked my lowest job—I had to inspect the pipes they used for the handles on the buggies—because I could take my copy of [Rimbaud's] *A Season in Hell* down in the basement and read.

How long did you last at the factory?

I only worked there in summers. I wanted to make money to go to college. It was just a schoolgirl thing.

But it wasn't written with a thought for anyone other than myself. That's why it's got that energy. When I wrote that piece, I didn't have any compassion for anybody else. I was fresh from having lived it, being ridiculed by those people, pushed around and roughed up.

Now I look at those same people with some compassion. I can imagine what their scenarios could have been: Maybe they were divorced, had five kids to take care of, nothing to look forward to. But I was sixteen, and I was concerned with myself.

Your new book about Robert Mapplethorpe, 'The Coral Sea,' is an almost mystical narrative written in an elegant, romantic style of prose, unlike any of your other published work.

That's because hardly any of my Eighties work has been published. I spent every day of the Eighties working on my writing, and I actually wrote...I hate to call them novels, more like novella-type pieces. And this particular work comes out of that. One morning I'd just sent Jackson off to school; it was about 7:30 in the morning, and the phone rang. I knew what it would be. It was Robert's brother; Robert had passed away.

I was watching A&E at the time. They had a long series on the Romantic poets, so I was deeply into Shelley and Byron. At the time he called me, I was actually watching the movie version of the opera *Tosca,* but when that was over, I was going to get my Romantic-era dose. I knew Robert was dying; I was on vigil that night. I had wept quite a bit in those last two years. So I just sat there and then became immediately energized. I felt rushes of energy, nearly chaotic. But I kept it together and started writing. And I didn't stop. Every morning after Jackson went to school, while Fred was sleeping, from March to May [1989], I worked on this.

The book describes a young man, M, undertaking a final journey before his death, but it does not recount Mapplethorpe's art or life in a literal sense.

No, it's encoded. It's not really about Robert, who had AIDS, and how he battled it. It encodes his process as an artist and things I knew about him, his childhood. The uncle in the piece is [his patron and mentor] Sam Wagstaff. Robert was very into the surrealists, Marcel Duchamp and Max Ernst—the idea of objects in boxes, making altarpieces. So the passenger M is also much like that.

Was it hard for you, after Mapplethorpe's death, to see him demonized by conservative politicians and right-wing activists who targeted the explicit sexuality in some of his work?

I thought it was ludicrous. If Robert was alive, he would have found it annoying. But he would also have been heartbroken by the idea of [Senator] Jesse Helms introducing Robert's pictures of children—he photographed children beautifully and in no unnatural way—as examples of child pornography. He would have wept over that.

Robert didn't like controversy. He didn't do his work politically. He was a pure artist. When he photographed two men kissing or a man pissing in another man's mouth, he was trying, as Jean Genet did, to portray a certain aspect of the human condition nobly, elegantly. I know the kind of man he was. If someone said, "This picture of a cock offends me," he would have taken it down and put a flower up. Because to him they were the same photograph. And they were. Robert's photographs of flowers were very evocative.

He had no problem with labeling his work. The small body of S&M photographs that he had, he put in a portfolio called X. He agreed with stickers that said one had to be over eighteen to walk into a room that had this work. It was not for everybody—he knew that.

You often use the word "work" when referring to your art. For someone who has been characterized as a bohemian poet and singer, you have a strong, focused work ethic.

I always have. I really developed a high work ethic through Robert. He had the strongest work ethic I've ever seen. Until practically the day he died, when he was almost paralyzed and half blind, he was still trying to draw. And my parents have strong work ethics. They both worked hard all their lives.

People think, "You romanticize all these indulgent, decadent French artists." I never romanticized their lifestyle, their waste. What I truly loved about them is the work they do. If someone had a great, romantic, self-indulgent life but did crappy art, I wouldn't be interested.

Do you miss rock & roll stardom at all—even just a little bit?

I didn't really experience a lot of that. On our last tour of Europe [in 1979], we were extremely popular, so I did see all the fame and fortune and fawning that I needed to see in a lifetime: paparazzi, people cutting my hair and pulling my clothes off. I felt like Elvis Presley for a month or two.

Fred's motto around the house—which I actually put in "Gone Again"—was "Fame is fleeting," which he took from General Patton, which General Patton took from Alexander the Great. And to strip oneself of all that is quite interesting. It's somewhat humiliating and painful at first, but once you do it, it's very liberating.

I don't look at all those things with contempt. I appreciate it when young bands say they were positively inspired by our work. And I'm proud that I can actually say, "Yes, for a brief period of my life, I was a rock & roll star." I cherish that.

But I don't need it now. Nor do I want it. That's youth's game. And quite a game. It can be an admirable, even treacherous game. But it belongs to youth.

DR. HUNTER S. THOMPSON

by P.J. O'Rourke

November 28, 1996

At the time you were writing 'Fear and Loathing in Las Vegas,' you implied that things had gone wrong with the Sixties, that it was a flawed era.

Well, the truth of the matter was, there was Kent State, there was Chicago, there was Altamont. The Sixties was about the Free Speech Movement long before it was about the flower children. I was more a part of the Movement than I was of the Acid Club. But you knew that something was happening. You have to remember that acid was legal. [Ken] Kesey was a leader of the psychedelic movement. Berkeley was a whole different thing. The music was another thing. There was the Matrix [club], Ralph Gleason, everything.

I had the best time of my life in the Sixties, and I rail and curse against it because I miss it. But when we really get to talking about it, and when I really get to remembering what actually happened, I recall that it was a horrifying period.

But we really had the illusion of power—the illusion of being in charge. Which was quite liberating. We did drive one president out of the White House.

You have given a pretty negative depiction of the effect of drugs in your work. Basically, nothing happy happens to people when they take drugs. Instead, it's Edge City. There's a lot of stuff that you've written that Nancy Reagan could have used — "Kids, this is what'll happen."

Whether it's negative or not, the reality of it is, you start playing with drugs, the numbers aren't on your side for coming up smelling like roses and being president of the United States. I did at some point describe the difference between me and, say, [Timothy] Leary's concept—you know, that drugs were a holy experience and only for, you know, the drug church. I am in favor of more of a democratization of drugs. Take your chances, you know. I never felt that, aside from a few close friends, it was my business to advocate things.

Do you think there's anything interesting about drugs for making art?

Yeah, totally interesting. But it took me about two years of work to be able to bring a drug experience back and put it on paper.

And not make it sound like a script for 'The Trip' with Peter Fonda.

To do it right means you must retain that stuff at the same time you experience it. You know, acid will move your head around and your eyes, and whatever else you perceive things with. But bringing it back was one of the hardest things I had ever had to do in writing.

You can kid about it. But to really put it down on paper, to be honest about it...

Well, that's what *Vegas* is about. It's about the altered perceptions of the characters. To me, that's really the bedrock of the book—their responses to one another's questions. It's like in the Three Stooges, that story where they were out in the rowboat in a lake and it sprung a leak. And the boat was filling up with water. So they decided to bash a hole in the bottom of the boat to let the water out. Now that's drug reasoning.

How do you write about it?

Well, you know, I wrote it in the process. I wrote it by hand at first, in notebooks. And in fear. Oscar had left me there with a pound of weed and a loaded .357, and some bullets in his briefcase.

And no money.

I couldn't pay the bill. And I was afraid. And I was waiting for the right hour to leave the hotel through the casino.

And earlier I'd slowly, you know, moved stuff down to the car, small amounts, in and out. But there was one big, metal Halliburton [suitcase] that there was no way to get out. I was trying to pick the right time to leave. I remember at 4:30 in the morning, a poker game was going on, nothing but poker games. I just walked through the casino nonchalantly carrying this big Halliburton. I was afraid. I was afraid of taking off, you know, in a red car, on the only road to L.A. I was afraid the whole time. I was in bad enough condition as it was. And, you know, I'm jumping a hotel bill out in Las Vegas and then trying to drive to L.A. in a red car.

Not entirely sober.

That's not your best way to go—a stolen gun, a pound of weed. There was this big bulletin board on the edge of Las Vegas: ATTENTION, TWENTY YEARS — FOR MARIJUANA.

For me, the key moment of the paranoia was the enormous, frightening sign outside the hotel window. Oscar wants to shoot it. But you say, "No, let's study its habits first."

We're feeding off each other. There's a knock on the door, and somebody says, "Well, it must be the manager ready to shoot our heads off." And the response from the other person is to immediately get a knife, open the door and slit the [guy's] throat.

But can you be productive on drugs? I mean, we know that drugs definitely give you different viewpoints, looking at the world through a fly's eye and so on.

Without the drugs, we would not have gone to Las Vegas. Well, we would have had completely different experiences. The logic of the whole thing was drug logic, and it was the right thought. But drugs get to be a problem when the actual writing time comes, except just as a continuation of the mood.

What do you tell people who say they want to become writers?

Ye gods, that's a tough one. I think that one of the things I stumbled on early, as really a self-defense mechanism of some kind, was typing other writers. Typing a page of Hemingway or a page of Faulkner. Three pages. I learned a tremendous amount about rhythm in that way. I see writing really as music. And I see my work as essentially music. That's why I like to hear it read out loud by other people. I like to hear what they're getting out of it. It tells me what you see. I like to have women read it. If it fits musically, it will go to almost any ear. It could be that that's why children relate to it.

And also you know if you're getting your reader to hear it the way you want it heard.

I like to hear them getting it. Boy, that's when you know you're on the same fucking frequency. Without the music it would be just a mess of pottage.

Did anybody read aloud to you as a kid?

Yeah, my mother did. We were big on stories in the family—fables, bedtime stories. The house was full of books.

There was no wall in the house that didn't have bookshelves. It's like this house [*points to rows of shelves*]. The library, to me, was every bit as much a refuge as a crack house might be to some gang kid today. You know, a library card was a ticket to ride. I read every one of those fucking things. My mother was a librarian for the Louisville [Kentucky] Public Library.

John Updike's mother told him that the whole Rabbit series read like an A student's idea of what a high-school athlete's life is like. . . .

Wow. To have his mother say it: "I knew there was a reason I was always disappointed in you, my son." Imagine the struggle that my mother had to go through.

How did she feel about your writing?

For ten years, the fact that I was a writer had little to do with the fact that I was seen merely as a criminal on a hell-bound train. My mother had to be down there on Fourth Street, at the main desk of the library, and had to have people come in asking for my book before she was convinced that I had a job.

What was the first book, the first whole book, you read?

Good lord, man—anybody who would remember that is probably in some kind of trouble or lying.

No, they say that drug addicts always remember the very first time they had the drug, or alcoholics remember the first drink.

[*Pauses*] Jesus, I think you're right.

I think I am, too.

Well, in my grandmother's bookcase there was a book called *The Goops.* I was maybe six, seven. It was a rhymed thing about people who have no manners—people who drooled. The Goops, they use the left hand; they chew all their soup. The Goops were always being punished for rudeness. My grandmother pulled it out for me to let me know that I was going against history. It was like a poem on every page, iambic pentameter definitely, and she gave me a sense of rules, and she managed to shame me for being a Goop—and being a Goop was like being a pig and lowlife. And it registered.

What about the first grown-up book that you read?

You've got to keep in mind that through high school, I was a member, actually an elected officer, of the Athenaeum Literary Association, which really governed my consciousness. It started out at Male High [in Louisville]. We'd gather around on Saturday nights to read. It was a profoundly elitist concept. It ended up being a kind of compensation for cutting school. You know, "What have you got? Where were you yesterday, Hunter?" "Well, I was down at Grady's, on Bardstown Road, reading [Plato's] allegory of the cave with Bob Butler and Norman Green, drinking beer." I don't know, it was fun. We were reading Nietzsche. It was tough, but when you're cutting school, you're reading for power, reading for advantage. I've always believed: You teach a kid to like reading, they're set. That's what we did with Juan [Thompson's son]. You get a kid who likes to read on his own, shit, you've done your job.

When you started reading on your own, who did you turn to?

When I was in the Air Force, I went into a feeding frenzy. I read contemporary stuff— *The Fountainhead.* I had Hemingway, Fitzgerald, Faulkner, Kerouac, e.e. cummings. The thing that was important to me about Hemingway at the time was that Hemingway taught me that you could be a writer and get away with it. The example he set was more important than his writing. His economy of words I paid a lot of attention to. That thing about typing other people's work was really an eye-opener to me. Nobody suggested it to me. I just started doing it. I had Dos Passos—that's where I got a lot of my style stuff, the newsreels up at the beginning of his chapters. I came to Fitzgerald early. At nineteen or twenty, *The Great Gatsby* was recommended to me as my kind of book.

I've said before, *Gatsby* is possibly the Great American Novel, if you look at it as a technical achievement. It's about 55,000 words, which was astounding to me. In *Vegas,* I tried to compete with that.

I didn't realize 'Gatsby' was that short.

It was one of the basic guiding principles for my writing. I've always competed with that. Not a wasted word. This has been a main point to my literary thinking all my life. Shoot, I couldn't match 55,000 no matter how I chopped. I even chopped the ending off.

There are few things that I read and say, "Boy, I wish I could write that." Damn few. The Book of Revelation is one. *Gatsby* is one.

You know Hemingway's concept: What you don't write is more important than what you do. I don't think he ever wrote anything as good as *The Great Gatsby.* There are lines out of *Gatsby*—I'll tell you why it's so good: Fitzgerald describing Tom Buchanan. You know—athlete, Yale and all the normal stuff, and the paragraph ended describing him physically. Fitzgerald said about Tom Buchanan's body, "It was a body capable of great leverage." Back off! I remember that to this day, exactly. You finish Gatsby, and you feel you've been in somebody else's world a long time.

You've said that you initially wanted to write fiction and that you saw journalism just as a way to make ends meet.

Essentially to support my habit, writing.

What is gonzo journalism?

I never intended gonzo journalism to be any more than just a differentiation of new journalism. I kind of knew it wasn't that. Bill Cardoso—then working for the *Boston Globe*—wrote me a note about the Kentucky Derby thing ["The Kentucky Derby Is Decadent and Depraved," *Scanlan's Monthly,* June 1970] saying, "Hot damn. Kick ass. It was pure gonzo." And I heard him use it once or twice up in New Hampshire. It's a Portuguese word [actually, it's Italian], and it translates almost exactly to what the Hell's Angels would have said was "off the wall." Hey, it's in the dictionary now.

Not many people get to add anything to the dictionary.

That's one of my proudest achievements. It's in Random House [and many other dictionaries]. I'm afraid to quote it.

Where did the phrase "fear and loathing" come from?

It came out of my own sense of fear and a perfect description of that situation to me. However, I have been accused of stealing it from Nietzsche or Kafka or something. It seemed like a natural thing.

What was the response when you filed 'Vegas'?

The staff then was a pretty tight group. We had dinner down at some Mexican restaurant we used to go to a lot, to celebrate the bringing in of the great Salazar saga. That was the event. We sat at a booth—white Formica table—there were four of us in there: Jane [Wenner], Jann, me inside and [former *Rolling Stone* editor] David Felton. I might have said something to Jann that afternoon like, "I got a little something extra."

But I remember sitting down there across from Jann—it was just the two of us at first—and I just said, "Hey, try this." I think the first day it was nine pages—somehow it went in nines. It was just my handwritten notes, which went on and on and on. That was the thing about *Rolling Stone* in those days: It was logical. Here I'd had one great triumph and said, "Hey, wait a minute, come over here, I got something better." And I knew somehow it was better. I knew it was special. It was a different voice. Jann read it. He was the one for a real judgment.

He made me an offer. Can you imagine anyone doing things that way now? But it was just entirely natural, and it's always been that way. It was, "Hey, hot damn, this is good. What else do you have?" I'd say, "This is a large thing; I'm full of energy here," and that energy meant finishing something. And he went right along with it.

You don't get that too often.

I've always appreciated that moment.

I've never been able to decide what makes me most envious of you as a writer, whether it is the "I feel a bit lightheaded; maybe you should drive" or when Oscar turned to the hitchhiker and said, "We're your friends. We're not like the others."

We happened to pick up this kid on another road, not on the road from L.A. to Las Vegas. I was driving; it was the first time around—the red car. I saw a kid hitchhiking. A tall, gangly kid. I said, "What the hell?" and I pulled over: "Hop in." "Hot damn," he said, "I never rode in a convertible before." And I said, "You're in the right place." I was really pleased. That was a true thing. I identified with him. I almost said, "You want to drive?"

Was Ralph Steadman in Las Vegas during any of this?

No, we sent it to him all at once when it was finished. When I went to Las Vegas, one of my jobs was to find physical art: things that we used, cocktail napkins, maybe photos—we didn't have a photographer. But that concept didn't work. I rejected it. It was a cold afternoon, Friday, on a deadline in the *Rolling Stone* offices, when I rejected [Art Director Robert] Kingsbury's art for the Vegas story. It was a real crisis: "What do we do now?" This is one of those stories that you read in bad books. I said, "What the fuck, let's get Ralph Steadman. We should have had him there in the first place."

We'd worked together on the Derby piece and also on the America's Cup nightmare. It never got published. *Scanlan's* had gone under. Ralph and I had become somewhat disaffected, estranged, because of his experience in New York—his one and only experience with psychedelics, with psilocybin. And he swore he'd never come back to this country and I was the worst example of American swine that had ever been born.

If I had had my way, Ralph would have gone with me to Las Vegas. It was some kind of accountant's thing: "Save on the art," you know. I didn't like the cocktail-napkin thing, but it wasn't that big a story, really. And, you know, Ralph wouldn't do it unless he was paid $100,000 or something like that. But when the other art was rejected, I think Jann was there: "Let's call Ralph." The story was done. It was one of those, "How fast can we get it to him? How fast can we get it back?" And, you know, we got him on the phone. You know [*British accent*], "Thot bastuhd. Well, ah'll hav a luk at it. Ah, yes, I cahn probably do it." The manuscript was sent off. He'd never been to Las Vegas.

I don't think it was probably necessary for someone to have been to Las Vegas to illustrate that story. I mean, the visuals were kind of "internal."

Yeah. But there was no more communication with him for, like, three days. We were all a bit nervous. And I would say, "Don't worry, he said he would do it." But his heart was full of hate. In about three to four days, a long tube arrived at the office. Great excitement. I was there when some messenger brought it in: a big, round thing. And we went to the art department. It was huge. Very carefully, we pulled the stuff out and unrolled it. And, ye gods, every one of them was perfect. It was like discovering water at the bottom of a well. Not one was rejected; not one was changed. This is what he sent.

Here's a question: Are you religious? Do you believe in God?

Long ago, I shucked off the belief that the people I was dealing with in the world, the power people, really knew what they were doing at all. And that included religion. The idea of heaven and hell—to be threatened with it—was absurd. I think the church wanted it to keep people in line. I've kind of recently come to a different realization that I'm in charge, really. That it comes down to karma. Karma is different things to different countries, but in the Orient, karma comes in the next generation.

And ours comes in the mail.

I've kind of updated Buddhism. In other words, you get your rewards in this life, and I think I'll be around again pretty quickly. Karma incorporates a measure of behavior, and in my interpretation, like everything else in this American century, it's been sped up—you know, the news, the effect of the news, religion, the effect of it. The only kind of grace points you get there is, they let you rest for a while sometimes. I may be sent back. I see myself as a road man for the lords of karma, and I'm not worried about my assignment. Of course, a lot of people have good reason to worry.

I think I know several people who are probably walking around as bugs right now.

Three-legged dogs on a Navajo reservation. Yeah, Pat Buchanan coming back as a rat on the great feeding hill in Calcutta. In Buddhism there is an acceptance of the utter meaninglessness and rottenness of life. I think Nixon got his karma in his time.

BILL CLINTON
by Jann S. Wenner

December 28, 2000

You're the youngest retiring president since Teddy Roosevelt. Do you compare yourself much to Roosevelt?

The time in which I served was very much like the time in which he served. His job was to manage the transition of America from an agricultural to an industrial power and from, essentially, an isolationist to an international nation. In my time, we were managing the transition from an industrial to an information age and from a Cold War world to a multipolar, more interdependent world.

Then, when Roosevelt got out, he felt Taft had betrayed his progressive legacy. So he spent a lot of the rest of his life in political affairs. He built a third-party political movement and was a very important force. But I think the impact he might have had was tempered by his evident disappointment at not being president anymore. That's not an option for me. I can't run again, because now there's the Twenty-second Amendment.

If there wasn't the Twenty-second Amendment, would you run again?

Oh, I probably would have run again.

Do you think you would have won?

Yes I do. But it's hard to say, because it's entirely academic.

Do you think the Twenty-second Amendment is a good idea? Is it really consistent with democracy to have this kind of term limit on a president?

On balance, the arguments for executive term limits are pretty compelling. I mean, I have an extra amount of energy and I love this job; I love the nature of this work. But maybe it's better to leave when you're in good. Maybe they should put "consecutive" in there, limit it to two consecutive terms.

One of the very first things you did in office was try to overturn the military's ban on gays. Why did this backfire, and what did you learn from that?

It backfired partly because the people that were against it were clever enough to push a vote in the Senate disapproving of the change in the policy. I wanted to do it the way Harry Truman integrated the military. He issued an executive order and gave the military leaders a couple of years to figure out how best to do it. But a lot of the gay groups wanted it done right away and had no earthly idea what kind of reaction would come. They were shocked by the amount of congressional opposition.

A lot of people think I compromised with the military. That's not what happened. If I was going to be able to do anything, I had to have a veto-proof minority in either the House or the Senate. But the Senate voted 68 to 32 against my policy, which meant that I could not sustain my policy in either house. And it was only then that I worked out with Colin Powell this dumbass "don't ask, don't tell" thing.

Would you do it any differently now?

I wish I had been able to get an agreement on the part of everybody involved to take this out of politics. But the Republicans decided that they didn't want me to have a honeymoon. They wanted to make me the first president without one, and—now that we were living in a twenty-four-hour news cycle—the press happily went along.

In your first year in office, you regularly talked with Richard Nixon.

I had him back to the White House. I just thought that I ought to do it. He had lived a constructive life in his years out of the White House; he had written all these books; he tried to be a force in world affairs. He paid a high price for what he did, and I just thought it would be a good thing for the country to invite him back. He told me he identified with me because he thought the press had been too hard on me in '92 and that I had refused to die, and he liked that. He said a lot of life was just hanging on. We had a good talk about that. I always thought that he could have been a great president if he had been more trusting of the American people.

What did you do when you heard the news about the shootings at Columbine?

I called the local officials and the school officials from the Oval Office. That was only the most recent and the most grotesque of a whole series of highly visible school shootings that we had. One of them, in Jonesboro, Arkansas, was in my home state — I knew some of the people who run the school.

I thought a lot of things. Number one: How'd those kids get all those guns? And how could they have had that kind of arsenal without their parents knowing? And I thought, after I read a little about it: How did they get so lost, without anybody finding them before they went over the edge? We had a spate of killings associated with a kind of darkness on the Net.

What do you mean, "darkness on the Net"?

Well, I mean, those kids were apparently into some sort of a satanic thing. I worried then — I'm worried now — about the people in our society, particularly children, that just drift off. Maybe one of those kids could have been saved if somebody had been there to help, and then all those other children would still be alive.

It seems shocking that we didn't get any major new gun-control legislation in the wake of that event.

The truth is that when legislation time comes, a lot of the people in Congress are still frightened of the NRA. The NRA is great at terrifying people with inflammatory rhetoric. Did you see the tirade that Charlton Heston carried on against Al Gore and me, saying that we were glad some of these people were killed, because it gave me an excuse to take people's guns away?

You got the Brady Bill and a partial assault-weapons ban through Congress in your first term. Why didn't you seize the opportunity, with this post-Columbine atmosphere? You called a White House conference on violence in movies and video games.

I thought Congress would be so shocked and the public so galvanized that we would have a window of opportunity.

So what happened?

The GOP leadership just delayed until the fever went down. They knew that they couldn't afford to have their members voting wrong on closing the gun-show loophole or banning the importation of large-capacity ammunition clips—which allows people to get around the assault-weapons ban. We finally got a majority vote for it in the Senate. Al Gore broke the tie. But we couldn't get a bill out of the conference committee in the House. If we could ever have gotten a clean vote—

Then you would have won that vote?

Oh, absolutely. We could win the vote today if we could get a vote. But the leadership in the Republican Party—as long as they're in the majority in both houses—can control things. You can write the rules so that you can just keep stuff from coming up.

I'll remind you that one of the reasons that Democrats are in the minority today is because of the Brady law and the assault-weapons law. There's not a single hunter that's missed an hour of hunting, not a single sport shooter has missed an event. They acted like it was the end of the world. But half a million felons, fugitives and stalkers haven't gotten handguns because of the Brady law.

How do you feel about the genocide in Rwanda? Is there anything that we could have done to prevent it? Do you feel any responsibility, personally?

I feel terrible about it. The thing that was shocking about Rwanda was that it happened so fast, and it happened with almost no guns. The idea that 700,000 people could be killed in a hundred days, mostly with machetes, is hard to believe. It was an alien territory; we weren't familiar. I think and hope that the United States will be much more involved in Africa from now on. If we had done all the things we've done since Rwanda in Africa—what would have happened is, the African troops would have moved in, they would have stopped it, and we could have given them the logistical support they needed to stop it.

Why do you think you were such a lightning rod for partisanship and bitterness and so much hatred during your terms in Washington?

There were a lot of reasons. Mostly, it's just because I won. [The Republicans] believed the only reason they lost in 1976 to Jimmy Carter was because of Watergate. They believed that from the time Mr. Nixon won in '68, they had found a foolproof formula to hold the White House forever. They really believed that America saw Republicans as the guarantor of the country's superiority in values and prudence in financial matters and that they could always turn Democrats into cardboard cutouts of what they really were. They could sort of caricature them as almost un-American. So I came along, and I had ideas on crime and welfare and economic management and foreign policy that were difficult for them to characterize in that way. And we won....And they were really mad.

I think, secondly, I was the first baby-boomer president. Not a perfect person—never claimed to be. And I opposed the Vietnam War. I think that made them doubly angry, because they thought I was a cultural alien and I made it anyway.

So you think the culture wars were very much a part of this atmosphere?

Mmm-hmm. I also think they were even more angry because I was a white Southern Baptist. They didn't like losing the White House, and they didn't like me. They didn't like what they thought I represented. They had worked very hard to have the old white-male Southern culture dominate the political life of America. And they saw me as an apostate—which I welcome. When I take on the NRA or do something for gay rights, to them, it's worse if I do it. It's like a Catholic being pro-choice.

Were you surprised by the difficulties you had in your own party? Pat Moynihan criticized your health care proposal and your economic plan.

I didn't take offense at that. Moynihan believed, first of all—with some justification—that he knew more about most areas of social policy than anybody else did. He felt we were making a political mistake not to do welfare reform first, which turned out to be right. Secondly, he felt that Washington could not absorb, in a two-year period, the economic plan, which he strongly supported. He said, "The system cannot absorb this much change in this short a time." They thought I was being bullheaded. And I think, in retrospect, they were probably right.

What was your relationship with Newt Gingrich like?

It depended on which Newt showed up. The good Newt I found engaging and intelligent; we were surprisingly in agreement in the way we viewed the world. We actually had a very cordial relationship. He was very candid with me about his political objectives. And he, in turn, from time to time, would get in trouble with the right wing of his own caucus, because they said I could talk him into too much.

On the other hand, when he did things like blaming every bad thing that happened in America on Democrats, the 1960s and all that—I thought it was highly destructive.

How did it make you feel personally?

At some point, probably around 1996, I got to the point where I no longer had personal feelings about those things—like the Whitewater investigation and the travel-office investigation. Newt was smart. He knew there was nothing in any of that stuff. It was all politics to him; it was about power. But he really did believe that the object of politics was to destroy your opponent. And he had an enormous amount of success. He won the Congress basically by having a take-no-prisoners, be-against-everything approach. He thought he was leading a revolution, and I was in the way. I thought he was a worthy adversary. I made a lot of errors, and he ran through them.

In the history books, it will say, of course, that you were the second president ever to be impeached. How does that make you feel? Will it cloud your real accomplishments?

The history books will also record, I think, that both impeachments were wrong. And that's why they failed. And I'm just grateful that, unlike Andrew Johnson, I was less embittered by it, and I had more support, from the public and in the Congress, and so I was able to resume my duties and actually get a lot done for the American people in the aftermath.

Did you ever get so angry during it that you think it clouded your judgment?

I got angry, but I always was alone with friends who would deflate me. I don't think it ever clouded my judgment on any official thing. I realized that, when it was all over, I would have the responsibility to work with the Republicans as well as the Democrats.

One of the things I had to learn—it took me almost my whole first term to learn it—was that, at some point, presidents are not permitted to have personal feelings. When you manifest your anger in public, it should be on behalf of the American people and the values that they believe in. I had very strong personal feelings about it, but I tried never to talk about it.

Do you think it was in some way a referendum on the nature, morality or character of the American people?

Not really. People strongly disagreed with what I did. I did, too. I think that they just were able to discriminate between a bad personal mistake and the justification for a constitutional crisis.

As president, you have a relationship with the press that's unique in the world: You are subject to more criticism, more attention—more everything. What's your take on the press in America?

The important thing is to try to hear the criticism. Because it's not always wrong, sometimes it's right. They're doing the best they can in a very new and different environment. I have a lot of sympathy for them. How can presidents hate the press? You can gripe all you want about all the negative coverage you get on the evening news or on the talk shows or being blasted in the newspaper or having them get on something when they're dead wrong, like Whitewater—where they're just dead wrong. But every day they're writing about all the things that affect the American people in their lives. Anytime you want a microphone to have your say, you've got it. So I think to be obsessively negative is a mistake.

What creature comforts are you going to miss the most about leaving the White House—about not living there?

What I will miss the most is not the creature comforts. It's the honor of living in the White House, which I have loved. And, even more than that, I'll miss the work. It's the job I'll miss the most—I actually love doing this job.

Do you just get off every single day when you get up?

Every day. Even on the worst day. Even in the worst times of that whole impeachment thing. I just thank God every day I can go to work.

What have you learned about the American people? You've had a unique exposure to them that nobody else has ever had.

I'll tell you this: When I leave office on January 20th, I will leave even more idealistic than I was the day I took the oath of office, eight years earlier.

The American people are fundamentally good, and they almost always get it right, if they have enough time and enough information. But the biggest problem we have in public discourse today is, there's plenty of information out there, but you don't know what's true and what's not, and it's hard to access it. It's all kind of flying at you at once. It's hard to have time to digest it. But if people have the information, they have time to digest it, they nearly always get it right. And if that weren't the case, we wouldn't be around here after 224 years.

Do you have any special message to young people? Any valedictory thoughts to the kids in school right now as you leave office?

This is a fascinating time to be alive, but it's not free of challenges. So I would say to the young people: You'll probably live in the most prosperous, interesting time in human history. But there are a lot of big challenges out there, and you'll have to be public citizens as well as private people.

THE DALAI LAMA

by Robert Thurman

May 24, 2001

Right now, the gap between rich and poor is increasing more and more. At least five hundred new billionaires have come up during the last twenty years.

Five hundred!

Yes, up from twelve in 1982, and now almost six hundred. But out of those, more than one hundred have come up in Asia. Though we think of Asia as poor, there are billionaires in Asia, and at the same time so many poor people in the West — so it's more like a worldwide system of rich and poor that has gone beyond East and West. You have said that the communists failed miserably in their attempt to force the rich people to share.

Yes.

So then what is the alternative in trying to get a better balance?

People have to decide on their own that it is good to share what they have, at least to some degree. I think that this can only happen through education, through increasing their awareness. In the long run, when there is one rich family surrounded by poor people, mentally they will not be happy. Their children will always receive some harassment from the poor community, so physically also they will constantly feel some sort of fear or threat. So in the long run, not only will they be morally unhappy but also they will be practically unhappy.

Then, you can think in terms of the murder rate or senseless violence in the community; in some cases an overly polarized economy can become one cause of a civil war. When there is too much of a gap, some agitators can easily organize the poor people, as they can claim to be fighting for equality or for justice. So therefore, if we return to an ever more huge gap, then due to such conditions within societies, many troubles are bound to come. That being the case, in the long run it is in the interest of the richer people themselves to make sure that there is a less-extreme gap between themselves and the poor around them. In this way, they will realize their enlightened self-interest in sharing.

Then also they can think more carefully about their own lifestyle. For example, except for the fact that richer people can think, "I am really rich!"—except for being able to hold this concept in their thoughts, I doubt if there is that much difference in the actual quality of their living, if they become more mindful of its actual details.

Except, as you already mentioned, on the physical level.

Even on the physical level, how much can anyone put into one stomach? Except perhaps you, as your belly seems quite expansive [*laughs*]! That being so, really, even in the practical, material facts of living, there's not that much special about being really rich. For example, you can drink a lot of wine or liquor, some really expensive kind, or you can eat very costly food. But if it is too rich, or if you eat too much, it will hurt your health. Then some people who don't work physically fear they are getting too unhealthy, so then they expend a tremendous amount of sweat doing strenuous exercises. Like me, I don't get out to walk very much, so I have to ride on my exercise bike every day! When you think about it, there isn't that much to it, is there?

As you say.

But in the thinking "I am rich, really rich!"—just the excitement of that concept gives a little energy. But this is really very little of a benefit, for some sort of self-image. Just for this, is it worth it to engage in all the stress of amassing huge wealth? Within one's family there will be unhappiness, within society there will be so many people feeling jealousy and malice and wishing you ill. And you will feel anxiety about that. And so one develops a more clear awareness of the realities of the state of extreme wealth.

On the other hand, if they instead think, "I'm so rich. If I help these poor ones in front of me, if I help their health, if I help them develop skills and good qualities, then these poorer people will really like me. Even though I'm rich, they will really feel friendly toward me." That way, the rich person will find real happiness, don't you think so? For example, if there is some tragedy in the thoughtless rich family, then the ordinary people might actually enjoy it. But in the opposite case, if something tragic happens to the generous rich family, then everyone is genuinely sorry. So if you get richer and richer and still share nothing, and the people around you really dislike you, how can you feel good?

Fundamentally, we are social animals, so when the surrounding people become more genuinely friendly, we feel more mutual trust and we are much, much happier. So the rich should make a conscious decision, on their own volition, to make their contribution, share the wealth that has come to them from their past good karma. When they increase their awareness of others' perspectives, they will naturally realize, "Helping others more, they will be happy, and then I will be happy myself!" That's what I am thinking.

Now for a really simple question: What is the essence of Buddhism?

Respect all forms of life, and then compassion and affection toward all sentient beings, with the understanding that everything is interdependent—so my happiness and suffering, my well-being, very much have to do with others'.

What prevents people from understanding this?

When people think it's all about doing tantric visualizations and rituals.

When I talk about the Buddhist dharma, I'm not talking about just chanting and rituals. If it's thought to be a philosophy, it's not that, either. The dharma, it's just the mind. I'm afraid that among the Tibetans, the Chinese and also some Westerners—the new Buddhists—in many cases they consider the practice of Buddhism is simply to recite something and perform some ritual, putting false expectations on the esoteric magic of tantra: "Oh, if I do this, I may get something amazing!" So they neglect the basic instruments that actually transform our mind. These instruments are the altruistic spirit of enlightenment [*bodhichitta*], the transcendent attitude, renunciation, the realization of impermanence, the wisdom of self-lessness. People who think they have a magic gimmick neglect these things. So their inner world, their inner reality, remains very raw.

Sadly, use of ritual can feed that neglect. Knowledge of philosophy can also feed that. It's a great tragedy. If Buddha came here, if Nagarjuna [a great Indian Buddhist philosopher, circa the second century C.E.] came here, I think they would feel very critical about this; they would give us a big scolding. Nagarjuna would say that all our complex philosophies are not meant just for academics, our elegant rituals are not just for theatrics.

What about those who think Buddhism is simply an unfair rejection of the world? Even today, the pope thinks Buddhism is too depressing and negative.

Most importantly, those people who consider themselves Buddhists must practice the Buddha's dharma sincerely—that will be the proof of the value of Buddhism. Some Tibetans today also say that in the past, the way of life was that the dharma almost served as a livelihood or a routine profession. The Buddhist was not thinking of nirvana, not caring for liberation, just how to make a living. Officials used it for their lives, monks, nuns and lamas for their lives. Inside, in their inner world, they were like ordinary people, lusting and hating. So the dharma became a poison in this way.

When there is too much focus on the Buddhist institution, and the country goes to waste, that's what it means when people say Buddhism ruined the country. According to that reality, these accusations become true.

Therefore, the best answer for this criticism is for ourselves to practice sincerely. We can aim for nirvana and Buddhahood. But in the meantime, we can be practical, develop the education field and improve the worldly life in various ways to benefit society and humanity. In this way, we can be fully engaged.

Are there particular dharma teachings that are especially useful for people at different ages—for example, for younger people filled with turbulent emotions or for older people worrying about death?

I don't think so. Buddha dharma is dealing with emotions. Young and old, the emotional world is the same. Some feelings closely associated with the physical body may differ in emphasis.

Then would you say that young persons benefit from meditating about death as much as older persons do?

Yes, in general. However, just to think about death alone, I don't know how useful it is. For a materialist who doesn't believe in future life, meditating on death might develop a bit more contentment, but it won't bring great benefit. In Buddhism, meditation on death is important in the context of the matter-of-fact expectation of limitless lives and the sense of the possibility to transform our mind while evolving through those lives. The time of this life with liberty and opportunity becomes very important, actually the most precious time; wasting such a lifetime is a great tragedy. So we concentrate and meditate on death and impermanence until we powerfully feel that our precious lives with liberty and opportunity might get wasted if we don't practice. In this case, since through ultimate wisdom you can attain ultimate freedom and even the exalted state of Buddhahood, you are energized by meditating on impermanence and death. Otherwise, just to do it in a materialist context might just make someone feel demoralized. That would be wrong, don't you think?

What do you think about the relationship of religion and politics?

I think politics is a technique or method to serve the community and to lead society. And what is the meaning of "religion"? Broadly speaking, religion is the warm heart. All human activities are furthered by the warm heart—the compassionate heart. Every human activity can be positive and also can be a religious activity. As for politics, unfortunately, some people consider that, in politics, there is no morality, it's just lies, bullying, cheating. That's not genuine politics. It's just savagery. Even religious teaching, when conducted with a motivation to deceive, exploit or dominate, is also quite immoral. On a general level in the West, religion means to believe in God the Creator, and with the motivation of serving God, one serves society and engages in politics, serves humanity or society morally as well as politically. And so there is no contradiction.

So in the Western dialogue about church and state...

Ah! That's different. "Church" means the religious institution. Of course that should be separate. Combining them causes too many difficulties. The spirit of democracy, competition and contest, as in the United States, is very important, so if religious leaders were to engage in such contests, it would lead to difficulties. Religious institutions should not get involved in the democratic competition— only individuals.

Turning to Tibet: You have said that Tibetans are basically more jolly and content than most of us in the West. Why?

There are many factors. First, Tibet maintained a small population, so generally speaking survival was not very difficult. The nomads have plenty of meat, plenty of cheese, plenty of milk, no problems. So it seems they can lie down all day; then, when they get hungry, they just get up and kill one yak. Of course, they have plenty of pasture, no boundary at all, everywhere. Then there are the farmers; perhaps they have to work more, but again, there is sufficient land for a small population. So these are economic factors for their contentment.

Then, Tibet had a lot of Buddhist teaching: the teaching of karmic evolution, the teaching of rebirth and the concept of the nature of suffering of the samsara [endless cycle of unhappy lives]. So no matter how difficult this life gets, still we put a lot of hope in the future. In daily life, at least some portion of our mind is thinking about the long-term future, just beginning with the next life. So when you face some difficulty in this life, since your whole mind is not focused only on it, even tragic things can happen, and you're not so disturbed. When your whole mind, your whole hope, is concentrated on something within this life, then when something happens, you have much more worry, much more anxiety. We often say, when some tragedy happens, it's all due to karma. In that way, we lay less blame on others; we feel at least less bitter.

BOB DYLAN

by Mikal Gilmore

November 22, 2001

In 1998, when you received the Grammy Award for Album of the Year, you said something that surprised me — maybe surprised other people as well. You said, "We didn't know what we had when we did it, but we did it anyway." That was interesting because 'Time Out of Mind' plays as an album made with purpose and vision, with a consistent mood and set of themes. Was it, in fact, an album you approached with forethought, or was its seeming cohesiveness incidental?

What happened was, I'd been writing down couplets and verses and things, and then putting them together at later times. I had a lot of that—it was starting to pile up—so I thought, "Well, I got all this—maybe, I'll try to record it." I'd had good luck with Daniel Lanois [producer of the 1989 album *Oh Mercy*], so I called him and showed him a lot of the songs. I also familiarized him with the way I wanted the songs to sound. I think I played him some Slim Harpo recordings—early stuff like that. He seemed pretty agreeable to it, and we set aside a certain time and place. But I had a schedule—I only had so much time—and we made that record, *Time Out of Mind*, that way. It was a little rougher....I wouldn't say rougher....It was...I feel we were lucky to get that record.

Really?

Well, I didn't go into it with the idea that this was going to be a finished album. It got off the tracks more than a few times, and people got frustrated. I know I did. I know Lanois did....I felt extremely frustrated, because I couldn't get any of the up-tempo songs that I wanted.

Don't you think a song like "Cold Irons Bound" certainly has a drive to it?

Yeah, there's a real drive to it, but it isn't even close to the way I had it envisioned. I mean, I'm satisfied with what we did. But there were things I had to throw out because this assortment of people just couldn't lock in on riffs and rhythms all together. I got so frustrated in the studio that I didn't really dimensionalize the songs. I could've if I'd had the willpower. I just didn't at that time, and so you got to steer it where the event itself wants to go. I feel there was a sameness to the rhythms. It was more like that swampy, voodoo thing that Lanois is so good at. I just wish I'd been able to get more of a legitimate rhythm-oriented sense into it. I didn't feel there was any mathematical thing about that record at all. The one beat could've been anywhere, when instead, the singer should have been defining where the drum should be. It was tricky trying to steer that ship.

I think that's why people say *Time Out of Mind* is sort of dark and foreboding: because we locked into that one dimension in the sound. People say the record deals with mortality—my mortality for some reason! [*Laughs*] Well, it doesn't deal with my mortality. It maybe just deals with mortality in general. It's one thing that we all have in common, isn't it?...You know, I'm not really quite sure why it seems to people that *Time Out of Mind* is a darker picture. In my mind, there's nothing dark about it. It's not like, you know, Dante's *Inferno* or something. It doesn't paint a picture of goblins and goons and grotesque-looking creatures or anything like that.

It was during the final stages of the album that you were hit with a serious swelling around your heart and were laid up in the hospital. You've said that that infection was truly painful and debilitating. Did it alter your view of life in any way?

No. No, because it didn't! You can't even say something like, "Well, you were in the wrong place at the wrong time." Even that excuse didn't work. It was like I learned nothing. I wish I could say I put the time to good use or, you know, got highly educated in something or had some revelations about anything. But I can't say that any of that happened. I just laid around and then had to wait for my strength to come back.

Do you think that the proximity of your illness to the album's release helped account for why reviewers saw so many themes of mortality in 'Time Out of Mind'?

When I recorded that album, the media weren't paying any attention to me. I was totally outside of it.

True, but the album came out not long after you'd gone through the illness.

It did?

Yes. You were in the hospital in the spring of 1997, and 'Time Out of Mind' was released in autumn that same year.

Okay, well, then it could've been perceived that way in the organized media. But that would just be characterizing the album, really.

I want to step back a bit, to those years preceding 'Time Out of Mind.' First, I'd like to ask you about an occasion at an earlier Grammy Awards, in 1991, when you received a Lifetime Achievement Award. At that point, America was deep into its involvement in the Gulf War. You came out onstage that night with a small band and played a severe version of "Masters of War"—a performance that remains controversial even today. Some critics found it rushed and embarrassing, others thought it was brilliant. Then, after Jack Nicholson presented you the award, you made the following comment: "My daddy [once said], 'Son, it's possible to become so defiled in this world that your own mother and father will abandon you. And if that happens, God will always believe in your own ability to mend your ways.'" I've always thought that was one of the more remarkable things I've heard you say. What was going through your mind at that time?

I don't remember the time and place my father said that to me, and maybe he didn't say it to me in that exact way. I was probably paraphrasing the whole idea, really—I'm not even sure I paraphrased in the proper context. It might've been something that just sort of popped in my head at that time. The only thing I remember about that whole episode, as long as you bring it up, was that I had a fever—like 104. I was extremely sick that night. Not only that, but I was disillusioned with the entire musical community and environment. If I remember correctly, the Grammy people called me months before then and said that they wanted to give me this Lifetime Achievement honor. Well, we all know that they give those things out when you're old, when you're nothing, a has-been. Everybody knows that, right? So I wasn't sure whether it was a compliment or an insult. I wasn't really sure about it. And then they said, "Here's what we want to do"...I don't want to name these performers because you know them, but one performer was going to sing "Like a Rolling Stone." Another performer was going to sing "The Times Are A-Changin'." Another was going to sing "All Along the Watchtower," and another was going to sing "It's All Over Now, Baby Blue." They were going to sing bits of all these songs, and then they were going to have somebody introduce me, and I would just collect this Lifetime Achievement Award, say a few words and go on my merry way. The performers, they told me, had all agreed to it, so there really wasn't anything for me to do except show up.

Then the Gulf War broke out. The Grammy people called and

said, "Listen, we're in a tight fix. So-and-so, who was going to sing 'Times Are A-Changin',' is afraid to get on an airplane. So-and-so, who was going to sing 'Like a Rolling Stone,' doesn't want to travel because he just had another baby and he doesn't want to leave his family." That's understandable. But then so-and-so, who was going to sing "It's All Over, Baby Blue," was in Africa and didn't want to take a chance flying to New York, and so-and-so, who was going to sing "All Along the Watchtower," wasn't sure he wanted to be at any high-visibility place right then, because it may be a little danger-ous. So, they said, "Could you come and sing? Could you fill the time?" And I said, "What about the guy who's going to introduce me [Jack Nicholson]?" They said, "He's okay. He's coming." Anyway, I got disillusioned with all the characters at that time—with their inner character and their ability to be able to keep their word and their idealism and their insecurity. All the ones that have the gall to thrust their tortured inner psyches on an outer world but can't at least be true to their word. From that point on, that's what the music business and all the people in it represented to me. I just lost all respect for them. There's a few that are decent and God-fearing and will stand up in a righteous way. But I wouldn't want to count on most of them. And maybe me singing "Masters of War"...I've said before that song's got nothing to do with being antiwar. It has more to do with the military industrial complex that Eisenhower was talking about. Anyway, I went up and did that, but I was sick, and I felt they put me through a whole lot of trouble over nothing. I just tried to disguise myself the best I could. That was more along the line of...you know, the press was finding me irrelevant then, and it couldn't have happened at a better time, really, because I wouldn't have wanted to have been relevant. I wouldn't have wanted to be someone that the press was examining—every move. I wouldn't have ever been able to develop again in any kind of artistic way.

But certainly you knew by playing "Masters of War" at the height of the Gulf War, it would be received a certain way.

Yeah, but I wasn't looking at it that way. I knew the lyrics of the song were holding up, and I brought maybe two or three ferocious guitar players, you know? And I always had a song for any occasion.

Truthfully, I was just disgusted in having to be there after they told me what they intended to do and then backed out. I probably shouldn't have even gone myself, and I wouldn't have gone, except the other guy [Nicholson] was true to his word. [*Taps his fingers rapidly on the tabletop*]

What about that statement you made, about the wisdom your father had shared with you? It could almost be read as a personal statement—you talking about your own life. Or was it about the world around you?

I was thinking more in terms of, like, we're living in a Machiavellian world, whether we like it or we don't. Any act that's immoral, as long as it succeeds, it's all right. To apply that type of meaning to the way I was feeling that night probably has more to do with it than any kind of conscious effort to bring out some religiosity, or any kind of biblical saying about God, one way or another. You hear a lot about God these days: God, the beneficent; God, the all-great; God, the Almighty; God, the most powerful; God, the giver of life; God, the creator of death. I mean, we're hearing about God all the time, so we better learn how to deal with it. But if we know anything about God, God is arbitrary. So people better be able to deal with that, too.

Some people have claimed starting in the 1990s your shows grew more and more musical. You've opened the songs up to more instrumental exploration and new textures and rhythmic shifts—like you're trying to stretch or reinvent then. And it seems that some of your most impassioned and affecting performances, from night to night, are your covers of traditional folk songs.

Folk music is where it all starts and in many ways ends. If you don't have that foundation, or if you're not knowledgeable about it and you don't know how to control that, and you don't feel historically tied to it, then what you're doing is not going to be as strong as it could be. Of course, it helps to have been born in a certain era because it would've been closer to you, or it helps to be a part of the culture when it was happening. It's not the same thing, relating to something second- or thirdhand off of a record.

You heard records where you could, but mostly you heard other performers. All those people, you could hear the actual people singing those ballads. Clarence Ashley, Doc Watson, Dock Boggs, the Memphis Jug Band, Furry Lewis—you could see those people live and in person. They were around.

What I was most interested in twenty-four hours a day was the rural music. The idea was to be able to master these songs. It wasn't about writing your own songs. That didn't even enter anybody's mind.

In a way, this line of talk brings us to your newest album, 'Love and Theft.' Its sense of timelessness and caprices reminds me of 'The Basement Tapes' and 'John Wesley Harding'—records that emanated from your strong folk background. But 'Love and Theft' also seems to recall 'Highway 61 Revisited' and that album's delight in discovering new world-changing methods of language and sharp wit, and the way in which the music digs down deep into ancient blues structures to yield something wholly unexpected.

For starters, no one should really be curious or too excited about comparing this album to any of my other albums. Compare this album to the other albums that are out there. Compare this album to other artists who make albums. You know, comparing me to myself [*laughs*] is really like...I mean, you're talking to a person that feels like he's walking around in the ruins of Pompeii all the time. It's always been that way, for one reason or another. I deal with all the old stereotypes. The language and the identity I use is the one that I know only so well, and I'm not about to go on and keep doing this—comparing my new work to my old work. It creates a kind of Achilles' heel for myself. It isn't going to happen.

Maybe a better way to put it is to ask: Do you see this as an album that emanates from your experience of America at this time?

Every one of the records I've made has emanated from the entire panorama of what America is to me. America, to me, is a rising tide that lifts all ships, and I've never really sought inspiration from other types of music. My problem in writing songs has always been how to tone down the rhetoric in using the language. I don't really give it a whole lot of soulful thought. A song is a reflection of what I see all around me all the time.

The whole album deals with power. If life teaches us anything, it's that there's nothing that men and women won't do to get power. The album deals with power, wealth, knowledge and salvation—the way I look at it. If it's a great album—which I hope it is—it's a great album because it deals with great themes. It speaks in a noble language. It speaks of the issues or the ideals of an age in some nation, and hopefully, it would also speak across the ages. It'd be as good tomorrow as it is today and would've been as good yesterday. That's what I was trying to make happen, because just to make another record at this point in my career...Career, by the way, isn't how I look at what I do. "Career" is a French word. It means "carrier." It's something that takes you from one place to the other. I don't feel like what I do qualifies to be called a career. It's more of a calling.

There's also a good deal of humor on this record—maybe more than on any record of yours since the 1960s.

Well...

C'mon, there are some pretty funny lines on this album—like the exchange between Romeo and Juliet in "Floater (Too Much to Ask)," and that knock-knock joke in "Po' Boy."

Yeah, funny...and dark. But still, in my own mind, not really poking fun at the principles that would guide a person's life or anything. Basically, the songs deal with what many of my songs deal with—which is business, politics and war, and maybe love interest on the side. That would be the first level you would have to appreciate them on.

This record was released on September 11th—the same date as the terrorist attacks on the World Trade Center and the Pentagon. I've talked with several people in the time since then who have turned to 'Love and Theft' because they find something in it that matches the spirit of dread and uncertainty of our present conditions. For my part, I've kept circling around a line from "Mississippi": "Sky full of fire, pain pourin' down." Is there anything you would like to say about your reaction to the events of that day?

One of those Rudyard Kipling poems, "Gentlemen-Rankers," comes to my mind: "We have done with Hope and Honour, we are lost to Love and Truth/We are dropping down the ladder rung by rung/ And the measure of our torment is the measure of our youth/God help us, for we knew the worst too young!" If anything, my mind would go to young people at a time like this. That's really the only way to put it.

You mean because of what's at stake for them right now, as we apparently go to war?

Exactly. I mean, art imposes order on life, but how much more art will there be? We don't really know. There's a secret sanctity of nature. How much more of that will there be? At the moment, the rational mind's way of thinking wouldn't really explain what's happened. You need something else, with a capital *E*, to explain it. It's going to have to be dealt with sooner or later, of course.

Do you see any hope for the situation we find ourselves in?

I don't really know what I could tell you. I don't consider myself an educator or an explainer. You see what it is that I do, and that's what I've always done. But it is time now for great men to come forward. With small men, no great thing can be accomplished at the moment. Those people in charge, I'm sure they've read Sun-Tzu, who wrote *The Art of War* in the sixth century. In there he says, "If you know the enemy and know yourself, you need not fear the result of a hundred battles. If you know yourself and not your enemy, for every victory gained you will suffer a defeat." And he goes on to say, "If you know neither the enemy nor yourself, you will succumb in every battle." Whoever's in charge, I'm sure they would have read that.

Things will have to change. And one of these things that will have to change: People will have to change their internal world.

OZZY OSBOURNE

by David Fricke

July 25, 2002

Did you try hard not to say fuck when you met the queen?

That word was temporarily on hold in my head. My wife said to
Camilla Parker Bowles [Prince Charles' girlfriend], "I think you're
fucking great." My eyeballs nearly flew out of my head. I said,
"Sharon, watch your language." And Camilla Parker Bowles says
[*affects posh accent*], "Oh, it's quite all right. We curse quite a lot
around here."

   When I went up to the queen, I tried to keep my hand in my
pocket. I was afraid she would faint when she saw the tattoo [O-Z-
Z-Y on the fingers of his left hand]. She said, "I understand you're
quite the wild one." I just went, "Heh, heh, heh" [*embarrassed laugh*].
One thing I noticed—she's got the greatest skin for a woman of
her age.

*If television cameras had followed you around as a child in Birmingham
[as they did on MTV's 'The Osbournes'], what would we have seen?*

My home was very poor. My father worked nights as a toolmaker.
He was the English Archie Bunker; he wouldn't change with the
times. He would never buy my mom a washing machine. We had
a boiler house in the garden—you'd put a fire under this copper
boiler, where you would boil the clothes to death. I used to sleep in

a bed with one of my brothers. We had no sheets. We had to use old coats.

When I was a young kid, my father would take me on Sunday mornings with my Uncle Jim to the pub, the Golden Cross. Since I wasn't allowed in, I'd sit on the step, and they'd bring me a shandy, which is half lemonade, half beer. I remember thinking, "Beer must be the best lemonade in the world. I can't wait until the age when I can drink it." When I had my first beer, I spat it out: "That can't be the fucking stuff. It's like dishwater." But then I got the glow. I didn't drink for the taste—I did it for the feeling.

What was your mother like?

She did her best. We never went without food. She stretched things to the limit. There was always a lot of bread and potatoes to fill us up. But money was very scarce. I used to have to ask the neighbors for a cup of sugar, a bottle of milk. One of my biggest fears is going broke. It's my insecurity, from when I was a child. I never went on holiday, never saw the ocean, until I was fourteen.

You left school at fifteen—because you wanted to or had to?

I wanted to. When I was in school, they didn't recognize dyslexia. I looked at the blackboard and it was like trying to read a Chinese menu, in Chinese. But I couldn't hold down a job. First, I worked at a jewelry company—they made napkin rings and cigarette boxes. Then I was a plumber, then a tea boy on a building site. Then I worked in a slaughterhouse. That was the longest job I ever had.

What did you do there?

Kill—at the end of it. It was automated, but the guys would let me shoot a cow now and then. My first job there was emptying sheep's stomachs of the puke. There was a giant mountain of the stuff. The stink was unbelievable. But you get used to it.

Then I got a job in a mortuary. My mother went ballistic: "You are crazy." The formaldehyde was awful. I'd have visions of the dead people's faces when I got home. Then my mother got me my first musical job—I tuned car horns. You were supposed to do 900 a day. Can you imagine being in a room with that fucking racket?

The big thing with working-class people in England was to work until retirement, and then they gave you a gold watch. That equation never made sense to me. I'm going to give you my life for a gold watch? I'd rather break a shopwindow and grab one.

You did some jail time, when you were seventeen, for burglary.

The best thing my father ever did for me was he refused to pay the fine. If you don't pay the fine, you go to debtor's jail. I went for a few weeks. He could have paid the fine for me, but after that, I never wanted to go back.

Describe Black Sabbath's earliest days. You were originally called Earth.

We played twelve-bar blues, like Ten Years After and the original Fleetwood Mac. We had a van full of equipment, and we'd go to gigs hoping the other band wouldn't make it, which happened several times. We used to play for nothing. We'd do wedding receptions.

We rehearsed at a community center near Tony Iommi's house, across the road from a movie theater. One morning, Tony says to us, "It's interesting. I was looking over at the theater." It was showing something like *The Vampire Returns*. "Don't you think it's weird that people pay money to be scared? Maybe we should write scary music." That's when we came up with "Black Sabbath" [*hums the guitar riff*]. That was the fucking change of my life.

Were you guys interested in black magic—even a little?

We couldn't conjure up a fart. We'd get invitations to play witches' conventions and Black Masses in Highgate Cemetery. I honestly thought it was a joke. We were the last hippie band—we were into peace.

In a lot of live Sabbath photos, you're flashing the peace sign.

I never did this black-magic stuff. The reason I did "Mr. Crowley" on my first solo album [*Blizzard of Ozz,* 1980] was that everybody was talking about Aleister Crowley. Jimmy Page bought his house, and one of my roadies worked with one of his roadies. I thought, "Mr. Crowley, who are you? Where are you from?" But people would hear the song and go, "He's definitely into witchcraft."

You were fired from Black Sabbath in 1978. Did you deserve it?

We deserved to fire each other. There was no one worse than anybody else. If the others had been churchgoing Bible punchers and I was fucking their wives, I could have expected it. But they were doing booze and quaaludes too.

In those days, we were well into cocaine. That turns you into a powder-seeking freak. The thing was, get the gig over with so we could get our bump of coke. We had a guy on tour with suitcases full of different strengths of coke.

We went head over heels. It made me incredibly afraid. I remember lying in bed at night, feeling my heartbeat, thinking "Please, God, let me sleep for an hour, so I'll be okay." Then I'd wake up and [*makes sniffing noise*] be straight into it again. We did it for years. Eventually it turned everything sour. One minute, we were a rock band doing coke. The next, we were a coke band doing rock.

You've been married to Sharon for twenty years. What was it that first attracted you to her?

Her laugh. She has the best laugh. She was so infectious, the way she laughed and cursed. I fancied her from a distance for quite a while. We'd pass in hotels, airports. Her father, Don Arden, managed Black Sabbath, and she worked in the office.

Then I got fired from Black Sabbath. I went to a hotel in L.A., locked myself in this room, ordered cases of beer and had a dealer bring me coke every day. I thought, "I'm on my last fling. I'm going to get well fucked up for a few months, then go home and call it a day." My idea was to open a bar—which is a brilliant idea for an alcoholic.

One day, there is a knock at the door. Someone in the band's organization had given me an envelope of cash I was supposed to give to Sharon. I blew it on coke. So she came round to tear me off a stripe. She comes in—I think she felt sorry for me. She goes, "If you straighten your act up, I want to manage you."

Everybody up to that point was going, "You dummy, you idiot, you can't do fuck-all." All my life, I used to be called a dummy. She was the one who didn't. She encouraged me. She got my ass in gear. We're the greatest team on earth.

You were arrested in 1989 for trying to kill her in a drunken rage.

It has not always been bliss. But when I was doing the Queen's Jubilee, there wasn't one rock star there, not one, with a wife who was the same age. They were all twelve or thirty-two or whatever. I know to get a young piece of skirt is one thing. But what the fuck do you talk about? "Oh, that was bad news about India and Pakistan." And it's so common. I wouldn't trade my Sharon for anything.

Are you amazed that, after everything you've been through and done to yourself with drugs and alcohol, that you're still here?

Absolutely. I've danced with death so many times, knowingly and unknowingly. You know what I do? Every year, since I was forty-five, I have a full physical: colonoscopy, prostate test; they shove things up my dick. And at the end, they go, "You're fine."

Nothing—touch wood [*he knocks on a table three times*]—has gone wrong with me. But if it does, it does. I've had a great run. The thing about life that gets me crazy is that by the time you learn it all, it's too late to deal with it. It should be the other way around. We should be born with all this sense and knowledge, and then get stupider as we get older.

If you could write your own epitaph, what would it be?

Just "Ozzy Osbourne, born 1948, died so-and-so." I've done a lot for a simple working-class guy. I made a lot of people smile. I've also made a lot of people go, "Who the fuck does this guy think he is?" I guarantee that if I was to die tonight, tomorrow it would be, "Ozzy Osbourne, the man who bit the head off a bat, died in his hotel room...." I know that's coming.

But I've got no complaints. At least I'll be remembered.

KEITH RICHARDS
by David Fricke

October 17, 2002

How do you deal with criticism about the Stones being too old to rock & roll?
Do you get pissed off? Does it hurt?

People want to pull the rug out from under you, because they're
bald and fat and can't move for shit. It's pure physical envy—that
we shouldn't be here. "How dare they defy logic?"

  If I didn't think it would work, I would be the first to say, "Forget
it." But we're fighting people's misconceptions about what rock &
roll is supposed to be. You're supposed to do it when you're twenty,
twenty-five—as if you're a tennis player and you have three hip surgeries and you're done. We play rock & roll because it's what turned
us on. Muddy Waters and Howlin' Wolf—the idea of retiring was
ludicrous to them. You keep going—and why not?

You went right from being a teenager to being a Stone—no regular job, a
little bit of art school. What would you be doing if the Stones had not lasted
this long?

I went to art school and learned how to advertise, because you don't
learn much art there. I schlepped my portfolio to one agency, and
they said—they love to put you down—"Can you make a good cup
of tea?" I said, "Yeah, I can, but not for you." I left my crap there and
walked out. After I left school, I never said, "Yes, sir" to anybody.

If nothing had happened with the Stones and I was a plumber now, I'd still be playing guitar at home at night, or get the lads around the pub. I loved music; it didn't occur to me that it would be my life. When I knew I could play something, it was an added bright thing to my life: "I've got that, if nothing else."

Do you have nightmares that someday you'll hit the stage and the place will be empty—nobody bothered to come?

That's not a nightmare. I've been there: Omaha '64, in a 15,000-seat auditorium where there were 600 people. The city of Omaha, hearing these things about the Beatles—they thought they should treat us in the same way, with motorcycle outriders and everything. Nobody in town knew who we were. They didn't give a shit. But it was a very good show. You give as much to a handful of people as you do to the others.

Do you have a pre-gig ritual—a particular drink or smoke?

I have them anyway [*laughs*]. I don't go in for superstition. Ronnie and I might have a game of snooker. But it would be superfluous for the Stones to discuss strategy or have a hug. With the Winos [his late-Eighties solo band], it was important. They were different guys; we only did a couple of tours. I didn't mind. But with the Stones, it's like, "Oh, do me a favor! I'm not going to fucking hug you!"

At the height of your heroin addiction, would you indulge before a show?

No. I always cleaned up for tours. I didn't want to put myself in the position of going cold turkey in some little Midwestern town. By the end of the tour, I'm perfectly clean and should have stayed sober. But you go, "I'll just give myself a treat." Boom, there you are again.

Could you tell that you played better when you were clean?

I wonder about the songs I've written: I really like the ones I did when I was on the stuff. I wouldn't have written "Coming Down

Again" [on 1973's *Goat's Head Soup*] without that. I'm this millionaire rock star, but I'm in the gutter with these other sniveling people. It kept me in touch with the street, at the lowest level.

On this tour, you're doing a lot of songs from 'Exile on Main Street'—for most people, the band's greatest album. Would you agree?

It's a funny thing. We had tremendous trouble convincing Atlantic to put out a double album. And initially, sales were fairly low. For a year or two, it was considered a bomb. This was an era where the music industry was full of these pristine sounds. We were going the other way. That was the first grunge record.

Yes, it is one of the best. *Beggars Banquet* was also very important. That body of work, between those two albums: That was the most important time for the band. It was the first change the Stones had to make after the teeny-bopper phase. Until then, you went onstage fighting a losing battle. You want to play music? Don't go up there. What's important is hoping no one gets hurt and how are we getting out.

I remember a riot in Holland. I turned to look at Stu [Ian Stewart] at the piano. All I saw was a pool of blood and a broken chair. He'd been taken off by stagehands and sent to the hospital. A chair landed on his head.

To compensate for that, Mick and I developed the songwriting and records. We poured our music into that. *Beggars Banquet* was like coming out of puberty.

The general assumption about the Stones' classic songs is that Mick wrote the words and you wrote the music. Do you deserve more credit for the lyrics—and Mick for the music?

It's been a progression from Mick and I sitting face-to-face with a guitar and a tape recorder, to after *Exile,* when everybody chose a different place to live and another way of working. Let me put it this way: I'd say, "Mick, it goes like this: 'Wild horses couldn't drag me away.'" Then it would be a division of labor, Mick filling in the verses. There's instances like "Undercover of the Night" or "Rock and a Hard Place" where it's totally Mick's song. And there are times when I come in with "Happy" or "Before They Make Me Run." I say, "It goes like this. In fact, Mick, you don't even have to know about it, because you're not singing" [*laughs*].

But I always thought songs written by two people are better than those written by one. You get another angle on it: "I didn't know you thought like that." The interesting thing is what you say to someone else, even to Mick, who knows me real well. And he takes it away. You get his take.

On Stones albums, you tend to sing ballads—"You Got the Sliver," "Slipping Away," "The Worst"—rather than rockers.

I like ballads. Also, you learn about songwriting from slow songs. You get a better rock & roll song by writing it slow to start with, and seeing where it can go. Sometimes it's obvious that it can't go fast, whereas "Sympathy for the Devil" started out as a Bob Dylan song and ended up as a samba. I just throw songs out to the band.

Did "Happy" start out as a ballad?

No. That happened in one grand bash in France for *Exile*. I had the riff. The rest of the Stones were late for one reason or another. It was only Bobby Keys there and Jimmy Miller, who was producing. I said, "I've got this idea; let's put it down for when the guys arrive." I put down some guitar and vocal, Bobby was on baritone sax and Jimmy was on drums. We listened to it, and I said, "I can put another guitar there and a bass." By the time the Stones arrived, we'd cut it. I love it when they drip off the end of the fingers. And I was pretty happy about it, which is why it ended up being called "Happy."

What would it take for the Stones to have hit singles now, the way you churned them out in the 1960s and 1970s?

I haven't thought like that for years. "Start Me Up" surprised me, honestly—it was a five-year-old rhythm track. Even then, in '81, I wasn't aiming for Number One. I was into making albums. It was important, when we started, to have hits. And it taught you a lot of things quickly: what makes a good record, how to say things in two minutes thirty seconds. If it was four seconds longer, they chopped it off. It was good school, but it's been so long since I've made records with the idea of having a hit single. I'm out of that game.

Charlie Watts gets an enormous ovation every night when Mick introduces him. But Charlie's also quite an enigma—the quiet conscience of the Stones.

Charlie is a great English eccentric. I mean, how can you describe a guy who buys a 1936 Alfa Romeo just to look at the dashboard? Can't drive—just sits there and looks at it. He's an original, and he happens to be one of the best drummers in the world. Without a drummer as sharp as Charlie, playing would be a drag.

He's very quiet—but persuasive. It's very rare that Charlie offers an opinion. If he does, you listen. Mick and I fall back on Charlie more than would be apparent. Many times, if there's something between Mick and I, it's Charlie I've got to talk to.

For example?

It could be as simple as whether to play a certain song. Or I'll say, "Charlie, should I go to Mick's room and hang him?" And he'll say no [*laughs*]. His opinion counts.

How has your relationship with Ron Wood changed since he gave up drinking?

I tell Ronnie, "I can't tell the difference between if you're pissed out of your brain or straight as an arrow." He's the same guy. But

Ronnie never got off the last tour. He kept on after we finished the last show. On the road it's all right, because you burn off a lot of the stuff you do onstage. But when you get home and you're not in touch with your environment, your family—he didn't stop. He realized he had to do it. It was his decision. When I found out about it, he was already in the spin dryer.

Ronnie has always had a light heart. That's his front. But there is a deeper guy in there. I know the feeling. I probably wouldn't have gotten into heroin if it hadn't been a way for me to protect myself. I could walk into the middle of all the bullshit, softly surrounded by this cool, be my own man inside, and everybody had to deal with it. Mick does it his way. Ronnie does it his way.

Do you miss having a drinking partner?

Shit, I am my drinking partner. Intoxication? I'm polytoxic. Whatever drinking or drugs I do is never as big a deal to me as they have been to other people. It's not a philosophy with me. The idea of taking something in order to be Keith Richards is bizarre to me.

Were there drugs you tried and didn't like?

Loads. I was very selective. Speed—nah. Pure pharmaceutical cocaine—that's great, but it ain't there anymore. Heroin—the best is the best. But when it comes to Mexican shoe scrapings, ugh. Good weed is good weed.

What about acid?

I enjoyed it. Acid arrived just as we had worn ourselves out on the road, in 1966. It was kind of a vacation. I never went for the idea that this was some special club—the Acid Test and that bollocks.

I found it interesting that you were way out there but still functioning normally, doing things like driving; I'd stop off at the shops. Meanwhile, you were zooming off. Methedrine and bennies never did appeal to me. Downers—now and again: "I've got to get some sleep." But if you don't go to sleep, you have a great time [*laughs*].

How much did your drug use in the 1970s alienate Mick?

He wasn't exactly Mr. Clean and I was Mr. Dirty. But I withdrew a lot from the basic day-to-day of the Stones. It usually only took one of us to deal with most things. But when I did come out of it and offered to shoulder the burden, I noticed that Mick was quite happy to keep the burden to himself. He got used to calling the shots.

I was naive—I should have thought about it. I have no doubt that here or there Mick used the fact that I was on the stuff, and everybody knew it: "You don't want to talk to Keith, he's out of it." Hey, it was my own fault. I did what I did, and you just don't walk back in again.

Describe the state of your friendship with Mick. Is friendship the right word?

Absolutely. It's a very deep one. The fact that we squabble is proof of it. It goes back to the fact that I'm an only child. He's one of the few people I know from my childhood. He is a brother. And you know what brothers are like, especially ones who work together. In a way, we need to provoke each other, to find out the gaps and see if we're on board together.

Does it bother you that your musical life together isn't enough for him—that he wants to make solo records?

He'll never lie about in a hammock, just hanging out. Mick has to dictate to life. He wants to control it. To me, life is a wild animal. You hope to deal with it when it leaps at you. That is the most marked difference between us. He can't go to sleep without writing out what he's going to do when he wakes up. I just hope to wake up, and it's not a disaster.

My attitude was probably formed by what I went through as a

junkie. You develop a fatalistic attitude toward life. He's a bunch of nervous energy. He has to deal with it in his own way, to tell life what's going to happen rather than life telling you.

Was he like that in 1965?

Not so much. He's very shy, in his own way. It's pretty funny to say that about one of the biggest extroverts in the world. Mick's biggest fear is having his privacy. Mick sometimes treats the world as if it's attacking him. It's his defense, and that has molded his character to a point where sometimes you feel like you can't get in yourself. Anybody in the band will tell you that. But it comes from being in that position for so long—being Mick Jagger.

You and your wife, Patti, have two teenage daughters, Alexandra and Theodora. And as a dad, you have a unique perspective on the mischief kids get up to, because you've done most of it.

I've never had a problem with my kids, even though Marlon and Angela [two of his three children by former girlfriend Anita Pallenberg] grew up in rough times: cops busting in, me being nuts. [Another son, Tara, died in 1976; he was ten weeks old.] I feel akin to the old whaling captains: "We're taking the boat out, see you in three years." Dad disappearing for weeks and months—it's never affected my kids' sense of security. It's just what Dad does.

What about serious talks? About drugs?

That's something you see on TV ads. Alexandra and Theodora are my best friends. It's not finger wagging. I just keep an eye on them. If they got a problem, they come and talk to me. They've grown up with friends whose idea of me—who knows what they've been told at school? But they know who I am. And they always come to my defense [*smiles*]. Which is the way I like it.

Describe your life at home in Connecticut: When you get up, what do you do?

I made a determined effort after the last tour to get up with the family. Which for me is a pretty impressive goal. But I did it—I'd get up at seven in the morning. After a few months, I was allowed to drive the kids to school. Then I was allowed to take the garbage out. Before that, I didn't even know where the recycling bin was.

I read a lot. I might have a little sail around Long Island Sound if the weather is all right. I do a lot of recording in my basement—writing songs, keeping up to speed. I have no fixed routine. I wander about the house, wait for the maids to clean the kitchen, then fuck it all up again and do some frying. Patti and I go out once a week, if there's something on in town—take the old lady out for dinner with a bunch of flowers, get the rewards [*smiles*].

Have you listened to the new guitar bands—the Hives, the Vines, the White Stripes? The Strokes are opening for you on this tour.

I haven't really. I'm looking forward to seeing them. I don't want to listen to the records until I see them.

But is it encouraging to see new guitar music being made in your image?

That's the whole point. What Muddy Waters did for us is what we should do for others. It's the old thing, what you want written on your tombstone as a musician: HE PASSED IT ON. I can't wait to see these guys—they're like my babies, you know?

I'm not a champion of the guitar as an instrument. The guitar is just one of the most compact and sturdy. And the reason I still play it is that the more you do, the more you learn. I found a new chord the other day. I was like, "Shit, if I had known that years ago..." That's what's beautiful about the guitar. You think you know it all, but it keeps opening up new doors. I look at life as six strings and twelve frets. If I can't figure out everything that's in there, what chance do I have of figuring out anything else?

A lot of people who were a big part of your life with the Stones are no longer here. Who do you miss the most?

Ian Stewart was a body blow. I was waiting for him in a hotel in London. He was going to see a doctor and then come and see me. Charlie called about three in the morning: "You still waiting for Stu? He ain't coming, Keith."

Stu was the father figure. He was the stitch that pulled us together. He had a very large heart, above and beyond the call of duty. When other people would get mean and jealous, he could rise above it. He taught me a lot about taking a couple of breaths before you go off the handle. Mind you, it didn't always work. But I got the message.

Gram Parsons—I figured we'd put things together for years, because there was so much promise there. I didn't think he was walking on the broken eggshells so much. I was in the john at a gig in Innsbruck, Austria. I'm taking a leak, and Bobby Keys walks in. He says, "I got a bad one for you. Parsons is dead." We were supposed to be staying in Innsbruck that night. I said fuck it. I rented a car, and Bobby and I drove to Munich and did the clubs—tried to forget about it for a day or two.

Have you contemplated your own death?

I let other people do that. They've been doing it for years. They're experts, apparently. Hey, I've been there—the white light at the end of the tunnel—three or four times. But when it doesn't happen, and you're back in—that's a shock.

The standard joke is that in spite of every drink and drug you've ever taken, you will outlive cockroaches and nuclear holocaust. You'll be the last man standing.

It's very funny, how that position has been reserved for me. It's only because they've been wishing me to death for so many years, and it didn't happen. So I get the reverse tip of the hat. All right, if you want to believe it—I will write all of your epitaphs.

But I don't flaunt it. I never tried to stay up longer than anybody else just to announce to the media that I'm the toughest. It's just the way I am. The only thing I can say is, you gotta know yourself.

After forty years, still doing two and a half hours onstage every night—that's the biggest last laugh of all.

Maybe that's the answer. If you want to live a long life, join the Rolling Stones.

EMINEM

by Touré

November 25, 2004

Who in your family loved you? Did any of the adults make you feel special?

My aunt Edna, which would be my great-aunt Edna, and my uncle Charles, my great-uncle Charles. This was in Missouri. They're from my dad's side. They took care of me a lot. My uncle Charles passed in '92 or '93, and Aunt Edna passed away just six months ago. She was, like, eighty-six. They were older, but they did things with me; they let me stay the weekends there, took me to school, bought me things, let me stay and watch TV, let me cut the grass to get five dollars, took me to the mall. Between them and my uncle Ronnie, they were my solidity.

Did they connect you with your dad?

They'd tell me he was a good guy: "We don't know what your mother's told you, but he was a good guy." But a lot of times he'd call, and I'd be there—maybe I'd be on the floor coloring or watching TV—and it wouldn't have been nothing for him to say, "Put him on the phone." He coulda talked to me, let me know something. 'Cause as far as father figures, I didn't have any in my life. My mother had a lot of boyfriends. Some of 'em I didn't like; some of 'em were cool. But a lot would come and go. My little brother's dad was probably the closest thing I had to a father figure. He was around off and on for about five years. He was the dude who'd play catch, take us bowling, just do stuff that dads would do.

When I saw you playing with [his daughter] Hailie back in February, you were so respectful. A lot of people talk down to little kids, but you talk to her like she's intelligent.

Thank you for seeing that. I just want her and my immediate family—my daughter, my niece and my little brother—to have things I didn't have: love and material things. But I can't just buy them things. I have to be there. That's a cop-out if I just popped up once in a while, didn't have custody of my daughter and my niece.

Do you have full custody?

I have full custody of my niece and joint custody of Hailie. It's no secret what's been going on over the past year with my ex-wife [Kim]. I wouldn't down-talk her, but with her being on the run from the cops I really had no choice but to just step up to the plate. I was always there for Hailie, and my niece has been a part of my life ever since she was born. Me and Kim pretty much had her, she'd live with us wherever we was at.

And your little brother lives with you.

I've seen my little brother bounce around a lot from foster home to foster home. My little brother was taken away by the state when he was eight, nine.

You were how old?

I was twenty-three. But when he was taken away I always said if I ever get in a position to take him, I would take him. I tried to apply for full custody when I was twenty, but I didn't have the means. I couldn't support him. I watched him when he was in the foster home. He was so confused. I mean, I cried just goin' to see him at the foster home. The day he was taken away I was the only one allowed to see him. They had come and got him out of school. He didn't know what the fuck was goin' on. The same thing that had happened in my life was happening in his. I had a job and a car, and me and Kim, we bounced around from house to house, tryin' to pay rent and make ends meet. And then Kim's niece was born, which is my niece now through marriage. Watched her bounce around from house to house—just watchin' the cycle of dysfunction, it was like, "Man, if I get in position, I'm gonna stop all this shit." And I got in position and did.

So you have joint custody of Hailie, but she lives with you and spends most of her time with you and not with Kim.

I don't know if I'm inclined, or allowed, to say more than what is fact. In the last year, Kim has been in and out of jail and on house arrest, cut her tether off, had been on the run from the cops for quite a while. Tryin' to explain that to my niece and my daughter was one of the hardest things I ever had to go through. You can never let a child feel like it's her fault for what's goin' on. You just gotta let her know: "Mom has a problem, she's sick, and it's not because she doesn't love you. She loves you, but she's sick right now, and until she gets better, you've got Daddy. And I'm here."

There are two songs about Kim on 'Encore.' In "Puke," you hate her so much she makes you want to vomit. Then in "Crazy in Love," you're like, "I hate you, yet I can't live without you."

It's a love-hate relationship, and it will always be that. We're talking about a woman who's been a part of my life since I can remember. She was thirteen when I met her. I was fifteen.

What was it like the first time you saw her?

I met her the day she got out of the youth home. I was at a friend's house, and his sister was friends with her, but she hadn't seen Kim in a while 'cause she was in the youth home. And I'm standing on the table with my shirt off, on top of their coffee table with a Kangol on, mocking the words to LL Cool J's "I'm Bad." And I turn around and she's at the door. Her friend hands her a cigarette. She's thirteen, she's taller than me, and she didn't look that young. She easily coulda been mistaken for sixteen, seventeen. I said to my friend's sister, "Yo, who was that? She's kinda hot." And the saga began. Now there's the constant struggle of "will I ever meet somebody else that's gonna be real with me, as real as I can say she's been with me?"

You get deep into your feelings about President Bush and Iraq on 'Mosh.' Do you think the war in Iraq was a mistake?

He's been painted to be this hero, and he's got our troops over there dying for no reason. I haven't heard an explanation yet that I can understand. Explain to us why we have troops over there dying.

There is no good answer.

I think he started a mess. America is the best country there is, the best country to live in. But he's fuckin' that up and could run our country into the ground. He jumped the gun, and he fucked up so bad he doesn't know what to do right now. He's in a tailspin, running around like a dog chasing its tail. And we got young people over there dyin', kids in their teens, early twenties, who should have futures ahead of them. And for what? It seems like a Vietnam II. Bin Laden attacked us and we attacked Saddam. We ain't heard from Saddam for ten years, but we go attack Saddam. Explain why that is. Give us some answers.

Are you voting?

I'm supposed to hand my absentee ballot in today. I'm going for Kerry, man. I got a chance to watch one of the debates and a piece of another one. He was making Bush look stupid, but anybody can make Bush look stupid. I'm not 100 million percent on Kerry. I don't agree with everything he says, but I hope he's true to his word, especially about his plan to pull the troops out. I hope we can get Bush out of there, and I hope *Mosh* wasn't too little, too late. That can sway some of the voters or open people's minds and eyes up to see this dude. I don't wanna see my little brother get drafted. He just turned eighteen. I don't want to see him get drafted and lose his life. People think their votes don't count, but people need to get out and vote. Every motherfuckin' vote counts.

There's a song on 'Encore' called "Like Toy Soldiers" where you get into issues around the battles you've had recently. It made me think about how you're a battle rapper who came up in an era where battling was pure, and now it's like, "Damn, if I really go too hard, somebody might get shot."

Someone might die.

It's gotta be ill to not be able to just battle out like you want to. Battling has been such a great part of hip-hop history.

It's sad. But I'm not gonna sit back and watch my people be hurt. It's like a Bush thing: You're just sending your troops off to war and you ain't in it. You're fuckin' playing golf and you sent your soldiers over to get killed. As you get older, you start to think that if you're just beefin' to be beefin' or tryin' to sell records, that's not the way to go. Because what usually ends up happening is somebody's entourage gets hurt. And it's not worth it. Battling always started out like a mind game: who could psych who out, who could look the scariest. Then it became people saying, "This is my life you're fucking with. This is everything I stand for, this is my career. If my career is gone tomorrow, then my life is gone tomorrow." That's how people end up losing lives.

Last year, 'The Source' uncovered a tape that you made when you were sixteen where you said "nigger." What was that about?

This is what we used to do. I'd go in my man's basement and do goofy freestyles, and we'd call 'em sucker rhymes, and the whole point of the rap was to be as wack as possible and warm up before we actually did songs that we wrote. And that ended up just happening to be the topic that day. I just broke up with a black girl, and the rest of the story I address on the album. I've got a song called "Yellow Brick Road," and it basically explains the whole story from beginning to end, how the tape derived.

When it came out, were you pissed?

I was angry at myself. I couldn't believe that I said it. The tone that I'm using, you can almost tell that I'm joking, but the words are coming out of my mouth. If there was never no Eminem, it wouldn't be so shocking, but given who I am and what I stand for today, then what else could be Eminem's Achilles' heel?

In our generation the word "nigga" is used by black and white kids as an expression of love, but even now you won't say it.

Yeah, it's just a word I don't feel comfortable with. It wouldn't sound right coming out of my mouth.

Do you see a similarity between "nigger" and "faggot"? Aren't they the same?

I've never really seen it that way. Growing up, the word "faggot" was thrown around. The two words were thrown around, they were always thrown around. But growing up, when you said "faggot" to somebody it didn't necessarily mean they were gay. It was in the sense of "You fuckin' dick."

But you don't see these two words doing the same thing?

I guess it depends on if you're using it in a derogatory way. Like, if you're using the word "faggot" like I just said, in the way of calling them a name, that's different than a racial slur to me. Some people may feel different. Some white kids feel comfortable throwing the word around all day. I don't. I'm not saying I've never said the word in my entire life. But now, I just don't say it in casual conversation. It doesn't feel right to come out of my mouth.

Let's talk about your process as a writer. How do you come up with hooks?

I think the beat should talk to you and tell you what the hook is. The hook for "Just Lose It" I probably wrote in about thirty seconds as soon as the beat came on. It was the last record we made for the album. We didn't feel like we had the single yet. That was a song that doesn't really mean anything. It's just what the beat was telling me to do. Beats run through my head—and rhymes and lyrics and wordplay and catchphrases. When you're a rapper, rhymes are just gonna come at you. Those words are usually inside that beat, and you gotta find them.

Have you ever tried the Jay-Z method of not writing the rhymes out, just coming up with them in your head?

Yeah, I've done that. If you've ever seen my rhyme pads, my shit is all over the paper, because it's a lot of random thoughts. But a lot of times I'll be short a couple of bars, and I'll have a couple of lines wrote down and then I just go in the booth and try shit, and see what I'll say. I'll lose my space on the paper and just start blurting out, and it'll just come out. Music for me is an addiction. If I don't make music I feel like shit. If I don't spend enough time at home with my kids I feel like shit. Music is my outlet, my kids are my life, so there's a balance in my life right now that couldn't be better.

So you were a teenager when you first heard the Beastie Boys, and they allowed you to feel like, "Oh, I could be part of hip-hop." 3rd Bass probably gave you more of that sense.

Yeah, but then along came the X-Clan. I loved the X-Clan's first album [*To the East, Blackwards,* 1990]. Brother J was an MC that I was afraid of lyrically. His delivery was so confident. But he also made me feel like an outcast. Callin' us polar bears. Even as militant as Public Enemy were, they never made me feel like, "You're white, you cannot do this rap, this is our music." The X-Clan kinda made you feel like that, talking [on *Grand Verbalizer, What Time Is It?*] about "How could polar bears swing on vines of the gorillas?" It was a slap in the face. It was like, you're loving and supporting the music, you're buying the artist and supporting the artist, you love it and live it and breathe it, then who's to say that you can't do it? If you're good at it and you wanna do it, then why are you allowed to buy the records but not allowed to do the music? That was the pro-black era—and there was that sense of pride where it was like, if you weren't black, you shouldn't listen to hip-hop, you shouldn't touch the mike. And we used to wear the black and green.

You wore an Africa medallion?

Me and a couple of my other white friends. And we would go to the mall.

Whoa.

I remember I had the Flavor Flav clock. The clock was so big and ridiculous, it was the perfect Flavor Flav clock. It was fuckin' huge. And me and my boy are in matching Nike suits and our hair in high-top fades, and we went to the mall and got laughed at so bad. And kinda got rushed out the mall. I remember this dude jumpin' in front of my boy's face and bein' like, "Yeah, boyyyeee! What you know about hip-hop, white boyyyeee!"

You must've had drama with the Africa medallion.

I'd be tryin' to explain to my black friends who didn't really feel like I should be wearin' it, like, "Look, I love this culture, I'm down with this." But you're a kid, so you're not really sure of anything, you haven't really experienced life yet, so you don't really know how to explain yourself to the fullest. You're tryin' to find your own identity and you're stuck in that whole thing of, who am I as a person? Walkin' through the suburbs and I'm getting called the N-word, and walkin' through Detroit I'm getting jumped for being white. And goin' through that identity crisis of, "Am I really not meant to touch the mike? Is this really not meant for me?"

And all this is inside you as you're coming up as a white rapper trying to enter this black culture.

Even growing up as a kid, being the new kid in school and getting bullied, getting jumped. Kids are fucked up, kids are mean to other kids. School is a tough thing to go through. Anybody will tell you that. I didn't really learn how to fight back till seventeen, eighteen. I reached my peak around nineteen, where people would call me and say, "Yo, I got beef with such and such — can you come help me out?" They knew I'd fight. I had a friend named Goofy Gary. He'd call me and say, "Yo, I just got jumped up at Burger King." And I'd say, "All right, Proof, we gotta go fight for Goofy Gary. Let's get in the car. C'mon." Then I found myself being the aggressor, which was a little strange from the few years prior to that being the loner kid who didn't fuck with nobody, wasn't lookin' for trouble.

Used to be Eminem was in the police blotter from time to time, but since that case you've made a conscious change.

Yeah. When I got off probation I remember sayin' to myself, "I'm never fuckin' up again. I'm-a learn to turn the other cheek." I took on boxing just to get the stress out. Plus I chilled out a lot as far as the drinking and the drugs and all that stuff. Just chillin' out on that made me see things a lot clearer and learn to rationalize a lot more. Sobering up, becoming an adult and trying to just become a businessman. Not sayin' that I don't still got it in me. Not sayin' I'm not still down for mine. But things changed.

What I want to do is make records, get respect, have fun, enjoy life and see my daughter grow up. I don't feel like I portray myself as a gangster; I feel like I portray myself as somebody who won't be bullied or punked. If I feel like I'm being attacked and somebody comes at me sideways with something I didn't start, then that's a different story. But I just try to do what I do, get respect, and that's it. If I can make people laugh and spark some controversy, good. It is entertainment.

BONO

by Jann S. Wenner

November 3, 2005

What was your childhood in Dublin like?

I grew up in what you would call a lower-middle-class neighbor-hood. You don't have the equivalent in America. Upper-working-class? But a nice street and good people. And, yet, if I'm honest, a sense that violence was around the corner.

Home was a pretty regular three-bedroom house. The third bedroom, about the size of a cupboard, they called the "box room"—which was my room. Mother departed the household early; died at the graveside of her own father. So I lost my grand-father and my mother in a few days, and then it became a house of men. And three, it turns out, quite macho men—and all that goes with that. The aggression thing is something I'm still working at. That level of aggression, both outside and inside, is not normal or appropriate.

You're this bright, struggling teenager, and you're in this place that looks like it has very few possibilities for you. The general attitude toward you from your father—and just the Irish attitude—was "Who the fuck do you think you are? Get real." Is that correct?

Bob Hewson—my father—comes from the inner city of Dublin. A real Dublin man but loves the opera. Must be a little grandiose himself, okay? He is an autodidact, conversant in Shakespeare. His passion is music—he's a great tenor. The great sadness of his life was that he didn't learn the piano. Oddly enough, kid's not really encouraged to have big ideas, musically or otherwise. To dream was to be disappointed. Which, of course, explains my megalomania.

I was a bright kid, all right, early on. Then, in my teenage years, I went through a sort of awkward phase of thinking I was stupid. My schoolwork goes to shit; I can't concentrate. I started to believe the world outside. Music was my revenge on that.

I got the sense that it was kind of a dead-end situation.

Its blandness—its very grayness—is the thing you have to overcome. We had a street gang that was very vivid—very surreal. We were fans of Monty Python. We'd put on performances in the city center of Dublin. I'd get on the bus with a stepladder and an electric drill. Mad shit. Humor became our weapon. Just stand there, quiet—with the drill in my hand. Stupid teenage shit.

Just to provoke people? Performance art?

Performance art. We invented this world, which we called Lipton Village. We were teenagers when we came up with this, a way of fighting back against the prevailing boot-boy mentality.

Were there a lot of fights?

Oh, yeah. The order of the day was often being beaten to within an inch of your life by roaming gangs from one of the other neighborhoods. When they asked where you were from, you had to guess right—or suffer. The harder they hit us, the more strange and surreal the response.

I mean, myself and my other friend, Guggi—we're still very close friends—were handy enough. We could defend ourselves. But even though some of us became pretty good at violence ourselves, others didn't. They got the shit kicked out of 'em. I thought that was kind of normal. I can remember incredible street battles. I remember one madser with an iron bar, just trying to bring it down on my skull as hard as he possibly could, and holding up a dustbin lid, which saved my life. Teenage kids have no sense of mortality—yours or theirs.

So that was your teen rebellion?

I don't know if that was rebellion. That was a defense mechanism. We used to laugh at people drinking. We didn't drink. Because people who spilled out of the pubs on a Friday night and threw up on the laneway—we thought we were better than them.

You were the smart-kid clique?

We were a collection of outsiders. We weren't all the clever clogs. If you had a good record collection, that helped. And if you didn't play soccer. That was part of it.

   Now, when you look back, there's an arrogance to it; it's like you're looking down, really...

At the jocks?

At the jocks, at the skinheads, at the boot boys. Maybe it's the same arrogance my father had, who's listening to opera and likes cricket. Because it separates him.

You wrote an extraordinary song about your father, "Sometimes You Can't Make It on Your Own." When I spoke to Edge, he said that you're turning into your dad.

He was an amazing and very funny man. You had to be quick to live around him. But I don't think I'm like him. I have a very different relationship with my kids than he had with me. He didn't really have one with me. He generally thought that no one was as smart as him in the room. You know that Johnny Cash song "A Boy Named Sue" where he gives the kid a girl's name, and the kid is beaten up at every stage in his life by macho guys, but in the end he becomes the toughest man.

You're the boy named Sue?

By not encouraging me to be a musician, even though that's all he ever wanted to be, he's made me one. By telling me never to have big dreams or else, that to dream is to be disappointed, he made me have big dreams. By telling me that the band would only last five minutes or ten minutes — we're still here.

It seems there's some power in this relationship that's beyond the ordinary father-son story. You were probably one of the most difficult children to have around.

I must've been a bit difficult.

He was trying to raise two children without a mother. And here you are, unforgiving and unrelenting, showing up at all hours, in drag and with all kinds of weird people. I think it's amazing he put up with you and he didn't just throw you the fuck out. Do you ever feel guilty about how you treated him?

No, not until I fucking met you! He loved a row. Christmas Day at our house was just one long argument. We were shouting all the time — my brother, me and then my uncles and aunts. He had a sense of moral indignation, that attitude of "You don't have to put up with this shit." He was very wise politically. He was from the left, but you know, he praised the guy on the right.

The more you talk about it, the more it sounds like you're describing yourself.

That is a very interesting way of looking at it, and I think there'll be a lot of people who might agree with you. I loved my dad. But we were combatants. Right until the end. Actually, his last words were an expletive. I was sleeping on a little mattress right beside him in the hospital. I woke up, and he made this big sound, this kind of roar, it woke me up. The nurse comes in and says, "You okay, Bob?" He kind of looks at her and whispers, "Would you fuck off and get me out of here? This place is like a prison. I want to go home." Last words: "Fuck off."

What were the first rock & roll records that you heard?

Age four. The Beatles—"I Want to Hold Your Hand." I guess that's 1964. I remember watching the Beatles with my brother on St. Stephen's Day, the day after Christmas. The sense of a gang that they had about them, from just what I've been saying, you can tell that they're connected, as well as the melodic power, the haircuts and the sexuality. Which I was just probably processing.

Then performers like Tom Jones. I'd see Tom Jones on Saturday night on a variety show—I must have been, like, eight years old—and he's sweating, and he's an animal, and he's unrestrained. He's singing with abandon. He has a big black voice, in a white guy. And then, of course, Elvis.

I'm thinking, what is this? Because this is changing the temperature of the room. And people stopped talking.

When did you run across Elvis?

I might have heard the songs, but it was the *Comeback Special,* when he was standing up—because he couldn't sit down to play. The thing was: He's not in control of this—this is in control of him. The abandon was really attractive.

Who else had a big impact on you, musically, when you were that age?

Before I got to the Who, the Rolling Stones and Led Zeppelin, and those kinds of things—I really remember John Lennon's *Imagine.*

I guess I'm twelve; that's one of my first albums. That really set fire to me. It was like he was whispering in your ear—his ideas of what's possible.

Different ways of seeing the world. When I was fourteen and lost my mother, I went back to *Plastic Ono Band*.

Bob Dylan at the same time. Listened to his acoustic albums. Then starting to think about playing those acoustic songs. My brother had a Beatles songbook—so trying to teach myself guitar, and him sort of helping.

And that song—which is actually such a genius song, now that I think about it, you're embarrassed the day after you learned it—"If I Had a Hammer." That's a tattoo, that song.

That was the first song you learned how to play?

"If I had a hammer, I'd hammer in the morning/I'd hammer in the evening/All over this land/I'd hammer out justice/I'd hammer out freedom/Love between my brothers and my sisters/All over this land." Fantastic. A manifesto, right there.

You're still doing the same song.

[*Laughs*] Right.

And so all that stuff was going on in London in the Sixties: the Beatles, the Stones, the Who, the Kinks. What kind of influence was that on you?

The Who: About age fifteen, that starts really connecting. In amongst the din and the noise, the power chords and the rage, there's another voice. "Nobody knows what it's like behind blue eyes…" And the beginnings of what I would discover is one of the essential aspects for me—and why I'm drawn to a piece of music—which has something to do with the quest. The sense that there's another world to be explored. I got that from Pete Townshend; I got that from Bob Dylan.

'Imagine' was the first really powerful thing to you?

Imagine and Bob Dylan. "Blowin' in the Wind"—all that stuff—and the folksy thing. Which is, I suppose, what set me up for John Lennon.

Dylan set you up for John Lennon?

Because it's folk. If you're interested in folk, in words and whisperings, that quiet thing. I was in my room listening on headphones on a tape recorder. It's very intimate. It's like talking to somebody on the phone, like talking to John Lennon on the phone. I'm not exaggerating to say that. This music changed the shape of the room. It changed the shape of the world outside the room; the way you looked out the window and what you were looking at.

I remember John singing "Oh My Love." It's like a little hymn. It's certainly a prayer of some kind—even if he was an atheist. "Oh, my love/For the first time in my life/My eyes can see/I see the wind/Oh, I see the trees/Everything is clear in our world." For me it was like he was talking about the veil lifting off, the scales falling from the eyes. Seeing out the window with a new clarity that love brings you. I remember that feeling.

Yoko came up to me when I was in my twenties, and she put her hand on me and she said, "You are John's son." What an amazing compliment!

About the band, you said, "We come from punk." What does that mean?

Now it's 1976. I was in school. It was the obnoxious-teenager phase. Schoolwork's gone to shit, angry, living at home with two men. My friends are all gonna have big futures, 'cause they're very clever. I'm probably not gonna be able to concentrate enough to be that clever.

I've always had these melodies in my head. In quiet times—at the local club, in a church hall—if I'm beside a piano, I put my finger on a key. I figured that if I press a pedal under that—boom—this note can fill the whole hall. Reverb, you know. It turns this church into a cathedral. I hear a rhyme for the note in my head—I really do. I can find another note that sounds good with it—but I've had no way to express it.

Then a note appears from this kid twenty-nine years ago last Saturday. Like really a kid—he's fourteen, and I'm sixteen. He wants to start a band. He plays the drums. So my friend Reggie Manuel says, "You have to go." He puts me on the back of his motorcycle, and he takes me out to this suburban house, where Larry Mullen lives. Larry is in this tiny kitchen, and he's got his drum kit set up. And there's a few other boys. There's Dave Evans [Edge]—a kinda brainy-looking kid—who's fifteen. And his brother Dick—even brainier-looking—who's built his own guitar. He's a rocket scientist—a card-carrying genius.

Larry starts playing the kit—it's an amazing sound, just hit the cymbal. Edge hit a guitar chord which I'd never heard on electric guitar. I mean, it is the open road. Kids started coming from all around the place—all girls. They know that Larry lives there. They're already screaming; they're already climbing up the door. He was completely used to this, we discover, and he's taking the hose to them already. Literally, the garden hose. And so that starts. Within a month I start going out with Ali [his future wife]. I mean, I had met her before, but I ask her out.

That was a good month.

Yes, a very good month. What's interesting is, in the months leading up to this, I was probably at the lowest ebb in my life. I was feeling just teenage angst. I didn't know if I wanted to continue living—that kind of despair. I was praying to a God I didn't know was listening.

Were you influenced by punk rock then?

No, this has nothing to do with punk. This is September of '76. Punk has just started in London that summer. Adam [Clayton] goes to London the next summer. London was burning. And he comes back with the Stranglers, the Jam, the Clash. Oddly enough, though, in our very first rehearsals, we were talking about what music we should play. Everyone got to make suggestions. I wanted to play the Rolling Stones, from the *High Tide and Green Grass* era, and the Beach Boys. I was getting tired of the hard-rock thing.

Hard rock being . . .

Big hair and extended guitar solos. I was saying, "Let's get back to this rock & roll thing." Then people said, "Oh, have you heard the Clash?" And then seeing the Jam on *Top of the Pops* in '76, just going, "They're our age! This is possible." Then the Radiators From Space—our local punk band—had a song called . . . "Telecaster" or something: "Gonna push my Telecaster through the television screen/'Cause I don't like what's going down." And it's a twelve-bar thing—so you can play it.

How far into the band are you now?

It's just occasional rehearsing. We're playing the Eagles. We're playing the Moody Blues. But it turns out we're really crap at it. We actually aren't able to play other people's songs. The one Stones song we tried to play was "Jumpin' Jack Flash." It was really bad. So we started writing our own—it was easier.

Were the Ramones the big punk influence on you? Or the Clash?

More Ramones than the Clash—though we saw the Clash first, in '77, in Dublin, and it was extraordinary. There was an air of violence, the sense that somebody could die. But their music didn't connect with us the same way that the Ramones' did.

What connected about the Ramones?

I didn't have the gravel or the gravitas of Joe Strummer. Joey Ramone sang like Dusty Springfield. . . . It was a melodic voice like mine.

Was David Bowie a big influence?

Gigantic, the English Elvis. Bowie was much more responsible for the aesthetic of punk rock than he's been given credit for, like, in fact, most interesting things in the Seventies and Eighties. I put his pictures up in my bedroom. We played "Suffragette City" in that first wedding-band phase.

We started to listen to Patti Smith; Edge starts listening to Tom Verlaine. And, suddenly, those punk chords are just not the only alternative. Now we've got a different kinda language and we started finding different colors, other than the primary ones.

What role did religion play in your childhood?

I knew that we were different on our street because my mother was Protestant. And that she'd married a Catholic. At a time of strong sectarian feeling in the country, I knew that was special. We didn't go to the neighborhood schools—we got on a bus. I picked up the courage they had to have had to follow through on their love.

Did you feel religious when you went to church?

Even then I prayed more outside of the church than inside. It gets back to the songs I was listening to; to me, they were prayers. "How many roads must a man walk down?" That wasn't a rhetorical question to me. It was addressed to God. It's a question I wanted to know the answer to, and I'm wondering, who do I ask that to? I'm not gonna ask a schoolteacher. When John Lennon sings, "Oh, my love/For the first time in my life/My eyes are wide open"—these songs have an intimacy for me that's not just between people, I realize now, not just sexual intimacy. A spiritual intimacy.

Who is God to you at that point in your life?

I don't know. I would rarely be asking these questions inside the church. I see lovely nice people hanging out in a church. Occasionally, when I'm singing a hymn like...oh, if I can think of a good one...oh, "When I Survey the Wondrous Cross" or "Be Thou My Vision," something would stir inside of me. But, basically, religion left me cold.

Your early songs are about being confused, about trying to find spirituality at an age when most anybody else your age would be writing about girls and trouble.

Yeah. We sorta did it the other way around.

You skipped "I Want to Hold your Hand," and you went right...

...Into the mystic. Van Morrison would be the inverse, in terms of the journey. It's this turbulent period at fifteen, sixteen, and the electrical storms that come at that age.

There was also my friend Guggi. His parents were not just Protestant, they were some obscure cult of Protestant. In America, it would be Pentecostal. His father was like a creature from the Old Testament. He spoke constantly of the Scriptures and had the sense that the end was nigh—and to prepare for it.

You were living with his family?

Yes. I'd go to church with them too. Though myself and Guggi are laughing at the absurdity of some of this, the rhetoric is getting through to us. We don't realize it, but we're being immersed in the Holy Scriptures. That's what we took away from this: this rich language, these ancient tracts of wisdom.

So is that why you were writing such serious songs when you're nineteen?

Here's the strange bit: Most of the people that you grew up with in black music had a similar baptism of the spirit, right? The difference is that most of these performers felt they could not express their sexuality before God. They had to turn away. So rock & roll became backsliders' music. They were running away from God. But I never believed that. I never saw it as being a choice, an either/or thing.

You never saw rock & roll—the so-called devil's music—as incompatible with religion?

Look at the people who have formed my imagination. Bob Dylan. Nineteen seventy-six—he's going through similar stuff. You buy Patti Smith: *Horses*—"Jesus died for somebody's sins/But not mine...." And she turns Van Morrison's "Gloria" into liturgy. She's wrestling with these demons—Catholicism in her case. Right the way through to *Wave,* where she's talking to the pope.

The music that really turns me on is either running toward God or away from God. Both recognize the pivot, that God is at the center of the jaunt. So the blues, on one hand—running away; gospel, the Mighty Clouds of Joy—running towards.

And later you came to analyze it and figure it out.

The blues are like the Psalms of David. Here was this character, living in a cave, whose outbursts were as much criticism as praise. There's David singing, "Oh, God—where are you when I need you?/You call yourself God?" And you go, this is the blues.

Both deal with the relationship with God. That's really it. I've since realized that anger with God is very valid. We wrote a song about that on the *Pop* album—people were confused by it—"Wake Up Dead Man": "Jesus, help me/I'm alone in this world/And a fucked-up world it is, too/Tell me, tell me the story/The one about eternity/And the way it's all gonna be/Wake up, dead man."

What is your religious belief today? What is your concept of God?

If I could put it simply, I would say that I believe there's a force of love and logic in the world, a force of love and logic behind the universe. And I believe in the poetic genius of a creator who would choose to express such unfathomable power as a child born in "straw poverty"; i.e., the story of Christ makes sense to me.

How does it make sense?

As an artist, I see the poetry of it. It's so brilliant. That this scale of creation, and the unfathomable universe, should describe itself in such vulnerability, as a child. That is mind-blowing to me. I guess that would make me a Christian. Although I don't use the label, because it is so very hard to live up to. I feel like I'm the worst example of it, so I just kinda keep my mouth shut.

Do you pray or have any religious practices?

I try to take time out of every day, in prayer and meditation. I feel as at home in a Catholic cathedral as in a revival tent. I also have enormous respect for my friends who are atheists, most of whom are, and the courage it takes not to believe.

How big an influence is the Bible on your songwriting? How much do you draw on its imagery, its ideas?

It sustains me.

As a belief, or as a literary thing?

As a belief. These are hard subjects to talk about because you can sound like such a dickhead. I'm the sort of character who's got to have an anchor. I want to be around immovable objects. I want to build my house on a rock, because even if the waters are not high around the house, I'm going to bring back a storm. I have that in me. So it's sort of underpinning for me.

I don't read it as a historical book. I don't read it as, "Well, that's good advice." I let it speak to me in other ways. They call it the *rhema*. It's a hard word to translate from Greek, but it sort of means it changes in the moment you're in. It seems to do that for me.

You're saying it's a living thing?

It's a plumb line for me. In the Scriptures, it is self-described as a clear pool that you can see yourself in, to see where you're at, if you're still enough. I'm writing a poem at the moment called "The Pilgrim and His Lack of Progress." I'm not sure I'm the best advertisement for this stuff.

ACKNOWLEDGMENTS

Thanks to four decades of *Rolling Stone* editors and writers for making this book possible. Corey Seymour, Lesley Savage and Andy Greene researched the *Rolling Stone* archives to find the best *Rolling Stone* Interviews. Charles M. Young, Eric Bates and Sean Woods helped to edit those interviews.

ABOUT THE EDITORS

Jann S. Wenner is the founder, editor, and publisher of *Rolling Stone* magazine and the owner of Wenner Media. He lives in New York City.

Joe Levy is the executive editor of *Rolling Stone*. He is also an adjunct professor in New York University's Clive Davis Department of Recorded Music.